Some biblical couples are famous, while others remain obscure. All of them have something to teach us, however, and I know of no book more searingly honest than the Bible. Robert and Bobbie have performed a true service by looking at the Bible through the prism of marriage — a relationship that was God's idea, after all.

PHILIP YANCEY

My husband, Ken, and I are always looking to learn from other couples, but never did it occur to us to do a study of couples in the Bible. But now, our good friends, Robert and Bobbie Wolgemuth, have made that possible — plus, more convenient. This is an *astounding* undertaking; the list of couples alone left us breathless. Reading about these remarkable relationships underscores how not only was God active in the past, but He is still pushing and prodding us today in our marriages — so this year Ken and I are choosing *Couples of the Bible* to read together. And we invite *you* to join us!

JONI EARECKSON TADA, Joni and Friends International Disability Center

This book may be one of the best investments you could ever make in your marriage and eternity. Reading this together brought us closer to God, to each other, and to the kind of life His Word abundantly promises. Piercing insights. Profound truth. Powerfully moving. This book helps you to take each other's hand — and the hand of God.

THE FARMER HUSBAND AND ANN VOSKAMP, author of the *New York Times* bestseller, *One Thousand Gifts*

We have been students of the Bible for most of our adult lives. However, we have never viewed Scripture through this particular lens. The approach our dear, long-time friends Robert and Bobbie take as they tackle this topic of marriage is fresh and creative. By exploring both negative and positive examples presented in the Bible, you can deepen and strengthen your marriage one day at a time.

MICHAEL AND GAIL HYATT

Robert and Bobbie Wolgemuth make an incredible team. Married for many years, their commitment to each other and to the faith they embrace is evident to all. As lifelong students of the Bible, their insights into the life and times of various couples of the Bible will prove invaluable to married couples and anyone considering marriage.

ANN SPANGLER, coauthor (with Jean Syswerda) of *Women of the Bible*

Dianna and I have known Robert and Bobbie nearly their entire married life and know their own relationship has been burnished to sterling in the fires of pain and testing. You'll find no better pair to lead you through daily devotions based on the marriages found in Scripture.

JERRY B. JENKINS, novelist and biographer

Robert and Bobbie Wolgemuth equip marriage partners on a rich adventure with couples throughout the Bible who struggled, turned to God, and overcame great odds in their own lives. Every week, you will learn how the Lord can bring you closer to Himself and each other, despite the challenges that come your way. This book will strengthen your union, no matter how long you've been together or what trials you face today and in the seasons to come!

LARRY AND AUTUMN ROSS, cofounders, A. Larry Ross
Communications

We've had the privilege of knowing Robert and Bobbie for many years and have long respected and admired their marriage. Their faithful and consistent walk with the Lord is evident in their lives individually and as a couple. You will be encouraged and challenged in your marriage relationship as you spend a year digging into real-life biblical examples of other couples.

RON AND JUDY BLUE

We should expect to be wonderfully helped by spending a year learning what it means to grow closer to Christ and to each other. Here is help for me first as a husband and then as a pastor.

ALISTAIR BEGG, PARKSIDE CHURCH, Cleveland, Ohio

There is no better way to build intimacy in your marriage than growing together spiritually. This devotional study is a great blessing to my wife, Laura, and me. I've known Robert and Bobbie for over three decades and have seen their relationship stand the test of time. I highly recommend this book *Couples of the Bible* to anyone who wants to grow.

RYAN AND LAURA DOBSON, speaker and author

High praise goes to Robert and Bobbie for crafting a biblical rendering of couples living in reality. The Wolgemuths are certainly not untested—their marriage has survived many of life's unexpected twists and turns, and yet they remain unreservedly committed to the Lord and each other. Enjoy the daily journey—you are in great hands.

DR. JERRY AND DR. CRISTIE JOHNSTON, executive director of Crossroads USA and Bible teacher

COUPLES
of the BIBLE

A One-Year Devotional Study to Draw
You Closer to God and Each Other

ROBERT & BOBBIE
WOLGEMUTH

ZONDERVAN.com/
AUTHORTRACKER
follow your favorite authors

We want to hear from you. Please send your comments about this book to us in care of zreview@zondervan.com. Thank you.

ZONDERVAN

Couples of the Bible
Copyright © 2013 by Robert D. Wolgemuth and Barbara J. Wolgemuth

This title is also available as a Zondervan ebook. Visit www.zondervan.com/ebooks.

This title is also available in a Zondervan audio edition. Visit www.zondervan.fm.

Requests for information should be addressed to:

Zondervan, *Grand Rapids, Michigan 49530*

Library of Congress Cataloging-in-Publication Data

Wolgemuth, Robert, 1948–
    Couples of the Bible : a one-year devotional study of couples in Scripture /
Robert Wolgemuth, Bobbie Wolgemuth.
      p. cm
    Includes bibliographical references and index.
    ISBN 978-0-310-33268-8 (hardcover, jacketed)
    1. Married people in the Bible. 2. Married people—Prayers and devotions.
I. Wolgemuth, Bobbie. II. Title.
BS579.H8W65 2013
220.9'2—dc23   2012039762

Any Internet addresses (websites, blogs, etc.) and telephone numbers in this book are offered as a resource. They are not intended in any way to be or imply an endorsement by Zondervan, nor does Zondervan vouch for the content of these sites and numbers for the life of this book.

Published in association with the literary agency of Wolgemuth & Associates, Inc.

Cover design: Curt Diepenhorst
Cover photography: Erich Lessing / Art Resource, NY
Interior production: Beth Shagene

Printed in the United States of America

13 14 15 16 17 18 19 /DCI/ 22 21 20 19 18 17 16 15 14 13 12 11 10 9 8 7 6 5 4 3 2 1

With thanksgiving and gratitude,
we dedicate this book to
Monroe and Susie Dourte,
married in 1911,
and to their eight children—

Grace Wolgemuth and her husband, Samuel;
Ruth Musser and her husband, Elias;
Mary Martin and her husband, Roy;
Allon Dourte and his wife, Jeanette;
Eber Dourte and his wife, Ruth;
Jesse Dourte and his wife, Wilma;
Esther Snyder and her husband, Paul;
Victor Dourte and his wife, Lois.

All of these were married "till death do us part."
Because of their love for God's Word,
they inspire us to become a couple of the Bible.

We are grateful for their lives, their faith,
and their example of endurance.

Contents

Foreword

Over the years, when we have looked for wisdom for our own marriage or for advice to give couples who came to us for counsel, we turned to the truth of Scripture. In our four decades of marriage, Scripture has been our compass. Based on God's clear message for marriages and families, our ministry, FamilyLife, was founded in 1976 and has sought to bring those blueprints to home builders around the world.

When we first heard about the idea of a book highlighting couples in the Bible, we were intrigued. Yes, biblical history is bursting with the stories of husbands and wives. Wouldn't it be convenient to be able to meet all these couples in one place?

As we thought about it, from beginning to end, the Bible is full of stories about relationships. God existed in perfection as Father, Son, and Holy Spirit even before He created Eden and carefully crafted humans — a man and a woman — to live in unbroken fellowship with each other and their Creator. Step by step, from Genesis to Revelation, the character of God — His grace, mercy, and love — can be traced through His encounters with men and women ... couples of the Bible. Learning about these couples provides an overview of the entire Bible and God's great love and grace for mankind.

Even if you have a limited understanding of the Bible, you may already know that it displays the lives of men and women as they really are, hiding none of their humanity — fears, mistakes, or rebellious ways. The honesty of Scripture allows us to see ourselves as people in process, learning what husbands and wives can do to grow into healthy and whole relationships with God and with each other.

Couples of the Bible will provide a view of marriage unlike any other book, because it takes dozens of Bible characters and unpacks the accounts of their lives and marriages. For fifty-two weeks, you will be able to spend a whole week with a biblical couple, learning their story and capturing life lessons from each one—lessons that, if applied, have the capacity to inspire and strengthen your marriage.

In this book, you may meet some couples you didn't know before. And you may be surprised by what you discover in the marriages of couples you thought you knew.

Someone has said, "Tomorrow you will be the same person you are today, except for the people you meet and the books you read." We could amend this by suggesting that tomorrow your marriage will be better than it is today because you have met these biblical couples and spent time in the Bible, observing God's gracious character.

If you want to be closer to each other and to God, we recommend looking at biblical examples of those who followed God faithfully, learning from their lives.

And finally, let us say a word about the authors. When you meet Robert and Bobbie Wolgemuth, it isn't just their last name that is distinctive. This is a couple that lives with distinction. We've watched them on their journey to mountaintops, and we've prayed for them as they've weathered storms *together*. They are serious followers of Christ who seek to surrender to Him and His lordship every day. They live where you live, and their authenticity is both refreshing and exhilarating. I may have met a more talented couple, but honestly, I'm not sure who that couple would be if it's not Robert and Bobbie. Singing, speaking, writing, leading, loving, laughing—they really are remarkable. And we like them.

Now we commend this helpful and insightful book to you. Whether it takes a year or even longer to meander your way through, you are going to really enjoy the journey.

Dennis and Barbara Rainey
Little Rock, Arkansas

Introduction

When you married, you started on a journey with your spouse. Without knowing what was ahead, you began walking an unfamiliar trail that was certain to surprise you with twists and turns, from pleasant valleys to steep rugged places—and plenty of unexpected terrain in between. Wouldn't you like to meet other couples who have walked ahead of you on some of the same paths you and your spouse may travel?

Couples of the Bible is a book about how God revealed Himself through the lives of men and women. It is a visit with some couples who trusted God in the midst of great trials and suffering, and with others who lived in deep darkness, doubt, and disobedience.

You'll encounter couples you already know and meet others for perhaps the first time. And you'll see how their lives reveal the wonder and power of God's loving nature and faithfulness. You'll experience the overarching plot of Scripture—creation, fall, redemption—all pointing to the main character, Jesus.

Reading the accounts of these couples will inspire you to draw closer to God and to each other. Shared victories, defeats, mistakes, and restored relationships form a common link across the centuries and will turn your attention to the God who was active in the past—and is still active today in your marriage.

As you read the stories of biblical couples, you are invited to listen to the voice of God, enjoy His companionship, trust His intervention in your marriage, and believe He is a God who will walk with you.

The Bible—a collection of sixty-six separate books—opens with creation ... a man and a woman in a perfect relationship, in a perfect place. And it ends with the marriage of believers—the church—to their perfect Groom, Jesus Christ. Between these bookends are many couples who offer us a road map to trace God's ways, see His character, trust His purposes, and receive His redemptive plan.

After Adam and Eve sinned in the garden of Eden, they were forced to leave Paradise. Yet, despite the rebellion of the first couple, God was merciful. Then and now He chooses and leads ordinary men and women to display His goodness.

Sometimes we're like Eve; we are prone to pluck at forbidden fruit. Other times we're like Jacob; we panic and try to manipulate situations to fit our needs. Or maybe we're like Zechariah and Elizabeth; we wonder if God will ever give us our longed-for blessing.

The biblical couples you will encounter will speak for themselves. Some will warn you and challenge you to make necessary changes. Others will encourage you to persevere and wait for God's perfect timing. All of them will show you new things about God.

The Bible is a living book. It is the inspired love story of the great King in heaven who woos His people and commits Himself to perfectly love them forever.

How the Book Is Organized

Couples of the Bible has fifty-two chapters. Each chapter highlights one couple in five ways:

Monday: *Their Story.* These pages highlight the relationship of each couple and how they faced challenges or celebrated victories. Although the narrative stays as close as possible to the biblical text, certain scenarios of what might have been happening at the time of the story are imagined. Some conversation in this and other sections is quoted directly from Scripture. Other dialogue is paraphrased. In many cases, Scripture references are given to help you in your study.

Tuesday: *Their Life and Times.* Knowing what it was like to live in the culture surrounding each couple will add to your understanding. A Jewish Christian researcher provided invaluable help with this feature about what life was like thousands of years ago.

Wednesday: *Can You Imagine?* On this day, you are invited to put yourself in the place of the couple in the story. What would it have been like to be there? To be them? To face the heartbreak of an unfaithful spouse or to hold a baby after a lifetime of barrenness? This day concludes with help "From God's Word."

Thursday: *Their Legacy in Scripture.* Several key Bible verses and questions are offered for application to your own life and marriage. This short study will be helpful to use by yourself, with your spouse, or with a group of friends eager to know what God says about the issues married couples face.

Friday: *Their Legacy of Prayer.* The week concludes with a time for reflection, listening, and prayers intended for you and your spouse.

As you read *Couples of the Bible*, we celebrate the exciting new things God can do in your hearts and in your marriage.

ROBERT AND BOBBIE WOLGEMUTH
Orlando, Florida

Whatever was written in former days was written for our instruction.

ROMANS 15:4 ESV

Perfect Companions

Adam and Eve

Meaning of Names:	*Adam* means "man" or "red earth." *Eve* means "living" or "life."
Their Character:	He was a good man who loved God and his wife. She was at peace with God and her husband, for whom she was created as a perfect mate.
Their Challenge:	They were restricted from eating from the tree of the knowledge of good and evil.
Their Outcome:	Their marriage and their relationship with their Creator represented God's original blueprint for both.
Key Scripture:	Genesis 2

Their Story

Monday

The Creator had done His work, removing a rib from Adam's side while he slept, fashioning a creature of grace without the man's knowledge or advice. As Eve's Father and Creator, God escorted her to the waiting Adam. The Creator gently took her, the first bride, to the first groom.

Adam's eyes danced at the sight of her. Eve returned his glance, her smile captivating his soul. "I thought that I had seen all the creatures," he said out loud. "How did I miss this one?"

Adam's arm drew his bride's soft form into his side. His hands touched her face, smoothing away wisps of hair. His heart raced. The Creator and giver of everything good had made this woman especially for him, to be a perfect companion and helper.

Delight and joy encircled them. Adam was no longer alone. He had someone with whom he would share ordinary moments and years of memories in their lush garden home. In Eve he found someone he could talk with, laugh with. They romped in the ecstasy of secret places as together they discovered joy in God's perfect design for their bodies. They worshiped their Maker in their union.

Adam loved Eve. He was strong for her, sheltering her. He anticipated how to bring her pleasure and delighted in her charms. He basked in her admiration, honored to serve her well and to provide a home for her.

As husband and wife, Adam and Eve were adept at listening and at empathizing. Their communication was open and transparent, and they never misunderstood each other. Their motives were selfless. Both put the other first. Adam loved and protected his wife as he loved and protected himself. Eve admired and respected her husband. Their relationship lacked nothing. It was perfect.

Evening was their special time with God. As the sun lowered in the sky, painting magenta streaks under the clouds, the Maker covered the couple with His presence. They walked together, these three. It was at these times that Eve felt spiritually complete. This was joy that could only be known from a perfect companionship with her husband and with God.

As they talked, they reviewed the day's discoveries. Trees, animals, plants, birds, blossoms, insects, cloud formations ... so many details, so much to learn from Elohim. The Creator taught Adam and Eve about the miraculous creations—from great soaring birds to tiny seeds dropped into the soil, producing lush vegetation and majestic trees.

Drinking in the Lord's words, the couple listened as their Creator and Divine Companion explained how their own children would fill the earth, how the seed of the man inside the woman would produce new life.

As the three continued to enjoy sweet communion in the garden, they strolled to the center, where two trees stood: the tree of life and the tree of the knowledge of good and evil. God had told Adam, and

Adam informed Eve, that eating from any tree was permissible, but that the fruit from one tree—the tree of the knowledge of good and evil—was off-limits.

Why God had given such a directive was a mystery, but during these evenings in the garden, it hardly concerned Adam and Eve. What *did* matter was the delight of being together in the presence of their Creator.

Then later, lying motionless in the nighttime darkness of Paradise, Adam and Eve looked upward and saw the wonders of the heavens —the sparkling radiance of the stars, the brilliance of the luminous moon. Adam tenderly stretched his arm behind his wife's shoulders and pulled her close. Gently resting her head on his shoulder, Eve reveled in the security of her husband's love.

She wanted this to last forever.

Their Life and Times

Tuesday

What Every Man Longs For, What Every Woman Needs

Adam and Eve, as God's first image bearers, were the ideal representatives of all that was good in the newly created world. The very story of creation is the story of good things.

God made light and declared it "good." He made open sky, oceans and dry land, vegetation, and all living creatures. Good, good, good, and good again. But suddenly and quite unexpectedly, God's review of all these good things came to an abrupt halt. God declared something "not good." "It is *not good* for the man to be alone" (Genesis 2:18, emphasis added).

God, who lacked nothing, was deliberate with these words. He was acknowledging the importance of relationship. Even the perfect Creator did not act alone. "Let *us* make mankind in *our* image, in *our* likeness ..." (Genesis 1:26, emphasis added). God created the universe and everything in it as a commission of three. The Bible reveals that our God is one in essence but is manifest in three Persons: Father, Son, and Holy Spirit—the Trinity or the "tri-unity." Everything

18

God did—and does—He accomplishes with the full knowledge and cooperation of the All-Three.[1]

After the creation was complete—the Grand Tetons and eyelashes, the galaxies and the fragrance of gardenias—God looked at His handiwork and said, "The creation isn't quite finished. Something is missing ... something is *not good*. Adam cannot be expected to live by himself."

Created in God's image, Adam—and all mankind—was made to live in relationship. Yet, for Adam, no friend was found among God's creation. No confidante. No lover. No equal.

So after He created Adam, God designed the man's companion for life. He created woman, a well-suited helper to the man.

In the millennia that have followed creation, the description of woman as man's "helper" has been misunderstood. And debated. And rejected. Does she live in her husband's shadow, available only at his whim? What exactly is the kind of "helper" God had in mind?

When Jesus, the Son of God—the Trinity's second Person—was telling His disciples that He was going to leave them and depart planet Earth, they were troubled. They had counted on His presence, His teaching, His wisdom, His power, His love. But in leaving, Jesus assured them that they would not be alone. He would send them the Holy Spirit, *all* of God in Spirit form, to be a Helper to them.[2]

So when God told Adam that Eve was his "helper," He was saying that bringing the woman to Adam was divinely intentional. The woman was precisely what the man needed, a suitable helper of the highest order. As his companion in marriage, she would listen to his dreams, affirm his aspirations, offer discernment for decisions, bring wisdom to his notions, bring him delight, and express gratitude for his love and protection.

And he was exactly what she needed. He provided security and strength. He would linger with her in unhurried conversation, express delight in her, acknowledge her many gifts. The man would give his full attention to her longings.

Husband and wife, each one strong and necessary. Elegant differences. Ideal symmetry. Perfect companions.

---

1. See Deuteronomy 6:4.
2. See John 15:26 ESV.

Can You Imagine?

Wednesday

Adam and Eve's relationship in their early days in Eden shows us what God intended marriage—your marriage—to be.

God's original pattern for marriage was impeccable. He designed you and your spouse to be whole in your relationship with God, to be completely satisfied in knowing and loving Him. He created your hearts and minds, as well as your bodies, to be the consummate match. A fit. Can you imagine such perfect companionship?

While in the garden of Eden, Adam and Eve had an undivided relationship. With their introduction to each other, God declared history's first human institution.

> The man said,
>
> > "This is now bone of my bones
> > and flesh of my flesh;
> > she shall be called 'woman,'
> > for she was taken out of man."
>
> GENESIS 2:23

In the Hebrew language, the word *flesh* not only refers to a person's physical body; it also means a person's whole being. When the Bible says partners in marriage become one flesh, it means they have become "glued" together as an indivisible person. A husband and wife are not only an exact fit physically, but his maleness and her femaleness *fill out* or *complete* one another in every respect. Imagine what your marriage could be if you and your spouse completed each other in this way.

When you said "I do" at the wedding altar before God, you and your spouse became one flesh. One person. Not competitors. Your concerns, hurts, victories, sorrows, awards, and recognition belong to each other.

Think back to the time when you fell in love and how you longed to be together. Conversation was effortless. You laughed often and forgave quickly.

Something higher, deeper, than infatuation joined the first couple together. Adam and Eve had the joy of God's purpose and presence in their marriage. This was the secret to Eden, and it is what God wants for your marriage.

From God's Word . . .

> "'So they are no longer two, but one flesh. Therefore what God has joined together, let no one separate.'"
>
> MARK 10:8–9

Their Legacy in Scripture

Thursday

1. **"So God created mankind in his own image, in the image of God he created them; male and female he created them"** (GENESIS 1:27).

    What is an *image*? What does it mean that we are made in God's image? In what ways can you reflect or become a picture of God on earth?

    What character traits or gifts of personality do you see in your spouse that display God's likeness?

2. **"The LORD God said, 'It is not good for the man to be alone. I will make a helper suitable for him'"** (GENESIS 2:18).

    Adam was alone. His wife had not yet been created. For a married couple living in a contemporary setting, aloneness still happens. For some couples, a great deal of time is spent apart. What are the dangers of too much time away from each other?

    When have you planned a special time with your spouse—a walk around the block, a dinner, an overnight getaway—and what was the benefit?

3. **"For in Christ all the fullness of the Deity lives in bodily form, and in Christ you have been brought to fullness. He is the head over every power and authority"** (COLOSSIANS 2:9–10).

    When Adam and Eve were together, they needed a third Companion to join, fill, and complete them. What is God's role in your marriage? How could you be more intentional about including Him?

Their Legacy of Prayer

Friday

Reflect On: Genesis 2:18–24

Praise God: For creating you as His image bearer; for making you
capable of displaying His goodness, glory, wisdom, and
love; and for designing your spouse especially for you.

Offer Thanks: That He offers His presence and speaks to you through
His Word and your spouse.

Confess: Your lack of gratitude for your spouse and for the good
things God has provided for your benefit.

Ask God: To teach you to honor His divine blueprint for marriage
and to help you listen carefully for His voice as He
speaks to you about your relationship with your spouse.

Listen: "Dear children, I created you to display My glory by
lifting up the best in each other. Consider My handiwork
and praise Me for making you the way you are."

Pray: *Father and Creator of our marriage, You have made us in Your
image and designed us to display Your glory. We need Your help
in order to honor our commitment to You and to each other. We
ask You to forgive us when we fail to appreciate each other as
the gift You have graciously given. We invite You to teach us how
to live and love the way You originally planned. Thank You for
being the Divine Helper in our marriage. Amen.*

Fractured Intimacy

Adam and Eve

Meaning of Names: *Adam* means "man" or "red earth." *Eve* means "living" or "life."

Their Character: She entertained thoughts that led her to disobey God. He blamed her for their disobedience.

Their Challenge: The enemy, Satan, convinced them to disregard God's instructions.

Their Outcome: They were separated from God and emotionally distant from each other, forced to live lives of toil and heartache, and eventually experience death.

Key Scripture: Genesis 3

Their Story

Monday

Adam and Eve had walked to the tree of the knowledge of good and evil. They knew they should turn away, but they decided to linger under its fragrant and fruit-laden branches.

While they were admiring the tree, a creature approached from a distance. Certain that they knew all the inhabitants of the garden, they were surprised by this one. He walked upright, but was not a man. His handsome face was almost luminous. The couple was captivated.

When the creature reached them, he looked directly at her and said, "Did God really say, 'You must not eat from any tree in the garden'?"

Eve knew the question was dangerous, and that they should ignore him and get away as quickly as possible, yet in her curiosity she lingered. Adam was equally intrigued, equally unwilling to resist.

"We may eat fruit from the trees in the garden," Eve said, masking her uncertainty. "But God did say, 'You must not eat fruit from the tree that is in the middle of the garden, and you must not touch it, or you will die.'"

"You will not die," the creature mocked her. "For God knows that when you eat of it, your eyes will be opened, and you will be like God, knowing good and evil."

Be like God? Eve wondered. *Like* God?

The creature walked up to the tree, plucked a piece of fruit off its branches, and held it out to her. Eve thought it was the most beautiful piece of fruit she had ever seen. *Oh,* she wondered, *what new taste might this fruit hold for me? What harm will just one bite do?*

She reached out and took the fruit, turned it slowly in her hand, admiring its ripe beauty—and then she did something she would soon come to regret. She took a bite. The nectar was sweet, its taste glorious. Reaching up, she picked another fruit and handed it to her husband. He also took a bite. Eve watched his face and saw it flood with pleasure.

But then her eyes moved from his face to his body. Her husband was naked! Scandalized, she quickly shifted her eyes to her own body and realized that she too was naked. She looked back at Adam and saw her own horror mirrored in his face.

What have we done? She glanced at the creature, and what she saw filled her with dread. He looked triumphant.

Adam threw down the half-eaten fruit and grabbed her hand, pulling her toward the underbrush, looking for a place to hide. In the deep woods, they found large fig leaves and wove them together, fashioning crude coverings and slipping them over their bodies.

And then a sound. The rustle of leaves. The cracking of twigs. God—their Friend—was coming to walk with them in the garden.

"Where are you?" God's voice was pure and strong.

Nervously Adam sputtered that he and his wife were ashamed because they were naked.

God asked, "Who told you that you were naked? Have you eaten from the tree that I commanded you not to eat from?"

Eve listened in disbelief as Adam blamed her. Leaping to her own defense, she blamed the serpent.

Unimpressed by their alibis, God banished Adam and Eve from the garden.

Now, the morning after, tears fell as Eve remembered what they had done. Things would never be the same. Innocence had vanished. Perfection had died. Eden was lost. Today, she and Adam would begin again in this new world, a different and harsh place of their own making.

Their Life and Times

Tuesday

Perfection Spoiled

Adam and Eve's home in the garden of Eden is the first identified stretch of property in recorded history. It was located in the Fertile Crescent, which was at the mouth of the Tigris and Euphrates rivers in the northwest corner of the Persian Gulf. The climate was comfortable. The terrain was gentle, the air clear and clean.

But because Adam and Eve had disobeyed God's command, they were evicted from perfection. Expelled from Eden, the trespassers were forced to settle elsewhere.

Displacement and wandering and anguish have plagued humanity for the rest of recorded time. Because Adam and Eve were banished from their original home, all people would wander, lost and longing for perfection. A fallen world — evil, sickness, warfare, pain, and natural disasters brought about by a cursed earth — replaced Paradise.

Adam and Eve's disobedience also ripped apart their unselfish intimacy. Hiding replaced transparency. Doubt replaced trust. Cruelty replaced kindness.

Sin harmed the first husband and wife, putting distance between them, just as it would all husbands and wives who would come after them. But even far from Eden, God's presence was — and is — the perfect provision for sustainable unity in marriage.

Lord, you have been our dwelling place
    throughout all generations.
Before the mountains were born
    or you brought forth the whole world,
    from everlasting to everlasting you are God.

PSALM 90:1–2

God punished Adam and Eve for their rebellion, but He did not leave them without clothing or without His presence. He dressed them and accompanied them in their exile. The animal-skin garments God provided were costly. Something had to die in order for Adam and Eve to be covered.

Here was a hint of God's merciful plan of salvation for all mankind.

Since Eden, husbands and wives have experienced both the rewards of obedience and the consequences of sin. Even though we are all made from the rebellious mold of our original parents, God graciously gives couples who choose to follow Him a taste of Paradise — intimacy with Him and with each other.

Can You Imagine?

Wednesday

Adam and Eve's perfection in Eden lay shattered at their feet. Can you imagine how desperately they wanted to return to the ecstasy of their former faultless relationship?

Slipping from the side of his sleeping wife, Adam walked across new territory. Beams of slanted light crisscrossed the unfamiliar terrain before him like glassy spindles. The sights and sounds were foreign.

His night had been restless even after making love to his wife. The experience had been selfish rather than spontaneous and joyful, coerced instead of rollicking. It was not good.

Trying to push back pangs of the guilt of his fruit-eating disobedience, Adam tried to talk with God, his Friend. But his words were hollow and awkward. God, who had once felt so close, suddenly felt far away.

Adam groaned audibly. He knew that what they had done in the garden had destroyed his perfect companionship with Eve. His relationship with his wife was now laced with misunderstanding and heartache. And strain. Just that morning he had spoken thoughtless and searing words intended to hurt in response to her unkind outburst. The reality of their foolishness trampled his spirit.

God had declared Adam and Eve guilty of sinning against Him and announced the sentence:

> "By the sweat of your brow
>   you will eat your food
> until you return to the ground,
>   since from it you were taken;
> for dust you are
>   and to dust you will return."
>
> GENESIS 3:19

In a moment, Eden was ruined. Paradise vanished. Its occupants, chased out.

Although Adam and Eve could not comprehend it at the time, their merciful Creator had made provision for human sin and failure. He promised future restoration. The hope for your life and your marriage was begun with God's gracious plan after the banishment from Eden. Even before you or your spouse knew to ask for His forgiveness, something new, something amazing, was made available … God's grace.

From God's Word . . .

"For if, by the trespass of the one man, death reigned through that one man, how much more will those who receive God's abundant provision of grace and of the gift of righteousness reign in life through the one man, Jesus Christ!"

ROMANS 5:17

Their Legacy in Scripture

Thursday

1. Read Genesis 3.

What was Satan's strategy in tricking Adam and Eve? Why do you think Adam didn't put up a fight when Eve was tempted by the serpent? What area of conflict would your spouse say is difficult to confront you about? How would you address a situation if you perceived your spouse was about to make a foolish decision?

2. "When tempted, no one should say, 'God is tempting me.' For God cannot be tempted by evil, nor does he tempt anyone; but each person is tempted when they are dragged away by their own evil desire and enticed. Then, after desire has conceived, it gives birth to sin; and sin, when it is full-grown, gives birth to death" (JAMES 1:13–15).

How do these verses match the experience of Adam and Eve? What is the "progression" or "pattern" of sin described here?

Why is it important to be alert for early stages of temptation? What specific safeguards can you put in place to protect your marriage (for instance, choosing not to friend someone on Facebook whom you once dated or were attracted to)?

3. "Where sin increased, grace increased all the more" (ROMANS 5:20).

If a good marriage is made up of two sinners who are good forgivers, what attitudes or actions do you need to address or confess to your spouse? What do you need to forgive?

Their Legacy of Prayer

Friday

Reflect On:	Genesis 3
Praise God:	For the grace He has offered to you, for forgiving you and your spouse for every confessed sin, and for providing a way to have fellowship and peace with Him and each other.
Offer Thanks:	That He has provided for you and your spouse the "covering" of Jesus Christ, who clothes you in beauty, grace, and righteousness.
Confess:	Your caustic or blaming tongue and occasional ill-treatment of your spouse when things don't go your way.
Ask God:	To give you strength to be gracious and forgiving toward your spouse, knowing that you too are in need of grace and forgiveness.
Listen:	"Dear children, though you were once far away from Me, I have chosen you to be part of My family. You are no longer children of wrath, but children of the King!"
Pray:	*Heavenly Father, You brought us together and made us one. When we sin and blame each other or act selfishly, we fall short of Your glorious ideal. We cannot make it in our marriage without You. We need Your forgiveness when we fail to measure up to Your standards. Today, we commit to be the companions You created us to be and to encourage each other to live faithfully with You. Help us to love You with all our hearts and each other more than we love ourselves. Amen.*

Violence in the Family

Adam and Eve

Meaning of Names: *Adam* means "man" or "red earth." *Eve* means "living" or "life."

Their Character: She learned the meaning of gratitude and how to cherish God's grace and mercy. He worked hard in order to provide food and shelter for his family.

Their Challenge: One of their sons held God in contempt and murdered his brother.

Their Outcome: They experienced the joy of God's abundant grace when He granted them another child, Seth, who sought God and became a righteous man. Seth was an ancestor in the messianic line.

Key Scripture: Genesis 4

Their Story

Monday

The baby slept in Eve's arms. Having just nursed, the little boy was satisfied and peaceful. His mother marveled at the tiny infant she cradled. "God has graciously granted me another child," she whispered.

With a third son nestled in her care, Eve was content. Adam gently reached his arm around her as he had long ago. In Eden.

Everything had changed since that day of their disobedience. Adam and Eve had been banished from Eden's perfection and lush

beauty. Now, burdened by problems and the struggles of their relentless work, Eve wondered if Paradise still existed.

The loss of the idyllic garden had been a stinging memory for
many years, but she and Adam rarely talked about Eden anymore.
Accepting the punishment God had pronounced, they did their best
to adapt to their new world. The land had been cursed, making it
reluctant to produce and difficult to tend. Exhausted at the end of
each day, Adam suffered the pain of his hard work. They had plenty
to eat—God saw to that—but only by Adam's labor did their land
yield food.

Soon after their dismissal from Paradise, Eve had awakened early
one morning with an unfamiliar sensation. In the coming months,
she marveled at the mystery of what was happening in her body.
When Eve gave birth to the baby that had been growing inside her
for nine months, she experienced pain, just as God had foretold.
Adam stood by her, helping Eve deliver their first son.

"Oh, Adam," she breathed out. "What a miracle. This is ours. Isn't
he beautiful?"

"He's so tiny," Adam exclaimed. "May I touch him? I have never
before seen anything like him."

Adam was not exaggerating. This *was* the first human being ever
to be born.

They named their child Cain, meaning "to bring forth," saying,
"With the help of the Lord I have brought forth a man."

Not long after Cain was weaned, Eve became pregnant again. She
gave birth to another son named Abel.

As the two boys grew, Adam and Eve saw a glaring difference
between them. Abel, the younger brother, was gentle and sweet,
always looking for ways to please his parents. Cain was a different
sort—selfish, distant, and aloof. His darting eyes expressed contempt,
and his affections were sparing. Cain thought only of himself.

Adam and Eve tried to discipline and praise their sons evenly, but
this proved to be a daily trial. Abel's spirit was teachable, Cain's defiant. And the struggle to shape Cain's spirit caused dissention between
his parents. They often argued about Cain.

As Cain and Abel matured, their differences became even more
pronounced. Abel was considerate and kind; Cain was sullen and
self-absorbed. Adam and Eve worried about their older son. They

warned Cain of the consequences for his rebellion, but they could not reach his heart.

Then one day, Eve saw Adam approaching after harvesting in the fields.

His hands were covered with blood. It looked like he had been slaughtering cattle. And then she saw the horror on his face. He stood dazed.

Adam was trembling. "I just buried Abel. His brother murdered him." Adam trembled. "And Cain has fled. The Lord has driven him away."

Collapsing to her knees, Eve wailed. "Abel is gone! What has Cain done?" Adam could not console her.

Now robbed of both their children, Adam and Eve experienced the full force of their sin. In the days to come, waves of despair crashed over them. They cried out to God. Sometimes they clung to each other; often they suffered alone.

Then one night, sometime later, brimming with God's healing balm, the couple shared a desire for each other that they had not experienced since the day of their son's murder. They shared their love, and Eve became pregnant again. After waiting nine months, she gave birth to Seth, the baby she now held.

"Oh, Adam," Eve said. "The Lord has been good to grant us another child. Why does He favor us so?"

Although they would never forget their beloved Abel, Adam and Eve rejoiced that the Lord had blessed them. God had visited them with His lavish grace, forgiveness, and sustaining love.

In the many years that followed, Eve bore more sons and daughters. But the timing of Seth's birth would always remind the couple of God's kindness and mercy.

Their Life and Times

Tuesday

Sin's Consequences, Grace Is Born

The Bible makes no attempt to cover up a reality that has been a mystery to parents from the beginning of time. Two boys, brothers raised by the same parents—Adam and Eve—turned out so differently. While one grew up with a desire to please God, the other rebelled and murdered his brother. When a child willfully displays ungodly character or chooses to walk a rebel path, parents can become confused and frustrated. The inability to change their child's heart often kindles disagreement and conflict between husbands and wives.

Scripture is clear that Adam and Eve's children were each accountable to God for their own actions and provides a picture of God's justice and wisdom. Thousands of years after Abel's murder, a specific warning was given: "Every man in Israel must appear before the Sovereign, the LORD" (Exodus 23:17 NLT). As difficult as it may be for parents to reconcile the rebellion of their child, sons and daughters are eventually responsible for their own choices and the consequences that result.

So what is the legacy of the sons of Adam and Eve?

After being exiled to the land of Nod, an area east of the garden of Eden, Cain eventually married, and his wife had a son named Enoch. Cain built a city and, wanting to honor himself rather than God, named it after his son.[1]

Little is said about Enoch's descendants until the birth of his grandson Lamech. With him, the selfishness and sin displayed by his great-grandfather Cain continued to plague the family.

Holding God's laws in contempt, "Lamech married two women, one named Adah and the other Zillah" (Genesis 4:19). This is the first recorded instance of polygamy in the Bible, a tragic departure from God's original intent for marriage and a precursor to chaos in the generations to follow.[2]

In a further display of irreverence toward God, Lamech said,

---

1. See Genesis 4:17–18.
2. See Genesis 2:24.

"Adah and Zillah, listen to me; wives of Lamech, hear my words. I have killed a man for wounding me, a young man for injuring me. If Cain is avenged seven times, then Lamech seventy-seven times" (Genesis 4:23–24).

Lamech's bravado and violent anger were appalling. When God had confronted Lamech's great-grandfather Cain about the murder of Abel, Cain tried to deny it. But Lamech boasted of his savage acts and reveled in them.

The descendants of Abel and his brother Seth are a different story.

Abel and his younger brother Seth acknowledged and honored God. Seth and his wife had a son named Enosh, and during this time, "people began to call on the name of the LORD" (Genesis 4:26).

Also from Seth's godly line came Enoch, not to be confused with Cain's son by the same name. (During this time there was only one baby name book!) Enoch's devotion to God was so intimate that the Lord whisked Enoch to heaven before he died: "Enoch walked faithfully with God; then he was no more, because God took him away" (Genesis 5:24). This descendant of Seth was a powerful evangelist and witness for the Lord.[3]

Enoch's grandson, also named Lamech, was a man of commendable character. Even though he shared the same name as the most contemptible man in Cain's line, this Lamech was far different. The good Lamech was the father of Noah, and he pronounced a blessing at his son's birth: "He will comfort us in the labor and painful toil of our hands caused by the ground the LORD has cursed" (Genesis 5:29). And Noah pleased God: "Noah was a righteous man, blameless among the people of his time, and he walked faithfully with God" (Genesis 6:9).

How completely different the two Lamechs were. The first one reviled God and sneered at His curse on Cain. The latter Lamech, like his ancestor Abel, lamented God's sentence on the earth and sought His comfort.

Each child of Adam and Eve chose the way they would go, and each was accountable to God for their actions. Their choices set a pattern for the generations that followed. Cain's family established a heritage of desperation and destruction, while Seth built a legacy of faithfulness that eventually brought to the world the Messiah.

---

3. See Jude 14–15.

Can You Imagine?

Wednesday

Adam and Eve lost both of their children in a single day—one was murdered, the other banished. Can you imagine the horror and pain they must have felt? How can a couple deal with that kind of deep sorrow and guilt?

Suffering has a way of putting our joy on trial. We can train our hearts to trust the character of God before we are faced with a tragedy. We can have confidence in the truth of God's Word even when we don't understand what He's doing. "Oh, the depth of the riches of the wisdom and knowledge of God! How unsearchable his judgments, and his paths beyond tracing out!" (Romans 11:33).

Adam and Eve may have thought their sin had thwarted any chance for future joy, but God redeemed the situation in His perfect time. He blessed the couple with another son in the wake of their bereavement and brought them comfort, graciously allowing Eve to conceive again. And this experience would be different.

When she had given birth to her firstborn, Cain, Eve had said, "With the help of the LORD I have brought forth a man" (Genesis 4:1). Notice that she takes credit for herself—"*I* have brought forth a man" (emphasis added). However, after suffering loss—the tragedy in the garden, the death of Abel, the banishment of Cain—Eve was humble and grateful. After Seth's birth, she was thankful: "God has granted me another child in place of Abel, since Cain killed him" (Genesis 4:25). This time, Eve gave all the credit to the Lord. After enduring failure and the inability to control or repair life on her own, Eve acknowledged God's kindness and mercy.

As a couple, you will face difficulties you cannot understand. You can prepare now by spending time in His presence and learning to trust His goodness, grace, and wisdom for whatever lies ahead.

From God's Word . . .

> "'I have told you these things, so that in me you may have peace. In this world you will have trouble. But take heart! I have overcome the world.'"
>
> JOHN 16:33

Their Legacy in Scripture

Thursday

1. **Read Genesis 4.**

   In one day, Adam and Eve lost both their sons. When have you or your spouse experienced a significant loss? How do you and your spouse express your grief differently? In what ways can you encourage your spouse when crisis comes?

2. **"'Do not let your hearts be troubled. You believe in God; believe also in me. My Father's house has many rooms; if that were not so, would I have told you that I am going there to prepare a place for you? And if I go and prepare a place for you, I will come back and take you to be with me that you also may be where I am. You know the way to the place where I am going.' Thomas said to him, 'Lord, we don't know where you are going, so how can we know the way?' Jesus answered, 'I am the way and the truth and the life. No one comes to the Father except through me'"** (JOHN 14:1–6).

   What promises from God can you cling to in times of pain and grief?

3. **"This is what the LORD says ... 'I will contend with those who contend with you, and your children I will save'"** (ISAIAH 49:25).

   What resources do you and your spouse hold on to when you're dealing with crisis? What promises in God's Word are especially meaningful to you?

Their Legacy of Prayer

Friday

Reflect On: Genesis 4

Praise God: For His gracious provision of redemption and restoration and for His ability to transform hearts, allowing His children to recover from sin, heartbreak, and failure.

Offer Thanks: That God knows exactly what you need in your most trying times. When you call to Him in prayer, God is never far away.

Confess: That in difficult times you and your spouse often seek temporary solutions instead of turning to God's Word for comfort. The Lord gave you to each other as teammates to seek Him together.

Ask God: For a heart that trusts God — to be able to react to bitter disappointment in a way that glorifies and honors Him.

Listen: "My dear ones, I am with you even in the confusion of your crisis. Though the pain is sharp, I will provide the healing balm your souls need. At all times, look to Me."

Pray: *Father in heaven, You are the God of creation. You form children in their mothers' wombs. You planned every day of their lives before the foundation of the world. Today, let us, along with our children, sense the miracle of Your design. Let them know the presence of Your Spirit guiding them in the direction You have chosen. Make clear the path of preparation we need to follow. Give us wisdom and strength to trust You. In the powerful name of Jesus. Amen.*

4

Daring to Stand

Noah and Wife

Meaning of Names: *Noah* means "rest" or "comfort." The name of Noah's wife is not given in the Bible.

Their Character: He was a man of integrity who walked righteously in an evil world. Though everyone mocked her husband, she followed him into the ark and supported his call.

Their Challenge: They sought to live holy lives in a corrupt society. They carried the grief of knowing God was about to punish the wicked.

Their Outcome: They survived a flood that covered the earth. Their children would begin to repopulate the world.

Key Scripture: Genesis 6:1–22

Their Story

Monday

Noah and his wife stood hand in hand, gazing at the newly finished boat. It was, by far, the largest structure they had ever seen. The couple was overwhelmed by the magnitude of what was about to happen.

"Words fail me," Noah whispered, his voice quivering.

"Then say nothing," his wife consoled him, giving his hand a squeeze of assurance. "This has been an ordeal for all of us. But remember—the people have brought this on themselves."

"I know, but ..."

"Noah, you're a good man. You have done exactly what God told you to do."

She always knew the right way to soothe him. For the length of their marriage, Noah's wife had reassured him with her smile and touch, melting his insecurity with her words. These days, Noah and his wife stood alone—along with their three sons, Shem, Ham, and Japheth, and their wives—in a culture that had gone terribly astray. God announced that He would destroy all humanity save these eight.

The Lord had made His intentions clear to Noah: "I am going to put an end to all people, for the earth is filled with violence because of them. I am surely going to destroy both them and the earth" (Genesis 6:13).

Then God directed him to build an ark, a very large ship that would house Noah's family and two of every living creature—thousands of animals. Noah and his family would be the only human survivors.

The news sickened Noah. With urgency, the humble man had tried to convince anyone who would listen that the Creator God sought their obedience and devotion. As he and his sons set about building the ark, he pleaded with the people to repent and change their evil ways, but they only scoffed at him and told him to go away.

It seemed the more he spoke to his neighbors about repentance, the more hardened they became. The more he lived out mercy and goodness, the more they mocked him.

Noah would lament to his wife, "It is unbearable to see our neighbors trapped in sin."

His wife was his consolation. "Noah," she would say, "together our family can show the world what it means to be children of the living God. He knows you, and He knows your heart. You can only see part of the plan. This is God's battle; you are only His mouthpiece."

"I must trust Him then," Noah replied, "and do what He tells me to do."

"With His help, you and I will obey God," she pledged.

Finally the ark was finished.

It had taken Noah almost a hundred years to complete construction. But he knew that the longer it took him to build the ark, the more opportunity his neighbors had to repent. Their confession, however, never came.

"We have prayed together every day for these people," Noah said to his wife.

"We have, Noah. Be at peace."

"Have we prayed enough? Did we do enough?"

"Please, Noah, leave it to God. We have done what He asked us to do."

"But maybe there was someone I missed. Perhaps I could have spoken to just one more person," Noah lamented.

Noah's wife turned toward him. Touching his face, her eyes revealed her steely conviction. "Noah," she said, "we and our children are the only ones. Her voice dropped, knowing the magnitude of what she was about to say. "May God's will be done."

Noah knew she had spoken the truth. God's will would be done and soon. And when the Lord executed His judgment wrath, Noah's family would be safe inside the ark.

Their Life and Times

Tuesday

Nice Boat

The story of one righteous man and his family gathering materials and building a boat many miles from open water has captivated Bible readers for centuries. It's hard to comprehend the challenges of constructing this massive wooden craft with the engineering limitations of the ancient world. But build it they did.

The reason the ark was to be constructed is described in detail in the Bible. The world of Noah's day had become evil beyond comprehension, and God had informed Noah of His intention to destroy the inhabitants of the earth with a flood. Every person would die except Noah, his wife, their three sons, and their sons' wives. God ordered Noah to build a huge boat to shelter them from the deluge He would soon unleash on the earth. The ark was also built to preserve animals, birds, and insects—a male and female of each—so they could reproduce after the flood. God's plan was to repopulate the earth.

Noah couldn't do this alone. God helped him construct a massive vessel. The Lord gave Noah the exact blueprint for the ark. It was to be 450 feet long, 75 feet wide, and 45 feet high. Its length would equal one and a half football fields and would be about half as wide. The ark would stand four stories high.

Built of "gopher wood"—cypress or perhaps pine or cedar—the ark had three decks, giving it over 100 thousand square feet—almost a million and a half cubit feet—of inhabitable space. The exterior of the boat was covered with water-resistant pitch—resin or perhaps sap from the trees, which sealed the seams and cracks between the boards.

Though the ark's mass would have been awesome to behold, it was not handsome. The huge rectangular structure was only designed for floating, not sailing. The ark had a clear function but no intended course. A floating box with those dimensions was capsize-proof, built for stability, not speed.

More remarkable than the size of the ark was its purpose: saving one family and thousands of animals from destruction. No one knows for certain how many pairs of animals went aboard the ship, but estimates range in the tens of thousands. And then there needed to be enough space to store food for their time on board.

The account of the faithful man and his wife who built the ark is true and powerful. But the symbolism of the story is even more amazing.

The interiors of many of the great cathedrals around the world have been constructed to resemble the inside of a ship, the walls and beams reminding people of the ark's vast hold. In one of His last conversations with the disciples, Jesus conjured up visions of Noah and his family safely inside the ark when He told them about the church that would protect His people for generations to follow. "I will build my church," He said, "and the gates of Hades will not overcome it" (Matthew 16:18).

> *The Lord's our Rock, in Him we hide,*
> *A shelter in the time of storm;*
> *Secure whatever ill betide,*
> *A shelter in the time of storm.*[1]

---

1. "A Shelter in the Time of Storm," lyrics by Vernon J. Charlesworth, circa 1880.

Can You Imagine?

Wednesday

For many years, Noah and his wife refused to buckle under the temptations of wickedness all around them. In fact, outside their immediate family, they did not have one friend who believed in God or was living a righteous life. Can you imagine what it must have been like to be so alone?

The town—and the neighborhood—where Noah and his wife lived was soaking in sinfulness. According to the Bible, the world of their day was literally "full" of immorality. So reprehensible was the behavior of these people that God regretted having created them in the first place and decided to wash the slate clean.

But on His way to starting over, God bumped into a faithful man named Noah, his wife, and their three sons and their wives. From the time their sons were small, Noah and his wife surely included them in conversations about God. They must have prayed together and spoken of the majesty of God's creation.

Deep inside this story is something very special. Noah and his wife opened their home to lost people. We know this because the women their sons married were counted among the righteous who came aboard the ark. This means that even though they came from homes where God was not worshiped, these women's lives were changed by the influence of a believing family that welcomed them and loved them.

For Noah and his wife, the choice was clear. In spite of temptations to conform to the culture around them, they—and their family —chose to serve the Lord. You and your family can do the same.

It may not look like it, but your house is a lifeboat. Your storm-tossed friends and your children's confused playmates need shelter. They need safety, instruction, and a display of love from a family that knows and worships the true God. Your family may be their only hope.

A safe little boat the shape of your house is floating in your neighborhood.

From God's Word ...

"'As for me and my household, we will serve the LORD.'"

JOSHUA 24:15

Their Legacy in Scripture

Thursday

1. **"All his laws are before me; I have not turned away from his decrees. I have been blameless before him and have kept myself from sin"** (2 SAMUEL 22:23–24).

   Samuel calls himself blameless. Noah was also referred to as blameless (Genesis 6:9). What does the word *blameless* mean? Were Samuel and Noah perfect or without sin? What would it mean for you and your spouse to have a "blameless marriage"?

2. **"Just as he who called you is holy, so be holy in all you do; for it is written: 'Be holy, because I am holy'"** (1 PETER 1:15–16).

   What does it mean to be holy? What are some ways you can encourage your spouse to live a holy life when the world around him or her offers an abundance of temptations?

   Withdrawing from society and living on a mountaintop is probably not a practical solution, so what steps can you take to combat destructive influences on you and your marriage?

3. **"The LORD then said to Noah, 'Go into the ark, you and your whole family, because I have found you righteous in this generation'"** (GENESIS 7:1).

   The home of Noah and his wife must have had some special qualities that welcomed the three young women who married their sons. What might that have included? What can you do to turn your home into a lifeboat? What would this look like to your neighbors?

Their Legacy of Prayer

Friday

Reflect On: Genesis 6

Praise God: That He has given you the gift of faith and a desire to live for Him.

Offer Thanks: That He has shown you what is good and how to walk humbly with Him.

Confess: That you sometimes succumb too quickly to destructive thoughts and habits in order to please yourself and forget to focus on pleasing God.

Ask God: To show you how your home can be a beacon of light and calm in a world of darkness and chaos. To use you to reach your lost neighbors.

Listen: "Dear children, I have called you to be separate from the world and to be a witness of My faithfulness. I am the One who called you out of darkness into light."

Pray: *Our great and wonderful God, empower us to live lives that please You. Help us to be winsome messengers of Your Word and to show others the love of Jesus. Use us to lead people to Christ. Amen.*

Obeying God

Abram and Sarai

Meaning of Names:	*Abram* means "exalted father." *Sarai* means "my princess."
Their Character:	He was a man of faith who was called by God and willing to obey. She was a strong woman who was willing to partner and venture out with her husband to a new land.
Their Challenge:	They twice had to leave behind the life and home they knew so well and head into the unknown.
Their Outcome:	They experienced the unique blessing of God and the promise that they would be the ancestors of a new nation.
Key Scripture:	Genesis 12:1–9

Their Story

Monday

The early-morning hours were his favorite. On many days, Abram gingerly slipped from beside his sleeping wife, stepped from their home, and walked toward the gardens. His gardens. All that disrupted the silence was the occasional chirrup of a songbird or the rustling sound of an animal scurrying through the underbrush foraging for the first morsel of the day.

Predawn darkness gave way to a new day. Just like sunrise had been in the Fertile Crescent where he had grown up, Abram loved the sight of the sun rising over the verdant land of Harran. Many years before, Abram had moved here with his father and his wife and achieved success well beyond his expectations. He had expanded his holdings in land and in livestock, with plenty of hired hands to tend to the daily rigors of agrarian life. Aside from the fact that Abram and Sarai had no children, life was settled and good.

But on this day, the serene beauty of the gardens did not calm his heart. Abram felt a deep sense of both adventure and uncertainty. Soon he and Sarai would be leaving Harran.

Something had happened. One day while Abram was out in the fields, the Creator of the universe spoke to him in a voice clear and strong: "Go from your country, your people and your father's household to the land I will show you" (Genesis 12:1).

Abram was awestruck. He had grown up in a land of myriad deities and idols, but this tangible encounter confirmed his belief that Yahweh was the one true God. From this day forward Abram belonged to Him.

As he walked along that morning, Abram pictured the questioning face of his beautiful Sarai, rehearsing how he would tell his wife about the plan to fold up their tents again and leave Harran. Many years before, at the command of Terah, his late father, Abram had moved Sarai from her homeland in Ur. But now, having lived and settled in Harran, Sarai probably would bristle at the announcement.

"God has spoken to me," Abram practiced out loud. "Now that my father is dead, we are to gather all of our possessions and continue the journey to an unknown place. We must leave Harran and follow God's instructions. We will wander like nomads until He tells us to stop."

The thought of making this pronouncement to his spirited wife made Abram's heart race. He had confronted her with difficult news in the past, and he was instinctively familiar with her emotional protests. Abram dreaded telling her the news. Even though He had clearly told Abram to leave Harran, God had not spelled out exactly where He wanted Abram and Sarai to relocate. Nor had God appeared to Sarai.

Abram was left to tell his wife that she would have to leave their home for an unknown destination. They would become vagabonds, living out of satchels, walking for hours, only stopping at nightfall, hammering tent pegs and cooking on the ground until God told them to stop. But Abram did not equivocate. Abram hoped that his wife would agree to this seismic change.

She did.

After predictable and emotionally charged questions, Sarai trusted her husband and his God. And she packed up her household and went.

And so the journey from Harran to the Promised Land began. Abram and Sarai—along with Lot, Abram's nephew, and their caravan of people, livestock, tents, and cooking supplies—left behind much that was cherished.

Abram believed the promises Yahweh had given him. The message would forever define God's covenant relationship with all future generations. "I will make you into a great nation, and I will bless you; I will make your name great, and you will be a blessing. I will bless those who bless you, and whoever curses you I will curse; and all peoples on earth will be blessed through you" (Genesis 12:2–3).

Adding to the mysterious assignment, the Lord told Abram that from his own body would come an entire nation. A strange pronouncement for a childless husband and wife.

Abram, age seventy-five, and Sarah, now sixty-five, set out for what would eventually become the homeland for the "great nation."

When they finally reached the place God had designated, Abram's urgent priority was to build an altar and worship Yahweh, the God who is.

God's redemptive plan to save the world would come from this very territory. This was Canaan. The Promised Land. The blessings of the future were assured by the faithfulness of the One who had spoken to a man who believed and obeyed—and to a woman who trusted her husband to follow God.

Their Life and Times

Tuesday

Moving Days

Ten generations after Noah, there were still believers in God on the earth. A remnant. A handful of people who listened to the Creator's voice and obeyed and gathered their children together and worshiped the true God.

In choosing the patriarch of a nation, God went back to where He started ... at the intersection of the Tigris and Euphrates rivers — the Fertile Crescent. Abram had been born in that region, but by this time, it was no longer a quiet, unspoiled paradise. Ur was a bustling, commercially vibrant Mesopotamian city.

It was from this place that God first moved Abram's family. Abram's father, Terah, was not a follower of Yahweh. The book of Joshua tells us that he "worshiped other gods" (Joshua 24:2). Other early Hebrew records report that Terah manufactured idols and sold them in the market. Even though we have no account of Terah ever acknowledging Yahweh as God, Abram's father providentially became part of God's plan. God orchestrated Terah's desire to move with his sons and their families to Canaan.

When they came to the city of Harran, built on a tributary of the Euphrates, Terah announced that the caravan would stop and settle there. So they set up tents and made Harran their home until Terah died.

Years later, God spoke to Abram, telling him to move again. Abram and Sarai gathered their extended family and their belongings and traveled to the land God had chosen. This is the place the Jews would call their homeland for the remainder of recorded history.

God made Abram an irrevocable promise, a covenant to make of him a great nation. "I don't understand how this could be," Abram could have replied. "How is this possible? I'm an old man, and my wife's biological clock stopped ticking a long time ago."

But what Abram did, immediately following God's covenant, reveals the true measure of his faith. "So Abram went, as the LORD had told him" (Genesis 12:4). No arguments. No push back. Not even a request for clarification, a second opinion, or further instructions. "So Abram went ..."

Approximately four thousand years after the message was delivered by God and received by Abram, the very same land can still be identified: Israel.

Homelands are important to God. He has a place for His treasured people. Their hearts, their families, and their homes are marked to be a blessing.

Yesterday, today, and forever.

Can You Imagine?

Wednesday

If you have ever moved, you have faced uncertainty. You know the hassle of boxing up all of your belongings and carting them to the new place. But Abram and Sarai had no idea where they were going. Can you imagine leaving your home not knowing your destination?

When God sent Abram and Sarai to Canaan, the wanderers went by faith. They could not see where their new home would be located or if they would like it. But they felt safe moving into the unknown because they trusted God, and they were following His instructions.

Homes are important to God. You may never have thought of God as a real estate agent; however, the Bible is filled with references to the importance of territory and land and your home, both here on earth and for eternity.

Though Abram would travel far to reach his new earthly dwelling, his ultimate goal was far greater: "He was looking forward to the city with foundations, whose architect and builder is God" (Hebrews 11:10). God had promised Abram an eternal home, and he looked forward to living there.

Abram and Sarai spent most of their lives wandering from town to town and living in tents. Actually, this is what you're doing. Even if it's built with brick and stone, your home has a shelf life. It's temporary. "For this world in its present form is passing away" (1 Corinthians 7:31).

When it comes to homes, God has something far better for you than anything you can imagine here on earth.

The home you live in now is temporary. Your permanent home is in heaven. And when moving day comes, unlike Abram and Sarai, you'll know exactly where you're going.

From God's Word ...

"'If I go and prepare a place for you, I will come back and take you to be with me that you also may be where I am.'"

JOHN 14:3

Their Legacy in Scripture

Thursday

1. "'Therefore I tell you, do not worry about your life, what you will eat or drink; or about your body, what you will wear. Is not life more than food, and the body more than clothes? Look at the birds of the air; they do not sow or reap or store away in barns, and yet your heavenly Father feeds them. Are you not much more valuable than they? Can any one of you by worrying add a single hour to your life?'" (MATTHEW 6:25–27).

   What would it be like to "not worry" about your life? God told Abram — who had to tell his wife — to relocate to an unknown place. What do you think could have caused Abram and Sarai to worry? What pressure does moving place on a couple? If you have moved, what was your experience?

2. "Now faith is confidence in what we hope for and assurance about what we do not see. This is what the ancients were commended for" (HEBREWS 11:1–2).

   Abram lived by faith. When God called him and Sarai to leave their home and move to a foreign land, what specific details did God give them about the future? With nothing but God's word to direct him, Abram moved. When has God called you or your spouse into unexpected territories? What would it be like to have your spouse tell you that God was calling him or her to do something that would require stretching on your part?

3. "So [Abram] built an altar [in Canaan] to the LORD, who had appeared to him ... There he built an altar to the LORD and called on the name of the LORD" (GENESIS 12:7–8).

   How did Abram celebrate his arrival in Canaan, far from anything familiar? What did an altar represent? In what ways do you and your spouse "call on the name of the LORD"?

Their Legacy of Prayer

Friday

Reflect On: Genesis 12:1–9

Praise God: For His sovereign ability to plan and control life and for having a distinct plan for your life.

Offer Thanks: That God's plan is for your good and His glory, no matter where He leads, and that He is always with you to guide and instruct you.

Confess: Your unbelief in God's goodness and ability to work on your behalf when you cannot understand your circumstances.

Ask God: To give you the gift of faith that will allow you to trust Him and His word, and to give you a calm willingness to accept where He is leading when doubts arise.

Listen: "Dear children, I have a great and wonderful plan for you —a plan that was established for you long before time began. Walk in My ways and follow My leading. I will be with you always."

Pray: *Father of our lives and future, we know that You have a wonderful and specific plan for us. Whether that means ministering right here in our home or going to the ends of the earth, we want to trust and obey You. Help us to be faithful to Your call, no matter what fears or doubts arise. Strengthen us with Your truth so we may go forward in faith, even into the unknown, and accomplish what You have planned for the future. Amen.*

Jesus Sees and Saves

Abram and Hagar

Meaning of Names:	*Abram* means "exalted father." *Hagar* means "flight" or "forsaken."
Their Character:	He was passive and not willing to wait for God's covenant promise. She was proud and insensitive to her mistress and ran away from her problems.
Their Challenge:	Abram was unhelpful to Hagar in her pregnancy. Rivalry broke out between Hagar and Sarai when Hagar became pregnant and gave birth to a son.
Their Outcome:	God was merciful and visited Hagar, doing what Abram would not do—bless her child.
Key Scripture:	Genesis 16

Their Story

Monday

Gazing at her newborn son almost erased the horror of the nightmares. He was unusually strong and seemed determined to lift his head.

Now one week old, baby Ishmael, with his sparkling eyes, thick black hair, and tiny fingers wrapped around her own, reminded the Egyptian servant girl of her mission. His sturdy legs kicked off his covers, and she replaced them, gently tucking the blanket under his small form. Hagar thanked God that her son had arrived and was healthy. The God of Abram had seen her misery and assured her that her son would have many descendants. It was more than she could have ever hoped for, considering her humble beginnings and station.

Taken from her homeland in Egypt, Hagar had come as a slave into the house of Abram and Sarai several years earlier. And though she was now Abram's wife, something else had changed. She had experienced a spiritual transformation. God had seen her.

Since becoming the property of the wealthy Hebrew couple, Hagar had heard the hushed chatter about Abram's promised son who was supposed to be born to Sarai. But along with every other servant in the house, Hagar could see that Sarai was well past her childbearing years and still wasn't pregnant. They whispered about it. How could their master believe such a thing? And yet he was unwavering, telling them of God's promise.

Then one day as Hagar was carrying a water jug to her master's house, Sarai had approached her. "My handmaid," she said, "you must do something for me."

Bowing low, Hagar replied, "My mistress."

"Look at me, Hagar," Sarai demanded. Hagar lifted her eyes.

"As you know," Sarai continued, "the God of Abram has promised him a son, one I believed would come through me. But this has not happened. Therefore, as an acceptable custom, I order you to go to my husband, lie with him, and produce a male heir for us."

Hagar's face flushed. A slave could not disobey. There were consequences for defiance. Though anguish filled her, she replied to Sarai, "As you wish, my mistress."

Hagar had no choice. And soon she succeeded where Sarai had not. The maidservant's belly swelled, alive with a baby. Hagar's pride ballooned as well.

"The child of my master," she quietly mused. "I carry his child!" The thought was exhilarating.

No longer just the lowly slave girl, Hagar had become an honored mother-to-be, second wife to the master. She was brimming with new life. She was young. She was beautiful. She carried the heir.

Ah, she thought in the conceit of her mind, *I am better than my mistress. My aged mistress. My graying mistress. My barren mistress!*

Now months later, Hagar regretted her arrogance toward Sarai. She had been a strident young woman in those days of early pregnancy, considering herself superior to her mistress. She despised Sarai and taunted her, saying cruel things such as, "You're too old to ever bear a child. At least *my* son is real, not some imaginary promise." The words were searing. Hagar ignored the pain in Sarai's eyes.

And then came Sarai's wrath.

Hagar paid for her insolence. She had underestimated Sarai, who unleashed her fury on the maidservant. Hagar feared for her life. And for the life of her unborn child.

Hagar could not bear the rejection any longer. "I must escape," she resolved. "I will run far away."

So she left ... under the cover of early-morning darkness with some meager provisions—a blanket, a loaf of bread, and a skin of water.

At first, Hagar's youth served her well. Traveling by day, she covered several miles. At night, she depended on the kindness of nomads to shelter her in their tents.

Soon, however, with the baby inside her draining her energy, Hagar grew weaker.

She was on the road to Shur, almost sixty miles south of Canaan from where she had begun her journey.

"It's too far," Hagar cried out as she collapsed near a spring. "My child and I will die. Why did my master, Abram, not protect me? He was silent when Sarai mistreated me. I cannot go on!"

Sobbing quietly in complete despair, she heard someone speak.

"Hagar."

Hagar lifted her face. *Who knows my name?* In the desolation of the wilderness, someone had called to her. Hagar looked and saw a man—a stranger—but she was not afraid.

"Slave of Sarai," the man continued.

Who knows this about me?

"Where have you come from, and where are you going?" he questioned.

Hagar slowly stood to her feet. The man smiled, His gentle countenance erased her fear.

"I'm running away from my mistress," she replied.

"Go back to Sarai, and submit to her." The man's words were kind and reassuring. "I will increase your descendants so much that they will be too numerous to count."[1]

---

1. Genesis 16:10.

The words stunned her. *Did he say, "I will?"* she asked herself. *"I will?" But who could promise to increase my descendants except ...*

Hagar's mind could barely finish the thought.

This is the angel of the God of Abram! He has come to me in my despair. He has ...

"Hagar," the angel interrupted her thoughts, "you will give birth to a son. You shall name him Ishmael, for the Lord has heard of your misery."[2]

With these words, Hagar's strength soared.

The angel added, "He will be a wild donkey of a man; his hand will be against everyone and everyone's hand against him, and he will live in hostility toward all his brothers."[3]

Wondering at the meaning of these mysterious words, Hagar turned.

The angel was gone.

She fell to her knees with hands lifted toward heaven. "You are *El-Roi*, the God who sees me!" she exulted in joy and wonder. "I have now seen the One who sees me."

Hagar turned and started back toward the home of her master and mistress. She would tell them about the God who sees, the One who had met her.

Days later, as Abram's house came into view, Hagar stopped.

Still thinking of the miraculous encounter, she spoke in a whisper, "God has seen me in my affliction. He has heard my prayer. He has blessed me."

Coming to Sarai's tent, Hagar bowed. "Forgive me. I will no longer trouble you," she promised.

When Hagar delivered her son, she named him Ishmael—"God hears." And now, with her baby squirming quietly in his bed, Hagar closed her eyes in gratitude.

"You heard me, Lord," she sighed. "And You see me."

2. See Genesis 16:11.
3. Genesis 16:12.

Their Life and Times

Tuesday

The God Who Is Always There

Sarai's relentless emotional torment of Hagar was too much for the maidservant to bear. Hagar considered herself an innocent victim. She had done exactly what Sarai had ordered her to do — and it had produced the hoped-for outcome. Hagar had conceived.

But it takes no stretch of the imagination to predict how Sarai could have changed her mind about offering the beautiful young Egyptian as a surrogate. Once her pregnancy was certain, Hagar began to despise Sarai. Like Hagar's waistline, the acrimony between them swelled.

As a slave of Sarai, probably acquired when she and Abram were in Egypt, Hagar was Sarai's property.[4] She had no rights of her own. She had obeyed her mistress by lying with her master. But in running from Sarai's anger, Hagar was breaking the law. She knew she must leave secretly and move quickly before her absence was discovered, or else she could be caught and punished. In those times it was not unusual for runaway slaves to be arrested and imprisoned. Perhaps executed.

When she fled Abram's home in Hebron, Hagar ran toward the desert on one of several trade routes that led to Shur. The terrain was barren and treacherous; the assault of dry, hot wind was relentless. The persistent danger of bandits and wild animals made this no easy journey for a pregnant woman traveling by herself.

Though she set out alone, Hagar could have met up with one of the many caravans traversing the well-traveled route, affording her a welcome source of security.

At the time, caravans were broad enterprises, some containing as many as three thousand donkeys, though five to six hundred were more common. As caravans followed routes located near fresh streams to water their animals, Hagar would have had plenty to drink. Merciful people — women — in the caravans would have given the pregnant runaway food to help her keep up her strength.

---

4. See Genesis 12:10–20.

Though companionship, food, and water were necessities for Hagar, they were not as important to her as protecting her unborn child. Depending on how far along she was in her pregnancy, Hagar would perhaps have traveled between six and nine miles a day. And even if she had the protection of others, traveling by foot would have been difficult, as the changing desert weather could range from searing heat in the midafternoon to almost frosty temperatures in the early-morning hours. If Hagar joined a family caravan, kindhearted people may have shared their tent with her.

As Hagar headed away, she stopped at "the spring that is beside the road to Shur" (Genesis 16:7) to fill her water skin.

It was here that the "angel of the Lord" visited Hagar. Many Bible scholars identify the angel of the Lord as Jesus, the preincarnate God in human flesh. Throughout the Old Testament, the angel of the Lord made many appearances, but the inaugural visit of an invisible God in visible form is this visit to Hagar. The angel could have appeared to Adam. Or Enoch. Or Noah. Or Abram. But he didn't. Instead, the angel of the Lord first appeared to a weak, frightened, and vulnerable Egyptian slave girl.

When Hagar set out to flee from her mistress, she could not have imagined an encounter with the God who created her. But that is exactly what happened.

God sees. God knows. God loves. God rescues.

Can You Imagine?

Wednesday

Hagar had run out of options. She had obediently slept with Abram in order to become a surrogate mother for her mistress. In that single act she conceived. That was her mistress's plan. Hagar's ability to do what Sarai could not do caused resentment.[5] The bitterness was mutual. Sarai and Hagar despised each other.

Hagar flaunted her pregnancy before Sarai. But Hagar was Sarai's property. She had no rights. Abram, the only person who could have

5. See Genesis 16:4.

helped her, refused to get involved.[6] He gave Sarai permission to treat Hagar in whatever way she thought best, so Sarai mistreated her pregnant servant. Hagar was in an impossible situation. Can you imagine?

Like Hagar, you or someone you know may be facing what feels like an impossible situation. It may be a spouse you think will never meet your needs or one you can never please. The breathtaking romance you once cherished is gone. Disrespect and constant fighting can make a person want to run away.

Like Hagar, leaving—emotionally, if not physically—may seem your only option. And sympathizing companions may foolishly encourage an escape. "You deserve better," they tempt. "You have every reason to leave."

When Hagar ran away from her problems, she learned something important. God saw her misery, and He trailed her. She could not run away from Him. Not letting her wallow in self-pity, the Lord asked her, "Where are you going?"

Hagar identified her feelings and spoke the truth. "I'm running away from my mistress" (Genesis 16:8).

But the transforming moment happened when the presence of the Lord surrounded Hagar. The desperate woman discovered that God had pursued her. He was *El-Roi*, the God who sees.

Being out of options can be a good thing. It can be the opportunity to turn to the compassionate One who sees. God knows your situation, and He can transform it into something good.

From God's Word . . .

> "I can do all this through [Jesus Christ]
> who gives me strength."
>
> PHILIPPIANS 4:13

---

6. See Genesis 16:6.

Their Legacy in Scripture

Thursday

1. **"Humble yourselves before the Lord, and he will lift you up"** (JAMES 4:10).

   What did Hagar do to earn Sarai's mistreatment? How did Abram contribute to Hagar's hopelessness? Think about a time when you felt invisible. What do you learn about God from Hagar's story that can change your outlook? Identify some attitudes you may have about your spouse or your marriage that need to be changed. What do you need to confess?

2. **"This is what the LORD says, he who made the earth, the LORD who formed it and established it—the LORD is his name: 'Call to me and I will answer you and tell you great and unsearchable things you do not know'"** (JEREMIAH 33:2–3).

   God tells us to cry out to Him when we feel weak and wrestle with difficulties. In trials He promises His presence. What was God's role in the story of Hagar? When in the past has God rescued you or your spouse from something beyond your control?

3. **"For I am the Lord your God who takes hold of your right hand and says to you, 'Do not fear; I will help you'"** (ISAIAH 41:13–14).

   God sent Hagar back to her difficult circumstances armed with something new. She had new information about her future. What was it? How do God's promises and presence change your attitude in your home?

Their Legacy of Prayer

Friday

Reflect On:	Genesis 16
Praise God:	For being the God who sees every painful situation and stands ready to respond to the cries of His children. For His perfect timing and goodness.
Offer Thanks:	That the Creator of the universe cares about you and can transform your attitude and give you His heavenly perspective regarding your circumstances, and that He is always planning for your good.
Confess:	The sin of self-pity. That instead of seeking God's Word for a remedy, you too often run to companions or unholy habits for relief.
Ask God:	To teach you how to magnify His presence in your life, even when your situation doesn't change, and to make you sensitive to Him and to open your heart to discuss your every thought and attitude in prayer with Him throughout the day.
Listen:	"My children, when I called you to be Mine, I didn't abandon you. I am with you every moment of the day. Never hesitate to cry out to Me in times of trouble. Run toward Me, not away from Me. I have a plan for you that is good."
Pray:	*Lord Jesus, the One who appeared to Hagar, we thank You that You always see us and come to our rescue. Though we cannot see You, we see the evidence of Your power. You are with us when we rise, as we move through the activities of our day, and when we go to sleep. Lord, we want to honor You with patient endurance and humble obedience.*

7

Angels Unaware

Abraham and Sarah

Meaning of Names:	*Abraham* means "father of a multitude." *Sarah* means "princess."
Their Character:	He believed God's promise and was alert to welcoming God's messengers. She joined her husband in entertaining and serving their guests.
Their Challenge:	It would have been inconvenient to serve visitors in the heat of the day.
Their Outcome:	They were surprised by three visitors with a divine message.
Key Scripture:	Genesis 18:1–15

Their Story

Monday

My, my, Sarah thought to herself, *Abraham is certainly in a spirited mood.*

And he was.

It was just after noon. The sun, unfettered by any clouds at all, pounded down on the little village near Hebron, between the towns of Bethel and Ai. Although the area was somewhat desolate, Sarah knew Abraham loved this place. The commotion of city life was never his choice. He and Sarah had pitched their tent here as a permanent—at least for now—home.

Ninety-nine-year-old Abraham had just come bursting into their tent, asking Sarah to prepare a loaf of bread. And quickly! *What is all the fuss about?* she wondered. *Why the rush?* At eighty-nine, Sarah was not exactly quick at anything anymore.

Three unexpected guests had come to visit, and Abraham was in full hospitality mode. Before Sarah had the chance to question her husband, he had already rushed out of the tent and was gone.

Unable to stifle her curiosity, Sarah followed Abraham at a distance. She watched as he quickly made his way to the herd, selected the best calf, and gave it to a servant to prepare as a lavish meal for his guests.

Sarah looked at the visitors. Three ordinary men. Nothing in particular stood out about them.

"Oh, well," she said, and made her way back inside her tent to bake bread.

Abraham had moved his family, servants, and flocks several times since their arrival in Canaan from Harran. Sarah longed for a permanent place to live. However, she followed her husband's will and dutifully relocated time and again.

Then, after more than a decade, they settled in the vicinity of Hebron, near the great trees of Mamre. It was there that God changed their names from Abram and Sarai to Abraham and Sarah. The long years of sojourning were over. Sarah had a home. At the time of the visit from the three men, they had been in the same place for thirteen years.

After preparing the bread, Sarah gave it to a servant to deliver to her husband. Because she hadn't been invited to the meal, Sarah stood just inside the flap of her tent, listening to the conversation between Abraham and his visitors as they ate.

The meal ended, and the men leaned back as they talked. Sarah could tell that the dialogue had taken a serious turn. She listened intently. Imagine her surprise when one of the men said to Abraham, "Where is your wife, Sarah?"

She heard Abraham hesitate, clearly taken aback by the curious inquiry. *How does this man know my name?* she wondered silently.

"There, in the tent," Abraham answered. She pictured him pointing to their home.

That's strange, Sarah said to herself. *Why would the stranger ask about me?* She leaned forward to look around the tent flap.

The guest unfolded his arms, leaned in, and looked directly at Abraham.

"This time next year, when I return to you, your wife, Sarah ..." —he paused—"will have a son."

Sarah laughed at the thought. *Have you seen my wrinkles, sir?* Her years of potential childbearing were long past. Her body was thoroughly incapable of carrying a child. Hers was a life of barrenness, and she had learned to accept it. *What madness is this message?* Sarah wondered. *After my body is worn-out and my dear husband is old, will I now have the privilege of giving him a child?*

Her mind dwelled on this strange proclamation. Either these words were bitter mocking, or they were prophetic. Sarah had no idea which. Her heart raced as she caught a glimpse of Abraham, who looked dumbfounded. Sarah could not contain a muffled laugh.

One of the visitors asked with a boldness that echoed in the silence that followed, "Why did Sarah laugh and say, 'Will I really have a child, now that I am old?' Is anything too hard for the Lord?"

His words pierced Sarah. *How could this man have known what I did not speak aloud?* She trembled.

Is anything too hard for the LORD? Sarah silently repeated. *Who is this man? Surely it is the Lord!*

The man continued. "I will return to you at the appointed time next year, Abraham, and Sarah will have a son."

To Abraham and his wife, these words were a pronouncement, a confirmation of the same promise they had heard many years before from the Almighty.

Without even realizing it, out of view but not out of earshot, Sarah spoke aloud, "I did not laugh." She didn't mean to lie, but she hadn't meant for anyone to hear her.

Once more she heard the Lord speak.

"You did laugh, Sarah."

Sarah could have been embarrassed. After all, the Lord had caught her in a lie. But somehow a sense of peace crowded out all other emotions. The Lord was not condemning her, but only confirming His identity and the certainty of His promise.

Sarah began to weep. *A son. The Lord spoke to me. He is finally giving me a son. He said so.*

She fell to her knees, grateful that her husband had chosen to entertain the strangers.

Her lips moved as she praised aloud, "Oh, Lord, nothing is too hard for You."

Nothing at all.

Their Life and Times

Tuesday

Guess Who's Coming to Lunch

During this time of the day, when the sun was directly overhead and its rays most penetrating through the clear, dry air, locals did their best to huddle under the shade of one of the trees or inside their tents. Never would they stand outside or travel, unless it was absolutely necessary.

So visitors to this part of the region were rare but especially in the heat of the day.

Yet one afternoon while sitting under the shadow of the door flap of his tent, Abraham looked up to see three men approaching. He was certain he had never seen them before. He couldn't put his finger on it, but there was something unusual about the three ... something curious.

In ancient Near Eastern culture, hospitality was an obsession. Being hospitable to any guest—invited or not—was never a choice; it was a duty. Even so, Abraham's response to the surprise guests appeared overly enthusiastic.

First, he hurried from his tent and pleaded with them to stop. Bowing low to the ground wasn't required for uninvited strangers, but in this case, Abraham believed it was right. He offered water so the men could rinse their feet and invited them to rest beneath his sprawling shade tree to cool down. Anticipating their every need, he also offered them food. All of these kindnesses were spoken in a single breath, not a conventional thing for a man nearly one hundred years old.

As the visit unfolded, Abraham and Sarah realized these three men were exceptional. They knew Sarah's name without asking. They were able to read her thoughts. And then they prophesied that in one year Sarah would bear a son, their words echoing the promise given by God to Abraham years before, when they were young.

These men were not mortals. Two were angels, and one was the angel of the Lord. These three beings appeared and disappeared without needing any transportation. Their bodies did not require any of the food Sarah had prepared.

God had sent these men to Abraham and Sarah to deliver the astounding news that Sarah would give birth to a child. The news foretold of Abraham's promised son ... Isaac, the boy of the covenant, who would be born miraculously to this elderly couple.

How could Abraham and Sarah have known the significance of their enthusiastic welcome of the visitors? How could they have ever predicted the blessing these men would bring?

More than a thousand years later, the writer to the Hebrews borrowed a page from this account of the three visitors to Abraham and Sarah. "Keep on loving one another as brothers and sisters. Do not forget to show hospitality to strangers, for by so doing some people have shown hospitality to angels without knowing it" (Hebrews 13:1–2).

No one ever knows for sure what may come by way of a visitor. Even the uninvited ones may bring a surprise. A blessing.

Can You Imagine?

Wednesday

Hospitality is a team sport. When you agree to an open-door policy in your home, amazing things can happen.

Welcoming an uninvited visitor into your home for a drink of water on a hot day may sound like kindness. But what if it were three visitors? And what if you and your spouse gave them a basin of warm water to clean their feet, a few slices of freshly baked bread, and a lavishly prepared veal dinner from scratch? Can you imagine doing all this for surprise guests?

The picture of Abraham frantic about accommodating three uninvited guests is almost comical. And his eagerness to involve Sarah in the welcome and her willingness to jump in are revealing. Perhaps they sensed these were no ordinary people.

Hospitality was a given in biblical times, but it isn't so much today. What about in your home? Do you have an open-door policy? Are you friendly to uninvited guests? That's good. Are you welcoming? That's even better. Are you lavishly hospitable? That's the idea.

Why is it important to welcome visitors?

The story of Abraham and Sarah and the three men gives us a delightful answer to these questions. You never know what blessings or rewards God may send your way through the people who enter your home. Of course, they may appear to be ordinary—neighbor kids with scraped knees from a bicycle pileup on the sidewalk or the guy who services your air conditioner.

Or your guests may be angels. Their visit to your home may be a divine appointment, a life-changing encounter for you or them with the transcendent God.

This was the case with Zacchaeus. One day, Jesus was walking through the city of Jericho. A despised tax collector, a short man named Zacchaeus, decided to climb a low-limbed fig tree to get a better look at the Messiah. To everyone's surprise, when Jesus reached the tree, He stopped and looked up at the little man. "Come down, Zacchaeus," Jesus said. "I'm going to stay at your house."[1]

---

1. See Luke 19:5.

What kind of hostess was Zacchaeus's wife? We know that Jesus invited Himself, but how welcoming was she? Scripture says that Zacchaeus "welcomed him gladly" (Luke 19:6), so surely he and his family must have had an open-door policy at their house.

That day, Zacchaeus's wife heard a knock at the door. Standing there was her husband, and with him stood another man. We don't know if she knew the identity of the visitor, but that didn't matter. She welcomed Him in, and soon discovered that the person in her home was the Creator of the universe, God in human form. Not only did her husband bring a new friend to their house; he brought the Savior of the world—the Savior of Zacchaeus's whole family.

When you open your door, you never know who might come in.

From God's Word . . .

"Keep on loving one another as brothers and sisters. Do not forget to show hospitality to strangers, for by so doing some people have shown hospitality to angels without knowing it."

HEBREWS 13:1–2

Their Legacy in Scripture

Thursday

1. "As Jesus and his disciples were on their way, he came to a village where a woman named Martha opened her home to him. She had a sister called Mary, who sat at the Lord's feet listening to what he said. But Martha was distracted by all the preparations that had to be made. She came to him and asked, 'Lord, don't you care that my sister has left me to do the work by myself? Tell her to help me!'" (LUKE 10:38–40).

   Sometimes hospitality means fastidiously scurrying around in the kitchen to find something to eat. And sometimes it only requires your undivided attention. Which kind of host or hostess do you tend to be? What kind is your spouse? What can you learn from each other?

2. "Then Jesus said to his host, 'When you give a luncheon or dinner, do not invite your friends, your brothers or sisters, your relatives, or your rich neighbors; if you do, they may invite you back and so you will be repaid. But when you give a banquet, invite the poor, the crippled, the lame, the blind, and you will be blessed. Although they cannot repay you, you will be repaid at the resurrection of the righteous'" (LUKE 14:12–14).

   Do you suppose that the door to the emergency room of the hospital near your home is ever locked? Why not? The word *hospitality* includes the word *hospital*. Why do people go to a hospital? What can happen to those who come to your home?

3. "Anyone who welcomes you welcomes me, and anyone who welcomes me welcomes the one who sent me … And if anyone gives even a cup of cold water to one of these little ones who is my disciple, truly I tell you, that person will certainly not lose their reward" (MATTHEW 10:40, 42).

   Think of someone you know who has "the gift of hospitality." How do you feel when you're in their home? Why is this quality called a "gift"? What does Abraham and Sarah's story say about the reward of using the gift?

Their Legacy of Prayer

Friday

Reflect On: Genesis 18

Praise God: For His generosity and hospitality. For His love and open-door policy. "Come to me," Jesus said, "all you who are weary and burdened, and I will give you rest."

Offer Thanks: For giving you friends and others who need you. Thank Him that there are many people around you to whom you can reach out and show the love of Christ through hospitality. For opening your heart to be sensitive to the things that please God, and that you are being molded into Christ's image daily.

Confess: Your busyness, inattention, and lack of hospitality to those in need and for hoarding your time and your things instead of offering them to God for His purposes.

Ask God: To instill in you a heart of generosity and to mold you into a giver. To give you the desire to help others without ever expecting anything in return.

Listen: "My children, everything you have, including your breath and your possessions, are gifts from My generous hand. I love you and constantly welcome you into My presence. Be content with what you have and entertain others with enthusiasm. I want you to share with others what I have given you."

Pray: *Gracious Father, You have blessed us with the riches of Your grace and Your good gifts. Alert us to the people You want welcomed into our hearts and home. Nudge us to know when and where to share these blessings from You with those You send our way. Lord, we want others to meet You because we are obedient to Your call to live generously. Amen.*

God's Promise Fulfilled

Abraham and Sarah

Meaning of Names:	*Abraham* means "father of a multitude." *Sarah* means "princess."
Their Character:	He was a man of faith and the grateful recipient of God's promised blessings. She was a doubter-turned-joyous worshiper who celebrated the birth of a son in her elderly years.
Their Challenge:	Unbelief, the human impossibility of childbirth in old age, and resentment within the family.
Their Outcome:	God's fulfillment of a great promise. Joy and laughter over the birth they never could have imagined.
Key Scripture:	Genesis 21:1–7

Their Story

Monday

Sarah had just finished nursing Isaac and had laid him down to rest on a padded mat. He stirred for a moment, his eyes closed. Then his little mouth puckered in a sucking motion, and he went to sleep. He looked so peaceful.

She returned to bed where Abraham had been watching her. He drew a breath to speak. "Who could this be, having just nursed a baby? Aren't you my ninety-year-old wife?" His chuckle filled the room, and Sarah hushed him, lest he wake the child.

Then she smiled and began to laugh like she had when she was a young girl.

It felt good to be so happy.

The elderly couple savored these moments of unexpected, irrepressible joy. During their long lives, times of levity had been rare. Now with the events of the past few days, laughter was easy.

Sarah tried to gather herself, but the giggles were hard to stop. Finally she calmed down when the baby turned his head, still asleep. "Oh, Abraham," she sighed, her eyes dancing. "What if we could have seen this day a year ago? Would we have dared to dream that this could really happen?"

"God is good," he said with a nod.

It was so satisfying to laugh. To have a reason to laugh.

With just a hint of remorse, she remembered a year ago, almost to this very day. She had laughed then too. But her attitude had been far different—not something she was proud of. Last year's laughter was cynical. It had even had a touch of outrage and mockery.

Last year, when she had overheard a conversation between Abraham and an angel, the heavenly messenger had promised that Sarah would give birth to a son "by this time next year."

Sarah's reaction to the absurdity of the visitor's prediction revealed her disbelief—bitter sarcasm and pessimism fueled by years of infertility and disappointment. She had endured Abraham's fathering of a child by her own slave girl, and the nasty emotional warfare that resulted. She had watched Abraham's son-by-another-woman grow, thriving in the love of his doting father. Though it was Sarah's own doing, her resentment must have cast a dark ugliness over her.

But the angel heard her thoughts and her laughter. "Nothing is too hard for God. Just wait and see. In a year I will come back, and you will have a son."

And three months later, the impossible happened. Sarah conceived. Why had she ever doubted? Of course nothing was impossible with God! They named him Isaac, meaning "he laughs."

Now, two weeks following the miraculous birth and one week after the ceremonial circumcision, Sarah bubbled with the exhilaration enjoyed by a new mom. Oh, how wonderful it was. How glorious to feel God's blessing at such a time of life. How merciful to have the lost years of youth, fertility, and joy restored.

An ageless God had fulfilled His promise and accomplished the impossible. The Sovereign Lord had stretched His gracious hand to an unbelieving old woman and confirmed His covenant pledge to her believing husband.

God gave them a boy.

And soaring, wonderful laughter.

Their Life and Times

Tuesday

Belonging to God, Becoming Identified as His

Abraham and Sarah celebrated the birth of Isaac and were careful to obey the Lord's command to fulfill the sign of the covenant — circumcision. "When his son Isaac was eight days old, Abraham circumcised him, as God commanded him" (Genesis 21:4).

As a covenant requirement for Abraham's descendant, God had identified circumcision as necessary for every man.[1] This ceremony — the cutting away of the male foreskin — had already been long practiced in the Middle East for health reasons.

However, when God instructed Abraham — and all generations of Hebrews from that day forward — to be circumcised, He gave it an entirely new meaning. Circumcision was God's way of saying, "The Hebrews belong to Me; circumcision is the mark of My seal on them."

Circumcision symbolized the cutting away of sin and the need to be cleansed. And this symbol was meant to be carried on from generation to generation, a fitting gesture since the male organ delivers the seed that produces descendants.

The male children of Israel carried a reminder of their covenant with God on their bodies. They were commanded to be aware of their obligation to that promise. Being faithful to God would result in His favor, but being unfaithful to God would bring consequences. Circumcision was a way of saying, "If I am not loyal to God in faith

---

1. See Genesis 17:9–14.

and obedience, then He may remove me and my offspring from His blessing."

Even with the outward sign, the Israelites did not always obey. When they strayed from His commandments, God warned the people, "Circumcise your hearts, therefore, and do not be stiff-necked any longer" (Deuteronomy 10:16). God demanded internal obedience as well.

God's spiritual covenant was for all Israelites, both men and women. Abraham was given the directive, but Sarah was included as a partner in the promises of God. The implications of being identified as God's people and separated to produce godly offspring included everyone.

God chose the most private part of a man's body — one that must be shared with his wife in order to produce descendants — to be marked as His possession. Together a couple was to please God by birthing godly offspring.[2]

And as faithful partners and nurturers of their children, both husbands and wives continue the building of God's kingdom on earth.

Under the new covenant established when Jesus came to earth, baptism became the equivalent of circumcision.[3] It is a mark of God's ownership of His people. In the water of baptism we are identified as God's covenant children, separated from the old nature and born into God's family.

And just as it was with Abraham and Sarah, our part in this covenant transaction is living by faith and obeying God's Word.

---

2. See Malachi 2:15.
3. See Colossians 2:8–15.

Can You Imagine?

Wednesday

Celebration and tears. Levity and surgery. Could the roller coaster swing more wildly? You have likely experienced these extremes in your own marriage.

On your wedding day, the minister spoke sobering words. "For better, for worse, for richer, for poorer, in sickness or in health, in joy or in sorrow." Can you imagine such a wide sweep of opposites?

If you've been married for a while, you remember the joy of falling in love and the pain of your first argument. You may recall both the ecstasy when your first child was born and the frustration of sleepless nights. You probably have known both the warmth of long walks with the spouse you adore and standing by the bedside of your companion who was too sick to move.

Someone has wisely compared marriage to a sailing expedition. You're headed across open water, sometimes enjoying smooth seas and sometimes — often — negotiating strong crosswinds. Times of serenity and joy. Moments of sheer terror.

Abraham and Sarah's lives were surely marked by extremes. Some of their pain — the death of Abraham's father in Harran, Sarah's childlessness, the constant moving, famine in Canaan — came to them in their innocence. Other travails — lying to the Egyptian pharaoh (see Genesis 12:10 – 20) and having a child through Hagar — were the results of their own foolish decisions and their lack of trust that God would do what He had promised to do.[4]

No matter what you face, as the pendulum swings in your marriage, God does not change and you are never alone. Because God is able to orchestrate all things for His redemptive purposes, He is your source for celebration.

> *The Lord is never far away,*
> *but through all grief distressing,*
> *An ever-present help and stay,*
> *our peace and joy and blessing.*[5]

---

4. See Genesis 12:10 – 20; 16:1 – 4.
5. "Sing Praise to God Who Reigns Above," lyrics by Johann J. Schütz, 1675.

It's God's desire for you to live by faith in His presence as you ride the roller coaster, knowing His faithfulness and grace will sustain you. As you experience God's presence through His Word and trust His sovereignty above your circumstances, you will be able to "rejoice in the Lord always" (Philippians 4:4).

Nothing can separate you from His love. His peace and joy are yours.

From God's Word . . .

"Consider it pure joy, my brothers and sisters, whenever you face trials of many kinds, because you know that the testing of your faith produces perseverance. Let perseverance finish its work so that you may be mature and complete, not lacking anything."

JAMES 1:2–4

Their Legacy in Scripture

Thursday

1. "Sarah said, 'God has brought me laughter, and everyone who hears about this will laugh with me.' And she added, 'Who would have said to Abraham that Sarah would nurse children? Yet I have borne him a son in his old age'" (GENESIS 21:6–7).

How is Sarah's laughter this time different from her laughter when she overheard the visitors speaking to her husband?[6]

What does Sarah's situation tell us about who God is and how to respond when life turns out differently than we expected? What does the birth of Isaac, despite Sarah's lack of faith, her doubts and missteps, even her bitterness, teach us about God's faithfulness?

2. "Shout for joy to the LORD, all the earth. Worship the LORD with gladness; come before him with joyful songs" (PSALM 100:1–2).

According to this verse, how are we to respond to the Lord at all times? What brings joy to you, to your spouse? What robs you of joy? Ask yourself, "Am I fun to live with?" and then do something creative to bring laughter and music into your home (read from a joke book after dinner, take a trip to the zoo, watch a funny animal video, sing "You Are My Sunshine" when your spouse comes into the room).

3. "'Blessed are you who hunger now, for you will be satisfied. Blessed are you who weep now, for you will laugh'" (LUKE 6:21).

Blessed in this verse means "happy." What heart issue is Jesus addressing here? What do Jesus' words imply about material and physical comforts? As a Christ-follower, how can you be joyful in the midst of the highs and lows of "for better, for worse, for richer, for poorer, in sickness or in health, in joy or in sorrow"?

---

6. See Genesis 18:12.

Their Legacy of Prayer

Friday

Reflect On: Genesis 21:1–7

Praise God: For the gift of smiles and laughter and for His power to transform anything that comes into your life. For His Holy Spirit that produces joy and inspires new growth.

Offer Thanks: That God considers you His precious child and strengthens you through trials. For moving you into a deeper relationship with Him and your spouse.

Confess: Your lack of joy and the critical or sarcastic things that roll off your tongue too often. Confess any ungratefulness and unforgiveness toward your spouse that robs you of joy.

Ask God: To give you the joy of the Lord and to help you accept the things you cannot change now. Ask to be transformed into a person who smiles and displays grace and joy.

Listen: "Dear children, I take great delight in you and am watching over every detail of your lives. Nothing can separate you from My love. I will be your supply of joy, which will never run dry. Ask Me, and I will fill you with My Spirit. There is much you cannot see right now. Trust Me. Sing. Rejoice in hope. Be patient; I am with you.

Pray: *God of joy and peace, we rejoice in Your strength and Your sovereign ability to steer us through every situation. You are adequate in all things. Help us to experience Your joy that is available for us today. We want to enjoy the fullness of unrestrained laughter with each other when things are great, and we want to praise You on days that are not so good. Make us strong to always rejoice in You. Amen.*

9

Pass the Salt

Lot and Wife

Meaning of Names:	*Lot* means "veil," "covering," or "hidden." The name of Lot's wife is not given in the Bible.
Their Character:	He was a good man but was easily lured by the prosperity of a corrupt society. She was disobedient to God and unwilling to surrender her comfortable lifestyle.
Their Challenge:	They lived in a wicked city that God was going to destroy.
Their Outcome:	Lot's descendants became the Moabites and the Ammonites, Israel's enemies. Lot's wife died when she disobeyed God's word.
Key Scripture:	Genesis 19:1–29

Their Story

Monday

"Don't look back," Lot had screamed. "Don't look back!" Running as swiftly as he could, Lot's words rose like the scalding fire that was leveling the city of Sodom behind him. He had warned his wife to obey the angel's command and not turn back or look at the reckoning that was destroying everything — their home, their possessions, and their friends.

But Lot's wife had turned to see the city she loved. Just one deadly, final time.

Now Lot shivered as he sat at the mouth of a cave looking at the smoke billowing from the plain. His two daughters slept, thoroughly worn-out from the chaos and from the shock of their mother's death.

But there was no respite for their father. Lot's mind was tangled in memories and misgivings. His wealth, dignity, and self-importance were gone. He sat stupefied and defeated.

A once-good Hebrew man who had slipped trying to balance on the tightrope of righteousness and sin, Lot could now do little more than breathe.

How far he had fallen.

Lot recalled the day long ago when his Uncle Abram came into his tent and announced that God—the true God—had spoken to him. God had directed Abram to step out with his wife, Sarai, and his nephew, Lot, and leave their home in Harran.

The news of such a mysterious adventure had ignited excitement in Lot back then, and he had agreed to make the journey. Packing his possessions and gathering his livestock, Lot set out with his uncle to travel five hundred miles southwest toward Canaan.

Sometime during the travels and settlements, Lot had chosen a wife. And over the next several years, two daughters were born to them.

Life in Canaan had been good until a drought caused a food shortage throughout the country. Abram and Sarai and Lot were forced to go to Egypt for a time. When they came back to Canaan, Lot's family and Abram's family together settled between the cities of Bethel and Ai. Ironically, the diversion to Egypt had been a boon to their business. They returned to Canaan far wealthier—with plentiful livestock and servants—than when they had left.

In fact, so vast were Lot and Abram's flocks that the men's holdings could no longer be managed together by their company of servants. The herdsmen were quarreling. Bitterness entangled Lot and his uncle. But trusting God's provision, the wise Abram suggested they go their separate ways. As the entitled elder, he could have chosen the best for himself, but Abram graciously offered his nephew first choice of the land.

Lot stood on a high hill overlooking the Jordan Valley to the east with its lush meadows, rich soil, and prosperous cities. He consulted his own best judgment and announced, "I'll go there." The area offered what they thought they wanted. It featured sprawling marketplaces, vast tracts of fertile land for their herds, and a comfortable lifestyle found nowhere among the sheep herders and tent dwellers of Bethel and Ai.

As Lot and his wife settled in, enjoying the things that pleased them, one thing was lacking—a place to worship. In their previous travels, Uncle Abram had always built an altar to Yahweh, leading the family in worship wherever they lived. The altar had become the centerpiece for their communion with a holy God. A place of prayer, confession, and reverence. But in Sodom, neither Lot nor anyone else had built an altar. No altar meant no regular worship, no fellowship with believers, and no maintenance of holy habits. No accountability.

Lot and his wife quickly adapted to metropolitan life. Soon their status rose as Lot assumed power in the hierarchy of the city. Lot's wife was proud of her husband, who held an honored position, sitting as a judge by Sodom's city gate. She basked in her privilege and the stature that came with being married to a wealthy, well-respected man.

The couple reveled in their lifestyle, relishing the romance ... the magnetic power and excitement of the city. Rationalizing the rampant immorality, Lot mingled with the people as a man of prestige. Even if the memories of Abram's faithful prayers and closeness to God haunted him, Lot succumbed to the pressures of his culture and ignored the tug toward righteousness. He decided to live with the tension because his family was happy. They loved Sodom.

One day, two visitors walked into the city. Sitting at his usual spot at the city gate, Lot rose quickly to greet them. "Stay at my home." When the two strangers resisted, Lot insisted they accept his hospitality. And so they went to Lot's home for safe lodging for the night.

The men—actually angels—had been sent by God to mercifully remove Lot and his family from Sodom.

> The two men said to Lot, "Do you have anyone else here— sons-in-law, sons or daughters, or anyone else in the city who belongs to you? Get them out of here, because we are going to destroy this place. The outcry to the LORD against its people is so great that he has sent us to destroy it."
>
> GENESIS 19:12–13

At dawn, the angels commanded Lot's family to hurry and leave. When Lot hesitated, the angels seized him, his wife, and two daughters by the hand and dragged them safely out of the city. As they were running, one of the angels turned to the family and shouted, "Don't look back, and don't stop anywhere in the plain! Flee to the mountains or you will be swept away!" (Genesis 19:17).

Lot joined in shouting the warning. "Don't look back," he shrieked to his wife and daughters.

"My home, my friends!" Lot's wife cried out.

"Don't look back," Lot screamed. "Don't stop!"

But Lot's wife ignored the warning and turned around to look, inescapably drawn back to the place of her treasures. In that moment, she froze in her place, becoming a lifeless statue of salt.

Later and at a safe distance away, Lot and his daughters huddled in a cave. The reflection of the boiling city danced on Lot's face. "My wife is gone forever. Everything is gone," he cried. "What have I done?"

Their Life and Times

Tuesday

The Consequences of Choices

Lot looked over "the whole plain of the Jordan toward Zoar," which was "well watered, like the garden of the LORD [Eden], like the land of Egypt" and "chose for himself the whole plain of the Jordan and set out toward the east." He "lived among the cities of the plain and pitched his tents near Sodom" (Genesis 13:10–12).

Lot's decision makes sense from a human perspective. The land was a fertile oasis of meadows and lush vegetation.

However, he refused to defer to his uncle and made the choice selfishly. Nowhere is it recorded that Lot acknowledged the Lord or sought Him for wisdom about which land he should choose. And there is no record that he scouted out the area to see if its people would be sound, respectable neighbors. So it seems likely that Lot did not know that "the people of Sodom were wicked and were sinning greatly against the LORD" (Genesis 13:13).

Sodom was the most significant city in a five-town settlement that included Gomorrah, Admah, Zoboyim, and Zoar. Sodom's great

wickedness indulged in social oppression, rampant adultery, the practice of homosexuality, lying, criminal activity, and immoral business
practices. The people were merciless and cruel. However, Sodom,
being a lush and fertile land, was quite prosperous, a place where citizens lived comfortably. The city thrived by selling its rich storehouse
of salt, bitumen, and potash deposits around the Dead Sea.[1] Sodom
also enjoyed wealth from the several trading centers it established for
caravans traveling north and south.

Although God had decided to destroy the wicked city, His mercy
toward Lot and his family was evident. Just before arriving in Sodom,
these same two angels had visited with Lot's uncle and spiritual mentor, Abraham.

Pleading with the angel of the Lord to spare Sodom, Abraham
wondered if even ten righteous people lived there, including Lot.
But there were not even ten people who followed God in that large,
bustling city.

Eventually, the angels removed Lot, his wife, and two daughters
from Sodom and destroyed the towns of the plain. But Lot's wife lost
her life when she disobeyed the angel's command not to look back.

Enticed by the euphoria of a glamorous place to live, Lot and his
wife chose an evil city. The result was ruinous.

Can You Imagine?

Wednesday

It's a tragic tableau. A poignant warning. A husband, a father whom
the Bible calls a "righteous man" (2 Peter 2:7), huddled with his
two daughters, grieving the loss of his wife and watching the things
he cherished consumed in a searing fire. Can you imagine the deep
regret Lot was feeling?

If in that moment Lot had been given the opportunity to rewind
the past events of his life, he surely would have.

He would not have moved his family to Sodom. When given a
choice of places to live, rather than consult the Lord, Lot had chosen

---

1. Bitumen is an oily substance that was used as a sealant to waterproof roofs and seagoing craft.
Potash was used in bleaching fabric and later for making glass.

the fertile land of the Jordan Valley and the fascination of the sprawling city.

For years, Lot had watched his uncle follow the Lord and build altars to worship the living God. If only Lot had built a family altar and prayed like Abraham had prayed. If only he had sought the community of godly people.

When it came to learning how to be prosperous, Lot had been Abraham's charmed student. But unlike his uncle, Lot did not nurture his family's faith in order to combat the deadly influence of their surroundings. In the lives of Abraham and Sarah, Lot and his wife had witnessed the example of a married couple who had faced remarkable struggles but had honored the Lord and each other. If only Lot and his wife had done the same in their marriage.

The picture and warning for us are clear. Lot's downfall started with a few poor choices. It came in increments. One small step, one seemingly insignificant decision, one small compromise at a time. Little misses. Big consequences.

But for Lot—and for you—God's grace is available. Even though Lot had made wrong choices, God offered a way out. Lot hesitated, but God's messengers mercifully dragged him out. No looking back. His wife's heart was divided, drawn back to people and things she would miss.

We make choices every day. When the overwhelming sinfulness of the world would capture us, we can trust God's strong hand to rescue us from evil. He wants to use our lives and our marriages to honor Him.

From God's Word ...

"For if God did not spare angels when they sinned ... and if he rescued Lot, a righteous man, who was distressed by the depraved conduct of the lawless ... if this is so, then the Lord knows how to rescue the godly from trials and to hold the unrighteous for punishment on the day of judgment."

2 PETER 2:4, 7, 9

Their Legacy in Scripture

Thursday

1. **"The men turned away and went toward Sodom, but Abraham remained standing before the LORD"** (GENESIS 18:22).

   The two angels who came to destroy Sodom had just been with Lot's uncle, Abraham. The Lord had informed Abraham about the coming destruction of his nephew's city. Abraham stayed in God's presence and pleaded for this sinful city. What do we learn about God's mercy and the need for intercessory prayer from this story? Name someone you can intercede for, asking God to rescue them from evil, addiction, or unholy entrapments.

2. **"Trust in the LORD with all your heart, and do not lean on your own understanding. In all your ways acknowledge him, and he will make straight your paths"** (PROVERBS 3:5–6 ESV).

   Almost everyone moves to a new location sometime in life. Lot's choice of a place to live affected his wealth, his faith, and his family. When you move, what are your priorities? How can you acknowledge the Lord in your choice of location, housing, friends, school, church, or work? What can a couple do to ensure they have a godly community around them?

3. **"For just as each of us has one body with many members, and these members do not all have the same function, so in Christ we, though many, form one body, and each member belongs to all the others. We have different gifts, according to the grace given to each of us"** (ROMANS 12:4–6).

   To be strong in their faith, believers need each other. Where do you think Lot and his wife went wrong in this area? Do you think they could have made a difference in the lives of other citizens of Sodom if there had been a community of believers? When have you felt overwhelmed by worldly influences? How did you escape?

Their Legacy of Prayer

Friday

Reflect On: Genesis 19

Praise God: For being a God who rescues and forgives. That He has given you the gift of faith and the Holy Spirit to help guide your actions.

Offer Thanks: For His Word to inform your conscience and His Spirit to counsel and lead you in daily decisions.

Confess: Your indifference to things that honor God and your failure to acknowledge Him in every choice. That you often neglect to ask God for what He wants for your life and marriage.

Ask God: To soften your heart toward the things that please Him. To help you trust His plan above pursuing your own desires. To help you to pray with discernment for your spouse and to obey instructions from the Holy Spirit.

Listen: "My children, the values of this world are temporal. I can see what you cannot, and I will direct you. I have provided a way of escape from evil. Seek Me in My Word and pray for insight so you may focus on those things that really matter. Cling to Me, and you will be truly successful.

Pray: *Father and Shepherd, You are holy and must deal with persistent sin. Forgive us for allowing anything to capture our hearts and separate us from each other and from You. We want to worship You and seek Your guidance always. You are the merciful and forgiving God who rescues lost people. Help us to avoid any decisions that would allow us to become entrapped by temporary values rather than following Your plan. Help us to encourage each other to do the right thing in every circumstance so our lives and our marriage may thrive in unity and holiness. Amen.*

10

Who Gives This Woman?

Isaac and Rebekah

Meaning of Names:	*Isaac* means "laughter" or "he laughs." *Rebekah* means "snare" or "to tie" or "to bind."
Their Character:	He was a prayerful man and open to God's leading. She was a hard worker, hospitable, and sensitive to God's call.
Their Challenge:	There was a great distance between their two homelands. She had to leave her family behind. They did not know each other before their arranged marriage.
Their Outcome:	Covered in prayer, they experienced a loving start to their marriage. They were recipients of family blessings and enjoyed God's favor.
Key Scripture:	Genesis 24

Their Story

Monday

Isaac looked north from the field where he had gone to pray. The huge plume of dust disturbing the desert floor signaled that a large group was approaching. This might be his father's servants returning with his bride. He had been wondering for weeks about whether the quest to find a wife for him had been successful. His heart raced at the thought of seeing his bride-to-be for the first time. He awaited her arrival with nervous expectancy.

For Rebekah, the travel from Harran to southern Canaan had been long. It was not a pleasant journey, though her youth carried her with little trial. All she could think about was meeting the man she would marry. Her heart fluttered with anticipation.

Two hearts waiting, wondering what they would discover.

As Rebekah approached, she squinted to see the figure in the distance.

The traveling party came to a stop. In humility and respect, Rebekah covered her face with a veil.

An elderly man named Eliezer, the servant of Isaac's father, Abraham, made his way from Rebekah to Isaac. The young girl knew that Eliezer would be telling Isaac that she was the answer to his prayer in Harran. How she had carried water for the man and his camels. And that she had run to tell her family about the mysterious visitor bringing news of their kinsmen in the land of Canaan.

Every detail of Eliezer's story confirmed one amazing thing to Isaac: God's providence had been at work in the selection of Rebekah as Isaac's bride. When he finished telling all that had happened, Eliezer with an outstretched hand invited Rebekah to approach.

Isaac, the child of promise, was forty but yet unmarried. God had chosen Abraham to be the patriarch of a new nation, the Israelites. To fulfill the promise, Isaac needed to marry someone from the proper line and have children with her. Abraham knew no local Canaanite woman would do. Isaac's bride had to come from his distant relatives living in Harran.

Eliezer's entourage of servants and ten camels had been dispatched to Harran, a journey of nearly 550 miles. The mission was to find and take home a bride for Isaac. Hoping they would be successful, Abraham had sent exquisite gold jewelry, expensive clothing, and gifts of silver to compensate and entice the woman's father. Isaac's father believed that God would go before Eliezer and provide a suitable bride for his son. But the question lingered: Would the girl's family agree to the plan?

When he arrived just outside the city, Eliezer stopped his camels by a well, and he humbly prayed, "LORD, God of my master Abraham, make me successful today … May it be that when I say to a young woman, 'Please let down your jar that I may have a drink,' and she says, 'Drink, and I'll water your camels too'—let her be the one you have chosen for your servant Isaac."[1]

---

1. Genesis 24:12, 14.

Before his prayer was even finished, Eliezer looked up and saw a stunningly beautiful and graceful young woman headed his direction. When she was within earshot, Eliezer asked for a little water from the jar she carried on her shoulder. "'Drink, my lord,' she said, and quickly lowered the jar to her hands and gave him a drink, saying, 'I'll draw water for your camels too, until they have had enough to drink.'"[2]

Eliezer wanted to be sure this was the one the Lord had chosen to be Isaac's bride. Offering gold jewelry from his satchel as a payment for her trouble, he asked about her father. "I am the daughter of Bethuel," she replied. Immediately Abraham's servant recognized the name. The girl was the daughter of his master's kin.

"We have plenty of straw and fodder," Rebekah offered, "as well as room for you to spend the night."[3]

Then the faithful old man bowed down and worshiped the Lord, saying, "Praise be to the LORD, the God of my master Abraham, who has not abandoned his kindness and faithfulness to my master."[4]

All that was left for Eliezer to do was to meet the family and reveal the purpose for his journey. Over dinner, Eliezer told Rebekah's father and her family about the mission, asking if he could return to Canaan with Rebekah.

Rebekah's father and brother replied, "This is from the LORD; we can say nothing to you one way or the other. Here is Rebekah; take her and go, and let her become the wife of your master's son, as the LORD has directed."[5]

But what did Rebekah think about leaving right away?

The following morning, her mother and brother asked her, "Will you go with this man?"

With calm resolve, Rebekah answered, "I will go."

So Rebekah, along with her nurse, Deborah, and her maidservants, returned to Canaan with Eliezer.

Isaac had waited for his bride. And now he beheld Rebekah. His heart was undone.

God had chosen her for him.

There was no doubt.

---

2. See Genesis 24:18–19.
3. See Genesis 24:25.
4. Genesis 24:27.
5. Genesis 24:51–52.

Their Life and Times

Tuesday

Arranged Marriage

The story of Isaac and Rebekah is an example of an arranged marriage. It was not the first one recorded in the Bible. The inaugural arranged marriage was orchestrated for the very first couple in history: "Then the LORD God made a woman from the rib he had taken out of the man, and he brought her to the man" (Genesis 2:22).

This is no "boy meets girl" scenario with the guy catching her eye across a crowded room, long getting-to-know-you talks, hand-in-hand walks, expressions of undying love, the proposal, and finally the wedding. Adam and Eve's betrothal and marriage were nothing of the sort.

In the story of the first bride and groom, Someone knew the man and the woman better than they knew themselves. The Creator designed Eve to be the ideal match for Adam and took her to him. "This is a woman you will love," God said to Adam. "She will be your own wife. You will live together and enjoy her companionship. The end."

When it came time for Abraham and Sarah's promised son to be married at age forty, God orchestrated the second recorded prearranged marriage. Knowing God's promised nation would come from Isaac's descendants, Abraham prayed for a suitable wife for his son and charged his chief servant with the task of finding a bride from Abraham's tribe in Harran.

The girl's father would have to approve the transaction. In biblical days, fathers made most of the important decisions for their under-age daughters until it was time for their betrothal.[6] When a girl was in her midteens, it was time for her father to choose the man she would marry.

If the family was wealthy and the daughter played a significant role in the running of the household, the father could delay marriage until the girl was in her late teens or early twenties. If the family was

---

6. Rebekah was already an adult so she was given the opportunity to make her own decision (see Genesis 24:58).

poor and needed the bride-price, the father often sought a husband for his daughter earlier.

When a potential spouse was identified, the father of the young bride would pay a visit to the prospective groom's home and begin negotiations with the man's parents. Marriage was a legal transaction. If the groom-to-be was older and living on his own, the daughter's father negotiated directly with him. Often the girl's father presented a gift — a dowry — to the boy's parents, as a down payment on the agreement. Because Jewish parents wanted their daughters to find love and happiness, most daughters were consulted and permitted to give their consent to their father's choice of a groom.

God's providence played an essential role in the joining of Rebekah and Isaac. On a God-appointed day, Rebekah was doing an ordinary task when Abraham's praying servant discovered her. And the prayers and blessings of many people surrounded Rebekah as she waved a final good-bye to her family and left her home to join Isaac and begin a new life.

When we trust in God's sovereignty, we can be sure He will redeem every circumstance. This makes even boy-meets-girl marriages sweetly prearranged by God's kind intervention and grace.

Can You Imagine?

Wednesday

The idea of marrying someone your parents chose for you and hoping to fall in love with each other after the wedding seems a bit risky, calculated, and unemotional to our Western sensibilities, doesn't it? Can you imagine what it would be like to have an arranged marriage?

When we were teenagers, the idea of an arranged marriage sounded primitive and unromantic, but now that we're grown-ups and understand the many facets that make up a marriage, it makes a lot more sense. The emotional and material expenses of courting can be overwhelming. And how can teenagers — children, really — know enough about themselves and that awesomely cool person on the other end of a text message to make a serious decision such as, "I think I'll just go ahead and decide to spend the rest of my life with you."

The story of Abraham sending his trusted servant, Eliezer, on a journey to find a wife for Isaac is one of the great romantic stories in the Bible. But instead of a syrupy, paperback-novel liaison, this love affair involves godly parents, a willing man, a disciplined and hardworking woman, and a God who is invited to the pre-engagement party.

Not every marriage begins with consulting God. But He knows how to redeem poor choices. It's what He has done throughout history. Even our uninformed and unfortunate decisions can be used for our good and His glory.

Regardless of who arranged your marriage, God can make it something wonderful.

From God's Word . . .

> "Houses and wealth are inherited from parents,
>   but a prudent wife is from the LORD."
>
> PROVERBS 19:14

Their Legacy in Scripture

Thursday

1. **"She quickly emptied her jar into the trough, ran back to the well to draw more water, and drew enough for all his camels. Without saying a word, the man watched her closely to learn whether or not the LORD had made his journey successful"** (GENESIS 24:20–21).

   After praying specifically for the chosen bride, Abraham's servant watched in amazement as Rebekah hurried to satisfy his ten camels — a thirsty camel can drink as much as twenty-five gallons! What exceptional qualities did Rebekah display? What do you admire about *your* spouse?

2. **"For we are God's handiwork, created in Christ Jesus to do good works, which God prepared in advance for us to do"** (EPHESIANS 2:10).

   Think about your first date and the day you became engaged. What details did God orchestrate in advance in order to bring you and your spouse together? How did you include God in your selection process when you were looking for a spouse?

3. **"Plans fail for lack of counsel, but with many advisers they succeed"** (PROVERBS 15:22).

   Isaac and Rebekah experienced the joy and confidence of knowing God had answered the prayers of others on their behalf. Identify the caring people who surrounded you when you were making the decision to marry. When have you been sustained because of the prayers of others? Who speaks into your lives and prays for your marriage now? If you do not already have a marriage mentor, who would you choose to play that role in your life?

Their Legacy of Prayer

Friday

Reflect On: Genesis 24

Praise God: For being a covenant maker and keeper. For His wisdom
to orchestrate intricate plans far in advance and His
ability to carry out His will in every detail. For His grace
in redeeming poor choices.

Offer Thanks: For God's divine guidance and the path He has chosen
for you, and for the gift of your marriage.

Confess: Your faultfinding and complaining to your spouse and
for forgetting to pray about the details of your life and
marriage.

Ask God: To give you wisdom and conviction as you seek to
identify what needs to be changed so your marriage
may flourish. Ask for divine power to model a healthy
relationship and to display the faithfulness of a covenant
bond.

Listen: "Dear children, I planned every day of your lives before
and since your wedding day. I am able to keep you close
to each other as you stay close to Me. Pray always, show
kindness, and love tenderly. I will continue to instruct
you and carry you so a new generation may know who
I am and what I've done."

Pray: *Father in heaven who created marriage, we want our relationship
to reflect the love You planned for us to share. Help us to be
faithful in prayer so we may display Your glory and model for
others a covenant-keeping marriage. May our hearts be full of
mercy like Your heart is, and may our choices be Your choices.
Amen.*

Trust and Obey

Isaac and Rebekah

Meaning of Names:	*Isaac* means "laughter" or "he laughs." *Rebekah* means "snare" or "to tie" or "to bind."
Their Character:	He was a stubborn man who stopped seeking God and listening to his wife. His appetite for food and his passive parenting style caused him to ignore God's word and keep secrets from his wife. She was spiritual but manipulative, trying to fulfill God's will by deceiving her husband.
Their Challenge:	They each had a favorite child and were caught in a battle of wills over which son should receive the family blessing.
Their Outcome:	They had a dysfunctional marriage and family and became lonely and alienated from each other. Their son Jacob, renamed Israel, became the father of the Israelite nation.
Key Scripture:	Genesis 27

Their Story

Monday

*T*his is Isaac's fault! Rebekah whispered to herself. *If only he had listened to me; if only he had offered the blessing to Jacob in the first place, none of this would have happened.*

Rebekah poured out her pain in prayer to the God she had heard when she was younger. Now she wondered if He had abandoned her. How had her life turned so dark and lonely? Her beloved son Jacob was almost five hundred miles away—a heartbreaking distance—living with her brother Laban. Jacob's twin, Esau, had vowed to kill his sibling for stealing his blessing, which is what drove Jacob away.

Jacob was gone, and her husband's blindness—both physical and spiritual—was to blame for Jacob's running away. Isaac had known that the Lord had decreed that Jacob would rule Esau, but he wanted none of that and tried to take the matter into his own hands. And this was the result.

Rebekah slowly lowered herself, collapsing against a large rock and wrapping her arms around her knees. Her head slumped. *What has happened to the godly man I married?*

Rewinding her memory, Rebekah was transported back in time.

Rebekah could see herself as a woman of thirty-eight, rejoicing in the miracle of a long-awaited pregnancy. She had been married to Isaac for twenty years, two decades marked by barrenness. She pleaded with her husband to pray for her—and, being the tender, spiritual husband he was, he did pray. To the couple's delight, the Lord responded bountifully, blessing Rebekah's womb with not one baby but with twin boys. Isaac and Rebekah celebrated what would soon be the doubling of their small family.

Then something strange and frightening happened. Rebekah felt jostling and great discomfort as the babies inside her began to thrash. Rebekah cried out to God for an answer. "Why is this happening to me?"

The Lord who was giving her these children was now equally gracious in responding to her prayer. "There are two nations in your womb, two peoples. One will be stronger than the other, and the older will serve the younger."[1]

Rebekah was puzzled. She mulled over His divine words, then settled on the last of them: "The older will serve the younger," she whispered. "The older will serve the younger," Rebekah repeated. Later she told Isaac what the Lord had said.

When the twins finally arrived, she looked on in bewilderment at Esau, who was ruddy and red and, for a newborn, rather hairy. Her

---

1. See Genesis 25:23.

firstborn appeared almost furry, as if he were wearing a woolen outer garment. His younger brother, Jacob—the one who would rule over the other—was, she noticed, smooth, fair, wide-eyed, and beautiful. The younger baby captured her heart.

Now, many years later as Rebekah sat grieving, she wondered where it had all started—the favoritism, the preferential treatment, the competition. Why was she so partial to Jacob, and Isaac to Esau? She rued the day when those battle lines were drawn. It had begun decades before when Isaac spent most of his time with the hunter twin, who alone could satisfy his father's hearty appetite for adventure and tasty stew.

And later, as an old and wealthy man, thinking he was at death's door, Isaac secretly summoned the rebellious Esau, promising a private audience for the family blessing. But Isaac knew of God's earlier decree: "The older shall serve the younger." Rebekah overheard her husband telling Esau of the clandestine meeting. She set in motion her own secretive scheme.

Now, as Rebekah replayed the scenario in her mind, she recalled every detail of her clever maneuver. Because Isaac's eyes had grown old-man dim, she plotted with Jacob to deceive his father into giving *him* the blessing of the firstborn, the one Isaac intended for Esau. To simulate Esau's hairiness, Rebekah covered Jacob's arms and neck with supple strips of goatskin.

To tempt and satisfy Isaac's palate, she prepared a tasty stew, seasoned just the way Esau would have cooked it. Jacob voiced concern that his father would discover the deception and curse him rather than bless him. With unbroken resolve, Rebekah proclaimed, "My son, let the curse fall on me."[2]

Her plan worked to perfection. Though Isaac was suspicious, he indulged his appetite and fell for the masquerade.

Convinced that the son standing before him was the hunter Esau, the blind patriarch heartily spoke his irrevocable blessing over Jacob. Rebekah savored her victory as her husband savored the stew. But it would soon turn sour, and her beloved Jacob would be threatened by his brother, Esau, and driven from their home.

Now, ten years later, Rebekah remembered the words her own

---

2. Genesis 27:13.

mouth had spoken. In the years following Jacob's departure, she and her husband hardly spoke to one another. Rebekah was lonely. The marriage that had begun with triumphant faith and tender love had become self-serving and distant. All their wealth meant nothing now. She would never again see her favorite son.

Their Life and Times

Tuesday

Birthright

In biblical times, the oldest son was granted power, wealth, and standing. As the future head of the family, he would define and carry on traditions and the family's direction. From the time he was born, the oldest son enjoyed more privileges and respect than his younger brothers. After the death of his father, he would receive twice as much inheritance. As the descendants of the firstborn grew into a tribe, his influence also grew in civilian and political matters.

Is it any wonder that the younger Jacob coveted Esau's birthright?

Jacob knew that God had told his mother, "The older will serve the younger." Because his father, Isaac, was a man of great wealth, with numerous flocks of sheep and goats, a large household filled with servants, and significant land holdings, this message would have stirred the boy's imagination. Because of God's promise—despite the birth order—the greater share of this wealth would become Jacob's at his father's death.

Acquiring the birthright—and the irrevocable words of his father's blessing—also meant that Jacob's descendants would someday enjoy the bounty and the land. Jacob recognized the power of the father's blessing and coveted it; Esau was reckless and disregarded its importance.

Jacob was mindful of the stakes one day when his brother went out to hunt in the fields. While Esau was shooting game, Jacob was hunting for the blessing. He prepared some vegetable stew—water, wild lentils, onions, and spices—to cook slowly for hours, finishing in a mouthwatering dish of thick, reddish-brown soup. Returning from the hunt, Esau didn't resist. "Quick," he demanded, "let me have some of that red stew! I'm famished!" (Genesis 25:30).

Jacob was ready. "You may have some soup," the younger brother replied. "But first sell me your birthright."

Esau agreed. No negotiating. No haggling over the price. Esau seemed unconcerned about the outcome of his brother's demand, and in a moment, the legal right to the birthright was transferred to Jacob.

Though Jacob's methods were not secretive, they were manipulative and self-serving. He used his own cleverness to claim what the Lord had already declared was his.[3] And Jacob was not the only one unwilling to wait for God's timing. His mother, Rebekah, was an instigator of the conspiracy. Though she had witnessed the working of God in the early years of their marriage, she didn't trust her husband—or her God to bring about His promises in His own good time. She set out to trick Isaac into thinking he was blessing Esau so he would bless Jacob instead.

Isaac knew about God's promise to Rebekah when the twins were born. But he had come to enjoy his wealth and the comfortable life—his hunting expeditions and the food he liked. Although Esau had ignored God's standards by marrying pagan Hittite women, Isaac was willing to overlook his favorite son's offenses and compromise the covenant heritage. And so he planned a private ceremony with Esau rather than the usual extended family celebration accompanying a father's final blessing.

Isaac received a spiritual jolt after unknowingly blessing Jacob. Trembling, he said to Esau, "Who was it, then, that hunted game and brought it to me? I ate it just before you came and I blessed him—and indeed he will be blessed!" (Genesis 27:33).

Isaac shuddered as he realized that he had been deceived and that he had unwittingly accomplished God's words to Rebekah.

Having learned of Esau's plot to murder Jacob, Rebekah said to Isaac, "I'm disgusted with living because of these Hittite women. If Jacob takes a wife from among the women of this land, from Hittite women like these, my life will not be worth living" (Genesis 27:46).

---

3. See Genesis 25:23.

Isaac was quick to accommodate his wife this time and immediately called for Jacob, commanding him to travel to Rebekah's kin to find a suitable wife.

Because they did not trust and obey God, both Isaac and Rebekah would suffer the consequences.

The recipient of the birthright was God's to decide, and He had told them His choice. But neither Rebekah nor Isaac fully trusted God's wisdom. Instead, they drifted into self-serving deceit and lost the sweet love they once shared. God did confirm the covenant inheritance to Jacob, but their family suffered.

Can You Imagine?

Wednesday

Isaac had a secret. He deliberately planned to disobey God.

When Rebekah discovered it, she could no longer trust her husband.

Instead of waiting for God to work out His plan, this husband and wife selfishly deceived each other. They didn't wait for God to act or even trust that He would act at all.

Secrets. They can ruin the unity in a marriage. When out of selfishness or fear you hide anything from each other, your relationship is weakened.

Can you imagine permitting your own inferior plans to replace God's work in your heart and marriage? Yet many people feel it's OK to hide things from their spouse—fantasies, unbudgeted purchases, wasted hours on the Internet. They say they trust God, but like Isaac and Rebekah, they struggle with selfish pleasures and deceit by keeping secrets from one another.

It doesn't have to be this way. God gives us the power to break any damaging cycle of dishonesty. He gives us the courage to talk openly with our spouse about hidden motives and actions. It's not easy to confront our own sin or to speak to our spouse about secrets. But when we confess, repent, and pray for each other, we can begin to experience the closeness with our spouse that God intended.

When you need to discuss a secret, make a specific appointment with your spouse. "After dinner tonight, can we talk?" Then with humility begin the conversation by affirming your love and your desire to do what is right. Confess what you've been withholding, and be specific with your concerns. Listen carefully and be willing to patiently wait for God's timing.

When we ask, we can be assured of God's presence every day as He is changing our hearts and our marriage. Take courage. Speak the truth in love.

From God's Word . . .

"Love does not delight in evil but rejoices with the truth."

1 CORINTHIANS 13:6

Their Legacy in Scripture

Thursday

1. "Isaac prayed to the LORD on behalf of his wife ... The LORD answered his prayer ... and she said, 'Why is this happening to me?' So she went to inquire of the LORD" (GENESIS 25:21–22).

    Isaac and Rebekah had experienced tender love and answered prayers earlier in their marriage. When have you prayed for your spouse and experienced answers to your prayers? If someone challenged you to pray specifically for your spouse for five minutes every morning, how would you respond? What would you ask your spouse to pray for you in response to the same challenge?

2. "When I kept silent, my bones wasted away ... Then I acknowledged my sin to you and did not cover up my iniquity. I said, 'I will confess my transgressions to the LORD.' And you forgave the guilt of my sin" (PSALM 32:3, 5).

    This verse is about not keeping secrets from the Lord. What is the result of full disclosure before God? How does this also apply to your spouse? What might openness and confession do to build closeness with your spouse? When and where can you schedule an appointment to start your own conversation about secrets?

3. "And this is my prayer: that your love may abound more and more in knowledge and depth of insight, so that you may be able to discern what is best and may be pure and blameless" (PHILIPPIANS 1:9–10).

    Isaac and Rebekah tried to control their circumstances, using secrets and deceit, but it destroyed their relationship. Every couple faces the temptation to hide things from each other. What changes can you make in your relationship to ensure that you won't keep secrets from each other so your marriage can flourish? What do you need to confess to God and your spouse?

Their Legacy of Prayer

Friday

Reflect On: Genesis 27

Praise God: For His control over all things and for His Spirit, who is able to lead you and your spouse into all truth.

Offer Thanks: That God offers you the benefits of His wisdom and discernment through His Word.

Confess: That you too often hide things from your spouse and try to control circumstances rather than trust in God. That too often you'd rather manipulate than tell the truth.

Ask God: To help you recognize what He wants to teach you or your spouse as you wait patiently for Him to act. To help you acknowledge that He is at work and to give you the power to abide in Him.

Listen: "Dear children, I desire truthfulness so you may walk with each other in unity. I will give you courage to confront deceit and confess sin. I will use your struggles to build your faith and strengthen your dependence on Me. I love you and want you to walk in truth and faithfulness. I am at work helping you want to obey."

Pray: *Loving God, You are mighty to save and able to control the things that concern us. Please help us to submit to You in all things when we are unwilling to be transparent. Your timing is perfect. Your ways are higher than our ways and Your thoughts are higher than our thoughts. Teach us to seek Your truth at all times, even when it is uncomfortable. Bind us together in spiritual closeness and keep us from the sins of pretense and deceit. Quiet our hearts as we trust in Your Word. Amen.*

Bait and Switch

Jacob and Leah

Meaning of Names: *Jacob* means "grasps the heel," "supplanter," or "deceiver." *Leah* means "weary" or "to tire."

Their Character: He was blessed by God, strong and clever but deceptive. She was unloved and highly competitive with her sister.

Their Challenge: Jacob was trapped in a deceptive and dysfunctional family. Leah experienced the heartbreak of being an unloved wife.

Their Outcome: Their family was engulfed in strife, jealousy, and bitterness. Their sons became six of the future twelve tribes of Israel.

Key Scripture: Genesis 29:14 – 30:24

Their Story

Monday

Now on her deathbed, Leah was still trying to decide what to make of Jacob's words. Her husband had assured her that she would be buried in the family gravesite where his grandparents, Abraham and Sarah, and his parents, Isaac and Rebekah, silently lay. In death, she and Jacob would join them there.[1]

But if this was supposed to be a victory over her sister Rachel, she didn't feel any satisfaction. It was too late. Too late for vindication. Too late for celebration. Too late to dry the countless tears. Too late

---

1. See Genesis 49:31.

to mend her unloved soul. Yes, she would receive the honor of being buried along with her husband and his ancestors, but she would die without ever experiencing his devotion.

From the day so many decades before when her cousin arrived in Harran from Canaan, she knew she would never be his. Not really. Yes, she was Jacob's wife, but his heart was captured by Rachel, her younger sister, whose notorious beauty caused merchants to neglect their dealings in the marketplace and shepherds to lose sight of their flocks.

Whenever she and Rachel were together, Leah felt invisible. Her little sister's black-haired beauty captured all eyes. Actually, it didn't matter whether Leah was with Rachel or not; even when she was out by herself, people hardly noticed her. She was Rachel's older, plain sister. She would never be anything else.

Every time she looked into Jacob's eyes, she was reminded again of this icy reality. Jacob had labored on her father's property for seven years, working for Laban in order to earn Rachel's hand in marriage. He was polite to Leah, but why not? She was the daughter of his employer and the sister of his betrothed. And even though Leah was older, it never entered his mind to consider marrying her.

At the end of the seven years, Jacob demanded of Laban, "Give me my wife. My time is completed, and I want to make love to her."[2]

Laban schemed. Jacob would indeed get a wife.

Leah never forgot the day her father said to her, "My daughter, once your sister is married, you will have no chance to marry." His eyes narrowed and shifted, his voice dropping to a whisper. "Do what I tell you."

Saying no to her domineering father was not something Leah contemplated. Father had never adored her, even when she was a girl. She wasn't pretty. For a proud man like Laban, that was unacceptable. Handing her the dense wedding veil to conceal her face, he sent her into Jacob's marriage tent under the cover of darkness. Although she felt like a lamb being led to the slaughter, she dutifully obeyed, slipping into the marriage bed next to Jacob.

After consummating their marriage, Leah hardly slept all night, fearing the first morning glow that would reveal her and her father's deception.

---

2. Genesis 29:21.

Awaking, Jacob moved close to nuzzle his bride, but when he gazed into Leah's eyes, she knew he had realized their treachery. "How did you come to be in my bed? Where is Rachel?" His confusion was quickly replaced by anger.

The look of shock and disappointment in Jacob's eyes would haunt Leah all her life. Still in their marriage bed and sobbing uncontrollably, Leah could hear her furious husband outside the tent railing at her father. "What have you done to me?" Jacob demanded. "I served you seven years for Rachel, didn't I? You deceived me!"

Soon, cooler heads prevailed, and a deal was struck. Jacob would fulfill his wedding week with Leah and then marry Rachel when it was over.

Two wives in seven days.

Of course, one thing was clear. Leah was the second-place wife, a loser with no victory party. Her marriage to Jacob was a constant reminder that she would live in the shadow of her pretty sister. Her husband would never look at her with winsome delight like he did with Rachel, would never rush to whisper affection meant only for her ears. Even with all the comforts of life — a spacious tent, servants, food, and drink to spare — nothing could satisfy Leah's yearning for the love she craved. Her husband did not adore her.

He never would.

But, love her or not, Jacob still performed his conjugal duty with Leah, and she gave birth to a son, Reuben. "Surely my husband will love me now," she said.[3]

He did not.

Then she gave birth to Simeon … and Levi. "Now at last my husband will become attached to me, because I have borne him three sons."[4]

No, he wouldn't.

Then came Judah. "This time," Leah said, "I will praise the Lord."[5]

God showed favor and love to Leah, and she was fertile — eventually giving birth to six sons and one daughter. Her sister, Rachel, was barren but had Jacob's love. All of it. And Leah had none.

Leah's soul ached. When the loneliness became unbearable, she

---

3. Genesis 29:32.
4. Genesis 29:34.
5. See Genesis 29:35.

cried out in prayer: "Lord, my husband doesn't love me. Do You see my misery?" In quietness, the Lord assured her that He had seen her broken heart and loved her. Her seven children were adequate proof of that.

The assurance was balm enough to sooth Leah's anguish and strength enough to enable her to endure the dishonor and emptiness. And now, with her days ebbing to a precious few, she learned she had at last earned a place of respect in Jacob's eyes.

In death. She was to have the honor of being buried in Jacob's family tomb in the field of Machpelah, the place where Jacob himself would be buried (Genesis 49:29–32).

A shallow victory at best. She would be going to her grave without ever knowing the desire and loving touch of a husband. But now, at the very end, a new hope. The love that had eluded her in life would mercifully be won in death.

Their Life and Times

Tuesday

One Man, One Woman

The account of Leah and Rachel provides clear evidence of the dangers and heartbreak of polygamy. As two wives of Jacob, these sisters had lives marked by unhealthy competition, deceit, jealousy, and bitterness. Is it any wonder that the Hebrew term for "second wife" is literally "rival wife"?

Polygamy was practiced among the Israelites until the era of the Babylonian captivity. Though men of that time may have had more than one wife, it was far from God's ideal standard for marriage.

Having multiple wives was often promoted for business and legal reasons. In many cases, most heads of household were desperate for workers, especially if they were herdsmen or farmers. If a man was blessed with many children, they could provide the help needed to water and herd animals or reap in the fields at harvest time. Family wealth flourished in direct proportion to the number of children who would become workers.

With the large number of children required to prosper a family business, a wife in a monogamous marriage had unrealistic pressure to produce many children. Few women were able to be so fruitful. Wanting to quickly grow the family or tribe, men would often marry as many women as they could afford. If one wife could not produce the desired number of offspring, especially sons, then the head of the house felt obligated to remedy the situation by taking another wife.

Because every marriage required a dowry paid to the bride's father, a man's accumulation of wives was often determined by his finances. A wealthy man could afford several wives.

A poor man who wanted more children than his wife could produce might purchase a slave to bear additional children. Though frowned on in Hebrew culture, this practice was accepted only in the case where a man's wife was barren. The most memorable cases of men having children with slaves were Abraham with Hagar (Sarah's slave), Jacob with Zilpah (Leah's servant), and Jacob with Bilhah (Rachel's servant). In each of these situations, the slave or servant was not regarded as the man's wife, but her children were accorded the full rights of heirs.

Despite the widespread practice of polygamy in Bible times, when the Old Testament prophets speak of God's relationship with Israel, they often use the analogy of a monogamous marriage.[6] Although some of the patriarchs did not follow God's original design for marriage—one man and one woman for life—their offspring were accepted and blessed.

Scripture is clear that the only marriage scenario God explicitly endorses is a monogamous one: "That is why a man leaves his father and mother and is united to his wife, and they become one flesh" (Genesis 2:24). The New Testament tells us that a candidate for spiritual leadership must be "the husband of one wife" (1 Timothy 3:2, 12; Titus 1:6 ESV). Passages regarding behavior between spouses speak exclusively of one husband and one wife.[7]

Polygamy was far from the ideal God intended for marriage.

---

6. See Ezekiel 16:32; Hosea 3:1; Malachi 2:14–15.
7. See Ephesians 5:22–23; Colossians 3:18–19; 1 Peter 3:1–7.

Can You Imagine?

Wednesday

You will experience disappointment in your marriage. Your spouse will fail you, perhaps not by ignoring you like Jacob ignored Leah, but no person will ever live up to all your expectations or meet all your needs. God sees, understands, comforts, and loves you with a perfect love. Can you imagine being His beloved?

The story of Leah, who shared her husband, Jacob, with her younger sister is tragic. Jacob adored Rachel but had no words of affection for Leah, the woman he was duped into marrying. Leah carried the sorrow of lovelessness to her grave.

But the Lord was Leah's strength and lovingly blessed her with six sons. About the birth of her firstborn, Reuben, Leah said, "It is because the LORD has seen my misery" (Genesis 29:32). Though no one else may know your agony, God notices His children's suffering. *God always sees.*

When Simeon was born, Leah said it was "because the LORD heard that I am not loved" (Genesis 29:33). A distracted spouse may not listen, but God hears the silent anguish of an aching heart. *God always hears.*

After her third son, Levi, was born, Leah voiced her yearning: "Now at last my husband will become attached to me" (Genesis 29:34). "For your Maker is your husband—the LORD almighty is his name" (Isaiah 54:5). *God embraces a longing heart.*

When Judah was born, Leah said, "I will praise the LORD" (Genesis 29:35). No matter what the circumstances, exalting Him is the proper response. God promises deep joy when we focus on Him.[8] *God is always worthy of worship.*

At the birth of Issachar, Leah sang, "God has rewarded me" (Genesis 30:18). The blessing He sends could be a tangible provision, or the gift could be spiritual. In every case, God promises eternal rewards for steadfast endurance.[9] *God prizes trusting faith.*

Then came Zebulun, and Leah rejoiced, "God has presented me with a precious gift" (Genesis 30:20). Although Leah could have

---

8. See Jeremiah 31:13.
9. See 2 Timothy 4:7–8.

complained that her husband wasn't meeting her needs, she chose instead to be thankful. *God is pleased with gratitude.*

God lavishes particular grace on those who suffer, those who feel unloved. His presence turns bitterness into understanding, tears into praise.

From God's Word . . .

"The peace of God, which transcends all understanding, will guard your hearts and your minds in Christ Jesus."

PHILIPPIANS 4:7

Their Legacy in Scripture

Thursday

1. **"The LORD saw that Leah was not loved"** (GENESIS 29:31).

   Leah lived with the pain of rejection from her husband. Despite this, in what ways did she persevere in hope? How did she acknowledge God's love?

2. **"I am convinced that neither death nor life, neither angels nor demons, neither the present nor the future, nor any powers, neither height nor depth, nor anything else in all creation, will be able to separate us from the love of God that is in Christ Jesus our Lord"** (ROMANS 8:38–39).

   How can God's love transform your attitude toward your spouse even in the face of disappointments in your marriage? If you were to counsel a friend who feels unappreciated or unloved, what would you say to bring hope to him or her from God's Word?

3. **"Blessed is the one who perseveres under trial because, having stood the test, that person will receive the crown of life that the Lord has promised to those who love him"** (JAMES 1:12).

   What does God promise, no matter what happens in your life? What do you need to accept and appreciate about your spouse rather than trying to change him or her? How can knowing you are God's beloved satisfy your longings?

Their Legacy of Prayer

Friday

Reflect On: Genesis 29:1–30:22

Praise God: For His love and faithfulness and for His ability to transform you and your marriage.

Offer Thanks: That He sees, hears, and knows everything about your marriage. For His tangible and spiritual gifts in your life.

Confess: That you too often focus on your problems and not your Provider. That complaining or perfectionism keeps you from seeing the situation from God's perspective.

Ask God: To give you the deep peace—a peace beyond human understanding—that He promises. To fill you with the joy of His salvation.

Listen: "You are My beloved children. I am able to transform your marriage completely. As you attach to Me, I will bind your hearts to each other with My perfect love. I know your longings. I will provide My presence to accomplish what you cannot."

Pray: *Heavenly Father, You see us. You hear us, and You know us better than we know ourselves. You are our greatest resource. Teach us to look to You to satisfy our longings and to please You by the way we love each other. Amen.*

13

The Blame Game

Jacob and Rachel

Meaning of Names: Jacob means "grasps the heel," "supplanter," or "deceives." *Rachel* means "ewe" or "sheep."

Their Character: He was a strong man who showed weakness with the women in his life. She blamed her husband for her inability to become pregnant.

Their Challenge: Jacob was either unable or unwilling to understand his wife. Rachel was barren and jealous of her sister, Leah, because she had children.

Their Outcome: Their descendants became three of the twelve tribes of Israel.

Key Scripture: Genesis 30

Their Story

Monday

Out of the corner of her eye, Rachel saw him smiling at her. Looking up, she squinted. "What?"

Jacob's responded with a boyish grin. "You're so beautiful."

Blushing at the comment, Rachel was content these days. God had at last heard her prayers and given her the one thing she most desired—a son of her own.

Jacob leaned down and kissed his wife, then turned and stepped away from the tent. She sat alone, savoring her husband's adoring look. And words. With two-week-old baby Joseph nestling in her arms, she had time to reflect.

"This is what I was made for," she whispered out loud, cuddling her newborn. She could hardly believe this little boy was really hers. She had all but given up hope that she would conceive and bear a child. Her heart flooded with gratitude. But during the long years of her infertility, Rachel had not always been so humble. Growing up, she had been the enviable one of Laban's two daughters. Her beauty made her the center of attention wherever she went. Her older sister, Leah, was never a source of competition. All eyes were on Rachel. Never on Leah.

Then, by a sleight of their father Laban's hand, within a week they both ended up married to the same man, Jacob. Rachel wasn't threatened by the fact that Leah was Jacob's first wife. Leah's presence in the marriage was an annoyance, but one that could be endured. After all, *she*, Rachel, was the sole object of her husband's desire. He had been tricked into marrying Leah. Her position as wife was a mere technicality.

Then the fertility wars began, piercing Rachel's pride. She may have had her husband's love, but it was her sister who won the pregnancy sweepstakes. Rachel was incensed, her anger dramatically on display. "How could this have happened?" she fumed to her servant. "I'm the one who was supposed to bear children first."

Each day as Leah's belly swelled with her firstborn, Rachel cringed. The spotlight shifted to Leah at Rachel's expense. Even Jacob, delighted and intrigued over the excitement of his first descendant, showed Leah more attention. Thoroughly consumed with her inability to conceive, Rachel bristled. "How can it be so easy for her to get pregnant and not me? It's all Jacob's fault!"

The day of little Reuben's birth was a nightmare for Rachel. The entire household feasted and celebrated Jacob's first son. All eyes were focused on the infant ... and on the mother who held him. Rachel gave her sister an obligatory kiss on each cheek and resolved that Jacob would be sleeping in her tent that evening. *He must give me a child*, she obsessed. *I cannot let my sister and her son steal his affections from me.*

Jacob did grace Rachel's tent that night. And the night after. And for many nights following. But nothing stirred inside Rachel's womb.

Then Leah announced one morning that she was pregnant. Again. Rachel's dignity took another dive. Driven by both resentment and fear, she aimed poisonous glares at Jacob, all the while wondering, *Does he even love me anymore?*

In the years that followed, Leah delivered two more babies. That made four.

The wounded Rachel lashed out with a vengeance. Storming into Jacob's tent one night—a breach of etiquette he was used to by now—Rachel pummeled him with her frustration.

"Give me children, or I'll die!" she demanded, her brow furrowed and her arms folded in defiance.[1] Angry tears streamed down her face.

Jacob remained untouched by his wife's emotional outbursts. Rachel's tears had been more effective when she was at the height of her beauty. But not so much now. "Am I in the place of God, who has kept you from having children?"[2] he fired back.

His bitter assessment shook her. His words cut deep and hurt, but Rachel was not about to give up. She shot Jacob another caustic glare and stormed from his tent.

Unwilling to concede, she devised a plan that followed tradition, demanding that Jacob adhere to custom and father a child through her servant, an idea Leah would not celebrate.

The deed done, Rachel's servant, Bilhah, conceived and delivered a son named Dan.

"God has vindicated me," Rachel said as she held Bilhah's baby in her arms. "He has listened to my plea and given my servant a son. And my sister is not his mother."

Taking credit for her servant's second child, Rachel proclaimed, "I have had a great struggle with my sister, and I have won."[3]

Leah's string of pregnancies had come to a temporary halt, and so, not to be outdone by her younger sister, she gave her servant, Zilpah, to Jacob, and Zilpah bore two boys. When Leah was able to conceive again, she had two more sons and a daughter. Without the servants' children, the count was now Leah seven, Rachel zero.

Rachel was defeated, and she knew it. The fight in her was

---

1. See Genesis 30:1.
2. See Genesis 30:2.
3. Genesis 30:8.

diminishing. Her bluster was gone. She was too tired to hate. To blame everyone else but herself for her problems. Rachel became quiet, ranting less. Crying more. She even cried out to God.

Then, one day, she felt something strange in her body. She suspected, but dared not let herself believe. Not even for a moment. *Don't get your hopes up, Rachel!* she silently warned herself.

But the pregnancy *was* real.

She was tempted to boast, but didn't. She wanted to flaunt her fertility like she used to parade her good looks; however, Rachel knew not to take the credit. The God who gives life and forms babies in the womb had finally heard her plea and enabled her to get pregnant. In the past she would have swaggered. But not now. In her brokenness, God had answered her.

The day Rachel delivered Joseph, she laughed and wept, thankful to be holding the son she had longed for. Rachel knew God had been merciful to her. Once proud and angry, she had been transformed into a grateful woman.

God had made this impossible moment possible.

Their Life and Times

Tuesday

The Many Sons of Israel

Jacob's sons became the twelve tribes of Israel. In birth order, these twelve sons — tribes — of Jacob (Israel) were Reuben, Simeon, Levi, Judah, Dan, Naphtali, Gad, Asher, Issachar, Zebulun, Joseph, and Benjamin.

Their descendants eventually spread all over the earth and are still identifiable today ... the Jews.

These twelve sons of Jacob were heirs to the covenant promise given to Jacob's grandfather, Abraham, when God pronounced, "I will make you into a great nation" (Genesis 12:2).

Jacob's first four sons — all born to Leah — were Reuben, Simeon, Levi, and Judah. Then came Dan and Naphtali, sons of Rachel's slave Bilhah. After that, Leah gave her slave, Zilpah, to Jacob, and she bore two sons, Gad and Asher. After the first four sons had been born to Leah, she gave birth to two more, Issachar and Zebulun. Finally, Rachel—Jacob's prized wife—gave birth to Joseph and Benjamin.

All of these sons of Jacob had been born in Canaan but had migrated to Egypt because of a famine. Joseph was the first to arrive, though not of his own choosing. His older and very jealous brothers sold him to a band of Midianite merchants who were on their way to Egypt. In God's providence, Joseph became very successful in Egypt and eventually welcomed his father, Jacob, and his eleven brothers to live there. The sons of Jacob and their families lived in Egypt—first as guests, then as slaves—for almost four hundred years.

At the end of his life, while all the Israelites were still in Egypt, Jacob gathered his sons together and spoke his final words over each one. Beginning with the oldest, Reuben, and ending with Benjamin, the youngest, Jacob pronounced a blessing on some sons and punishment on others.[4]

Although the largest portion of a father's inheritance was traditionally bequeathed to the first son, Jacob bypassed Reuben. Neither did he bless Simeon or Levi, sons two and three. Jacob had special words, however, for his fourth son. He did not pass the official birthright to Judah, but what he had to say was prophetic:

"Judah, your brothers will praise you …
The scepter will not depart from Judah,
    nor the ruler's staff from between his feet,
until he to whom it belongs shall come
    and the obedience of the nations shall be his."

GENESIS 49:8, 10

Fifteen centuries later, in a vision of Jesus Christ reigning over all the earth, the apostle John wrote, "See, the Lion of the tribe of Judah, the Root of David, has triumphed. He is able to open the scroll and its seven seals" (Revelation 5:5).

Jacob's pronouncement to his fourth son rang down through the ages. His family would carry the Messiah.

After Jacob delivered his dying message to Judah, the patriarch spoke to the next six sons. No rich blessings. No birthright. Jacob waited until he spoke to Joseph—his eleventh son—to deliver a

---

4. See Genesis 49:3–27.

special patriarchal blessing. Joseph's two sons, Ephraim and Manasseh, were each given full ranking as tribal leaders. These two sons of Joseph were given the "double portion" when Jacob bequeathed to them the oldest brother, Reuben's, birthright. This meant a double inheritance. The tribe Joseph is not identified by his name but by the two tribes of his two sons, Ephraim and Manasseh.

By the time the Israelites had settled back in Canaan, all but one of the twelve tribes were given land to raise their families. Jacob had called each tribe by the names of his sons when they were still in Egypt: Reuben, Simeon, Judah, Dan, Naphtali, Gad, Asher, Issachar, Zebulun, Ephraim, Manasseh, and Benjamin.

The one tribe not given land was that of Levi. Because of the temple responsibility given to the descendants of Levi, these people were set apart as God's special inheritance and were not given land to occupy. So when the tribes are identified, the tribe of Levi is not included.

Can You Imagine?

Wednesday

Blaming each other. It's a malady as old as the garden of Eden but maybe as fresh as yesterday at your house. Adam blamed Eve. Eve turned and pointed her finger at the serpent. Now Rachel is carping at Jacob for her barrenness. And Jacob, also angry and tired of her complaints, rails right back at his wife, saying that it is God's doing.

Can you imagine how different the outcome might have been if Adam and Eve had each humbly said to the Lord, "I'm sorry I took the fruit from the tree. It was my fault. Please forgive me." And what if Rachel had embraced Leah's children and thanked God—and her husband—for the good things that were already hers instead of blaming her husband for her childlessness?

Rachel, who had grown up with beauty and favor, may have planned her future to easily include the offspring she desired with Jacob. When it did not happen, she chose anger and bitterness over contentment and humility.

Without a grateful heart, hostility and anger build between you and your spouse. When life hands you something you cannot control or when you are disappointed with your spouse's behavior, blaming is a dangerous response. The grinding feeling in your stomach tells you something is terribly wrong. You know that sensation, don't you?

When a conflict has your spirit in knots, stop and think: *Is this worth it?* Before you blame and glare at the person you promised to love and cherish, truthfully examine your own heart. Ask yourself: *What is my underlying fear? Can I assume my spouse's best intent? What is the truth?*

Repentance, after truthfully identifying your own sinfulness, frees you and transforms your heart.

Without confession, repentance, and forgiveness, you and your spouse could fall into the same trap of anger and resentment that caused Rachel to blame Jacob for their infertility.

The secret of slowing the hard-charging horses of disrespect and chaos in your marriage is quite simple. Ready? You go first.

"I'm sorry. I was wrong. Will you please forgive me?"

From God's Word . . .

"'I have listened attentively, but they do not say what is right. None of them repent of their wickedness, saying, "What have I done?" Each pursues their own course like a horse charging into battle.'"

JEREMIAH 8:6

Their Legacy in Scripture

Thursday

1. **"'You intended to harm me, but God intended it for good to accomplish what is now being done, the saving of many lives.' ... And [Joseph] reassured them and spoke kindly to them"** (GENESIS 50:20–21).

   Jacob and Rachel's firstborn son, Joseph, did not blame the brothers who had wrongfully sold him into slavery and hurt him with words and actions. He had faith that God would work on his behalf. What pattern of faith and forgiveness are you setting up in your home today that will impact your children years from now?

2. **"Be kind and compassionate to one another, forgiving each other, just as in Christ God forgave you"** (EPHESIANS 4:32).

   God went first in forgiving you and me. In your marriage, who is the most likely to forgive first? Think back to a dispute with your spouse and replay it, replacing blame or any unkind words with, "I'm sorry. I was wrong. Will you please forgive me?" What do you think the outcome would have been?

3. **"Therefore confess your sins to each other and pray for each other so that you may be healed"** (JAMES 5:16).

   How might Rachel and Jacob have applied this in their marriage? Why do you think confession is necessary and so powerful in relationships? When was the last time you confessed something to your spouse, and what was the outcome? What do you need to confess to your spouse now? How can you pray for your spouse?

Their Legacy of Prayer

Friday

Reflect On: Genesis 29; 30:1 – 22

Praise God: For going first in forgiving you and providing pardon through Jesus' death on the cross.

Offer Thanks: For all the good gifts you have already received. For your spouse and for the healing power of kind words, forgiveness, and compassion.

Confess: Your discontent and failure to trust God for what you cannot control. Your inclination to rush to blame your spouse rather than humbly repenting for your own misdirected anger and shortcomings.

Ask God: For the ability to see your spouse from His perspective, and to soften your heart and enable you to confess, repent, and forgive quickly.

Listen: "My children, I am the great Forgiver, and I will provide everything you need to live in peace. I have your children in mind as I enable you to model tender love and compassion toward each other. Ask Me, and I will give you every resource you need."

Pray: *Forgiving Father, You are full of mercy, and we are grateful that You loved us when we were unlovable. We ask for Your help in our home. We acknowledge to You first, and then to each other, our need to say, "I'm sorry. I was wrong. Will you please forgive me?" Amen.*

14

Family Ties

Judah and Tamar

Meaning of Names: **Judah** means "praised" or "celebrated." *Tamar* means "palm tree."

Their Character: He was hypocritical and immoral but recognized her righteousness. She was determined and pursued justice.

Their Challenge: He lied and refused to give his third son in marriage to the family widow. She was deceived and unjustly hindered from preserving her first husband's family line.

Their Outcome: Judah eventually was honorable and recognized Tamar's right to bear his sons, preserving the family line. Tamar's firstborn son, Perez, was included in the lineage of Jesus Christ.

Key Scripture: Genesis 38

Their Story

Monday

Although Judah was one of the twelve sons of God's covenant with Jacob, he had separated from his brothers and assimilated into the immoral culture of Canaan.[1] There he married a woman named Shua, and they had three sons together.

The firstborn's name was Er, and as he grew, he had no regard

---

1. See Genesis 38:1–2.

for God. When it was time for him to marry, a teenager named Tamar was chosen as his bride. But because of Er's greedy, selfish, and immoral ways, God "put him to death."[2]

Because Tamar had no children—and had produced no sons for him—Er's line would not be perpetuated. So, as was the custom, Judah ordered his second son, Onan, to marry Tamar in order to produce a son to carry on Er's name. Onan, knowing that the first son born to Tamar would be considered his dead brother's child and would receive double the family inheritance, refused to impregnate her.[3]

God could not allow this disobedience regarding widows' rights to go unpunished, so one day Tamar awoke to find Onan dead.

Still Tamar had no children.

Her father-in-law had only one son left—Shelah—but he was just a boy. Judah instructed Tamar to return to her father's house, promising her his third son when he was of marrying age. But when Shelah was old enough to marry, Judah did not bring him to Tamar, fearing Shelah would also die, as his brothers had.

After years of waiting, Tamar knew that Judah, seemingly unconcerned about the survival of his line, had no intention of ever giving his third son to her. He had unjustly deceived and lied to her.

Then, when Judah's wife died, Tamar conspired to protect the inheritance rights of her first husband through the one family member left who could father her child. She planned. She plotted.

One day, knowing the route that Judah would take to the sheep-shearing festival, Tamar removed her widow's garments and covered her face with a harlot's veil, appearing as a prostitute. Provocatively dressed, she took her place at the town gate of Enaim. She caught Judah's glance as he passed by on the road. He stopped, looked again, and then approached her, asking for her services.

Tamar began to negotiate. "How will you pay me?" she asked.

Judah offered to send her a young goat.

"Give me your signet ring and the cord from around your neck and the staff in your hand as a pledge."

Judah surrendered the three pieces of identification and immedi-

---

2. Genesis 38:7.
3. See Genesis 38:9.

ately went in to the woman he thought was a prostitute. And Tamar conceived.

The man who had lied to her and treated her unjustly by not providing for her as the law dictated napped. Tamar removed her disguise, gathered the contraband, and left.

Three months later, Judah heard the news that his widowed daughter-in-law was pregnant. He was outraged. Demanding her execution, he sent several men to her father's home to seize Tamar. "Bring her out and let her be burned," they demanded.

Tamar never flinched. She was prepared. As she was being brought out, Tamar produced the signet ring, the cord, and the staff. She told the men to take them to Judah. "I am pregnant by the man who owns these," she said. And she added, "See if you recognize whose seal and cord and staff these are."[4]

The philandering Judah had been found out. He sent word back to the men holding Tamar. "She is more righteous than I, since I wouldn't give her to my son Shelah."[5]

There would be no execution. The incident was over.

Judah acknowledged his shameful neglect and commended Tamar for her attention to the inheritance rights of her family line.

Six months later, Tamar delivered twins, Perez and Zerah.

Judah's watchful God had come to her rescue. He had seen the injustice done to her and had vindicated her and preserved the family legacy of her deceased husband. The line of Judah was rescued. Despite the violations in this story, Tamar's oldest son would be part of the messianic line, paving the way for the birth of Israel's Messiah, the Lord Jesus Christ.

---

4. Genesis 38:25.
5. Genesis 38:26.

Their Life and Times

Tuesday

Levirate Marriage

Judah called Tamar "righteous" because of her focused intention to preserve the family lineage. As a childless widow, she could expect the enactment on her behalf of what was described in Deuteronomy as the levirate marriage law:

> If brothers are living together and one of them dies without a son, his widow must not marry outside the family. Her husband's brother shall take her and marry her and fulfill the duty of a brother-in-law to her. The first son she bears shall carry on the name of the dead brother so that his name will not be blotted out from Israel.
>
> DEUTERONOMY 25:5–6

This law required a man to marry his widowed sister-in-law as a way of assuring an heir for the deceased man and perpetuating the name of his brother who died without a son. It also secured property for the original family. Without a son, a man's holdings could end up in the possession of an outsider, leaving the widow with no rights to it. A levirate marriage also provided a widow with a male heir who would care for his parents—particularly his mother—in their old age. In ancient Israel, the continuity of each family and the control of its land were important to God, who championed the significance of both the individual and the family.

Despite God's desire that the widow be provided for and that property remain within the family, the levirate law could be avoided. Some brothers balked at such an arrangement because they did not want to share their inheritance with a son who would be considered the son of the older brother, as was the case with Onan.

A provision, however, was made for a brother who did not want to fulfill the law: "His brother's widow shall go up to him in the presence of the elders, take off one of his sandals, spit in his face and say, 'This is what is done to the man who will not build up his brother's family line.' That man's line shall be known in Israel as The Family of the Unsandaled" (Deuteronomy 25:9–10).

God was disgusted with Onan, not just because he failed to obey the levirate law, but also because of Onan's sin of pretense, making others believe he was fulfilling his obligation to Tamar. A man who refused to take his brother's widow would carry the "unsandaled" stigma with him the rest of his days, making him an object of contempt and humiliation to the town elders. The harm done to his reputation would make him an unfavorable business partner and one of questionable values.

On the other hand, a man who unselfishly provided the levirate marriage for his brother's widow reflected love for his deceased sibling and compassion for the woman, who otherwise would be left destitute. The desire to carry on his brother's line affirmed the dignity and honor of the family.

The levirate law was a reflection of God's loving and caring nature. He is the champion of those who cannot fight for themselves. "A father to the fatherless, a defender of widows, is God in his holy dwelling" (Psalm 68:5).

Can You Imagine?

Wednesday

Although she was not an Israelite, Tamar would have learned about the Jewish custom of the levirate marriage law at the time she married into Judah's family. So Tamar pursued her rights when she became a widow.

Despite the injustices dealt to Tamar, one truth is clear: God is sovereign and is able to redeem any circumstance.

When the church was first established, God's people were specifically instructed to care for widows.[6] Even though believers today are not bound to Jewish levirate law, the call to embrace women in need could also apply to unmarried and single divorced women.[7] God deeply cares for each one of His daughters.

Your local church is a family—brothers and sisters who offer loving help for single women who are sick, hurting, lonely, or struggling to provide for themselves or their children. As church members, you and your spouse are the hands and feet of Jesus, fulfilling God's clear promise to defend the cause of the fatherless and the widow and to love the foreigners living among us.[8] Even when we suffer injustice or employ misguided methods, God is able to bless us and use us for His glory.

God's providence revealed through Judah and Tamar's story may be the reminder you need to confront someone who is promoting evil or to serve people who have no resources. You can be the ambassador of God's truth and grace.

Can you imagine that you are the answer to someone's prayer?

From God's Word . . .

"God sets the lonely in families."

PSALM 68:6

---

6. See Acts 6:1–4.

7. By some accounts, more than 50 percent of the adult women in America are living without a spouse (see Sam Roberts, "51% of Women Are Now Living without Spouse," *New York Times* (January 16, 2007), www.nytimes.com/2007/01/16/us/16census.html?pagewanted=all (accessed September 13, 2012).

8. See Deuteronomy 10:18.

Their Legacy in Scripture
Thursday

1. **"Religion that God our Father accepts as pure and faultless is this: to look after orphans and widows in their distress and to keep oneself from being polluted by the world"** (JAMES 1:27).

   What widows or single women in distress do you know whom you can pray for? What acts of loving-kindness can you share with them?

2. **"When you are harvesting in your field and you overlook a sheaf, do not go back to get it. Leave it for the foreigner, the fatherless and the widow, so that the LORD your God may bless you in all the work of your hands"** (DEUTERONOMY 24:19).

   The chances are good, whether or not you're a farmer, you're not going to be able to "overlook a sheaf." (Even if you do live on a farm, binding wheat into sheaves isn't the way you harvest!) If you were asked to rewrite this verse using an example you can identify with, what would it say? What is God's promise to you if you take care of "the foreigner, the fatherless and the widow"?

3. **"The LORD was gracious to [the Israelites] and had compassion and showed concern for them because of his covenant with Abraham, Isaac and Jacob. To this day he has been unwilling to destroy them or banish them from his presence"** (2 KINGS 13:22–23).

   The story of Judah and Tamar is the account of God's plan to preserve His people, the Jews. And over the centuries, He has done exactly that. This promise now includes all of us, whether or not we are Jewish. "He redeemed us in order that the blessing given to Abraham might come to the Gentiles through Christ Jesus, so that by faith we might receive the promise of the Spirit" (Galatians 3:14). What does God's faithfulness look like in your marriage?

Their Legacy of Prayer

Friday

Reflect On: Genesis 38

Praise God: For His love and justice to the disenfranchised and for fulfilling His sovereign plan.

Offer Thanks: That the Lord provides care and resources through His sons and daughters in the church.

Confess: That as a couple, you too often look for friendships among other couples, overlooking single people who need the love of a family.

Ask God: To identify the people with whom He wants you to share your home, your resources, and the love of Jesus.

Listen: "Dear children, I am able to do far more through you than you can imagine when you obey Me. Ask Me, and I will guide you and send you to befriend the lonely, help the helpless, and provide for the needy."

Pray: *Father in heaven, all the resources of the universe are at Your disposal. Who is a God like You, who cares for the hurting and sets the lonely in families? Give us hearts like Yours, and fill us with compassion so that we may be Your hands and feet. Thank You for the joy that comes from You when we serve others. Amen.*

15

Distraction, Dalliance, and Deceit

Potiphar and Wife

Meaning of Names: *Potiphar* means "belonging to the sun" (referring to the sun-god Ra). The name of Potiphar's wife is not given in the Bible.

Their Character: He was proud and preoccupied with his work and too passive to question his deceptive wife. She was immoral, discontented, self-indulgent, vindictive, and deceitful.

Their Challenge: His busyness and unwillingness to pursue the truth. Her dalliance and deception.

Their Outcome: They continued living together in the palace, while the innocent Hebrew man they sentenced prospered in prison.

Key Scripture: Genesis 39:1–20

Their Story

Monday

Potiphar lay wide-awake in the early morning hours. There was nothing to look at but the darkness. Though she slept next to him this night, his wife was no companion. The palace where they lived had become a lonely dungeon. His wife, who cared only for herself, snored away the hours in tranquility. The opulence of his surroundings and the companionship of his priceless collections did nothing to fill the hollowness in his soul. No, though she lay next to him this night, Potiphar's wife was no companion. He remained unsettled.

As the captain of Pharaoh's guard, he was well compensated. A man of power, Potiphar had been rewarded with many benefits, including a beautiful wife. The pharaoh took ample care of those who served him.

Despite these trappings, Potiphar lived with a smoldering rage. Taking little satisfaction in the glitter of his home, he yearned for the morning light so he could return to his busyness. Work was the only opiate for his troubled heart.

In official business, Potiphar was intelligent and aggressive, pleasing the pharaoh with his resourcefulness and ability to manage the kingdom's military affairs. He was especially adept at spotting talent. One day, when a band of Ishmaelite merchants came through town vending an impressive seventeen-year-old Hebrew, Potiphar secured the bright teenager and took him home. The boy was handsome, sturdy, smart, and fluent in the Egyptian language. Potiphar knew a bargain when he saw one.

Most slaves were not afforded the honor of being addressed by their name, but Potiphar liked the young man so much that he called him Joseph. The Hebrew's dignity earned it. The master was satisfied with his new purchase. Potiphar's fortunes soared from the time Joseph joined his employ. Everything the young man touched turned a hefty profit. Before long, Potiphar realized the indispensability of the man who ran his estate.

Potiphar was pleased with Joseph. He was not the only one.

So was his wife.

Potiphar was too preoccupied with building his fortune to notice her salacious eye for the handsome man who had been assigned the supervision of the entire palace. No longer in her prime but assuming her own desirability, Potiphar's wife set her sights on the man young enough to be her son.

One day she cornered Joseph and boldly propositioned the Hebrew. "Come to bed with me!"[1]

But Joseph was steadfast. "How then could I do such a wicked thing and sin against God?"[2]

---

1. Genesis 39:7.
2. Genesis 39:9.

Day after day, Potiphar's wife continued her solicitations. And Joseph refused her advances.

Now as it happened, one day Joseph was going about his work in the palace when no others were there, except for Potiphar's wife. Seizing her opportunity, she pawed at his cloak and demanded again, "Come to bed with me!" But he left his cloak in her hand and ran out of the house.[3]

Embarrassed and furious, Potiphar's wife decided to make Joseph pay for refusing her flirtings. She summoned her servants and lied to them about what had happened, plotting the story she would tell her husband when he returned home.

In a few hours, Potiphar arrived at the palace. His long day at work left no room in his spirit for any grace at all. So when he walked through his door and was met there by his wife, he suspected trouble. The look in her eyes confirmed it.

"Do you recognize this cloak?" she snapped, throwing the garment at him. "Your slave assaulted me! Is this the kind of man you bring into this house? He ran away when I screamed, leaving his cloak in my hand. How will I ever recover from this?"

Her tears were fake, but her lie was real.

Potiphar was enraged.

All the servants were watching. Protecting his honor, Potiphar acted impulsively.

"Joseph!" he screamed.

The young man came running.

"What is this you have done!"

It wasn't a question.

"But sir ..."

With no discussion, Joseph was led away to the prison reserved for royal servants. As the faithful Hebrew disappeared from sight, a faint breeze of uncertainty blew across Potiphar. His wife's accusations against Joseph had blindsided Potiphar, and he had reacted. But as he reflected on her story and on Joseph's exemplary behavior, doubt began to flood his mind. Was there more to the story than his wife had told him? What had happened, *really*? But not willing to

---

3. See Genesis 39:12.

question his wife, Potiphar avoided the messiness of unearthing the truth, and he passively allowed the record to stand. He didn't want to challenge his wife, even if it turned out that Joseph was innocent.

And now, one year since Joseph's arrest, Potiphar's doubts and guilt were keeping him up all night.

Their Life and Times

Tuesday

Egypt

The land of Egypt played a sustaining role in the history of God's chosen people and in the story of redemption. One of the oldest on earth, Egyptian civilization began with settlements springing up over three thousand years before the birth of Christ. Egypt's land along the Nile River was lush and verdant.

Early Egyptian settlers were primarily farmers and fishermen until the discovery of copper. Because this valuable metal was desired by other nations, Egypt began to grow as an industrial leader.

Kings, called pharaohs, ruled over this prosperous nation.[4] These monarchs developed and supervised a successful labor force to manage construction and agriculture. They also established lucrative trade routes. The Egyptians were resourceful people, making notable advances in architecture, art, technology, and the establishment of a sophisticated judicial system.

The most celebrated of Egypt's architectural wonders were the mighty pyramids. These giant crypts entombing some of the nation's rich and famous people — mostly pharaohs — stand as monuments to Egyptian brilliance. The movement and fitting together of stones weighing as much as fourteen thousand pounds each is a testament to the people's ingenuity.

The first pyramids date back to the year 3000 BC and were designed like Mesopotamian temples. Called ziggurats, these temples were massive stone structures with steps leading all the way to the top. Egyptians transformed the original ziggurat model into some-

---

4. Joseph became Pharaoh's vizier (his second-in-command) in about 1885 BC.

thing much grander—a glorious pyramid fit for a king after his death.

It was the idea of the pharaoh Djoser in 2630 BC to build and use a pyramid as a tomb where he—and subsequent pharaohs—would continue to be worshiped long after their deaths. Entombing a pharaoh in a spectacular burial edifice would maintain the supposed immortality that kings claimed for themselves.

Djoser recruited a talented architect named Imhotep to design a pyramid as his eventual mortuary. Soaring 180 feet (eighteen stories), this monument still stands today in Saqqara, near Memphis, Egypt. Deep within the pyramid is Djoser's burial chamber, which was carved out of rock.

Each pyramid took about twenty years to construct. The area for the casket was only 8 feet long by 4 feet wide, but the main gallery —or entryway—could be as high as 36 feet and as long as 160 feet. The last pyramid was built about 1790 BC.

During the years Abraham and Sarah were moving from place to place (about 2100 BC and following), they made a short visit to Egypt because of the famine in Canaan, where they lived (Genesis 12:10–20). Word had spread throughout the known world that the Egyptian economy was strong and that the country had plenty of food. So the patriarch and his wife traveled there in order to survive the famine. Abraham and Sarah would have marveled at the sight of the pyramids when they entered Egypt.

Unlike his great-grandfather Abraham, Joseph's presence in Egypt was not voluntary. He had been sold by his brothers to a band of Ishmaelite merchants traveling through Canaan toward Egypt. Joseph was later purchased by the powerful Potiphar, the captain of the guard in Pharaoh's army.

Though put in prison by Potiphar, Joseph prospered and later became Pharaoh's second-in-command. When Egypt faced a famine of its own, Joseph may have used the pyramids as his primary warehouses. They could accommodate the enormous amount of grain needed to feed millions of people for seven years.

In God's providence, the land of Egypt also provided food for Joseph's extended family, the Hebrews, and became a temporary place of rescue for them.

Can You Imagine?

Wednesday

Potiphar's wife didn't lack anything, at least materially. Married to one of the most prominent men in Egypt, she was living the dream. She lived in a palatial home with endless resources and servants. To every appearance, she had a faithful husband who worked hard to sustain their opulent lifestyle. Yet this wife was willing to risk all she had for some moments of stolen pleasure with Joseph. Can you imagine?

The temptress decided to seduce Joseph with more than words. "She caught him by his cloak" (Genesis 39:12). Don't you wonder if that morning she dressed and accessorized and perfumed with this specific plan in mind?

Her advances were entirely about meeting her own needs. Her undying love ... for herself. And she had no qualms about making her busy husband an accessory to injustice, robbing an innocent man of his honor.

What would make a wife intentionally act like this? Restlessness? Boredom? Despite all the accoutrements of her lifestyle, she was discontent and looking for something to fill up her emptiness. Her story is a warning not to listen to that whisper about being stuck in the life you have. And the danger of escaping into the novel tucked away in a secret place that takes you somewhere you should never visit; the open bottle of wine when your husband is on a business trip; the rush that comes when an old flame makes contact on the Internet.

And what of Potiphar? Given Joseph's stellar record, did this husband really believe his wife's accusations? The Bible doesn't tell us about what was going on behind the scenes in this relationship, but it seems plausible that Potiphar loved his work more than he loved his wife. And why did he allow his wife to be left alone with a handsome young manager in the palace? Maybe he was too distracted with his work to set safeguards at home. Or maybe he was clueless about his wife's secret fantasies.

Potiphar's distraction with his work and the treachery of his wife's discontent, restlessness, and deception trapped them in an unhealthy marriage.

From God's Word . . .

"Godliness with contentment is great gain. For we brought nothing into the world, and we can take nothing out of it. But if we have food and clothing, we will be content with that. Those who want to get rich fall into temptation and a trap and into many foolish and harmful desires that plunge people into ruin and destruction."

1 TIMOTHY 6:6–9

Their Legacy in Scripture

Thursday

1. "[Potiphar's wife] kept [Joseph's] cloak beside her until his master came home. Then she told him this story: 'That Hebrew slave *you* brought us came to me to make sport of me'" (GENESIS 39:16–17, emphasis added).

   Blaming ... it's the oldest trick in the book. Where have we seen this before in the Bible? Why do marriage partners avoid confession and resort to blaming so quickly? What in this scenario is a warning to you for the next disagreement you have with your spouse?

2. "When his master heard the story his wife told him, saying, 'This is how your slave treated me,' *he burned with anger*" (GENESIS 39:19, emphasis added).

   When making a decision that cost Joseph his freedom and Potiphar the loss of his loyal and wise manager, anger ruled the moment. What do you think could have been some other reasons for Potiphar's angry outburst?

   Anger can be a relationship killer. What triggers angry outbursts in your marriage? What can you do to restore your relationship with your spouse when it has been damaged by hurtful words?

3. "I know what it is to be in need, and I know what it is to have plenty. I have learned the secret of being content in any and every situation, whether well fed or hungry, whether living in plenty or in want" (PHILIPPIANS 4:12).

   Potiphar's wife longed for what she didn't have. Ask yourself, "What am I allowing my imagination to dwell on that stirs up discontent in my heart? In my marriage?"

   Potiphar was preoccupied and too busy to address the problems at home. What do you need to identify, confess, stop doing, or start doing in order to correct discontent in your marriage?

Their Legacy of Prayer

Friday

Reflect On: Genesis 39

Praise God: Because He is a bountiful God who gives you everything you need for a godly life and provides His Holy Spirit to guide you in your marriage.[5]

Offer Thanks: For His divine power to set you free from the things that would ruin your marriage and harm your relationship with God.

Confess: Any discontent, blaming, angry outbursts, or secret fantasies that hinder a clean conscience and openness with your spouse.

Ask God: To forgive you for these sins and replace them with His truth, joy, and peace. For strength to acknowledge those places where you and your spouse need divine help.

Listen: "Dear children, when I gave you eternal life, I equipped you with the Spirit of truthfulness and a desire for perfect unity in your marriage. I want you to be content. You please Me when you love one another with the holy love I provide."

Pray: *Dear Father in heaven, You have empowered us in all things to display Your peace. Teach us how to be content in every situation. We are grateful for the spiritual and temporal blessings that You lavish on us. Please give us eyes to see Your manifold bounty in our lives and our marriage. We desire to honor You with contentment and joy. Amen.*

---

5. 2 Peter 1:3.

A Time to Heal

Joseph and Asenath

Meaning of Names:	*Joseph* means "May He [God] increase" or "adds." *Asenath* means "worshiper of Neith" (Egyptian goddess of weaving, hunting, and war).
Their Character:	He was a godly man of honor, integrity, and perseverance in the face of adversity. She was a gift to Joseph from Potiphar and embraced Joseph's God.
Their Challenge:	Joseph entered marriage with the wounds of family rejection and unjust treatment, including ten years in prison. Asenath had grown up worshiping false gods.
Their Outcome:	Two sons were born who would be the patriarchs of two of Israel's twelve tribes — Manasseh and Ephraim.
Key Scripture:	Genesis 41:45–52

Their Story

Monday

The eleventh of twelve brothers growing up in the shepherding family of Jacob, the Hebrew living in Canaan, Joseph was his father's undisputed favorite, much to his brothers' indignation. It didn't help matters when Joseph began having dreams that hinted at his future ascendency over them. Joseph showed no restraint in telling his family of these night visions. It served only to stoke his siblings' rage, and neither Joseph nor his father had any idea of the calamity in store for the boy.

One day, while Joseph visited his brothers in the fields, they saw a way to rid themselves of their brother who was torturing them with his incessant ramblings. His brothers seized the unsuspecting seventeen-year-old, tossing him into a deep pit. As they sat down to eat before deciding what to do with him, they saw a caravan of Ishmaelites on their way to Egypt. "Oh, this is rich!" Judah beamed. "Well, brothers, I think we found the solution to our problem."

They sold their brother to the Ishmaelites, and soon Joseph's hands were shackled, and he was sent on his way to Egypt. Joseph had no idea where he was headed or what he was headed for. Like property, Joseph was sold to the highest bidder in Egypt. Then came his assignment to the household of Potiphar, captain of Pharaoh's police force. But with God's help, Joseph prospered, and Potiphar put him in charge of everything he owned.

Potiphar's wife, it turned out, had an eye for younger men, especially strong and good-looking ones. Her fantasies had Joseph's name scrawled on them. However, the young Hebrew was devoted to his God and refused to dishonor Him by bathing in the pleasures of another man's wife. Accustomed to getting what she wanted, Potiphar's wife did not take kindly to Joseph's rebuffs and arranged for him to find a new place of residence—Pharaoh's prison.

It was a grievous twist of fate for the promising teenager who once dreamed of ruling over his brothers. Joseph was young, handsome, strong, talented—and locked up in an Egyptian dungeon. Yet the Lord was constantly with him and prospered him. Soon the warden put him in charge of all operations; but still, Joseph was in prison … and would remain there for more than a decade.

Then one day, an opportunity. Fellow inmates—Pharaoh's baker and his cupbearer—each had a dream that needed interpreting, and Joseph gave each of them an accurate interpretation. "Remember me when you return to Pharaoh," Joseph told the cupbearer. But when he was released from prison, he didn't remember.

Two years later, another opportunity. This time a more promising one. Pharaoh himself had some very disturbing dreams about seven ugly cows devouring seven fat cows, and seven scrawny heads of grain on a stalk swallowing seven healthy heads of grain. Pharaoh's highly paid officials were clueless about what the dreams meant.

Then the cupbearer remembered Joseph, and the thirty-year-old Hebrew man was summoned. The king told Joseph about his dreams. Joseph, through God's divine enabling, correctly interpreted the dreams. First the good news: seven years of abundance awaited Egypt. Then the bad: seven years of famine would follow.

Joseph then boldly gave Pharaoh some unsolicited advice: "Look for a discerning and wise man and put him in charge of the land of Egypt."[1] Joseph told Pharaoh to store food during the prosperous years so there would be plenty for the lean years.

The king, impressed with the wisdom of the prisoner's counsel, decreed, *You're the one, Joseph!* "You shall be in charge of my palace, and all my people are to submit to your orders. Only with respect to the throne will I be greater than you."[2]

And then Pharaoh bestowed on Joseph the accoutrements of power. The king's signet ring. Costly garments. Chains of gold. An ornate chariot. Unlimited authority. And the gift of a wife named Asenath. After years of injustice, mistreatment, abandonment, and loneliness, Joseph had a companion—a wife who later would bear the two boys he would raise to fulfill God's promise.

What his brothers had meant for evil, God had indeed used for good.

Their Life and Times

Tuesday

Dreams

It was no coincidence that Joseph had the ability to interpret dreams. God had given him this special skill for a greater purpose. And eventually Joseph knew it.

In the ancient world, dreams were so significant that people often determined the course of their lives by them. Dreams were con-

---

1. Genesis 41:33.
2. Genesis 41:40.

sidered a means by which unreachable gods revealed the future to mere humans. Dreams were believed to be communications from the gods, veiled messages whose mysterious meanings needed to be deciphered and unpacked.

Because of this dependency on dreams, an entire dream-interpreting "industry" was forged in both Egypt and Babylon. *Onei-romancy*, the practice of interpreting dreams, flourished during the time of Joseph. Dreams, the people believed, functioned as keyholes, allowing a peek into the future.

Dreams were the obsession of the era of both royalty and commoners. In Egypt, many dream books were written, their focus being the scientific study of sleep-induced visions. People believed these visions foretold of either good fortune or looming disaster.

In fact, Egyptians and Babylonians were so preoccupied with their dreams that they would often spend a night sleeping, or incubating, in the temple of their favorite deity in hopes that the god would give them the answers to their indecipherable visions.[3]

As the decades passed, the Egyptians and Babylonians became experts in dream interpretation, compiling detailed dream manuals. Ordinary people had no choice but to consult these dream guidebooks because they were incapable of interpreting their dreams by themselves.

People who were superstitious could be easily preyed on by those claiming to have all the answers when it came to dreams. However, the Lord warned the Israelites about false interpretations. He told Moses to tell the people of Israel:

> If a prophet, or one who foretells by dreams, appears among you and announces to you a sign or wonder, and if the sign or wonder spoken of takes place, and the prophet says, "Let us follow other gods" (gods you have not known) "and let us worship them," you must not listen to the words of that prophet or dreamer. The LORD your God is testing you to find out whether you love him with all your heart and with all your soul.
>
> DEUTERONOMY 13:1–5

---

3. Jean-Pierre Isbouts, *The Biblical World: An Illustrated Atlas* (Washington, D.C.: National Geographic, 2007), 95.

So, what was God's view of dreams? The Lord used dreams for specific purposes—to clearly communicate His absolute will and wishes. Dreams were not intended to fool or confuse people. For example, God used a dream of a stairway to heaven to confirm to Jacob the Abrahamic covenant. He gave the weak-willed Gideon a dream that he would be victorious in an upcoming battle. The Lord appeared to Solomon in a dream and urged him to ask of the Lord anything the new monarch desired. He sent Joseph of Nazareth a dream, telling him he should take the pregnant Mary into his home to be his wife.[4]

When looking at the dreams recorded in the Bible, remember the difference between those induced by the imaginations of the human mind and those sent by the Lord, which have the unmistakable mark of truth, clarity, and His perfect will.

In the case of Pharaoh, God penetrated the mind of a pagan king to accomplish divine purposes. In a single night, the king of Egypt had two dreams that would change Israel's history. "Your dream was no accident," Joseph told Pharaoh, "nor did it come from your false deities. It came from the God of Israel, the Creator of heaven and earth, who is both the Author and Interpreter of dreams."[5]

In God's hands, dreams were a powerful tool in accomplishing His will. His goal was always the good of those who loved Him.

Can You Imagine?

Wednesday

When two people get married, they always bring their pasts into the marriage. Two completely different histories. This was true for you and your spouse, and it was true for Joseph and Asenath.

We know little about Asenath except that she was an Egyptian and the daughter of a pagan priest. She grew up in the city of On, where temples were built for the worship of multiple gods. As the

---

4. See Genesis 28:12; Judges 7:13–14; 1 Kings 3:5; Matthew 1:20.
5. See Genesis 41:16–40.

daughter of a priest of the sun-god Ra, Asenath did not share Joseph's faith in the one true God

While we know little about Asenath, we know quite a bit about Joseph's childhood and young adulthood. Until his arranged marriage with Asenath, Joseph's biography was filled with rejection and inequity. His resentful brothers sold him like common property to slave traders. In Egypt, Joseph was purchased, promoted, and then thrown into prison for thirteen years on a false charge. He did not marry Asenath until he was released from prison and elevated again to favor and prestige. Can you imagine entering marriage with wounds as painful as the ones Joseph carried?

These two very different people were thrown together into an arranged marriage. No getting acquainted in courtship. No engagement period with long talks about beliefs and hopes and fears. Can you imagine one day being single and strangers and the next day being husband and wife?

Although your own marriage was probably not arranged, and you and your spouse may not have backgrounds as different as Joseph's and Asenath's, you have surely faced the challenge of understanding and embracing each other's history. You both have stories that include hopes and victories, failures and brokenness. Can you imagine what your marriage could be if you and your spouse would choose to help each other identify dreams, validate past hurts, and bear one another's burdens?

Each of you married a person with a sacred history. And each of you has the privilege of understanding the other's joy and pain, seeking God's guidance toward healing, and holding on to the hope of the dreams God has given you.

From God's Word . . .

"Love does not delight in evil but rejoices with the truth. It always protects, always trusts, always hopes, always perseveres."

1 CORINTHIANS 13:6–7

Their Legacy in Scripture

Thursday

1. **"'I know the plans I have for you,' declares the LORD, 'plans to prosper you and not to harm you, plans to give you hope and a future'"** (JEREMIAH 29:11).

   When we first meet Joseph, he is given two dreams. What do they reveal about his future? Before fulfilling the dreams, what confusing events did God allow to humble him? What dream of yours—or your spouse's—has been detoured by a humbling experience?

2. **"Pharaoh gave Joseph the name Zaphenath-Paneah and gave him Asenath daughter of Potiphera, priest of On, to be his wife. And Joseph went throughout the land of Egypt"** (GENESIS 41:45).

   Joseph and his wife came from different backgrounds, contrasting families of origin. Their first adjustment must have included a recognition of their contradictory faiths. How have you impacted your spouse's spiritual life? How has your spouse's life impacted yours? What do you and your spouse do to cultivate a deeper walk with God?

3. **"Carry each other's burdens, and in this way you will fulfill the law of Christ"** (GALATIANS 6:2).

   How can you uncover your spouse's dreams or wounds? What does it mean to "carry" them? According to this verse, what is God's plan for you and for your marriage?

Their Legacy of Prayer

Friday

Reflect On: Genesis 40:1 – 41:40

Praise God: For His sovereignty over all things and for giving you a spouse with a unique story.

Offer Thanks: That although you and your spouse have different dreams and wounds, you have a God who loves you and will cover your marriage with redemption and hope. For His provision for healing.

Confess: That you too often ignore your spouse's needs and concerns.

Ask God: To give you insight and sensitivity to embrace your spouse's needs and for patience and grace when perceived flaws frustrate you. To use your marriage to display His kindness.

Listen: "Dearly loved ones, I have designed you to be healers to each other as I empower you with tenderness, patience, and love. Be sensitive and alert to each other's needs and encourage each other every day. Your spouse is a gift to treasure."

Pray: *Heavenly Father, You designed us to bless and provide healing for each other. Empower us to love You and to follow Your plan for our marriage. Help us to walk together in hope, understanding, and the fulfillment of all the dreams You have for us. Amen.*

17

Heroes at Home

Amram and Jochebed

Meaning of Names:	*Amram* means "exalted people" or "exalted nation." *Jochebed* means "Yahweh is glory."
Their Character:	He was a man who supported his wife in a trying time. She was a woman of faith, ingenuity, and courage.
Their Challenge:	Because Pharaoh had declared that all Hebrew male children were to be thrown into the Nile, this couple had to overcome fear and trust God to preserve the life of their infant son.
Their Outcome:	Moses would be raised in Egyptian court and later become Israel's great leader, leading them out of slavery.
Key Scripture:	Exodus 2:1–10

Their Story

Monday

Had it not been for God's overruling presence, neither Amram nor his wife, Jochebed, could have survived. Toughened by a lifetime of Egyptian bondage, Amram had enough strength in his body and spirit to carry Jochebed through the traumatic ordeal.

Jochebed's anguish had begun when she discovered she was pregnant with her third child—her daughter, Miriam, was ten; her son, Aaron, only three. Pregnancy was a frightening prospect for Israelite women because of Pharaoh's fatal edict. Fearing the irrepressible growth of the enslaved Israelite population, the pharaoh had warned his officials, "If we go to war there will be no stopping them. These Hebrews will side with our enemies and overpower us." His final solution was to kill all newborn male children. "Drown them in the Nile!"[1]

Hebrew women were terrorized by the prospect of delivering a male child. While pregnant, they would plead, "Lord, may the child in my womb be a girl." And so Amram and Jochebed were thrust into months of trepidation. "Amram, what if I carry a son in my womb? Then what will we do? How can we bear to let him be killed?"

Amram listened, but he had no answer. Only tenderness and prayers.

Then one day while enduring the slave labor and endlessly hauling water from the Nile to the troughs for brick making, Amram noticed something in the river. Near the shoreline marsh he saw one of the Egyptian papyrus and reed boats used for hunting fowl. He had often seen these vessels before, but this time an idea caught him. He mentioned it to Jochebed and left it at that.

She played out various scenarios.

The day she delivered a baby boy, she wept. At the sight of their child's soft face and the sound of his sucking, Jochebed's heart became stout, and she formed a plan. Going to the banks of the Nile to fetch water for each day's use, she had noticed Pharaoh's daughter in the distance. Surrounded by her attendants, the princess would bathe at the edge of the river—and always at the same time of day. Jochebed observed the kindness of the princess toward the children of the servants who accompanied her.

It was obvious that the princess loved babies. If she were to find a baby floating in the bulrushes, seemingly abandoned, would she not want to keep the child? *Dear God, let it be so*, Jochebed pleaded with Yahweh.

As she cuddled her baby, Jochebed began to believe something holy was happening. God could hear her prayers. This son would not die at the hands of the Egyptians.

Jochebed planned and prayed and discussed her plan with Amram. He agreed it was their only hope. Yet, Jochebed couldn't bear the thought of giving up her little boy so soon. Miraculously, she was

---

1. Exodus 1:22.

able to hide him for several months, a grace they never could have imagined.

When Moses was three months old, she swaddled his tiny body in soft pieces of cloth and lowered him into the little papyrus boat she had meticulously coated with tar and pitch. She gently steadied the basket in the shallow backwater, an eddy in the Nile where the water was quiet because the current hardly reached it. Hurrying from the spot but with a watchful eye, Jochebed stood at a distance waiting for the princess and her attendants to approach. Stepping into the water, the princess spotted the small ark. Curious to see what it contained, she called one of her servants to retrieve it. As she pulled back the cloth to see what was in the basket, she gasped at the sight of the beautiful baby. Clearly smitten and laughing with pleasure, the princess picked him up and claimed the cooing infant as her own.

Jochebed's heart pounded at the sight. On cue, young Miriam ran to the Egyptian women, innocently asking if the princess wanted her to find a Hebrew woman to breast-feed the child. When the princess said yes, Miriam fetched Jochebed, and Moses' mother was immediately hired — paid well with Pharaoh's funds — to raise her son until he was weaned.

Her plan had worked, and the death sentence was thwarted. Baby Moses would live — and be held and nursed and taught by his own mother for the first few years of his life.

However, the precious time passed too quickly. Moses was weaned. "It is time," Amram spoke softly to his wife. "This is the day we return our son to the princess." Jochebed and Amram shared a prayer and a last meal together in their simple dwelling before the afternoon exchange. "You are going to a new home, my son." Amram quietly whispered the unthinkable words to his little boy.

The princess's entourage was waiting. This was an exhilarating moment for the daughter of Pharaoh, and she treated it with the flourish it deserved. She was kind and gracious to Jochebed, unaware of the pathos of the mother's heart.

An official stepped forward and handed Jochebed a purse of money. She bowed in gratitude. Separating Moses from his mother, a courtier gently took the toddler's chubby hand and transferred it to the hand of the Egyptian princess.

Jochebed could barely breathe. She told her eyes not to blink tears.

Pulling the boy closer, Pharaoh's daughter gathered Moses as her own and crisply turned away. Her entourage dutifully followed.

Jochebed watched her toddler walk away, his small body nearly concealed in the mass of officials. As the party turned a corner, a glimpse of his chunky legs and thick curls split her heart. He was looking back, straining to see her. Then little Moses disappeared, swallowed up in the procession to the great palace.

In their home later that night, Amram and Jochebed knelt together, pouring out their hearts to Yahweh. "Thank You for sparing Moses, Lord God. Please watch over him since we cannot. Help him remember who You are and what You have done. Remind him how much we love him."

Jochebed collapsed into Amram's strong arms. "We can rest now, Jochebed," he soothed her. "The Lord has heard our prayer. He will be with Moses and watch over him. The child does not belong to us. You have taught him well, and he is in God's care."

Their Life and Times

Tuesday

Israel's Emancipator

The Hebrews were first welcomed as guests in Egypt to avoid the famine in Canaan. By God's providence, Joseph had been sent ahead to preserve his family. But three hundred years later, the hospitality changed. Dramatically.

With the rise of Egypt's Eighteenth Dynasty in 1557 BC, the affliction of the Hebrew people began.

At that time, the new pharaoh was Ahmose I of Thebes. Egypt had declined to a lesser world power as the ancient Babylonians, Assyrians, and Hittites began their ascension. Ahmose resolved to restore Egypt's lost greatness and launched an ambitious building program that included temples, defense cities, palaces, and granaries.

In order to complete these grand construction projects, cheap labor—and lots of it—would be necessary. Foreigners—including the vast population of Hebrews—were enslaved and forced to build and rebuild Egypt.

When Ahmose I died, this aggressive work was continued by the next pharaoh's successors, Amenhotep I (1524–1503 BC) and Thutmose I (1503–1493 BC). Each successor was more cruel than his predecessor and made life difficult for the Hebrew slaves.

Moses' father, Amram, was a Hebrew slave in Egypt during the reign of Amenhotep. Amram and thousands of his countrymen rose at dawn and reported to the site where they worked making bricks. Under the hand of merciless taskmasters who were ready to lash them with a whip at the slightest hint of dallying or falling behind, the Israelites were treated like common chattel.

Laboring under Egypt's scorching sun, slaves would haul large, empty pottery jars to the Nile, fill them with heavy mud, and carry them back to the brick makers. The sludge was poured into a pit and mixed with straw, sand, and water. The slaves delivering the mud returned to the Nile, repeating the grueling process for the next twelve hours.

Another group of slaves was assigned the task of tramping the mucky content in the brick-making pits. They stomped until the mixture was the right consistency. When their aching legs and feet could no longer move, the slaves used wooden pickax-like tools called mattocks to break up the thick mud. The work continued all day.

Another division of slaves carried the blended mixture in large clay jars to be poured into wooden, brick-shaped molds and smoothed out. When partly dry, the newly formed bricks were removed from the molds, arranged in stacks, and left to dry in the hot sun for eight days.

For the Hebrew men, there was no escape from the punishing work.

The distress of the Hebrews, however, did not escape the compassionate eye of their God. "I have indeed seen the misery of my people in Egypt. I have heard them crying out because of their slave drivers, and I am concerned about their suffering" (Exodus 3:7).

God planned the birth of a leader who would deliver the Israelites from the ruthless hand of Egyptian tyranny. The son born to Amram and Jochebed was that leader. The life of Moses was preserved during impossible times. God raised him up to lead His people out of bondage in Egypt.

Can You Imagine?

Wednesday

The story of Amram and Jochebed is a story of letting go. Surrendering. This is a difficult reality, but in marriage, in parenting, and in the Christian life, it's necessary to embrace.

Letting go applies to your relationship with your spouse, and it began the moment you said "I do." Before you were married, you had plenty of independence. But when you took that long walk down the aisle or stood waiting at the altar, you relinquished your individual rights.

When you marry, all your resources are pooled. No longer do you make major decisions without the involvement of another person. Of course, you happily exchanged your freedom for a partnership with this person you love — but still, marriage requires letting go of total control over your schedule, your finances, your freedom. The Bible calls this living in mutual submission to each other.[2] Marriage entails surrender as you love and serve your spouse, sometimes at the expense of your own comfort.

Having children requires you to surrender at a new level. It begins when your child is old enough to go off to kindergarten. If you've already done this, you know about the struggle. Someday, "letting go" will be about their driver's license, high school, college, entry into the workforce, and, most likely, marriage. You know these challenging milestones are coming. No surprises.

Amram and Jochebed had to let go of their little boy because of an evil decree in Egypt. First, Jochebed gingerly let go of the basket filled with her newborn son, and then she and her husband were forced to say good-bye when Moses was only three. Before she set the little boat into the shallow water, Jochebed did everything she could to ensure the basket's safety. Can you imagine how carefully this mother must have examined every crevice in the little craft?

As followers of Christ, letting go — surrendering — is a daily pursuit. Each day we lay aside precious time to seal our minds with

---

2. See Ephesians 5:21.

God's Word. And to pray. We ask God to direct our steps and help us to submit to the Holy Spirit's leading.

Amram and Jochebed willingly placed their baby in the basket because they trusted God with the outcome. They let go. We must learn to do the same.

From God's Word ...

> "This is what the LORD says—your Redeemer, the Holy One of Israel: 'I am the LORD your God, who teaches you what is best for you, who directs you in the way you should go.'"
>
> ISAIAH 48:17

Their Legacy in Scripture

Thursday

1. "But when she could hide [Moses] no longer, she got a papyrus basket for him and coated it with tar and pitch. Then she placed the child in it and put it among the reeds along the bank of the Nile. His sister stood at a distance to see what would happen to him" (EXODUS 2:3–4).

   What emotions do you think Jochebed and Amram felt when they placed their infant son into a basket and left him in the reeds? What inspired their plan?

   What uncertain times have you experienced during your marriage? In what ways did God inspire you with fresh ideas?

2. "My soul is weary with sorrow; strengthen me according to your word" (PSALM 119:28).

   When you are faced with a difficult situation, what resources are available to you and your spouse? What Bible verses can you pray for your spouse when you are seeking God's strength as a couple in desperate times?[3]

3. "Do nothing out of selfish ambition or vain conceit. Rather, in humility value others above yourselves, not looking to your own interests but each of you to the interests of the others. In your relationships with one another, have the same mindset as Christ Jesus" (PHILIPPIANS 2:3–5).

   God modeled letting go. His Son—all of Himself in human form—came to earth, but in this coming Jesus did not claim the rights that were already His. He laid them aside. He was humble, and He looked out for our interests instead of His own. He surrendered. In what areas of your marriage have you had difficulty letting go? What choices can you make to change this?

---

3. Our favorite Bible prayers for each other (and for our kids) are Ephesians 1:15–23; Philippians 1:3–11; and Colossians 1:9–14.

Their Legacy of Prayer

Friday

Reflect On: Exodus 2:1–10

Praise God: For His perfect plan, which He is working out even in difficult times.

Offer Thanks: For the peace God is able to provide to your hearts. For people who listen, understand, and offer love and support to you.

Confess: That you focus too often on the trial instead of looking up and trusting that God will make a way through the difficulty, and that you tend to complain about the situation rather than being thankful for all the good things God has done and will do.

Ask God: For His wisdom and inspiration and to give you His perspective on your circumstances.

Listen: "Dear children, I know the plans I have for you, and I will bring good out of every trial you face. You do not know what I know. Ask Me to show you glimpses of My grace, and I will open to you a rich storehouse of wisdom."

Pray: *Father in heaven, nothing is a surprise to You. Long before this day, You knew what we would face and have provided peace for us as we focus on You. Give us grace to endure any difficulty You allow. Help us to walk together, following Your lead and encouraging each other. We trust You to accomplish what we cannot. We love You with all our hearts. Amen.*

18

Taking Good Counsel

Moses and Zipporah

Meaning of Names:	*Moses* means "to draw out" or "to deliver." *Zipporah* means "bird" or "beauty."
Their Character:	He was a protector of the women being harassed by greedy shepherds. He accepted the wise advice of his father-in-law and became a great leader. She was a hard worker and a woman of action. Later she used her resources to rescue her husband.
Their Challenge:	Moses was a fugitive without a home or family and later he struggled with a job that overwhelmed him. Zipporah had to leave her family and homeland and embrace a new faith.
Their Outcome:	Zipporah's father blessed his daughter's marriage to Moses, affirmed the couple's mission, and offered counsel that would prepare Moses to lead. Moses accepted God's call to deliver the Hebrews from Egyptian bondage.
Key Scripture:	Exodus 2:11–21; 18:1–27

Their Story

Monday

Moses first met Jethro when Moses was a fugitive traveling in the wilderness. Moses had murdered an Egyptian who was abusing a Hebrew slave, and Pharaoh set out to kill him, forcing Moses to flee to Midian.

On his way, Moses came to a well where rude shepherds were pushing aside seven sisters who were attempting to draw water. He rescued the women and graciously helped them fill the troughs to water their father's flock. The sisters returned home much earlier than expected with news of a kind Egyptian who had come to their rescue and saved them hours of labor. When Jethro, their father, heard the story, he immediately invited Moses to their home for dinner. Together they enjoyed a fine meal of goat meat, vegetables, cheese, and wine, sitting on a mat on a dirt floor.

Won over by his strong character and desiring to keep Moses in the family, Jethro soon offered his daughter Zipporah to be Moses' wife.

Moses and Zipporah settled in Midian for the next forty years and raised their family. Even though he had grown up surrounded by the opulence of royalty, this was Moses' first real home since his parents, Amram and Jochebed, had surrendered him to the pharaoh's daughter. Little did Moses realize that God used this time in the wilderness as preparation for his return to Egypt when he would lead the Hebrews out of slavery. Forty years after Moses arrived in Midian, God called this couple from tending their flocks to pastoring His people. As a shepherd with a wife, a wise father-in-law, and a large extended clan, Moses was being prepared by God to return to Egypt and lead the Hebrews.

In marrying Zipporah, Moses also "inherited" her father, who was the priest of Midian. Moses quickly came to appreciate his father-in-law. Life in the wilderness was a far cry from the privileged life Moses had enjoyed in the palace. The young groom needed the discernment of an older man.

Jethro celebrated the marriage of Zipporah to Moses, and he encouraged their independence. When after forty years in Midian God called Moses to return to Egypt to free the Hebrews, Jethro willingly blessed his daughter and her husband. "Go, and I wish you well," he said.[1]

Jethro knew what God had done for Moses and the Israelites when he traveled from Midian to visit his son-in-law. It was the first reunion since Moses and Zipporah had left Jethro's home to

---

1. See Exodus 4:18.

move to Egypt. During that time, Moses had successfully led two million Hebrews out of Egyptian slavery and had set up camp in the wilderness.

Seeing Jethro approaching, Moses ran to meet him, bowed in reverence, and then stood to embrace and kiss his father-in-law. Soon the two were seated in Moses' tent. Jethro wanted to hear first-hand the story of God's faithfulness. Listening like a friend, Jethro delighted in all the Lord had done to rescue Israel. Overwhelmed with God's providential care for His children, Jethro offered a sacrifice to the Lord. Moses and his father-in-law worshiped together.

The next day, Jethro watched as Moses, surrounded by the crowds, took his seat as their judge. Moses was faced with a daunting challenge. He alone was responsible to arbitrate disputes among the people ... and there were *always* disputes. Moses took it upon himself to listen, offer counsel, and bear the weight of every decision. Unable to keep pace with the demands, Moses was exhausted.

Jethro offered his wisdom to Moses. "What you are doing is not good. You and these people who come to you will only wear your-selves out. The work is too heavy for you; you cannot handle it alone" (Exodus 18:17–18). Moses knew his father-in-law was right. Jethro continued:

"Listen now to me and I will give you some advice ... Select capable men from all the people ... and appoint them as officials over thousands, hundreds, fifties and tens. Have them serve as judges at all times, but have them bring every difficult case to you; the simple cases they can decide themselves. That will make your load lighter, because they will share it with you. If you do this and God so commands, you will be able to stand the strain, and all these people will go home satisfied."

EXODUS 18:19–23

Moses did everything just as Jethro had advised, and the consuming burden was lifted from him.

With several hundred capable men doing the work he once had done alone, Moses was able to enjoy time with his family ... and his father-in-law.

Their Life and Times

Tuesday

The Midianites

Moses faced quite a dilemma. He had killed an Egyptian, been discovered, and fled from Egypt. Which way should the fugitive run? South would take him into Sudan where settlements would not offer a good place to hide. North would take him into Canaan. But for the same reason, that area would offer no secure cover for him. The stark and scorched Sinai Desert east of Egypt was his only option. Moses could easily find refuge in the vast and rugged mountains, and surely no Egyptian could find him there.

Though Moses knew this was the best route of escape, it was a potentially suicidal mission. How could a pampered prince raised in the affluent courts of Egypt survive the rugged surroundings of the deadly desert? Moses probably knew enough to bring along a pair of donkeys that could carry plenty of water bags. And he would have to rely on nomads to direct him to the nearest oasis or well.

Moses' flight eventually took him to the city of Midian, about four hundred miles from Egypt. A strong forty-year-old man, Moses likely covered between ten and fifteen miles a day, arriving in Midian thirty to forty days after leaving Egypt. Midian may not have been Moses' original destination—it didn't seem that he had one—but a providential meeting caused him to settle there.

The Midianites were descendants of Abraham. Midian was the fourth of six sons born to Abraham's wife Keturah, whom Abraham married after Sarah died (Genesis 25:1). As Midian's tribe grew, its people became nomads, wandering the desert regions east of the Jordan River, eventually settling in the Arabian Peninsula along the Gulf of Aqaba, which is modern-day Jordan. These people were famous for their work in copper, which they mined from the mountains of Sinai. They would hammer the metal into utensils and weapons and trade them for grain and other goods.

The Midianites were also shepherds, and this became Moses' assignment. Day after day of caring for and protecting Jethro's flocks and herds became important preparation and training for Moses.

Jethro was a priest of Midian.[2] Though his people lived near the pagan Edomites, Ammonites, and Moabites, it is possible they acknowledged the true God of their ancestor Abraham. Jethro's other name, Reuel, means "friend of God."[3] Jethro may not have been a true worshiper of Yahweh when Moses first met him, but later the Midianite priest recognized the power of Moses' God and worshiped Him.

"Praise be to the LORD," Jethro said, "who rescued you from the hand of the Egyptians and of Pharaoh, and who rescued the people from the hand of the Egyptians. Now I know that the LORD is greater than all other gods" (Exodus 18:10–11).

Can You Imagine?

Wednesday

Spending endless hours judging his people's civil cases, Moses was overwhelmed. Can you imagine being in charge of the daily needs of hundreds of thousands of people — with no one to help you? Providentially, God sent Moses' father-in-law at the right time to provide practical advice.

In your marriage, you also need to seek wise counsel rather than trying to decide every matter yourself. "The way of fools seems right to them, but the wise listen to advice" (Proverbs 12:15). God has intentionally put others in your path to help you navigate life's difficulties. He did not design us to go it alone. He wants us to first acknowledge Him and seek instruction from Him. "To God belongs wisdom and power; counsel and understanding are his" (Job 12:13). We are also to rely on our spouse to share in decision making, as well as listen to the people God sends our way to speak truth into our lives.

The next time you and your spouse face a significant decision or begin a new, bold project, arm yourselves with sound wisdom. Find godly people who will tell you the truth. Moses found Jethro, who identified his problem and gave him perspective. As in the case of

---

2. See Exodus 3:1.
3. See Exodus 2:18.

Moses, your best resource may be in your own extended family. But if not, ask God to send you a mentor who lives a Christlike life—a person willing to shepherd you with tenderness and truth in order to strengthen your life and your marriage.

"If any of you lacks wisdom, you should ask God, who gives generously to all without finding fault, and it will be given to you" (James 1:5).

Wise advice, guidance, and discerning counsel are gifts from God.

From God's Word . . .

"Carry each other's burdens, and in this way you will fulfill the law of Christ."

GALATIANS 6:2

Their Legacy in Scripture

Thursday

1. **"Your statutes are my delight; they are my counselors"**
   (PSALM 119:24).

   Why do you think the psalmist calls God's Word "delightful"? How satisfied are you with the amount of time you spend studying God's book of wisdom, the Bible? What can you do to improve? When has a strong word from Scripture been a "counselor" to you or to a friend?

2. **"Listen, my son, to your father's instruction and do not forsake your mother's teaching. They are a garland to grace your head and a chain to adorn your neck"** (PROVERBS 1:8–9).

   Though these verses apply to parents, they could include parents-in-law. What kind of relationship do you have with your in-laws? To what degree do they influence your decisions? What can you do to let them know you value their counsel and yet maintain your independence as a couple? How can you show your in-laws more love, honor, and respect?

3. **"Plans fail for lack of counsel, but with many advisers they succeed"** (PROVERBS 15:22).

   How good are you at taking counsel from your spouse? How would your spouse rate you as a listener? Who are your mentors? Your spouse's mentors? What wise couple would you most like to spend an evening getting to know?

Their Legacy of Prayer

Friday

Reflect On:	Exodus 18
Praise God:	For His perfect wisdom and for making it available to you and your spouse through His Word. For giving you in-laws who can help and guide you when you need help and guidance the most.
Offer Thanks:	For your spouse, your in-laws, and the extended family He has given you. For the way He is working through them to make you more like Jesus.
Confess:	That you want to control everything yourself. That you sometimes criticize, ignore, or resent your extended family.
Ask God:	To give you a teachable spirit and a willingness to listen to wise counsel from others.
Listen:	"My children, listen to Me. I have the riches of wisdom and complete understanding. Sit with Me, study My Word, and wait for My guidance. I will open your eyes to see your spouse and your extended family the way I see them. Learn from Me how to listen and love."
Pray:	*Father in heaven, You are the Fountain of wisdom and truth. We humbly ask You to fill us with Your Spirit and give us understanding so we may know the right thing to do. Help us to be attentive to Your Word and to watch for the people You send to instruct us. Thank You for our marriage and for speaking to us through each other. Amen.*

This Land Is Our Land

Othniel and Aksah

Meaning of Names:	*Othniel* means "lion of God" or "God is might." *Aksah* means "anklet."
Their Character:	He was a warrior with fierce determination. She was bold in seeking a blessing and exercising faith.
Their Challenge:	There were enemies in the land where they wanted to settle. Daughters did not receive inheritance and property equal to sons.
Their Outcome:	Othniel led Israel in conquering its enemies. He became the first ruling judge. Aksah obtained land and springs of water as an inheritance from her father, Caleb.
Key Scripture:	Joshua 15:13–19; Judges 1:12–15; 3:9–10

Their Story

Monday

The water splattered on his face as it had a hundred times before. Othniel knew it was coming.

"Well?" his wife said with a grin. "I just splashed you. What are you going to do about it?"

Four decades before, the powerfully built warrior would have swooped up his bride and hurled her into the middle of the springs that ran through their property. But Othniel and Aksah were now in their sixties, and such horseplay was in their past.

"Ah, you're no fun anymore," she teased, making a fist and gingerly punching her husband's arm.

Othniel smiled, glancing at his wife. She didn't notice as she closed her eyes, lifting her face to the hot desert sun. This was fine with Othniel. He would just as soon consider her beauty than do anything else. It amazed him that he was still every bit as infatuated with her as he had been in his youth.

Ah ... his youth. Those were great days for Othniel—and for all Israel—for they had conquered Canaan, evicting the inhabitants and staking out their promised property, tribe by tribe.

Caleb—the legendary spy during Israel's desert-wandering days —had led the tribe of Judah in battle against the pagan Anakites, a menacing brood of giants who occupied that land. Though eighty-five years old, Caleb never flinched and still welcomed a good fight. Othniel admired that about the old man. So, when Caleb gathered the troops and told them to make quick work of the Anakites, Othniel drew his sword and joined in the battle. The Israelites handily won the campaign, and Othniel shared in Caleb's victory.

Hebron was theirs, but Caleb wanted more, so he set his sights on Kiriath Sepher, a town five miles to the southwest. However, sensing that his soldiers were spent from the fighting, Caleb sweetened the pot. "Listen up, men," his voice echoed through the valley. "I want Kiriath Sepher, but you don't seem to be with me. So I'll make you a deal. I will give my daughter, Aksah, in marriage to the man who attacks and captures it. What do you say?"[1]

The offer inspired Othniel with resolve. Aksah? Marriage? Beautiful Aksah? Just for capturing this godless town? Of course. Of course! "I'll do it!" he shouted, though he only stood a few feet from Caleb. Some of the other men laughed knowingly at his eagerness to win the prize of Caleb's only daughter, but he didn't care.

"I'm not surprised, soldier," Caleb said. "In that case, choose the best men and take the town. Fair exchange, Othniel. I win Kiriath Sepher, and you win Aksah."

Again the men laughed, and again Othniel ignored them. Such was Othniel's love for Aksah that the battle almost seemed an afterthought. And when it was over, she was his. He had conquered their enemies; Aksah had conquered his heart.

---

1. See Joshua 15:16.

The young bride and groom were a great match. Kids at heart and strong, they raced on horseback, shot slings, and hurled spears to see whose would fly farther. Always sporting. Always together.

Then one day while they were out walking and discussing where they wanted to settle, Aksah suggested to Othniel that he ask her father to give them a field he owned so they could build their home. He did, and Caleb was generous and the land was theirs.

There was something else they talked about and wanted for their homestead. Because the land was arid, Aksah asked Othniel to go back to her father and ask for the springs. But before Othniel could even make his request, Caleb asked his daughter, "What can I do for you?"[2]

"Do me a special favor," Aksah replied. "Since you have given me land in the Negev, give me also springs of water."[3]

So Caleb gave Aksah and Othniel the land ... and the springs.

But then life in Israel turned dark. Because the nation had embraced idol worship, God issued justice by subjecting His people to the cruelty of a vile, pagan monarch. The king brutalized the nation, making life unbearable for the Israelite people.

"Our people are suffering," Aksah lamented to her husband. "How long will we be able to endure?"

"The Lord has not yet allowed me to attack," Othniel replied.

Then after eight years, the time was right. The people of Israel cried out to the Lord. And the Spirit of the Lord came on Othniel, and Othniel went out to war. So he led the armies of Israel into battle, and God gave them victory.

Because the Spirit of the Lord was on Othniel, he became Israel's first judge—its unofficial ruler—and brought to his fellow inhabitants forty years of peace.[4]

And now years later, Othniel and Aksah sat on their own land with their feet soaking in the cool water of the springs.

Aksah closed her eyes, enjoying the sun's rays. Othniel simply stared ... and thanked God for her.

---

2. Joshua 15:18.
3. See Joshua 15:19.
4. See Judges 3:7–10.

Their Life and Times

Tuesday

Israel's First Judge

At the heart of Othniel and Aksah's story is God's faithfulness to provide land and leadership for His people. He calls and uses individuals and couples to accomplish His purposes and plans.

The account of this couple comes at the beginning of Israel's darkest period, a time when "Israel had no king; everyone did as they saw fit" (Judges 17:6). But the lives of Aksah—the daughter of a warrior—and Othniel—a warrior and leader—stand in stark contrast to Israel's rebellion.

When God safely delivered the children of Israel to Canaan, He ordered Aksah's father, Caleb, to wage war against its pagan inhabitants and claim the land to be parceled out to each family. After her marriage, when Aksah wanted land, she asked Othniel to ask her father for a field. Why didn't she ask him herself? In biblical days, land passed from fathers to sons, not fathers to daughters. While the Bible doesn't record what happened next, we know Caleb gave them land, so it's probable that Othniel played the role of "son" in boldly making his—and Aksah's—request known to his father-in-law.

But because the field Caleb had given the couple was located in the Negev—Israel's desert region in the south—Aksah asked Caleb to give them springs of water as well. Caleb provided a pair of springs so Othniel and Aksah were able to flourish on their land. But others in Israel were not as bold in claiming the land God had promised. God said He would grant it to them if only they would obey Him. But they didn't. Israel needed a godly leader to be an example for them.

Enter Othniel, a fearless man who was God's chosen leader. Othniel's father, Kenaz, came from a family of warriors. And Caleb, Othniel's brave father-in-law, was one of the twelve spies sent to Canaan when the Israelites were still wandering in the wilderness. Ten of the spies gave a fainthearted report and discouraged the people from entering the land. Caleb, along with Joshua, disagreed and assured the people of God's presence and their certain victory. Then God spoke: "Because my servant Caleb has a different spirit and follows me wholeheartedly, I will bring him into the land he went to, and his descendants will inherit it" (Numbers 14:24).

Aksah most likely grew up hearing this story from her father, including God's promised reward. She and her husband would be among the blessed descendants.

By the time Othniel and Aksah married, the sinful Israelites had been subjected to the cruelties of a pagan king, Cushan-Rishathaim. After eight years of suffering, the Israelites cried out to God for relief. Othniel was God's answer. We don't know exactly how Othniel delivered the people, only that he "saved them" (Judges 3:9) and "overpowered" the king (Judges 3:11). Because Othniel obeyed the Lord, "the land had peace for forty years, until Othniel son of Kenaz died" (Judges 3:11).

Othniel, Israel's first judge, brought leadership and a peace to the nation that lasted four decades.

Can You Imagine?

Wednesday

God called Othniel to lead the nation of Israel as its first judge. But God never calls anyone without also calling his or her spouse. Nor does He give them an assignment and expect them to carry it out on their own. He joins them and works through them to accomplish His purposes.

Othniel had impressive warrior credentials and leadership abilities, but that wasn't what made him a good judge of Israel. For that, he needed God's presence and help. And God provided enough wisdom and direction to do the job. Scripture tells us that "the Spirit of the LORD came on him, so that he became Israel's judge and went to war" (Judges 3:10).

Even though you may not be asked to lead a nation, God has something for you to do. Have you asked Him to empower and use you? He has an assignment for you and your spouse. He's looking for hearts that ask for His presence, seek His wisdom, and obey the promptings of His Spirit. What might God do through you? Can you imagine how He could use you to mentor a young person or a new believer, lead a Bible study, or share your hospitality with families on your block?

When you feel inadequate to display godly character or volunteer for action, God will transform you to do His work. "So Christ himself gave the apostles, the prophets, the evangelists, the pastors and teachers, to equip his people for works of service, so that the body of Christ may be built up" (Ephesians 4:11–13).

For a couple to join God in the work He has planned requires more than cleverness, credentials, or skills. As we pray together, we ask God to use us. We read His Word to inform and instruct us. We knock on doors that seem like opportunities from God, and we wait for His timing.

When a husband and wife together seek what God desires, they'll experience His transcendent power.

From God's Word . . .

> "Being confident of this, that he who began a good work in you will carry it on to completion until the day of Christ Jesus."
>
> PHILIPPIANS 1:6

Their Legacy in Scripture

Thursday

1. "'Everyone who asks receives; the one who seeks finds; and to the one who knocks, the door will be opened'" (MATTHEW 7:8).

   How has God prepared and equipped you and your spouse for roles of leadership at home, church, and work, or among friends? In the past, when did you feel inadequate for a task? How did God surprise you or your spouse with strength to do the job He had given you?

2. "The LORD is my shepherd, I lack nothing. He makes me lie down in green pastures, he leads me beside quiet waters" (PSALM 23:1-2).

   Where you live is important to God. How did you and your spouse find your first place to live? How did you sense God's leading or His preparing you for your decision? What role did your family or your friends play in helping you locate a place to settle?

3. "One day when [Aksah] came to Othniel, she urged him to ask her father for a field" (JOSHUA 15:18).

   Othniel and Aksah needed help at the beginning of their marriage in setting up a homestead. What obstacle did they face in securing land? What does this verse tell us about Othniel and Aksah's relationship to each other and to Caleb?

Their Legacy of Prayer

Friday

Reflect On: Joshua 15:13–19

Praise God: For His abundance and wisdom as the gracious giver of all good gifts. For providing for your future.

Offer Thanks: That He has provided through His Spirit springs of living water that will sustain and nourish your marriage.

Confess: Your selfish tendency to seek the presents rather than the presence of the Giver, and for neglecting to thank Him for your spouse, your partner in receiving God's inheritance.

Ask God: To give you a bold but patient heart as you determine His timing for every decision. For His love so you will continue to appreciate, esteem, and honor your spouse.

Listen: "My children, I delight in giving you a place to live where you can honor Me and share My love with others. It is My pleasure to give you good gifts. I will lead you where you should go. I love you so much and want you to trust Me."

Pray: *Heavenly Father, the greatest prize You have given us is salvation in Jesus Christ. Teach us how to trust You as You lead us. We want to seek wisdom in Your Word and Your guidance in every decision. We want to enjoy the gifts You delight to provide for our marriage and family. Amen.*

20

The Best Man for the Job Was a Woman

Lappidoth and Deborah

Meaning of Names: *Lappidoth* means "torches." *Deborah* means "bee."

Their Character: He was likely a man of integrity who was supportive and comfortable with his wife's "fame." She was a decisive woman with godly wisdom, a prophetess with deep love for her nation.

Their Challenge: The Israelites faced a powerful pagan enemy that threatened their existence. Women were not ordinarily involved in military leadership.

Their Outcome: God gave Israel a rousing victory, and the credit went to a woman.

Key Scripture: Judges 4

Their Story

Monday

Blessed with wisdom and discernment, Deborah led the nation of Israel during its darkest period. With their country ruled by the Canaanite King Jabin and his ruthless general, Sisera, Israel's northern region was oppressed. Sisera took great pride in tormenting the outnumbered Israelites, making traveling from village to village a perilous plight for anyone foolish enough to attempt it. Pagan marauders lined the roads, assailing unsuspecting merchants trying to conduct business.

Even though he was the leader of the Israelite forces, Barak the commander said he would not go to war without Deborah at his side. She agreed to accompany him. It wasn't much of a battle. With the Lord of hosts fighting for Israel, the conflict was a rout, and General Sisera was killed, but not by Barak. He was killed by a woman named Jael.

Now back at home with her husband, Lappidoth, Deborah began venting. "I cannot understand why the commander of the army would willingly step aside and allow the honor to go to a woman. It's a mystery to me!"

"But Deborah," Lappidoth reasoned, "Israel has won a great victory. It's over."

Her husband was right.

It was also a mystery to her that God had chosen to stir in her a heart of outspoken bravery and had established her as a source of comfort, wisdom, and counsel for the nation. Recognizing that God's hand was on his wife, Lappidoth encouraged her when people began streaming to her for advice. She listened with grace to everyone's problems and had just the right words for each one.

As word of her insight spread, Deborah's popularity grew, and their small home became a gathering place for people seeking her wisdom. Soon there wasn't enough room, and so she set up her counseling chair under a honey tree near their property. The people came to Deborah for advice and to have their disputes settled.

Her fellow Israelites recognized her as an anointed woman. A prophetess. There were days when the people's quandaries, questions, and quiverings were both time-consuming and overwhelming. Yet God was faithful to speak to His people through her. Sometimes after hearing her own words, Deborah would humbly think, *That thought didn't come from me. Thank You, great God of Israel.*

Lappidoth watched her day after day, amazed at the gift God had given her. He remembered well that morning not long ago when God had spoken specific instructions for Deborah to give to Barak. The Lord told her to summon the commander of the army and announce to him an impending victory over Israel's oppressors. Although Barak was known as Thunderbolt for his skills as a soldier and military strategist, he did not live up to his name.

Not that day.

As Barak stood before Deborah, God spoke through her. "Barak," she said, "the LORD, the God of Israel, commands you: 'Go, take with you ten thousand men of Naphtali and Zebulun and lead them up to Mount Tabor. I will lead Sisera, the commander of Jabin's army, with his chariots and his troops to the Kishon River and give him into your hands."

Barak replied, "I will go, but only if you go with me. If not, I will not go."

Deborah was incredulous at his timidity. After all, the Lord had assured Barak of victory. What more could a person want?

But without scorn, Deborah told the commander exactly what the Lord had ordained. "Certainly I will go with you," she said. "But because of the course you are taking, the honor will not be yours, for the Lord will deliver Sisera into the hands of a woman."[1]

Now, a short time after the great victory, Deborah was once again occupying her prophetic seat under her honey tree.

Their Life and Times

Tuesday

A Woman's Courage and Wisdom

Except for telling us that Lappidoth was the husband of Deborah, the Bible says nothing more about him other than his name. Perhaps the reason is that he was humble and gave Deborah the freedom to serve in her anointed role as prophetess and leader of Israel.

At a time when Israel desperately needed a strong and decisive military leader, Barak, the standing commander of the Israelite army, failed to take charge. So God raised up an unexpected leader, a woman named Deborah. After hearing from the Almighty, she announced to Barak that the Lord promised Israel a sure victory.

Barak's case of cold feet demonstrated disbelief in God. Even with a divine vow, Barak would not enter the battle unless Deborah was with him. Why such trepidation for a capable military leader? Perhaps the key to understanding Barak's fearful resistance is the fact that his enemy, Sisera, had nine hundred iron chariots. These chariots were not only numerous; they were virtually indestructible. Convinced

---

1. See Judges 4:6–9.

this would be an impossible war to win, Barak was defeated before it began.

For much of its early history, Israel was behind the times when it came to technology. By the time the Hebrews finally claimed Canaan after forty years of wilderness wandering, they were backward in weapons sophistication. While their enemies were fighting with metal swords, daggers, shields, and chariots, the Israelites were toiling on the battlefield with inferior swords and wooden shields. Unlike their enemies who had horses, they were fighting mostly on foot. The Iron Age had come boldly to the Near East, and Israel missed it. So when Barak looked at his weapons of wood and bronze, he must have figured they were no match against iron.

But he failed to consider that his powerful adversaries did not have the Lord fighting for them. This made all the difference. And Deborah knew it. With God's help, Israel could have defeated the Canaanites with paper swords and cardboard shields. For Barak, the battle ahead was a matter of sight, not faith. Deborah had spoken the clear word of the Lord to him, but he did not believe her.

Recognizing her as a spokesperson for God, Barak wanted Deborah along as God's representative. With the prophetess by his side, Barak maneuvered his ten-thousand-man army up the steep slopes of Mount Tabor, where the chariots couldn't reach them. Sisera led his chariots to the beautiful Jezreel Valley below along the Kishon River. There, the chariots would have plenty of space to maneuver.

It was a good plan.

Except for one thing.

Sisera wasn't counting on God fighting for Israel. The Lord caused an unseasonable downpour of rain on the region, resulting in the flooding of the Kishon River and the entire valley. Suddenly, the hard ground became a muddy bog, and the iron chariots were rendered useless. Israel descended on her hapless enemy and easily won.[2]

The Lord chose to use a righteous woman to speak His word to Barak. The commander failed to realize that the battle was neither his nor Deborah's.

The battle was the Lord's.

---

2. See Judges 5:19–22.

Can You Imagine?

Wednesday

Deborah had a husband and a career, and she also became a woman of great influence. Her wisdom was renowned. Individuals were impacted and her nation was saved because Deborah heard from the Lord.

You can also become a person of discernment by studying God's Word and asking for His wisdom. Can you imagine the impact you and your spouse can have on neighbors, friends, and family when you hear from God and are careful to speak His words to them?

You know people who are discouraged because of health and financial problems, wayward children, or difficult marriages. Are you willing to spend time with Jesus so you can be equipped to take His encouragement to them?

And you can be the one to pray for your spouse. You can offer thoughtful counsel and provide insight, enriching your spouse's life with kindness and truth.

To become the people God created you to be—people of character, maturity, and spiritual wisdom—your spouse needs you and you need your spouse. You can strengthen each other. "As iron sharpens iron, so one person sharpens another" (Proverbs 27:17).

Who is timid or fearful and needs your encouragement today? Ask the Lord to give you His words for someone who is weak and unable to battle a seemingly impossible enemy.

From God's Word . . .

> "Strengthen the feeble hands, steady the knees that give way; say to those with fearful hearts, 'Be strong, do not fear.'"
>
> ISAIAH 35:3–4

Their Legacy in Scripture

Thursday

1. **"Two are better than one, because they have a good return for their labor: If either of them falls down, one can help the other up"** (ECCLESIASTES 4:9–10).

   How has your spouse helped to shape you into the person you are today?

   Deborah must have been extremely bright, sold-out for God, and passionately zealous for Israel. She had a degree of fame and popularity that may have outshone her husband in the eyes of the people. Are you married to a gifted spouse who is highly respected? How can you better embrace this reality?

2. **"[Deborah] held court under the Palm of Deborah between Ramah and Bethel in the hill country of Ephraim, and the Israelites went up to her to have their disputes decided"** (JUDGES 4:5).

   Have friends come to you or your spouse for counsel? How could listening to other people's problems create conflict in your marriage? How can you and your spouse work together to focus on strengthening and improving your own marriage?

   Though we are called to "bear with each other" (Colossians 3:13), when have you said no to others for the sake of your marriage?

3. **"Submit to one another out of reverence for Christ"** (EPHESIANS 5:21).

   Lappidoth supported his wife's gifts and calling. What are some of your spouse's unique strengths? How do you support your spouse's dreams and call from God while balancing your own aspirations?

Their Legacy of Prayer

Friday

Reflect On:	Judges 4:4–8
Praise God:	For His wisdom and power and for designing you and your spouse to strengthen each other.
Offer Thanks:	That God is allowing both of you to serve Him according to the gifts He has blessed each of you with.
Confess:	Your unbelief in God's leading, your selfishness, and your lack of sensitivity to your spouse and his or her unique gifts.
Ask God:	To give you a more accepting and less critical heart. To help you notice what inspires your spouse and to be an encouragement.
Listen:	"My child, I created you and your spouse with unique strengths. I brought you together because your individual gifts are the perfect complement. I will empower you to be the companion I want you to be. Love each other as I have loved you."
Pray:	*Father in heaven, You have made us in Your image and have generously given us just what we need to serve You and each other. We want to live creatively, delighting in the good gifts of each other. We rely on Your strength to make us bold to live in unwavering faith and humble obedience to Your Word. Amen.*

Hear Me Roar

Heber and Jael

Meaning of Names:	*Heber* means "alliance," "partner," or "enclave." *Jael* means "mountain goat."
Their Character:	He was a traitor, given to compromising and seeking alliances with the enemy. She was determined, resourceful, and courageous in the face of evil.
Their Challenge:	He was friendly with Israel's enemies. She defied her husband by standing on her convictions, defending her people.
Their Outcome:	Jael killed the enemy's general, helping to end the Canaanite threat to Israel.
Key Scripture:	Judges 4:17–22; 5:24–27

Their Story

Monday

Heber was furious.

His wife, Jael, stood with her arms crossed, disgusted with her husband's churlish rants.

"Imagine my surprise," he spewed, "as I passed through an Israelite village and listened to the people singing songs of praise for their victory over Sisera! And what do you think I heard them say, Jael?"

"I don't know, Heber. Tell me."

"People were celebrating ... about a woman."

"Deborah?"

"No, not Deborah—you!" He was almost shouting. "The people

are singing, 'Most blessed of women be Jael, the wife of Heber the Kenite ... Her hand reached for the tent peg, her right hand for the workman's hammer. She struck Sisera, she crushed his head, she shattered and pierced his temple.'"[1]

Jael winced. She was not aware that her exploits had become known — and so quickly. The short-lived war between Israel and Sisera, general of the Canaanite armies, was not even a day old. It was a rousing victory for Israel.

"A tent peg?" Heber raged. "A tent peg? You hammered a tent peg through his skull! This is what you've done to our friend?"

"He was no friend of mine," Jael pushed back, "or of Israel's God."

Heber scowled at his wife, but she was unfazed. If it was a battle of wills, it was a short one. Jael would not be shamed.

"A demon for a wife, I have!" Heber spit out, and then he exploded from his wife's tent in a frenzy of indignation.

Jael's face broke a thin smile. *Imagine me, the subject of a song.* Slowly moving toward the corner of her tent, she dreamily picked up an unused tent peg and turned it slowly in her hands, savoring the sweet adulation. She had simply done what she believed was her duty.

Years earlier, when Jael was given to Heber as his wife, she had no objections; this was, after all, the custom of the day. She was given her own tent, separate from her husband, but one he could visit whenever he liked. A metalworker and businessman, Heber was shrewd and sometimes ruthless. It wasn't long before Jael witnessed his severe tantrums and compromising ways. She quickly abandoned expectations of tenderness from this man.

If there was any consolation, living in southern Judah among the Hebrews suited Jael. Her people, the Kenites, and the Israelites had warm relations, forged over a century earlier when Moses married into the family of Hobab, an ancestor of the Kenites.

But one day, her husband announced that the family was moving north.

"Why would we do such a thing?" Jael challenged.

"Because in the north they have iron chariots and weapons, and I deal in metal. You figure it out, wife."

Over the years, the Canaanites, under King Jabin and General

---

1. Judges 5:24–27.

Sisera, had oppressed the Hebrews. Relocating to Canaan made Jael feel like a traitor, but she had no choice. Her husband believed he could profit from commerce with people she regarded as the enemies of Israel. And so they went.

Jael held the Canaanite enemies in contempt for their treatment of the Israelites. She detested their army general, Sisera, who had become friends with her husband and was a regular guest to Heber's tent. Jael cringed every time Sisera visited, knowing she was obligated to offer him all the traditional hospitality she could muster.

One day Heber invaded the privacy of her tent, announcing that Israel's leader, Deborah, and its general, Barak, had formed an army and led them to Mount Tabor. "I wonder if Sisera knows about the war plan," Heber wondered aloud.

"Why do you fret?" Jael asked. "Sisera can take care of himself."

"Haven't you learned anything as my wife?" Heber scorned. "Don't you realize that a victory by Israel over Sisera will be very bad for my business?" Without waiting for her response, Heber rushed from the tent in a panic.

Awaking one morning after a night of torrential wind and rain, Jael noticed that one of the tent pegs had come loose. As she had done hundreds of times before, she picked up the heavy wooden mallet that lay close by and skillfully drove the peg firmly back into the ground, then returned the tool to its place.

Later that day, while the afternoon sun burned hot, she heard a voice calling faintly from outside her tent.

"Jael, Jael, are you there?" The voice was weak and strained. It sounded familiar, but she couldn't quite place it.

Lifting the door flap, she was stunned to see the mighty—and horseless—Sisera, who stood muddy, bloody, bent, and bewildered.

His face softened, "Ah, wife of Heber, you are here. Praise the gods," he mumbled. "I have been injured in battle, and Barak pursues me. I need a place to hide."

Although dismayed and unsettled, Jael acted quickly. "Come in, my lord. Come right in," she said, pointing to a mat on the ground. "Lie down right there."

Sisera collapsed in exhaustion.

"I'm thirsty," Sisera said. "Please bring me some water."

Water? she thought as a plan unfolded. *I can do better than that.*

She brought him a skin of goat's milk, knowing it would help him sleep. He propped himself up and drank it ravenously, the overflow dripping down his beard.

"Now stand watch at the entrance of the tent," he ordered. "If someone comes by and asks you if anyone is here, say no."

Jael nodded. Sisera lay back down, and Jael covered him with a blanket. But instead of standing guard for him, she stood over him, scrutinizing the exhausted general on the floor. He quickly fell asleep.

Jael bent down and gently touched his shoulder to be sure. Then she quietly lifted the mallet and one of her many unused tent pegs —the sharpest one she could find.

Kneeling next to Sisera's sleeping form, Jael chose the spot on the side of his head she wanted to strike—the temple, a soft target. Settling the sharp point of the peg, she took a deep breath and raised the mallet above her head. Using all her strength, she swung the mallet and struck the peg, driving it deep into Sisera's head. His body flinched, and straightened, then settled. It was over.

She stood up, trembling. Israel's foe lay dead at her feet. She had done the right thing to preserve God's chosen people. For now, that was all that mattered.

Their Life and Times

Tuesday

Using What You Have

It's easy to cringe at the way Jael killed a man by hammering a tent peg through his head. But because it was wartime, Jael was determined to defend the Hebrews by eliminating the enemy general responsible for the slaughter of many Israelites. Her resolve and inner courage were equaled only by her physical strength to be able to do such a thing.

In biblical times, women needed to be energetic, industrious, and sturdy for the tasks of homemaking. While the men were out tending sheep and goats, doing business in town and neighboring communities, hunting game, or standing guard over the village, the women were taking care of everything else.

A woman's work often began at dawn, carrying one or two large jars to the local well and filling the containers with the day's supply of water.

At home, backbreaking chores were her daylight routine. She churned milk into butter in goatskin bags, an activity that sculpted her powerful arms. Her fingers kneaded heavy dough that she shaped into flat loaves before baking the bread over hot stones.

Then there was laundry to be done. Cleaning the clothes of a large family could take hours. A woman had to dip the family's wash into a heavy bucket of water, squeeze it, pound it over smooth rocks, and spread it out to dry.

Milling grain was also a woman's job. She ground hard kernels of wheat and maize using a heavy stone mortar and pestle. This required muscled arms and strong shoulders and built calluses on her hands.

If she could not afford to buy tunics and undergarments at the market for her family, a homemaker was responsible for sewing them. Using wool from her husband's flocks, she would spin fleece into coarse thread, dye it, and weave it on a handmade loom.

Like that of weaving clothes, the process of tentmaking was time-consuming. Tents were made of goatskin, and the work was arduous. The family dwelling had to be big enough to shelter many children, who almost always slept with their mother, while the father often had the luxury of his own tent.

Not only did women make the tents, but they were also responsible for setting them up. And when the tents wore out, it was a woman's job to mend them.

Meal preparation was also a woman's responsibility. Staples for dinner often included figs, grapes, wine, honey, olives, bread, cooked meat, and roasted fowl. Although meat came primarily from the wild game brought in by the community's hunters, the women had to prepare and cook it.

And there also was the work that took place during the planting and reaping season. In late October, when Israel's winter rains began, the people planted wheat and barley in terraced fields carved into the hills. Though men did most of the heavy labor, they depended on the women to spread seed in long, narrow trenches dug by the men with bronze-tipped wooden plows. The women, sometimes with their older children, sprinkled the seeds.

In March, when the harvest came in, the men cut down the flax and gave it to the women to be dried and spun into linen fiber. In May, the men cut the wheat crop and took it to communal threshing floors where both men and women beat the stalks with stones to separate the grains from the stalks.

A woman also had the primary responsibility of raising the children.

Is it any wonder that Jael was strong enough to snuff out the life of an enemy general with one swing of her mallet?

Can You Imagine?

Wednesday

Heber and Jael must have lived with profound conflict. He sided with the enemy for profit; she stood on firm convictions, unwilling to compromise.

Jael was a common tent dweller; yet, when it came time to defend God's people, she used her ordinary skills to accomplish what military power could not. Jael looked around for what was familiar and courageously used it to do something heroic for God. Can you imagine what God can do in your home with what He has already given you?

Just as the Canaanites threatened the Hebrews, the Enemy is targeting your marriage. This Adversary wants to divide you and your spouse and to ruin your home. He attacks you both with temptations toward selfishness, unholy habits, constant complaining, overwork, and the delusion that you can control everything yourself.

With God's help, you don't have to succumb to these attacks. Look to Him as the source for success. To be the person God wants you to be in your marriage, you must have a heart that loves Jesus Christ, a faith that trusts Him, and a humble spirit that submits to His commands. He will equip you to do what you aren't able to do in your own power.[2]

God used what Jael had at home to save a nation. What's in your hand that you can use to strengthen your marriage? Your mallet and

2. See John 15:5.

peg may be making a batch of homemade cookies, asking forgiveness for an unkind word, taking a walk around the block while holding hands, unloading the dishwasher without being asked, or filling the car with gas for your spouse. Ordinary and simple acts of kindness may transform the atmosphere in your home and push back the distance and the conflict your Enemy hopes will destroy your marriage.

When you ask for His help, God's grace is available to do what you cannot do. He is your source of power for every assignment.

From God's Word ...

"But [the Lord] said to me, 'My grace is sufficient for you, for my power is made perfect in weakness.' Therefore I will boast all the more gladly about my weaknesses, so that Christ's power may rest on me."

2 CORINTHIANS 12:9

Their Legacy in Scripture

1. "Now Heber the Kenite had left the other Kenites, the descendants of Hobab, Moses' brother-in-law, and pitched his tent by the great tree in Zaanannim near Kedesh" (JUDGES 4:11).

   Heber decided to move away from God's people and forced his wife, Jael, to move into an unfavorable situation. If you've ever disagreed with your spouse over a major decision, how did you handle it? What were your feelings toward your spouse and how did you express them?

2. "'The eyes of the LORD range throughout the earth to strengthen those whose hearts are fully committed to him'" (2 CHRONICLES 16:9).

   How does it make you feel to know that God sees everything you do? What does it mean to be fully committed to Him? What difference does a desire to please God make in your relationship when you're in conflict with your spouse?

3. "'Do not be afraid. Stand firm and you will see the deliverance the LORD will bring you today'" (EXODUS 14:13).

   When have you been afraid because your marriage was threatened? What would it look like to "stand firm" in God's strength when a situation seems impossible to resolve? What ordinary things can you do to strengthen your relationships with God and with each other?

Their Legacy of Prayer

Friday

Reflect On: Judges 4:16–24

Praise God: For being the One who is always watching over you and your marriage for good.

Offer Thanks: That the Lord understands your circumstances and will enable you to fulfill His purposes.

Confess: Any fear and lack of faith when obstacles seem insurmountable in your home. Your failure to believe that God can transform your hearts and save your marriage.

Ask God: To help you stand firm in the strength He provides and unselfishly serve your spouse in ordinary ways at home.

Listen: "Dear children, I see your desire to please Me and to love each other. When you are weak, I am strong. I delight in protecting your marriage and will empower you to overcome the things that threaten your relationship. Always look to Me, and I will lift you up."

Pray: *Father in heaven, we want hearts that love You and put You first, faith to trust You, and humility to submit to Your plans. We don't have the power to sustain our marriage on our own. Thank You for providing what we need and the courage to use what You have already given us. We want our relationship to reflect Your grace. Amen.*

22

God with Us

Manoah and Wife

Meaning of Names:	*Manoah* means "rest" or "place of rest." The name of Manoah's wife is not given in the Bible.
Their Character:	He was hospitable and a man of prayer who wanted more information from God and chose to obey His direction. She was a woman of faith who was sensible and obedient.
Their Challenge:	They were a godly but barren couple who lived during Israel's dark time when many had resigned themselves to enemy domination. They didn't recognize the Lord when He first appeared.
Their Outcome:	They became the parents of Samson, who grew up to be a deliverer and a judge in Israel.
Key Scripture:	Judges 13

Their Story

Monday

Manoah lived with uncertainty about the future. He and his wife longed for a child, but she was barren.

Then one day, alone in the field gathering grain, she looked up and saw a mysterious and awesome visitor. She squinted and scanned her memory, wondering if she had ever seen him before. She hadn't. There was something compelling and calming in the stranger's bright appearance. He stepped closer and began to speak. "You are barren and childless, but you are going to become pregnant and give birth to a son," the man told her.[1]

She dropped her basket of grain. *Perhaps he is a prophet*, she thought.

But the man was not finished speaking. "You will become pregnant and have a son whose head is never to be touched by a razor because the boy is to be a Nazirite, dedicated to God from the womb. He will take the lead in delivering Israel from the hands of the Philistines."[2]

Astonished, she wondered if she had heard him right. She looked away, her mind a flood of wonder. But when she turned back to ask him to repeat what he had said, he was gone. "I must go quickly and tell Manoah," she said aloud.

Cinching up her skirt, she began to run, imagining how she could describe the messenger and the announcement to her husband. *How I wish Manoah had been with me! Will he believe me? Who was the messenger? Am I really going to have a baby? What could this mean?*

Her thoughts outran her legs as she approached the field where Manoah was walking behind two yoked oxen, pulling a wooden blade that split the ground for seeds.

"Manoah, oh, Manoah!" she said when she reached her husband. "A prophet of God came to me in the meadow. Maybe he was an angel. I don't know. He was spectacular. He spoke to me. About us. You must stop. Something wonderful is going to happen." And then she recounted everything the stranger had said.

Manoah listened, trying to interpret the pieces of her story. When she was finished, he called a nearby servant to spell him from the field work, and turned over control of the oxen to the helper. Then Manoah and his wife walked to the generous shade of a large tree to talk.

Manoah wanted more details. "Where did the man come from? Why didn't you ask his name?" Suspecting that the message was from God, Manoah paused, tilted his face upward, and prayed. "Pardon your servant, Lord. I beg you to let the man of God you sent to us come again to teach us how to bring up the boy who is to be born."[3]

---

1. See Judges 13:3.
2. Judges 13:5.
3. Judges 13:8.

The following days, Manoah teetered between doubt and faith, frustrated over the limited information he had received. *Was the message really from God?* He continued to plead for a return visit from the man.

Then the angel of the Lord appeared a second time. But it was again to Manoah's wife ... alone in the field. Seeing him, she ran at once to fetch her husband. Hearing the news, he sprinted to the spot. The visitor was still there.

"Sir," Manoah stammered, "are you ... are you the man who talked to my wife?'

"I am," the angel of the Lord replied.

"When your words are fulfilled," Manoah queried, "what is to be the rule that governs the boy's life and work?"[4]

The angel's instructions were the same.

Manoah nervously offered the visitor a special meal. "We would like you to stay until we prepare a young goat for you."

"I will not eat any of your food," the man said. "But if you prepare a burnt offering, offer it to the Lord."

Overcome and still curious, Manoah attempted to wheedle more information. "I must ask you, what is your name, so that we may honor you when your word comes true?"

"Why do you ask my name?" the angel of the Lord answered. "It is beyond understanding."[5]

Manoah and his wife were convinced their visitor was more than a mere man. Hastily, they left to secure the goat as they had promised, while the messenger from God patiently waited. When they returned, Manoah and his wife built a fire on a rock altar and obediently sacrificed the goat, along with a grain offering.

Then the angel of the Lord went up with the rising flame from the altar, blazing toward heaven. He and the fire were one as they disappeared. And then there was silence.

Awestruck, the couple fell to the ground, their faces pressing against the dirt. They had seen the angel of the Lord!

"We're doomed," Manoah moaned. "We will surely die. We have seen God. We have seen His face, and now we will die!"[6]

---

4. See Judges 13:12.
5. See Judges 13:15–18.
6. See Judges 13:22.

But instead of entering into her husband's hysteria, his wife spoke with calm resolve and common sense. "Manoah," she reassured him, "we will not die. If the Lord had meant to kill us, he would not have accepted a burnt offering and grain offering from our hands, nor shown us all these things or now told us this. Be at peace, Manoah."[7]

Standing to their feet, the couple took each other's hand as they walked away, leaving the hot stones of the altar behind them.

Almost four years later, the sunlight danced on their toddler's curls. Little Samson laughed as his father threw him into the air.

"Again," the boy squealed. "Again, Daddy."

His giggles flooded his mother's heart with joy and gratitude. They had waited so long for this special child, and God had heard their prayer.

Their Life and Times

Tuesday

The Philistines

When Samson was promised to Manoah and his wife, Israel had already endured forty years of Philistine oppression. And although the couple lived on a beautiful plot of land in the Shephelah—a region of low hills in south-central Israel—there was anguish in their nation. Their land was just a short distance from the enemy that had caused Israel centuries of distress.

Proud and fearsome, the Philistines collected military victories at sea and on land ever since migrating from Crete to Palestine. The most famous Philistine was Goliath, the nine-foot warrior who instilled terror in the hearts of Israel's entire army during the days of King Saul.[8]

Known as one of the "Sea Peoples," the Philistines eventually settled on a swath of land forty miles long and twenty miles wide along the Mediterranean Sea. The Philistines made life miserable for their neighbor Israel for more than two hundred years.

---

7. See Judges 13:23.
8. See 1 Samuel 17:4.

The Philistines were pagans, worshiping the fish-god Dagon, Baal-Zebub, Ashtoreth, and other deities.

A bright and industrious people, the Philistines were technologically advanced. They pioneered iron smelting that afforded them weapons and tools vastly superior to the bronze instruments used by the Israelites. They also introduced the composite bow and arrow, an offensive weapon that outranged all others. Their razor-sharp, iron swords were fearsome against the Israelites on the battlefield.

The Philistines were also politically sophisticated. Their five city-states—Ashdod, Ashkelon, Ekron, Gath, and Gaza—were independently ruled by different kings, but they united during times of war to create a formidable fighting force. The people in one of Israel's tribes, Dan, were so terrified of the Philistine warriors that they abandoned their inherited land and resettled in the region far to the north of Israel.[9]

Living in close proximity to the Israelites, the Philistines and their pagan ways threatened to corrupt Israel and her worship of Yahweh. Up until then, since their exodus from Egypt, the Israelites had remained organized in tribes under the rule of judges. Their King was the Lord God Himself. However, fear of their enemies —particularly the Philistines—influenced them to seek a central government headed by a man instead of God.

It was in this ominous setting that Manoah and his wife sought and clung to the God of the Hebrews. The angel of the Lord visited them and announced that God had not abandoned His chosen people. Even without requiring the nation to first repent, God would send and set apart Samson to begin to deliver Israel from oppression.

---

9. Manoah was a Danite.

Can You Imagine?

Wednesday

This is a story about God's providence. It's a reminder of how God wants His curious and anxious children to trust Him and wait for Him to act.

The political landscape outside Manoah and his wife's home was treacherous. Inside their home, there was childlessness. God seemed to be silent on both accounts. And then, right in the middle of the ordinary, He showed up. Manoah's wife was not in the synagogue when the Lord spoke to her. (She wasn't even attending a women's conference!) She was in the field gathering wheat.

God had plans for the couple and their people all along. First a son for the couple. Then a deliverer for their nation. The angel's message was brief and incomplete. Then and now, God answers on a need-to-know basis. Our part is not to focus on "what" or "why" but rather to find refuge in Him.

In the face of uncertainty or fear, you and your spouse can pray. Seek a strong word from Scripture and cling to it. Consult with each other and struggle together as you seek to know what God wants you to do — pursuing a new job, moving to a different address, choosing a school, deciding on the best treatment for an illness, or figuring out the right care for aging parents. Seek God's will together.

Like Manoah's wife, you are called to go about your routines, calmly trusting God to intervene and to direct you.

And He *will* answer. It may be in a place or at a time you least expect — in the laundry room as you fold clothes or in a car at a stoplight, from a friend's phone call or during the wide-awake minutes when you can't sleep at night. God will always answer ... in His own time and in His own way.

From God's Word ...

"I sought the LORD, and he answered me; he delivered me from all my fears. Those who look to him are radiant; their faces are never covered with shame. This poor man called, and the LORD heard him; he saved him out of all

his troubles. The angel of the LORD encamps around those
who fear him, and he delivers them."

PSALM 34:4–7

Their Legacy in Scripture

Thursday

1. **"God heard Manoah, and the angel of God came again to
the woman while she was out in the field; but her husband
Manoah was not with her"** (JUDGES 13:9).

   The angel of the Lord deliberately chose to answer Manoah's
   prayer by appearing to his wife when she was alone. Why do you
   think the messenger came to her and not to her husband? When in
   your marriage has God given you insight or a call to action through
   your spouse? In what ways do you and your spouse seek each other's
   input when making a small or large decision?

2. **"The woman hurried to tell her husband ..."** (JUDGES 13:10).

   You and your spouse are a team. How easy do you make it for
   your spouse to come to you with good news, bad news, a vision or
   dream, or just a "crazy" new idea? How would you rate yourself as
   a listener and empathizer? What might you do to become adept at
   these important skills?

3. **"The one who calls you is faithful, and he will do it"**
   (1 THESSALONIANS 5:24).

   Although Manoah's wife was the first to hear from the Lord, the
   message was for both of them. When have you shared with your
   spouse an inspiration you received from God's Word? What concerns
   can you and your spouse pray about together? According to this
   verse, what gives you confidence that answers will come?

Their Legacy of Prayer

Friday

Reflect On: Judges 13:1–24

Praise God: For His infinite power, wisdom, and love and for His gift of faith to believe that He is in control of all things.

Offer Thanks: That the Lord hears your prayers and will answer in His way and in His time. For enabling you and your spouse together to understand His will for your lives.

Confess: That you choose to be fearful and impatient rather than to concentrate on God's majesty and goodness. Your tendency to demand instant answers to prayer instead of asking for more holiness in your character.

Ask God: For faith to believe that nothing is beyond God's control and for the patience to wait for His direction.

Listen: "My children, I love you with unconditional and immeasurable love. Nothing is beyond My awareness, concern, or the reach of My power. My desire is for you to live in relationship with Me. I want to extend to you the fullness of My mercy and blessing. Focus on My strength and allow Me to direct you in your marriage and your future."

Pray: *Sovereign God, You are unlimited in knowledge and worthy of our praise. We are earthbound and have limited understanding. We ask You to visit us and tell us what we need to know. Enable us to eagerly seek Your will and to stand strong in the face of adversity and to move into the unknown future without fear. Help us to be good listeners and empathetic with each other as we wait for Your guidance. We want what You want and together are willing to patiently trust You. Amen.*

23

Keeping Secrets

Samson and Delilah

Meaning of Names:	*Samson* means "like the sun" or "little sun." *Delilah* means "dainty one" or "delight."
Their Character:	He possessed divinely bestowed physical strength but was an arrogant, carnal man controlled by his appetites. She was a wicked and manipulative pagan willing to betray her husband for money.
Their Challenge:	Their relationship was an "unequal yoke," and they allowed unholy desires to snare them.
Their Outcome:	Samson was stripped of his strength, blinded, imprisoned, and humiliated. He died a violent and premature death. The Bible does not record the end of Delilah's life, but it is possible she was one of the three thousand Philistines killed when Samson pulled down the temple columns.
Key Scripture:	Judges 16:4–31

Their Story

Monday

Appointed before his birth as Israel's deliverer from the oppressive Philistines, Samson — the joy of his parents — had been marked as a Nazirite. His body had been divinely endowed with extraordinary strength, and his life was devoted to God for a redeeming purpose. As he grew up, Samson was drilled with the rules that were to govern his life — no wine, no haircuts, no touching of dead bodies. His prophetic call to leadership of the Hebrews included marrying only a spiritually matched Israelite woman.

Ironically, even though he was called to be a liberator, Samson was enslaved to his own passions. When there was wine he wanted, he drank. When there was a woman he desired, he took her. Ignoring the decree about marrying outside his Hebrew family, Samson chose to violate God's marriage regulation and took a Philistine wife.[1] Then there was a foolish dalliance with a prostitute.[2]

Finally, there was Delilah.

A Philistine woman from the Valley of Sorek where Samson spent most of his days, she was perfumed, charming, witty, and available. Samson never thought twice about his wife or his vow. *I must—and will—have her.*

For Delilah, luring men with devilish deceit was a specialty. Samson, Israel's unmatched killer of Philistines, was her pathway to wealth. For two decades, the rulers of her people had been trying to subdue Samson but had found it impossible. His prowess was legendary, and the Philistine army could not rid itself of this troublemaking Hebrew champion. It would pay an enormous price to take him out. A bribe was promised to Delilah—fifty-five hundred shekels of silver.[3] A king's ransom for conspiring against her lover.

Samson regarded his power as an entitlement and assumed there was nothing Delilah—or anyone else—could do to take it away. He thought he was invincible on the night she filled him with wine, placed his head on her lap, stroked his long locks, and purred, "Tell me, my lover, what is the secret of your great strength and how you can be tied up and subdued?"

"That's simple," he teased, thinking up a silly lie. "If anyone ties me with seven bowstrings that have not been dried, I'll become as weak as any other man."

She delivered the secret to her Philistine allies the next day. That night, they hid in Delilah's home while she again lulled Samson with wine. With him asleep on her lap, Delilah tied him with seven bowstrings. Suddenly waking him, she shouted, "Samson, the Philistines are upon you!"

---

1. See Judges 14:1–3.
2. See Judges 16:1.
3. Roughly $8 to $10 million, given the approximate value of silver today.

Samson sat up and snapped the bowstrings as easily as if they had been yarn set on fire.[4]

When he saw the look on the faces of the would-be attackers, Samson, naive to Delilah's treachery as an enemy agent, threw back his head and laughed.

The charade replayed itself twice more with the same results.

Then came the scheme that took Samson down. "How can you say you love me when you won't confide in me?" Delilah pleaded, feigning hurt feelings. "This is the third time you have made a fool of me and haven't told me the secret of your great strength."[5]

Her final weapon—false tears—melted Samson's heart. Day after day, Delilah persisted. "Tell me, Samson. You would tell me if you loved me."

The strong man who could conquer Philistines with his bare hands could not topple his wife's deceitful charms. Becoming a traitor to himself, he confessed everything. "No razor has ever been used on my head because I have been a Nazirite set apart to God since birth," he admitted. "If my head were shaved, my strength would leave me, and I would become as weak as any other man."

Samson had broken faith with God. He had trifled with his sacred calling and succumbed to the wiles of a pagan woman. While Samson slept that night, Delilah summoned the enemy to her quarters. Quietly and quickly they sheared Samson's hair that had grown uncut for forty years. When it was gone, so was Samson's divine strength.

Samson awakened to Delilah's cry. "Samson, the Philistines are upon you!"

The mighty Samson was undone. Like a helpless child, he was bound with bronze shackles and led away. His foes gouged out his eyes and carried him away to the city of Gaza. Far from home, Samson languished in a prison cell by night and was forced to grind grain like a beast by day. Round and round he pushed the heavy stone mill. No break. No respite. His life was sightless, humiliating drudgery.

This once-renowned judge in Israel was defeated. Samson, supernatural strong man and tormentor of Philistines, was now a grinder, doing the work of a mindless animal. Robbed of his might, the bald and blind slave would soon be dead.

---

4. See Judges 16:6–9.
5. See Judges 16:15.

But there would be one more surge of strength for his final act of revenge on Israel's enemy—Samson's tumbling of a temple, killing three thousand Philistines. Even in this, however, there was no glory for him.

Samson's legacy would be that of a man who had a noble beginning but whose disobedience to God allowed sensuality and secrets to ruin him.

Their Life and Times

Tuesday

The Nazirites

When the angel of the Lord visited Manoah and his wife, he told them their son would be a Nazirite. Samson, along with the prophet Samuel and John the Baptist, was one of the few "lifetime" Nazirites of the Bible.[6] These men could not drink wine, touch a dead body, cut their hair, or marry outside the Hebrew people.

For God to appoint someone as a lifetime Nazirite was a great privilege, one embraced by Samuel and John but disregarded by Samson. He was called to walk uprightly all his days. Instead, Samson chose to ignore God's sacred purpose for his life.

God created the law of the Nazirite because there were devout Israelites who truly wanted to serve Him but were not from the tribe of Levi and so could not be priests. The priests were the overseers of Israel's religious life and the Levitical system, offering daily sacrifices for the people's sin. Only men who were descendants of Levi—one of Jacob's sons—could serve in the various priestly and Levitical offices. All priests were Levites, but not every Levite was a priest.

God established the law of the Nazirite to provide all Israelites —men and women—a means by which to serve Him in a special way. By this law, any Israelite could take a vow to separate himself or herself for a set time—ranging from a month to a lifetime—in service to God. Bringing daily offerings and living righteously were not enough. Some people wanted a more sacrificial experience. So these people were given the privilege of taking a Nazirite vow.

Samson was set apart to be a lifetime Nazirite before his birth. Even though Samson became entrapped in sin, God had ordained him as a special leader and used him for a time to bring the Lord's revenge on the Philistines.

---

6. See 1 Samuel 1:11; Luke 1:15.

Can You Imagine?

Wednesday

Samson and Delilah both had secrets. Samson's long hair was the key to his divine strength, but he didn't tell that to Delilah. She was a coconspirator with an enemy band of Philistines who wanted to kill Samson. She didn't tell him her secret either.

Samson kept the secret about his hair because he didn't trust Delilah with the information. She wasn't truthful about the conspiracy because her motives were selfish.

And so the terrible—and predictable—story unfolded. Their relationship was conceived in selfishness. Can you imagine the destructive power that deceit of any kind might inflict on your marriage?

Dishonesty, false tears, and manipulation can close down the open and trusting relationship you want to build with your spouse. Secrets and deception are like wooden Trojan horses. Their dark and hollow bellies are filled with enemy soldiers who eventually break out and destroy your union with the one you love. So how do you arm against this threat?

To be a healthy couple, the first step is to work on yourself. You must be honest and assess your motives by asking, "Do I really want what is best for my spouse?" and "Am I willing to set aside my own agenda for the good of our marriage?"

Then you need to become a loving listener—a safe person who guards your spouse's expressions of their dreams, failures, and deepest needs. The more your spouse trusts you, the more they will want to be transparent. Your spouse needs to know that you unselfishly care and want God's best for the future.

We are inadequate to love our spouses in a way that invites trust until we confess our selfishness and receive the power to love that only Christ can give.

From God's Word . . .

> "If we walk in the light, as he is in the light, we have fellowship with one another, and the blood of Jesus, his Son, purifies us from all sin."

1 JOHN 1:7

Their Legacy in Scripture

Thursday

1. "'No one lights a lamp and hides it in a clay jar or puts it under a bed. Instead, they put it on a stand, so that those who come in can see the light. For there is nothing hidden that will not be disclosed, and nothing concealed that will not be known or brought out into the open'" (LUKE 8:16–17).

   Trouble often comes into relationships when things are *not* said, not when things *are* said. Secrets between you and your spouse can create an emotional and potentially destructive separation. Why do you think marriage partners are sometimes afraid to reveal secrets? How do you think your spouse would react if you confessed a secret habit, unholy attitude, or sin?

2. "If we claim to be without sin, we deceive ourselves and the truth is not in us. If we confess our sins, he is faithful and just and will forgive us our sins and purify us from all unrighteousness" (1 JOHN 1:8–9).

   God sees inside our hearts. He knows our secrets. We cannot hide anything from Him. What does the Bible say about sin that is confessed? How does God treat us when we repent? What attitude or sinful action do you need to confess to God? To your spouse?

3. "The word of God is alive and active. Sharper than any double-edged sword, it penetrates even to dividing soul and spirit, joints and marrow; it judges the thoughts and attitudes of the heart. Nothing in all creation is hidden from God's sight. Everything is uncovered and laid bare before the eyes of him to whom we must give account" (HEBREWS 4:12–13).

   When we diligently study the Bible, God's Holy Spirit reveals harmful things that we have not admitted to Him and have hidden from our spouse. What is your plan for uncovering secrets? What safeguards do you and your spouse discuss regarding sensuality or inappropriate behavior outside your marriage?

Their Legacy of Prayer

Friday

Reflect On: Judges 16

Praise God: For knowing all about you and yet loving you unconditionally. For His forgiveness and ability to cleanse you from every sin, and for His redeeming grace for broken and wayward people.

Offer Thanks: That God loves you and is constantly guiding you into all truth and enabling you to live as Jesus did. That He is strengthening you to obey Him.

Confess: Your rebellion and your fear of giving up your secret indulgences and sins. Your leniency toward your own sensuality or sins and your unforgiving attitude toward your spouse's sins.

Ask God: To give you the ability to face your fears, confess your sins, and live in the fresh newness of the life He offers. To protect your marriage from destructive indulgences, sensuality, and secrets.

Listen: "Dear children, I love you with an everlasting love and will welcome you with forgiveness when you repent of your sins. I am able to make you clean on the inside so you are radiant with spiritual strength and dignity. Your purity is a gift to your marriage. I want to help you live with loving hearts focused on Me and each other. Call to Me, and I will answer you and give you clean hearts and pour out on you My peace."

Pray: *Dear Father in heaven, we confess that we try to hide our sin because we want our way, not Yours. You desire truth in our marriage. Give us strength to offer our purity to each other by focusing on Your goodness and holiness. We want Your gracious presence and an indestructible closeness with each other. We depend on Your ability to help us break the power of sin so that our marriage can display Your love and forgiveness. Amen.*

24

Never Alone

Elimelek and Naomi

Meaning of Names: *Elimelek* means "my God is King." *Naomi* means "my delight" or "pleasant."

Their Character: He didn't trust God to provide for his family and unwisely moved them to a pagan land. Although she was happy in her youth, she was bitter following the deaths of her husband and two sons.

Their Challenge: There was a famine in their homeland, so they moved with their sons and lived among a pagan people, away from God's Land of Promise.

Their Outcome: Elimelek died in Moab. Their sons married Gentile women and then also died. Naomi went back to her homeland with her daughter-in-law, Ruth, who married a Hebrew. Their son, Obed —Naomi's grandson—was in the lineage of Jesus Christ.

Key Scripture: Ruth 1

Their Story

Monday

The little boy squirming on Naomi's lap stirred warm memories of her own babies so many years before. The women of Bethlehem were gathered around, making a glorious fuss about Naomi's infant grandson, Obed. Over the squabble, Naomi heard Ruth's voice among the voices of the women calling out, "Praise be to the

Lord, who this day has not left you without a guardian-redeemer. May he become famous throughout Israel!"[1]

The words startled Naomi. "Ruth," she gently called to her daughter-in-law and the mother of the boy, "come and hold Obed for a while."

"Are you all right, Mother?"

Naomi smiled, lifted the baby to Ruth, and stood to leave.

A guardian-redeemer? Naomi repeated to herself, walking outside toward the field where she and Elimelek had once harvested together. "Praise be to the Lord," she sighed. She was remembering when circumstances seemed impossible and her faith was shattered.

Naomi looked around and continued walking in the silence of the empty field where she and her husband had stood together a decade before, wondering how they would survive in a land where no rain had fallen. She remembered deep cracks in the soil swallowing any hope they had to feed their two sons. She could see Elimelek raising his calloused hand, shading his eyes from the scorching sun. "I have never seen the land in Bethlehem this unyielding," he had lamented. "If we stay here, we will die."

"But the Lord has promised to uphold us in this land," Naomi had said. "He will sustain us and give us food."

Fearing the worst if they stayed in Bethlehem, Elimelek had considered his options, including traveling thirty-five miles to Moab where he had heard there was food. He had tried to hold on to his wife's hope in God, but when day after day there was no rain, Elimelek finally surrendered. "We are going to Moab," he announced.

So Elimelek, Naomi, and their sons, Mahlon and Kilion, gathered their belongings and headed southeast to the pagan land of Moab where alien gods were worshiped and Hebrews were hated. Elimelek and Naomi and their sons knew they would need to be discreet about their identity in this foreign country.

But soon after their arrival in the land of plenty, tragedy struck. Elimelek died, leaving Naomi to care for her sons. When they came of age, Mahlon and Kilion took Moabite wives, Ruth and Orpah. Naomi found little comfort in her sons' choices to marry Gentiles, as it was forbidden. This was not how she had expected her life—or theirs—to unfold.

---

1. Ruth 4:14.

And then, before their new wives had borne any children, Mahlon and Kilion were suddenly taken away in death. The three women mourned. The sons and husbands they had depended on were gone. In less than ten years, there were three lonely widows and three Hebrew graves in a pagan land.

"Where is the good hand of Your providence, Lord? Why has this happened?" Naomi asked tearfully.

When the official time of mourning for her sons ended, Naomi heard that the famine in Bethlehem was over. She could go home. Knowing her sons' widows would be considered outsiders in Canaan, Naomi urged Orpah and Ruth to remain in Moab, remarry, and start new lives among their own people.

Orpah eventually agreed to stay with her relatives. But Ruth was different. Pleading with Naomi, she said, "Don't urge me to leave you or to turn back from you. Where you go I will go, and where you stay I will stay. Your people will be my people and your God my God."[2]

So Naomi, comforted by Ruth's love and determination, agreed to let her daughter-in-law accompany her to Bethlehem.

News of Naomi's return arrived before the two widows entered the city. Some women, remembering Naomi's former glory, were skeptical about her and the young Moabitess. Prepared for the dubious reception, Naomi responded angrily. "Call me Mara, because the Almighty has made my life very bitter."

Naomi was not finished with her litany. "I went away full, but the Lord has brought me back empty. The Lord has afflicted me; the Almighty has brought misfortune upon me."[3] And so the wife of Elimelek, who had left Bethlehem with her husband and two sons, reentered the city of her joyous youth without them.

But Naomi had Ruth. And for the next few years, Naomi delighted in their friendship. She watched in amazement as the Lord blessed her faithful daughter-in-law with a generous Hebrew husband named Boaz.

And God had given Ruth a son.

The Lord had been gracious, for the child born to Ruth and Boaz was Naomi's descendant. This boy, when he was grown, would

2. Ruth 1:16.
3. See Ruth 1:21.

provide for Naomi until she died. Her friends' words sang in her ears. "[Obed] will renew your life and sustain you in your old age. For your daughter-in-law, who loves you and who is better to you than seven sons, has given him birth."[4]

This little boy filled Naomi's emptiness and loss with comfort.

And now as she walked the field alone, she thanked her God who had carried her. "Blessed are You, O Lord, for You have not left me without a redeemer." With her hope restored, Naomi turned and walked back to her home. Greeting Ruth with a smile and open arms for her grandson, Naomi sat down and held him close.

It had been a long time since she felt this satisfied.

A very long time.

Their Life and Times

Tuesday

God's Provision for Widows and Foreigners

The book of Ruth reveals God's tenderness and temporal provision for those in need. God's instructions in the Old Testament for the care of society's disenfranchised were clear. His people were commanded not to overlook the orphaned, poor, or homeless and to generously give them an opportunity to provide for themselves.

Naomi and Ruth were widows without resources, marginalized in a culture where husbands were the providers. What made the fate of widows so hopeless was that they, as women, could not go out and earn a marketplace living. If they were fortunate, they would become servants or nursemaids, but even if such arrangements included room and board, there was no living wage. A servant was more like a slave. Although the widow could leave when she wished, often there was nowhere to go.

The wisdom of God's directive to His people to care for widows and orphans was clear. Ruth was provided grain from the fields of Boaz and said to Naomi that she would "pick up the leftover grain behind anyone in whose eyes I find favor" (Ruth 2:2).

---

4. Ruth 4:15.

Allowing strangers to enter a field and gather food was a way of life and commanded of the Israelites.

The law went like this:

> When you are harvesting in your field and you overlook a sheaf, do not go back to get it. Leave it for the foreigner, the fatherless and the widow, so that the LORD your God may bless you in all the work of your hands. When you beat the olives from your trees, do not go over the branches a second time. Leave what remains for the foreigner, the fatherless and the widow. When you harvest the grapes in your vineyard, do not go over the vines again. Leave what remains for the foreigner, the fatherless and the widow."
>
> DEUTERONOMY 24:19–21

God also cared about the foreigners who were drawn to worship the true God of Israel. Israelites often looked suspiciously at such people as inferior and shunned them. To the Lord, this was unacceptable behavior considering that the Israelites were once foreigners in Egypt ... and had been divinely provided and cared for by their generous God.

Not only were God's laws a temporal display of His goodness and provision; they were also a way of giving the destitute a sense of pride. Gleaning on someone else's property—as Ruth did in the field of Boaz—was laborious work, but it gave the needy worker dignity. This opportunity spared them the humiliation of begging or accepting welfare.

Although the landowners were better off than the poor, not all of them were affluent. Some barely grew enough crops and grain to feed their own families. But God promised a reward to everyone who obeyed. If His people were kind and generous, God would supply all they needed too. To such a kind person, Naomi pronounced, "Blessed be the man who took notice of you! ... The LORD bless him!" (Ruth 2:19–20).

God's people were to demonstrate His generosity and mercy. They were to embrace those in need, and their generous obedience in caring for each other assured their own blessing.

Both would experience miraculous provision.

Can You Imagine?

Naomi's comfortable life crumbled. Her husband died; her two sons married outside their faith, and then they also died. These events happened in the decade right after Naomi, her husband, and their sons faced a famine in their homeland. Thinking that life would be more secure in the pagan land of plenty, they had moved to a foreign country where God was not worshiped. Can you imagine dealing with such disastrous circumstances and feeling totally alone?

This is what happened to Naomi.

How did she survive? How was she able to hope again? What did God provide for her? Naomi's redemption finally came through the noble love of a young Moabite widow and the generosity of a man named Boaz.

Everyone will face loss. Jesus told us to expect suffering.[5] We misunderstand God's ways when we interpret His love for us by our circumstances. Even though Naomi could not see the solution to her troubles, God had not abandoned her. He provided Ruth for Naomi. As inconvenient and challenging as it must have been for Ruth to leave her birthplace and the people she knew, she clung to Naomi and Naomi's God and went with her to Canaan. Once there, God provided again—Boaz for Ruth.

When someone you love is experiencing trials, God may be calling you to faithfully come alongside them. You may be the answer to someone's prayer. Or in His kindness, God may send someone to you.

God had a good plan for Naomi before creation and handpicked her to be the recipient of His grace through Ruth and Boaz. Naomi became the grandmother of Obed, who was in the lineage of Jesus Christ.[6] He is our Savior—the great Consolation, Companion, and Redeemer of all mankind.

The One who provides and never lets go.

---

5. See John 16:33.
6. See Matthew 1:5.

From God's Word ...

> "Praise be to the God and Father of our Lord Jesus Christ,
> the Father of compassion and the God of all comfort,
> who comforts us in all our troubles."
>
> 2 CORINTHIANS 1:3–4

Their Legacy in Scripture

Thursday

1. **"'Don't call me Naomi,' she told them. 'Call me Mara, because the Almighty has made my life very bitter. I went away full, but the LORD has brought me back empty'"** (RUTH 1:20–21).

   Naomi was convinced that the Lord was the cause of her distress. According to her, it was the Lord who made her life bitter and empty. When people suffer, in what ways do you think God is at work? How can you acknowledge the purposes of God in the midst of trouble?

2. **"My God will meet all your needs according to the riches of his glory in Christ Jesus"** (PHILIPPIANS 4:19).

   This is one of God's great promises of His power. Although the answer may not be on your list of wants, you can be confident in God's provision. When have you or your spouse faced a trial or something beyond your control? In what ways did God supply your needs?

3. **"Consider it pure joy, my brothers and sisters, whenever you face trials of many kinds, because you know that the testing of your faith produces perseverance. Let perseverance finish its work so that you may be mature and complete, not lacking anything"** (JAMES 1:2–4).

   Who has God used to be a comfort or healing to you? How has God used failure or pain in your or your spouse's life to strengthen your character?

Their Legacy of Prayer

Friday

Reflect On: Ruth 1–4

Praise God: For being a God of comfort, compassion, and hope, who has a redemptive plan for your life.

Offer Thanks: That God never leaves you alone. For showing mercy to you through the loving-kindness of others during dark times.

Confess: Your unbelief and disobedience and bitterness toward God when things don't go your way.

Ask God: To help you see your circumstances in the light of His all-encompassing love for you and your spouse. To alert you to someone who needs to experience His love through you.

Listen: "My children, I have been faithful and am able to supply your needs in the present and make all grace abound to you. Nothing comes into your life that has not first passed through My hands. I will give you the ability to see the big picture. Trust Me. I will never leave you or forsake you."

Pray: *Father in heaven, we acknowledge Your divine power and ability to shape the future when we see no hope. Thank You for sending Your Holy Spirit to be with us every moment. We look to You for answers and the path that leads us to be more like Jesus. Give us courage to obey Your Word and to please You in every decision we make. Because of Your great love we place our lives in Your capable hands. Amen.*

25

Will You Marry Me?

Boaz and Ruth

Meaning of Names: *Boaz* means "strength" or "swiftness." *Ruth* means "friend" or "companion."

Their Character: He was an older man of integrity, generosity, faith, and compassion. She was a young Moabitess, a loyal and kind woman who confessed faith in Israel's God. She was also a diligent worker and made great sacrifices for her mother-in-law.

Their Challenge: He would have to publicly claim his right as Naomi's "guardian-redeemer" in order to marry Ruth. The death of Ruth's first husband left her in the vulnerable state of being a widow and a foreigner in Naomi's homeland.

Their Outcome: Through the kindness of Boaz, God provided protection and food for Ruth. Boaz later became her bridegroom. They had a son, Obed, who was in the messianic line.

Key Scripture: Ruth 2–4

Their Story

Monday

It was mid-June, the end of wheat harvest. Ruth lay down, covering herself and carefully tugging at the blanket's edges to fend off the crisp evening air. She pulled gingerly so as not to disturb the sleeping owner. Her covering was in fact the hem of Boaz's long and heavy outer garment. In order to protect the day's harvest from thieves, he was spending the night on his own threshing floor.

Ruth had been living in Israel since early April, the start of barley harvest in Bethlehem. Several years earlier, while in her native Moab, she had married a fine Hebrew man named Mahlon and admired his widowed mother, Naomi. Ruth embraced their faith in the one true God of Israel.

But before Ruth and Mahlon had any children, her husband died. And his married brother also died. Crushed and dismayed over the death of her husband and two sons, Naomi decided to return to her homeland, Israel. She urged Ruth and her other daughter-in-law, Orpah, to remain in Moab with their families. Orpah agreed to stay, but Ruth clung to Naomi, eager to embrace her mother-in-law, the Hebrew people, and their God.

And so the two women traveled and talked on the thirty-five-mile journey away from Moab. Naomi encouraged Ruth with stories about the benevolence of landowners in Bethlehem, and how widows and foreigners were eligible to glean from the fields.

Once in Bethlehem and without resources, Ruth rose early one morning, setting out to find food. Her hope swelled as she happened upon a vast barley field swarming with harvesters holding armfuls of sheaves. As they carried the grain, they purposely let some stalks fall to the ground.

Ruth found the foreman and spoke to him. "Please let me glean and gather among the sheaves behind the harvesters."[1]

He nodded kindly and motioned where she should start.

As her hands began collecting the dropped barley stalks, her mind busied with thoughts of Naomi. *My mother will be delighted with this provision tonight.*

Ruth had been gleaning for hours when Boaz, the wealthy and generous owner, approached the field of workers and lifted his voice. "The Lord be with you!"

"The Lord bless you!" the harvesters chorused back in response.

Then Boaz addressed the overseer and inquired about her, the new gleaner. "Who does that young woman belong to?"

---

1. Ruth 2:7.

"She is the Moabitess who came back with Naomi," he replied. "The woman has toiled all day, except for a short rest in the shelter."

Ruth watched as Boaz turned and walked in her direction. Her face flushed.

"My daughter, listen to me." His kind eyes warmed her as he spoke. "Don't go and glean in another field and don't go away from here. Stay here with the women who work for me. Watch the field where the men are harvesting, and follow along after the women. I have told the men not to lay a hand on you. And whenever you are thirsty, go and get a drink from the water jars the men have filled."[2]

Overwhelmed, Ruth bowed low and softly said, "Why such goodness, my lord?"

"I heard of the kindness you have shown the widow Naomi," Boaz said. "May the Lord repay you for what you have done. May you be richly rewarded by the Lord, the God of Israel, under whose wings you have come to take refuge."

"May I continue to find favor in your eyes, my lord." Captivated by his manners and gentleness, Ruth went on. "You have put me at ease by speaking kindly—though I do not have the standing of one of your servants."[3]

Boaz was attentive to the new worker and later at mealtime, he offered Ruth as much roasted grain as she could eat. Then he told his men to watch over her and to drop plenty of stalks in her path.

As she walked home that evening with a shawl full of barley (an ephah, or about thirty pounds of grain), Ruth rehearsed the remarkable events of the day. After greeting Naomi, she told her about the field, the gleaning, the grain ... and the gracious man named Boaz.

Naomi celebrated. "The Lord bless him! God has not stopped His kindness to us. That man is our close relative; he is one of our guardian-redeemers."[4]

The next day, Ruth returned to the same field and worked under Boaz's protection. She gathered a bountiful supply of grain every day for two more months. And then the harvest season ended.

"Now it is time to find a home for you," Naomi said to Ruth one day. "I think Boaz is the man who could provide what you need."

2. Ruth 2:8–9.
3. See Ruth 2:13.
4. See Ruth 2:20.

Ruth listened carefully as Naomi continued. "Boaz will be winnowing barley on the threshing floor tonight. Wash and perfume yourself, put on your best clothes and go. Do not let him know you are there. Wait until he finishes eating and falls asleep, and then lie down at his feet, covering yourself with the hem of his garment. He will know what to do when he awakes."

Ruth trusted Naomi and, with a surge of excitement, went to the threshing floor that evening. And now she was waiting. What would Boaz say when he awoke?

A dog barked in the distance.

Boaz stirred and awakened. Lifting up on one elbow, he leaned forward and saw someone lying at his feet. "Who are you?" he asked.

"I am your servant Ruth," she replied softly, her heart racing with fear and expectation. "With the corner of your garment please cover me. You are a guardian-redeemer of our family."[5]

"The Lord bless you, my daughter," Boaz replied. "You have not run after the younger men. Don't be afraid, my daughter; I will do for you as you asked."

Ruth's heart soared. Boaz was willing to take her as his wife.

God had provided.

---

5. See Ruth 3:9.

Their Life and Times

Tuesday

The Guardian Redeemer

Family has always been important to God. The perpetual lineage of those who knew and trusted Him was essential, even if some new — non-Hebrew — family members needed to be grafted in. Like Ruth the Moabitess.

She was an outsider. Ruth had no Jewish blood. But because of Boaz, the guardian-redeemer, Ruth became an ancestor of Jesus Christ. The purity of the Savior's line came not by way of genetics but through God's grace and mercy.

The Hebrew word for "redeemer" is *gāʾal*. In ancient Israel, a *gāʾal* was like a conquering hero riding on his horse, coming to save the day. Boaz was a "guardian" *gāʾal*. He was also a relative. Boaz was a kinsman on a special mission: redemption.

In biblical times, the guardian-redeemer was expected to save in the following three situations.

1. If a person fell on hard times, they needed a rescuer to avoid being sold into slavery. One of their close relatives — an uncle, cousin, or anyone in their clan — was the provision to redeem them.[6] Acting on behalf of the needy relative was both generous and unselfish because the redeemer gained nothing for himself.

2. When there was a loss of land because of economic hardship, the *gāʾal* purchased the property to keep it in the family. "If one of your fellow Israelites becomes poor and sells some of their property, their nearest relative is to come and redeem what they have sold" (Leviticus 25:25).

3. If a woman's husband died without leaving children, the deceased man's brother (if single) was to marry the widow and provide her with a son. If there was no brother, or if the brother was already married, a more distant male relative was required to perform this duty. This was called the law of levirate marriage, which could only be fulfilled by the guardian-redeemer.[7] The relative

---

6. See Leviticus 25:47–49.

7. See Deuteronomy 25:1–10; for more on levirate marriage, see the Judah and Tamar story (Their Life and Times), pp. 122–23.

who eventually married the woman would become the *gāʾal*—her redeemer and protector. Boaz exemplified this example of a *gāʾal*.

Naomi's and Ruth's circumstances were unusual. Both women were widows and childless. Naomi's husband, Elimelek, and her two sons were dead. One of the sons, Mahlon, Ruth's husband, died without leaving Ruth any children. His brother, Kilion, also died childless.

Naomi was too old to have children and Ruth was not a Hebrew, facts that would have presented concerns for an Israelite man who wanted his offspring to be purely Jewish. But Boaz, a close relative of Naomi (possibly Elimelek's cousin), had already shown Ruth surprising generosity. So Naomi devised a plan, hopeful that Boaz would see himself as the *gāʾal* and marry Ruth.

While Boaz slept on the threshing floor, Ruth lay at his feet, covering herself with the lower part of his garment. Boaz recognized this as Ruth's appeal to him to provide the protection due her as the widow of his relative, Elimelek. As a Moabitess, Ruth had no obligation to marry within the family and could have married any single man. However, she loved Naomi and Naomi's God and wanted to honor both by giving birth to an heir. Any son born to Boaz and Ruth would extend the line of Elimelek and Mahlon.

Boaz, probably much older than Ruth, was touched by her overture. He was drawn to her, but a closer relative to Naomi had the legal right to claim Ruth as his wife. Being a man of honor, Boaz offered this relative the opportunity first. But the closer relative refused to take Ruth, allowing Boaz the freedom to become her bridegroom, which he promptly did.

In God's providence, the first child born to Ruth and Boaz (Ruth 4:13), a son named Obed, would one day become the man King David of Israel would call "grandfather."

The love story of Boaz and his Moabite wife is a portrait of God's faithfulness to everyone who believes in Him.

Can You Imagine?

Wednesday

This is one of the Bible's great love stories. A gracious and wealthy landowner named Boaz shows kindness to a foreigner, a lowly widow in his fields. Boaz finds Ruth at her work and falls in love with her. They marry and in time become the great-grandparents of David, the man after God's own heart—David, the king of Israel.

Can you imagine how it must have felt to be Ruth, looking for just enough barley to survive and then finding the one who would redeem and love her?

Tedious physical labor for a gleaner under the hot sun was hard. But because she and her mother-in-law were hungry, Ruth was resourceful and found this work. Then something unforeseen happened. The drudgery of her toil eased. Her heart was filled with hope. She no longer felt the sting of isolation. She went about her duties with joy.

What lifted Ruth's heart? The answer is very simple: Boaz's attention and kindness.

Marriage is hard work. It begins with two selfish people who hardly know each other committing to a lifetime of living together. Relentless demands discourage and isolate us. But the story of Boaz and Ruth reminds us that kindness matters.

From your first words of the day—"I love you"—to your last words of the evening—"always kiss me good-night"—you have the ability to lift the heart of your spouse. Throughout the day, you have multiple opportunities to show kindness: a grocery store purchase to let him know you remembered what he likes, a text message that lets her know you're thinking about her, and a smile when you see each other at the end of a busy day.

Every enthusiastic expression of your love for your spouse can inspire hope for the hard work of marriage.

From God's Word . . .

"Gracious words are a honeycomb, sweet to the soul and healing to the bones."

PROVERBS 16:24

Their Legacy in Scripture

Thursday

1. **"Be devoted to one another in love. Honor one another above yourselves. Never be lacking in zeal, but keep your spiritual fervor, serving the Lord"** (ROMANS 12:10–11).

   When Naomi and Ruth moved back to Bethlehem, theirs was a desperate situation. They were two widowed women with no one to care for them. Naomi was stuck in despondency and bitterness when Ruth chose to honor her mother-in-law with loyalty, loving devotion, and hard work. How might Ruth's example inspire you in your relationship with your spouse's parents?

2. **"May these words of my mouth and this meditation of my heart be pleasing in your sight, LORD, my Rock and my Redeemer"** (PSALM 19:14).

   Who has impacted your life with helpful words? Whether or not you heard enthusiastic affirmations as a child, God can empower you to fill your home now with pleasant words. What you say and how you say it can be an inspiring gift. How can you show kindness to your spouse with your words?

3. **"'Even to your old age and gray hairs I am he, I am he who will sustain you. I have made you and I will carry you; I will sustain you and I will rescue you'"** (ISAIAH 46:4).

   God was at work in the lives of Naomi, Ruth, and Boaz, regardless of their age or circumstances. What does this verse say about the unchangeable character of God to care for people at every stage of life? In what ways has God "sustained" you and your spouse? This verse also says that God will "rescue" you? In what ways has God already rescued you?

Their Legacy of Prayer

Friday

Reflect On: Ruth 3–4

Praise God: For His unchanging character and for rescuing and redeeming people.

Offer Thanks: For God's kindness in seeking you when you were lost, and for the gift of His Word, which feeds and sustains you. For providing you with everything you need for a godly life.

Confess: That you sometimes neglect to focus on kindness in your relationships with your spouse and his or her extended family, and that you do not seek to please the Lord with the words you speak.

Ask God: To fill you with His graciousness and enable you to see others as He sees them. To give you loyalty, patience, and gratitude for your spouse and others.

Listen: "Dear children, I am always looking out for you and will sustain you in every season of your life. I am planning what is best for your future. In My kindness I brought you together and will enable you to treat each other in a way that pleases Me."

Pray: *Our good and kind Redeemer, thank You for rescuing us and giving us the abundance of Your love and provision for our marriage. Give us a heart like Yours when we are tempted to be selfish, uncaring, or unforgiving. In our poverty You have supplied our needs. We thank You. In response to Your abundance we want to lift each other up with the words we speak, the devotion we show, and the moment-by-moment choice we make to be kind. You are a tender and merciful God who provides. Amen.*

26

Before God and These Witnesses

Elkanah and Hannah

Meaning of Names:	*Elkanah* means "God has created" or "possession." *Hannah* means "gracious," "favor," or "God has favored me."
Their Character:	He was a Levite who worshiped and served God. A transparent and tender man, he loved his wife deeply. She was a godly woman, overcoming adversity with prayer and humility.
Their Challenge:	Even though Hannah was a godly and righteous woman, she was barren. Elkanah had taken another wife to solve their problem of infertility, causing family rivalry and dysfunction.
Their Outcome:	God listened and responded to their worship and prayers, giving Hannah a child named Samuel who would grow up to be a prophet in Israel.
Key Scripture:	1 Samuel 1:1–20

Their Story

Monday

When they married, Elkanah and Hannah were happy and brimming with youthful optimism. She was confident that someday she would deliver a child to her Levite husband. The script Hannah had envisioned for the years ahead included motherhood.

But the lovely story she had authored for herself did not unfold. Hannah was barren.

So Elkanah took a second wife, Peninnah, in the hope that she would bear him a child. Although it was never God's design, during biblical times it was culturally acceptable in order to preserve the family estate for a man to take a second wife when the first was unable to produce an heir.

Hannah mourned her infertility. Even though Elkanah continued to love Hannah, nothing stirred within her belly. Her barrenness hung over her like a banner of shame. "There goes Hannah," she imagined the people of Ramah saying, "a woman as barren as the Sinai."

Her humiliation was softened by her husband's kindness. He affirmed his love for her often. And she knew he meant it. Elkanah made no secret that he loved Hannah more than Peninnah. Aware of her loveless role, Peninnah bitterly resented it.

With every son or daughter Peninnah delivered to Elkanah, his passion and affection seemed to grow ever more fervent ... for Hannah. Elkanah's preference for Hannah goaded Peninnah into mocking Hannah's womanhood while flaunting her own fertility. The relentless harassment went on year after year. Hannah often wept and would not eat.[1]

Trying to assuage his wife's emotional turmoil, Elkanah asked, "Don't I mean more to you than ten sons?"

His words were met with silence as Hannah contemplated the weight of her answer. She knew her kind and generous husband was trying to say how much he loved her by calling to mind the patriarch Jacob, who had ten sons by other women but loved his barren wife, Rachel, the most. His efforts were well-intentioned, and Hannah was grateful for his attempts to comfort her.

But his love did not numb her longing.

Or put an end to Peninnah's abuse.

Then one day Elkanah took Hannah, Peninnah, and her gaggle of offspring to the tabernacle at Shiloh to celebrate one of Israel's annual feasts. As a Levite, Elkanah was required to go.

Unable to join in the festivities, Hannah stood in the temple courtyard and expressed her sorrow to God. She poured out her pain to the Lord with tears.

---

1. See 1 Samuel 1:7.

"Lord Almighty, if you will only look on your servant's misery and remember me and give me a son, then I will give him to the Lord for all the days of his life."[2]

Hannah's vow was a marker in her surrender to a God who was mighty enough to grant her request. She asked God for a son—as she had so often done before—but this time she didn't seek a child for herself. If God would be so gracious to give her and Elkanah a son, she promised to give him back to the Lord. Hannah humbly left the temple that day, trusting the outcome to God. Peace surrounded her.

Soon after the visit to the tabernacle, she and Elkanah enjoyed their marriage bed. And God remembered Hannah, initiating a new life in her womb. Knowing the depth of his wife's desire to please God, Elkanah wept when he heard the news.

"Oh, Elkanah," Hannah said tenderly, "you really do mean more to me than ten sons."

Elkanah was a good and godly man, God's gift to Hannah, even more precious than a son. Together they would fulfill their vow to the Lord Almighty, the giver of life.

Their Life and Times

Tuesday

Infertility in Ancient Times

Elkanah was an ancestor of Levi, the third son of Jacob and Leah. The descendants of Levi were set apart to shoulder the priestly duties among the Hebrews. This included the physical dismantling, moving, and reassembling of the tabernacle as the Israelites wandered in the wilderness.

The Levites were also responsible for coordinating the elements of worship. Their appreciation for beauty in the appointments to the tabernacle enhanced the experience for the Hebrews. Since hymns and spiritual songs were an essential part of worship for the Israelites, many Levites were musicians.

---

2. See 1 Samuel 1:11.

When Elkanah and Hannah were first married, they hoped for children. As a Levite, Elkanah needed heirs to provide a legacy of future temple workers. According to the Hebrew Scripture, sons and daughters were seen as a confirmation of God's blessing on their union.

For example, Deuteronomy 7:13–14 reads, "[God] will love you and bless you and increase your numbers. He will bless the fruit of your womb, the crops of your land ... none of your men or women will be childless, nor will any of your livestock be without young."

And the psalmist writes, "Like arrows in the hands of a warrior are children born in one's youth. Blessed is the man whose quiver is full of them. They will not be put to shame when they contend with their opponents in court" (Psalm 127:4–5). In this passage, children are associated with strength, honor, and protection.

Though meant to praise the virtues of parenthood, the people of Israel, especially women, wrongly interpreted these passages as also saying that *not* having children was a sign of God's displeasure. It seems likely that Hannah saw barrenness as God's punishment, even though Scripture never states that. When Peninnah's body swelled with Elkanah's first child, Hannah's despair did as well. Her husband clearly had the ability to sire a child with another woman, so the infertility must be her own fault. She bore the guilt for her situation. If Hannah had been able to bear children, Elkanah would not have needed to marry another woman.

God never intended for barren women to be made to feel inferior and cursed. On the contrary, His love manifested itself to all women, their greatest joy coming from a loving relationship with Him. "He raises the poor from the dust and lifts the needy from the ash heap; he seats them with princes, with the princes of his people. He settles the childless woman in her home as a happy mother of children" (Psalm 113:7–9).

Can You Imagine?

Wednesday

One day you stood with your spouse in front of a minister and repeated vows. You promised to love, honor, and cherish, forsaking all others, remaining true and faithful to each other. You said you would love in sickness or health, in poverty or wealth. Surrounded by friends and family and flowers, you may have been so distracted by the excitement of getting married that you didn't pay much attention to what you were saying. Or, despite the distractions, you may have felt the impact of the words. Either way, you and your spouse made promises to each other. These were mutual promises, and you made them "before God and these witnesses."

When Hannah and Elkanah were first married, they had not envisioned they would have to endure the unquenchable pain of waiting for a child to be conceived. It was the surprise that challenged their vows. Real life always puts our marriage promises to the test.

At the altar, you pledged faithfulness, not knowing what difficulties you would face. Can you imagine if you had been able to see into the future and had known the adjustments you were about to experience? What if you had known what was ahead?

Christian marriage starts by making vows to God and then to each other. When we first promise to love, honor, and cherish the Lord, remaining true and faithful to Him, then we can face with His power whatever storms come our way.

God is watching over you and your marriage. He is your hope and sustainer. No trial or difficulty will remove you from His wise care and loving presence.

He is Immanuel — God with us.

From God's Word . . .

"Be strong and courageous. Do not be afraid or terrified ... for the LORD your God goes with you; he will never leave you nor forsake you."

DEUTERONOMY 31:6

Their Legacy in Scripture

Thursday

1. **"Early the next morning they arose and worshiped before the LORD and then went back to their home at Ramah. Elkanah made love to his wife Hannah, and the LORD remembered her"** (1 SAMUEL 1:19).

Elkanah worshiped God consistently and took his family to the temple regularly. Hannah loved the Lord with all her heart, soul, mind, and strength. A vigorous prayer warrior, she poured out her longings before the Lord. She was hopeful and thankful, resting in His providence for their marriage and their future.

What habits have you established as a couple that will fortify your confidence in God for the future? Recall together God's past faithfulness to you as a couple and recount the miracle of how you were introduced to each other.

2. **"Hannah prayed and said: 'My heart rejoices in the LORD ... There is no one holy like the LORD; there is no one besides you; there is no Rock like our God"** (1 SAMUEL 2:1–2).

Hannah decided to delight in the Lord even though she didn't have what she wanted—children of her own. Can you recall a time in your life when you were unsettled or tempted to despair over an unfulfilled dream? What was your attitude toward God while you waited? How did you choose to react when others received the very things you desired? What inspires you about Hannah's attitude during her times of disappointment?

3. **"In the course of time Hannah became pregnant and gave birth to a son. She named him Samuel, saying, 'Because I asked the LORD for him'"** (1 SAMUEL 1:20).

Hannah pleaded with the Lord for years. All she wanted was a child. And then one day, before Samuel was even conceived, she experienced God's peace. Why did her attitude change? Think back on a time when you rejoiced over receiving something for which you had waited. What is the cry of your heart right now? How does God's past faithfulness encourage you to trust that God is initiating some future good on your behalf? In what ways can you reflect holy calm, avoid complaining, and inspire your spouse to trust God's timing?

Their Legacy of Prayer

Friday

Reflect on: 1 Samuel 2:1–10

Praise God: For His omnipotent strength and His faithfulness.

Offer Thanks: For His sovereignty and timing in every good thing and trial.

Confess: Your tendency to fix problems on your own before pouring out your longings to God and waiting for His intervention.

Ask God: To give you patience as you focus on His character, worship, and wait for Him to initiate His work in you, around you, and through you. For His strength to avoid comparing yourself to others, which leads to jealousy or pride.

Listen: "My children, I am always aware of your thoughts and your deepest needs. I am your Rock and your Sustainer. I will always listen to your prayers when you humble yourself before Me and trust My ability to initiate what is beyond your control. Surrender your desires to Me, and I will lift you up and fulfill My good plans for your lives."

Pray: *Father in heaven, when we remember Your past goodness, we worship You and humbly acknowledge and thank You for Your faithfulness to us. You've brought us together, led us through good times, and been with us in every difficult time. When we're anxious, we will run to You for the peace that passes human understanding. Hear us. Help us. Deliver us. You are our Rock. There is no One besides You. May our lives be consistent in worship; may they be a demonstration to others of our trust in Your unfailing goodness. We rejoice and rest in who You are. Thank You for hearing our prayer. In the strength of Your great name, Jesus, we hope, wait, and pray. Amen.*

Lopsided Love

Nabal and Abigail

Meaning of Names: *Nabal* means "fool" or "senseless." *Abigail* means "my father" or "my father's joy."

Their Character: He was a selfish, stingy, foolish, and hard-hearted man. She was a discerning, gracious, wise, and resourceful woman.

Their Challenge: Nabal's own rude insults and ungracious behavior posed a deadly threat to his family and servants. She had to endure life with a negative, mean-spirited, and unapproachable husband.

Their Outcome: Abigail's wise actions averted the vengeance planned against Nabal's household. Nabal died prematurely, and Abigail became the wife of Israel's future king.

Key Scripture: 1 Samuel 25

Their Story

Monday

Even as a young girl, Abigail displayed wisdom beyond her years. Her charm, intelligence, and beauty made her the desire of wealthy wife hunters. Her father was thrilled with the number of suitors vying for his daughter's hand. He sat back and waited for the right offer.

"Right" meaning "most prosperous."

The winner was a wealthy landowner and shearer of sheep named Nabal, a descendant of the great Hebrew warrior Caleb. Boasting a lineage from the tribe of Judah, Nabal shamelessly flattered Abigail's easily impressed father and offered a dowry no other suitor could match.

Abigail's mother, concerned over her daughter's future, was wary that although Nabal was rich, he was also known as a mean and surly man, every bit the "fool" his name meant. In her view, Nabal's wealth was not enough for her daughter. Would the man treat their cherished daughter harshly?

Abigail's father, however, saw only shekels.

And so Abigail became the trophy wife of a cruel man who added the lovely young jewel to his vast possessions.

If Abigail was discontent as Nabal's wife, she overcame it with dignity. Soon she won over the caretakers, shepherds, stewards, and slaves. They were taken by her kindness and confided in her. She was their protection and strength, a safe barrier between them and their master's rudeness. The servants honored her and loved her. But they cringed at Nabal's sloppy treatment of this precious gem.

Despite his uncouth manner, Nabal recognized his wife's value and had no objection to her managing the household. He was praised for his choice of a spouse, and he reveled in displaying the beautiful Abigail at his parties.

As the years passed, Abigail endured Nabal's selfishness and disregard with goodness.

Then one day—one extraordinary day—her faithfulness was rewarded. A servant came running to her. Desperate and frightened, he told her that something terrible had happened.

It was sheep-shearing time, when supplies were abundant and spirits were high. Nabal was surrounded by revelry and lavish festivities in Carmel, a region not far from his home in Maon. David —Israel's greatest general—and his men had long protected Nabal's shepherds from bandits and his land from poachers, preserving their lives and Nabal's possessions in Carmel. And now, during the celebration when wine flowed and food was abundant, David sent ten of his men to greet Nabal, understandably requesting something for them. Perhaps a little of the wine and food.

Disregarding that David was from his own tribe of Judah, Nabal rejected the request in scathing terms, maligning the leader. Mocking the man who had protected him and deserved his favor, Nabal snarled, "Who is this David? Who is this son of Jesse?"[1]

When David's men returned empty-handed and reported what had happened, their commander was infuriated and told his men to put on their swords. David strapped his on as well. His mission was to slaughter every male in Nabal's household. He would take revenge on the ungrateful miser.

One of Nabal's shepherds who had observed his master's insolence toward David hurried to alert Abigail. She listened with growing alarm as the shepherd described how David and his men had been a wall of protection around them day and night. Grasping the urgency of the situation, Abigail lost no time in responding. But she did not reveal her plan to Nabal.

Abigail gathered together a peace offering, loading up heaps of bread, wine, grain, raisins, and figs and setting out to intercept David. The general had sworn vengeance against Abigail's husband and his possessions. David and his four hundred hungry fighters were on their way to carry it out.

Nabal's wife had recognized the deadly threat and the future king's power and decided to act. Now she would see if mercy was woven into his royal tapestry.

Meeting David as he and his men descended a mountain ravine, Abigail quickly dismounted her donkey and ran toward the commander. She fell on her face at his feet, assuming the full blame for her husband's treachery. "My lord," she humbly pleaded, "please let your servant speak to you; hear what your servant has to say."[2] Abigail urged David not to take vengeance, assuring him he would one day be king of Israel. She confirmed his high calling and reminded him that the Lord would protect his men and meet their needs.

Realizing that Abigail was a messenger from the Lord, David announced, "Praise be to the Lord, the God of Israel, who has sent you today to meet me. May you be blessed for your good judgment and for keeping me from bloodshed this day."[3]

---

1. 1 Samuel 25:10.
2. 1 Samuel 25:24.
3. See 1 Samuel 25:32–33.

Accepting the food Abigail had brought, David said to her, "Go home in peace. I have heard your words and granted your request."[4]

Abigail returned to Maon, where Nabal was hosting a grand party. He was in high spirits and very drunk, so she said nothing until daybreak. Her timing was impeccable. The next morning, when her husband was sober, Abigail told him what had happened. At that moment, Nabal suffered a heart attack. Ten days later, he was dead.

When David heard the news, he praised the Lord for upholding his cause and keeping him from doing the wrong thing.

Remembering Abigail's grace and discernment on his behalf, David then decided to seek the wise widow to be his own, and he asked her to become his bride.

Abigail would begin a new life as the cherished wife of the future king of Israel.

Their Life and Times

Tuesday

Protecting Assets

In ancient Israel, wealth was measured in land and livestock. Nabal had plenty of both. One thousand goats and three thousand sheep represented only part of his portfolio. Because the barren wilderness around Maon was insufficient for grazing so many animals, Nabal acquired territory in nearby Carmel, where he could feed his herds and flocks. Nabal was a member of the tribe of Judah and a descendant of the great warrior Caleb.

The occupation of sheepherder goes all the way back to Abel, the second son of Adam and Eve. Sheep and goats supplied wool, meat, and milk that was sometimes made into cheese. It was the duty of shepherds to lead their flock to adequate pastures and streams and keep them from straying—shielding their animals from danger.

The terrain owned by Nabal in Carmel was rocky and hilly, not suitable for farming. But it was well suited for his sheep and goats,

---

4. 1 Samuel 25:35.

which were adept at navigating the difficult landscapes in search of vegetation.

The shepherd's work was to carefully watch over every animal in case one fell down, strayed, or was stricken with sickness. And if he saw a wolf or wild animal stalking one of his flock, the shepherd acted quickly. Often with a slingshot, he would frighten away the predator with an airborne stone or kill it with the kind of accuracy that earned David the head of Goliath.

Marauders or warriors seizing an opportunity for plunder or an easy meal posed another threat to a man's flocks. Because Nabal's land was so vast and his sheep and goats so numerous, his men alone could not fully protect them. David's army, dwelling in Nabal's territory, graciously took it upon themselves to safeguard the holdings of a fellow Israelite.

Twice a year, Nabal's shepherds left the grazing hills and gathered their flocks in designated plains for a grand celebration of shearing.

It was at this festival time that David sent messengers to Nabal requesting a reward of meat, bread, and wine for David's hungry troops. Because his army had protected Nabal's possessions, David assumed the wealthy landowner would be grateful and generous.

But Nabal's political leanings prevailed. His likely loyalty to David's adversary, Saul, made him unwilling to provide a meal for David's men.

When she received the report of what her husband had said, Abigail quickly prepared an abundant feast for David and his four hundred men. Taking two hundred loaves of bread, two skins of wine, five dressed sheep, sixty pounds of roasted grain, a hundred cakes of raisins, and two hundred cakes of pressed figs, she and her servants loaded the meal onto donkeys. After traveling many miles, Abigail presented the meal to David as a peace offering.

Can You Imagine?

Wednesday

Abigail slept with a fool every night of her marriage. She was intelligent and beautiful; her husband was unbending and mean. From the beginning, and with no opportunity to escape, Abigail was in a bad marriage. Can you imagine the anger and resentment that could have resided in her spirit or the temptation for her to simply become a victim?

Like Hagar, she could have rebelled. Like Leah, she could have sulked. Like Delilah, she could have schemed her husband's demise. But instead, Abigail gives us a sterling template for women caught in desperate situations. She cloaks herself with strength and dignity and, like Jesus, adopts the attitude of self-sacrificing humility and sets out to redeem others.[5] Abigail's response to her woeful circumstance is honorable, purposeful, sacrificial, and strong.

Upon hearing the report that her husband had denied David's men with cruel and blundering words — an experience with a painful ring of familiarity — she responded thoughtfully. Rather than lashing out at her husband's arrogance or cowering in fear of the aggression of David's powerful forces, Abigail forged a plan.

After listening carefully, she took inventory of available resources, and she acted. From her full pantry, she gathered enough to feed David's hungry army and hurried out the door, determined to present her case — and lots of food — to the general himself.

In those days, women didn't negotiate with military generals, offering alternate recommendations. Nor did they volunteer for duty without their husband's approval. But with humility and empowered by the strength of the Lord, Abigail broke the rules and risked her life. She subordinated her own happiness to secure the salvation of her family. She trusted the God of Abraham, Isaac, and Jacob. And in the end, God rewarded her kindness, her sacrifice, and her faith.

5. See Philippians 2:3–5.

From God's Word ...

> "'Whoever tries to keep their life will lose it,
> and whoever loses their life will preserve it.'"

Their Legacy in Scripture

Thursday

1. **"Now think it over and see what you can do, because disaster is hanging over our master and his whole household. He is such a wicked man that no one can talk to him"** (1 SAMUEL 25:17).

   Abigail was a master strategist. What do you admire about her character and the way she handled the servants, her husband, and David? What do you think would have happened if she had told Nabal about her rescue plan? How can you show both respect and wisdom to a spouse who acts foolishly and brings potential harm to your family?

2. **"'Even though someone is pursuing you to take your life, the life of my lord will be bound securely in the bundle of the living by the LORD your God'"** (1 SAMUEL 25:29).

   Abigail's words expanded David's vision during a potentially disastrous moment. She did not bend to Nabal's self-imposed calamity with mindless compliance but focused on God's ability to redeem both David and her household. What does her bold act of faith tell you about her relationship with God? What difficulties have forced you to draw on God's supernatural strength?

3. **"If it is possible, as far as it depends on you, live at peace with everyone"** (ROMANS 12:18).

   What does this verse say to you about dealing with impossible people or difficult family members? How can you do a better job of living at peace with them?

Their Legacy of Prayer

Friday

Reflect On: 1 Samuel 25

Praise God: For His omniscience and timing to orchestrate His plan
in every situation.

Offer Thanks: For the Holy Spirit and for His ability to conform you
to the image of Christ through the difficulties you face.

Confess: Your unwillingness to see the possibility of God's
intervention to accomplish His will, and your lack
of focus on God's mercy when others act foolishly.

Ask God: For the grace to walk in dignity, strength, honor, and
humility in every uncomfortable circumstance and
difficulty. To use your marriage to help make you more
like Jesus.

Listen: "My children, I am able to give you the patience,
perspective, and power to endure any person or situation
that threatens you. I always act with both justice and
mercy. I am a forgiving God, and I will empower you
to reflect My grace in every conversation."

Pray: *Heavenly Father, You are loving and kind and compassionate.
Thank You for Your wisdom and for the insight to know exactly
what to do. We are listening to You. We admit our weaknesses
and rest in Your strength. Help us to display the gracious mercy
to others that You pour on us. Amen.*

28

Family Un-Ties

David and Michal

Meaning of Names: *David* means "beloved." *Michal* means "who is like God" or "stream."

Their Character: He was a courageous warrior who was determined to honor God when he became king. She was a princess who was wounded by her father's schemes, and she became spiritually hardened and critical.

Their Challenge: David was anointed as the future king of Israel and his wife's father, King Saul, hated him and forced Michal to marry another man. Michal was not attuned to her husband's spiritual commitment and ridiculed his unbridled worship of God.

Their Outcome: David became king of Israel when Michal's father, Saul, died. Michal lost favor in David's eyes and never had children.

Key Scripture: 2 Samuel 6

Their Story

Monday

Michal was altogether smitten with her father's greatest military commander and hero. The second daughter of King Saul, she lauded the daring young David, as did everyone else in the kingdom.

Desperately jealous of the acclaim given to David, King Saul plotted to destroy him. First, the king offered David his older daughter, Merab, in exchange for victory in battle, hoping the young soldier would be felled. Not knowing that Saul was trying to protect his own throne by having David killed, the handsome hero's refusal was naive and humble. "I am from a lowly family and am not worthy to become the king's son-in-law," David said.[1]

David prevailed, and the Philistines did not kill him as Saul had intended. But the king withdrew his offer to David, and Merab was given to another man.

Saul was pleased when he later learned that his second daughter, Michal, was in love with David. Seizing another opportunity to snare David, Saul offered Michal as a reward for his death-defying assignment. Messengers were sent to flatter the young warrior privately. "Look, the king likes you, and his attendants all love you; now become his son-in-law."[2]

Again, assessing his own unworthiness and inability to produce the dowry necessary to become the king's son-in-law, David answered, "I'm only a poor man and little known."

When the envoy reported what David had said, Saul attempted to manipulate the warrior's sense of duty and gave David an opportunity to earn his daughter's dowry. He offered Michal as the reward for David's having met a daunting challenge—the killing of one hundred Philistines. Saul's hope was that David would fall in battle.

David exceeded the bride-price by slaying *two hundred* Philistines, pleased to merit the right to become part of the royal family. Michal was delighted to marry the renowned victor.

The newlyweds reveled in their youth, energy, elevated rank, and good looks. But all of the attention on David agitated Saul. He realized the Lord was with David and that the hearts of his subjects were now favoring the youthful champion. An evil spirit fell on Saul, and his resentment descended into bitter hatred.

One night while David was playing his harp to soothe Saul's ragged nerves, the king hurled his spear at David and tried to pin him to the wall. David jumped aside, fled home to Michal, and described what her father had done.

---

1. See 1 Samuel 18:18.
2. 1 Samuel 18:22.

Peering outside, Michal saw the king's henchmen lurking in the dark. She warned David, "If you don't run for your life tonight, tomorrow you'll be killed."[3] After helping David escape through a window, Michal placed a life-sized idol on his bed and carefully covered it. The next morning when Saul's men came inside to capture David, she lied, saying her husband was sick in bed.

As David began a life of hiding from her father, Michal did not know it would be ten years before she would see her husband again.

Saul continued to harbor hatred for his fugitive son-in-law. One day, hoping to publicly disgrace David, Saul summoned Michal to his tent and ordered her to marry another man named Paltiel. Michal had no say in the matter. But in time her spirit gradually became hardened like her father's.

Then, ten years after David had disappeared from the court of King Saul, the enemies of Israel prevailed, and Saul was killed. The elders of Israel conferred, and a messenger was sent to David, asking him to become the new king.

"Good," said David. "I will make an agreement with you. But I demand one thing of you: Do not come into my presence unless you bring Michal daughter of Saul when you come to see me."[4] David assumed that the reunion with Michal—a Saul loyalist—would strengthen his claim to the throne and validate his standing.

Michal knew the request was politically motivated and that she was being used as a buffer between David and those who still supported the legacy of Saul. Taken by force from her husband, Paltiel, Michal was publicly delivered to David's house.

One day, she heard the sound of people celebrating in the streets. David had retrieved the treasured ark of the covenant—representing the presence of the Lord—and was joyfully returning it to Jerusalem. His exuberance for God was on display. Watching from her upper room, Michal caught sight of David celebrating. Wearing a simple priestly garment rather than his royal robe, he was shamelessly dancing and singing with all his might as the instruments played and the people shouted.

Michal was disgusted at this exhibition by the king of Israel.

3. 1 Samuel 19:11.
4. 2 Samuel 3:13.

When David returned home, his wife came out to meet him. "How the king of Israel has distinguished himself today, going around half-naked in full view of the slave girls of his servants as any vulgar fellow would!"[5]

Disgusted and disappointed, David retorted, "It was before the Lord, who chose me rather than your father or anyone from his house when he appointed me ruler over the Lord's people Israel—I will celebrate before the Lord."

David was unwavering in his determination to be the spiritual as well as temporal leader in Israel. He fled from Michal's presence. This time, however, his desire would not return. As her husband, David never came to her room again. The years of her fertility expired.

Michal was sentenced to a life of barrenness.

Their Life and Times
Tuesday

Paying the Bride-Price

In Bible times, a groom or his parents paid a bride-price for his future wife or their future daughter-in-law. The bride-price for Saul's daughter Michal was one hundred dead Philistines. Though this compensation seems violent, it was acceptable to the Hebrews of ancient Israel. Michal was David's reward for his military valor.

The practice of kings or generals giving their daughters in marriage to war heroes is also recorded in the book of Joshua when the mighty warrior Caleb offered his daughter Aksah "to the man who attacks and captures Kiriath Sepher" (Joshua 15:16). Othniel secured the battle and the bride.

Winning the daughter of a national leader was a distinguishing accomplishment for soldiers, especially if they came from an unheralded clan and wished to align themselves with a more notable family. For a soldier of modest means, battlefield daring was a way to negotiate the bride-price. He could never afford her, but he could fight for her.

---

5. 2 Samuel 6:20.

Prospective grooms could also pay a bride-price through hard work. That's what Jacob did. He earned the right to marry Laban's daughters with fourteen years of labor.[6]

Sometimes the groom's parents paid the bride-price. Abraham, through his servant Eliezer, gave fine jewelry and valuables in exchange for his son Isaac's wife, Rebekah: "Then the servant brought out gold and silver jewelry and articles of clothing and gave them to Rebekah; he also gave costly gifts to her brother and to her mother" (Genesis 24:53).

The purpose of the bride-price was to give the father compensation for the loss of his daughter and insurance for her support if she were to become a widow. The bride-price was often based on the social importance of the bride's family. The more honored and esteemed, the greater the price. But even a poor young soldier could afford the bride-price for a general's or king's daughter through military heroism.

Can You Imagine?

Wednesday

The twists and turns of David and Michal's marriage make for a sordid tale. Saul, Michal's father, offered his daughter to David as a reward for killing one hundred Philistines, secretly hoping that David would be killed in the battle, thereby eliminating the threat he posed.

Because the Lord's blessing was on David, he conquered two hundred enemy combatants. Saul had no choice and gave his daughter to David. But the bride's father continued to be resentful and jealous of his son-in-law: "When Saul realized that the LORD was with David and that his daughter Michal loved David, Saul became still more afraid of him, and he remained his enemy the rest of his days" (1 Samuel 18:28–29).

Can you imagine the stress on a marriage when the bride's or groom's parents selfishly oppose their child's spouse?

---

6. See Genesis 29:16–30.

The day you were married, two families were linked together. A minister asked, "Who gives this woman to be married to this man?" The response was a vow intended to transfer the protection, obligation, and commitment from the father of the bride to a new man in her life. And the same transfer was a necessary change for the parents of the groom.

In the Bible story, Michal is referred to as "David's wife" only one time. The other times she is called "Saul's daughter." David and Michal were not able to guard their allegiance to each other.

Your parents may need a gentle reminder to release control of you so that your marriage can flourish. You and your spouse need to lovingly set up boundaries to protect your marriage. You can say things like:

> We need to look at our calendar before we decide if those holiday plans will work for us.
>
> Please give us a call before you visit.
>
> We appreciate your offer to help, but we'd rather take care of this ourselves.

Although your parents' involvement in your lives is undoubtedly well-intentioned, your first loyalty must be to your spouse. Love and honor your parents, but don't allow them to separate you from the most important person in your life.[7]

From God's Word . . .

"That is why a man leaves his father and mother and is united to his wife, and they become one flesh."

GENESIS 2:24

---

7. Robert D. Wolgemuth, *She Still Calls Me Daddy: Building a New Relationship with Your Daughter after You Walk Her Down the Aisle* (Nashville: Nelson, 2009), 29.

Their Legacy in Scripture

Thursday

1. **"As the ark of the LORD was entering the City of David, Michal daughter of Saul watched from a window. And when she saw King David leaping and dancing before the LORD, she despised him in her heart"** (2 SAMUEL 6:16).

   David was exuberant and outspoken about following the Lord in his occupation and private life. Michal did not embrace her husband's love for God or his personal style. What does this verse tell you about her identity, her beliefs, and her attitude toward David? In what ways do you support your spouse's personality, passions, and personal style? How do you react when your spouse acts differently from those in your family of origin? What are your spouse's unique strengths and talents that require your special understanding and attention?

2. **"I am afraid that when I come I may not find you as I want you to be, and you may not find me as you want me to be. I fear that there may be discord, jealousy, fits of rage, selfish ambition, slander, gossip, arrogance and disorder"** (2 CORINTHIANS 12:20).

   Like her father, Michal displayed contempt toward David. Saul demonstrated many of the evils the apostle Paul warns about in these verses. Which of these attitudes or sins could become a snare in your marriage? How can you break a negative cycle that began in your family of origin?

3. **"When David returned home to bless his household, Michal daughter of Saul came out to meet him ..."** (2 SAMUEL 6:20).

   Although Michal may have treasured David when they were first married, she did not honor her husband with her words later in their marriage. David had just given gifts and words of encouragement to all the people after celebrating the arrival of the ark in Jerusalem. According to this verse, what was his intention and what did Michal miss because of her reaction? How do you greet your spouse every morning and at the end of your day? Smiles, enthusiasm, and kind words go a long way to encourage a spouse. In what ways can you nurture or enhance these behaviors?

Their Legacy of Prayer

Friday

Reflect On: 2 Samuel 6:16–23

Praise God: For His faithfulness in accomplishing His purposes in history and for sustaining His people in the midst of trials.

Offer Thanks: For your spouse and both of your families of origin. For His presence and His Spirit, which enables you and your spouse to break any cycle of sin, selfishness, and cynicism that could harm your marriage.

Confess: That you have spoken unkind words, had a critical spirit, or have been unwilling to change harmful habits.

Ask God: To help you to love and honor Him by the way you embrace your unique and gifted spouse. For discernment as you seek to lovingly set healthy boundaries with your parents-in-law.

Listen: "My children, I am your faithful God. I created and blessed you with gifts for each other. I am fully able to help you break every sinful pattern that could destroy your marriage. Ask Me, and I will give you the patience, gentleness, and wisdom you need in order to love and honor each other and your parents. Your marriage was designed to display My grace."

Pray: *Father in heaven, thank You for never taking Your love away from us and for the transforming power of Your presence in our lives. We need Your help to offer grace to each other and to our parents. Help us to speak encouraging words, radiate joy on our faces, and serve each other willingly. Help us to worship You in a way that will draw us closer to You and to each other. Amen.*

"You Are the Man!"

David and Bathsheba

Meaning of Names: *David* means "beloved." *Bathsheba* means "daughter of the oath" or "daughter of the promise."

Their Character: He was a prayerful, repentant man who loved God but was not careful to resist temptation. She was a beautiful woman who succumbed to the king's will and sinned against God.

Their Challenge: They spent an adulterous night together, and she became pregnant. He displeased the Lord when he committed adultery and was an accessory to murder.

Their Outcome: To cover up their sin, David ordered the death of Bathsheba's husband on the battlefront. The child conceived died when he was one week old. David's family was plagued by death and deception for the rest of David's life.

Key Scripture: 2 Samuel 11

Their Story

Monday

He wasn't sure what had awakened him, but for King David, there would be no more sleep on this night. At least not now. Getting up and slipping on his robe, he poured himself a drink. Stepping onto the palace rooftop, his eyes scanned the stillness across Jerusalem as thoughts of how much he loved the city filled his mind.

Inside a house along the street below him, he spotted a glowing lantern. And in the flickering light he saw someone. He moved to a place where he could see more clearly.

Sure enough. It was a woman, bathing. David knew he should look away, but he couldn't take his eyes off her. Slowly she dipped a sponge into a basin and then let the water run down her alabaster skin. She returned the sponge to the basin, leaned back, and lifted it again, allowing the water to gently trickle down her neck. Her body was beautiful. Elegant.

The king's heart rushed. His mind raced. *Who is this woman?* he wondered. *Why have I not seen her before?*

David stood and watched for a while. Slowly his imagination became a delicious plan. A scenario.

He summoned an aide who in moments, even at this hour, joined him on the roof.

"Who is that woman?" David asked, pointing to the lighted window.

"Bathsheba, your majesty," the man answered. "She is the wife of Uriah the Hittite."

Knowing that his troops were doing battle with the Ammonites in Rabbah and that Uriah was among his soldiers, David realized that Bathsheba was alone, so he sent for her. Soon his fantasy of passion would become real. After all, he was the king. Nothing was outside his grasp. Not even another man's wife.

"The king is summoning you," the messenger said to Bathsheba. At this time of the night, David's intentions must have been clear. He was the king. She had no choice.

Soon Bathsheba was lying in David's bed. Pushing aside any thoughts that what they were doing was wrong, they focused solely on each other. The night was ecstasy. For them both. David was with the luminous beauty; she was with the most powerful man in the country.

The next morning, David sent Bathsheba back to her house. Except for an occasional flashback and a missed heartbeat that followed, the tryst was forgotten.

Weeks went by. And then one day a messenger interrupted the king with the delivery of a note. The writing was not familiar, but the words immediately revealed their author: "I am with child."

The king panicked ... then quickly focused. A warrior and a strategist, David knew exactly what to do. "Send me Uriah the Hittite."[1] The message from the king went straight to Joab, the commander on the battlefront. David's plan was to have Uriah return to Jerusalem, surprising his wife with an unplanned conjugal visit. Then the unborn child could be credited to Bathsheba's husband.

Uriah soon was standing in front of his commander in chief, who told him to shower and shave and go to his wife. But Uriah did not want to do as he was ordered. How could he sleep with his wife when his comrades were in a battle? So the loyal soldier spent the night on the palace steps. The next night, David served Uriah dinner with plenty of wine. And more wine. Still, Uriah refused to sleep with his wife.

Bathsheba's husband returned to the battlefront, carrying a sealed message from David to Joab that read: "Put Uriah in the front lines where the fighting is the fiercest. Then pull back and leave him exposed so that he's sure to be killed."[2] This time David's plotting was successful. In the next skirmish, Uriah was killed in action. David's sin was compounded.

Word was delivered to Bathsheba that her husband had been slain. Crowds gathered around the widow to comfort her. Wailing echoed throughout the city. For seven days, the mourning continued. King David watched from the familiar place on his rooftop. Guilt consumed him. He chose to ignore it.

After Bathsheba's time of mourning was over, David brought her to the palace, and she became his wife. In time, Bathsheba delivered a son to the king. The parents were delighted with this new life.

Then the prophet Nathan came calling. He found David in the palace, and they walked to a solitary spot, speaking in hushed tones. As though he was seeking the king's wisdom, the man of God told David a story of a rich man and a poor man who lived in a nearby town.

In the story, the rich man possessed a large number of sheep and cattle. The poor man had only one little ewe lamb that he loved and nurtured like a household pet. The lamb shared food from the table,

---

1. 2 Samuel 11:6.
2. See 2 Samuel 11:15.

often slept in his arms, and was like a child to the poor man. The day came when a traveler visited the rich man, who felt obligated to prepare a feast. But instead of taking one of the thousands of his own livestock, the rich man took the poor man's only ewe lamb and killed it. A hearty dinner was served at the expense of the poor man.

Having risked his own life to protect lambs like this one when he was a shepherd boy, David exploded with anger. "The man who did this must die!"

Nathan stood in silence while David gathered his composure. The prophet looked deep into the eyes of the king and spoke in low and deliberate tones. "You are the man!" Nathan said.[3]

In that instant, David's treachery was revealed. Collapsing under the sheer horror of his sin, the king wept.

Their Life and Times

Tuesday

God's Mercy and Forgiveness

The story of David and Bathsheba is troubling. David, king of God's people and man after God's own heart, commits adultery with Bathsheba and then plots her husband's death.

In Old Testament times, both actions warranted the death penalty. But while the prophet Nathan pronounced severe judgment on David, he also spoke words of pardon. "The LORD has taken away your sin. You are not going to die" (2 Samuel 12:13).

It may seem like Nathan was offering a special favor to David in exchange for all the great things he had done for Israel. But this is not what was happening. David's many good and even heroic deeds didn't justify the king's sin. David was guilty of adultery and murder, and according to the law he deserved the death penalty.

Old Testament law mandated that "if a man commits adultery with another man's wife — with the wife of his neighbor — both the adulterer and the adulteress are to be put to death" (Leviticus

---

3. 2 Samuel 12:7.

20:10). The same punishment was meted out for premeditated murder. God's judgment for this predated Israel's birth as a nation. Following the great flood, He said to Noah and his family, "Whoever sheds human blood, by humans shall their blood be shed; for in the image of God has God made mankind" (Genesis 9:6).[4]

God was not overlooking David's sins of adultery and murder. He never ignores sin. But because David was contrite and repented, God extended grace, something only He can do.[5] Why God forgives and spares any sinner is a mystery. God is the only One who can see a person's heart. Forgiveness is the exercise of His unmerited favor —His amazing grace.

From the beginning of time, God's grace was at work. God told Adam and Eve, "You are free to eat from any tree in the garden; but you must not eat from the tree of the knowledge of good and evil, for when you eat from it you will certainly die" (Genesis 2:16–17). Yet they ate from the tree—and didn't die immediately. Although their sin did result in spiritual—and eventually physical—death, at the moment of their fall, God had already made a provision for their redemption. Restoration was planned and grace was given through His Son, Jesus Christ.

When Cain murdered Abel, Cain deserved death. But God allowed him to live, even though Cain was sentenced to a life of wandering. When Cain expressed his concern that someone might kill him for what he had done, God vowed His protection. Again, with no explanation for the grace issued to Cain, God gave it freely.[6]

Throughout Israel's history there are many examples of God's mercy, forgiveness, and grace. Over and over, God told His people not to worship idols, yet they disobeyed Him. God eventually punished them with exile, but the fact that He allowed them to live is an extraordinary act of grace.

The Bible is clear about sin. "All have sinned and fall short of the glory of God" (Romans 3:23). Everyone has sinned and desperately needs a Savior. God, in His grace, freely provides salvation.

Why did God spare David and Bathsheba? Why did He spare

---

4. See Exodus 21:12.
5. See Psalm 51.
6. See Genesis 4:8, 15.

Cain? Why did He spare Israel? Whenever God withholds punishment, it is because He has decided to issue mercy and forgiveness.

Grace.

It's His sovereign choice.

Can You Imagine?

Wednesday

I nfidelity causes chaos. Every time.

Why would a king who has everything risk his peace of mind and his entire future for one night of sexual pleasure? This is beyond logic.

Unless you're a man.

When David walked onto the rooftop that night and gazed at a sensual sight, he made a decision. A terrible decision. His fantasy and unholy passion overruled his good judgment.

A married woman needs to understand what happens to her husband's emotions when he sees something provocative. His pounding heart does not mean he is a dirty and lecherous man. This is the way God designed him. The intended purpose for this visual stimulation is to draw a man to attach to his wife.

It takes discipline and accountability to keep a man sexually pure. The same is true for a woman. You and your spouse both need someone to confide in as a sounding board to disclose and defuse poisonous thoughts that could destroy you and your marriage.

In the story of David and Bathsheba, there's a moment when David summoned "someone" to tell him the name of the bathing woman. Can you imagine what would have happened if that person had mustered the courage to challenge David's thoughts? "Why does Your Majesty want to know her name? She's Eliam's daughter. And she's married!"

Truthful conversation might have provided David the mirror he needed to see his heart and to consider the consequences of his plan. And it can do the same for you and your spouse.

A wife who loves her husband will encourage him to find a godly group of men who will dare to hold him accountable. And a husband will support his wife's friendships with godly women.

Pray for your spouse and ask God to help you both stay pure.

From God's Word . . .

After David had been confronted and had repented of his sin, he wrote:

"Create in me a pure heart, O God, and renew a steadfast spirit within me. Do not cast me from your presence or take your Holy Spirit from me."

PSALM 51:10–11

Their Legacy in Scripture

Thursday

1. **"Be still, and know that I am God; I will be exalted among the nations, I will be exalted in the earth"** (PSALM 46:10).

   David penned these words. Here we are admonished to "know" God, to understand Him as best we can. The King James Version of the Bible uses the word *know* to describe intimate sexual relations between a husband and wife. Adam "knew" Eve and she conceived.[7] Loving your husband is to know him; loving your wife is to know her. What does this mean?

2. **"Against you, you only, have I sinned and done what is evil in your sight; so you are right in your verdict and justified when you judge"** (PSALM 51:4).

   David sinned against Bathsheba and Uriah, and yet the words he wrote above do not even mention these two people. How should all sin be evaluated? How does this make you feel about your sin?

3. **"If we claim to be without sin, we deceive ourselves and the truth is not in us. If we confess our sins, he is faithful and just and will forgive us our sins and purify us from all unrighteousness"** (1 JOHN 1:8–9).

   These verses describe the power of confession, repentance, and forgiveness. How have you experienced God's faithfulness? What emotions did you feel after you last confessed to God or your spouse and asked for forgiveness? What keeps you from confessing and repenting more often?

---

7. See Genesis 4:1 KJV.

Their Legacy of Prayer

Friday

Reflect On:	2 Samuel 11–12
Praise God:	For His abundant mercy and great compassion for sinners.
Offer Thanks:	For God's restoration and a new beginning every time we confess, repent, and turn away from our sin.
Confess:	Your selfish and poisonous thoughts that lead to behaviors that displease the Lord. That your unholiness causes chaos in your heart and hurts others.
Ask God:	To give you a greater love for Him so you will want to please Him and see your sin as He sees it. For an undivided heart that is attracted and attached to your spouse only.
Listen:	"Dear children, I created your inmost parts and delight in your love for each other. Your marriage is a mirror that can reveal your character and reflect My beauty. In My design, you are to be accountable to each other and to live in the joy of purity. I will give you the strength and willpower to resist temptation so that you and your marriage can display My holiness, mercy, and grace."
Pray:	*Father in heaven, You see our hearts and still love us. Thank You for Your faithfulness to forgive our sin. You know what is best. You hate sin, but we foolishly embrace it. You despise iniquity, but we cling to it. Through Your Holy Spirit please alert us to every danger that would ruin our marriage and every sin that would separate us. Thank You for the gifts of purity, holiness, and righteousness. Give us hearts like Yours so our marriage can honor You. Amen.*

Walking Together

Mephibosheth and Wife

Meaning of Names: *Mephibosheth's* original royal name, Mirab-Baal, meant "opponent of Baal." His name was changed after his father, Jonathan, and his grandfather, Saul, were killed. His new name means "out of my mouth proceeds reproach" or "one who scatters shame." The name of Mephibosheth's wife is not given in the Bible.

Their Character: He was a crippled man who felt the shame of his disability from age five to adulthood, but later rejoiced in King David's honor and restoration. She embraced her husband's disability.

Their Challenge: Mephibosheth was not able to walk. As a descendant of a disgraced dynasty, he probably would have been executed if he had been able-bodied.

Their Outcome: Mephibosheth was granted royal favor by King David, who had loved Mephibosheth's father. He and his wife had a son named Mika.

Key Scripture: 2 Samuel 4:4; 9:1–13

Their Story

Monday

Hanon's[1] servant came running to find his portly master, who was in the vineyard overseeing the pruning after harvest. "A messenger from the house of King Saul is here, my Lord," the man gasped as he approached Hanon, bowing slightly. "His name is Ziba, and he is asking for you."

Hanon thanked his servant, turned, and hurried the short distance back to his home, rehearsing the likely reasons for such a visit. It had been almost twenty years since Saul and Jonathan had been killed in the bloody battle at Jezreel. *So why would Ziba be calling on me?* Hanon wondered.

By the time Hanon reached his home, his mind was whirling with the implications of a royal visit.

After a greeting, the messenger Ziba spoke. "The son of my lord Jonathan, the late royal prince of Israel, has expressed interest in marrying your daughter," he said. "If it pleases you, we will talk further. I will return here at the third hour tomorrow morning to discuss the matter, if you wish."

"My daughter?" Hanon replied.

Ziba hesitated. Then a winsome smile crossed his face. "Because his father is dead, Prince Jonathan's son has chosen me to speak to you concerning the betrothal of your daughter." The envoy waited a moment while Hanon processed the request and then asked, "Will you be here?"

"Yes, I will," Hanon responded. "Yes, I will," he firmly repeated.

Ziba thanked Hanon, turned, and stepped away from the house, moving toward his waiting entourage.

Although it was proper to wait until guests were nearly out of sight before shutting the door, Hanon neglected protocol. "I must tell my wife," he said aloud, closing the door behind him. "And, of course, I must tell my daughter."

He found his wife kneading dough and preparing loaves of bread. "Our daughter is going to marry Prince Jonathan's son," he

---

1. A made-up name. Mephibosheth's wife's father is not identified by name in the Bible.

exclaimed. She stopped. Her eyes widened. "Praise be to the Lord," she said, almost in a shout.

Over dinner, Hanon's family chattered about the visit from King Saul's servant. No one remembered hearing of Prince Jonathan's son. Now that David was on the throne of Israel, very little was said about Saul's progeny. Still, it seemed strange that no one had any memory of a son, an heir of Jonathan.

The following morning at the appointed third hour, Ziba returned as promised. After a cordial embrace, the men sat on the floor. Hanon's wife brought tea and quickly retreated. This conversation would not include her.

"On behalf of Mephibosheth, son of Prince Jonathan, grandson of King Saul, I am formally asking for your daughter's hand in marriage." Ziba sounded like he was reading from a decree. "We are no longer a family of great means," Ziba added, reducing the formality and speaking to Hanon as though he were a friend. "But my master's family is trustworthy. My lord Mephibosheth is a kind and honorable man. He loves and serves Yahweh God and would be pleased to marry your daughter."

"We are also not a family of wealth," Hanon responded. "But I will offer a generous gift to the groom and his family for this honor." Ziba extended his hand, and Hanon took it into his own. His daughter would wed the son of Prince Jonathan. It was settled.

Ziba was about to speak but hesitated. Hanon saw the uncertainty and waited. There was something else Ziba needed to say, and Hanon could see he was looking for the right words. For a few more moments, Ziba searched in vain. Then he spoke. "My lord Mephibosheth has not walked since he was a small boy," Ziba said, dropping his eyes toward the floor. "His lameness was the result of a careless accident, not a disease," he added reassuringly.

Now it was Hanon's turn to be silent. The two men sat quietly for some time. Ziba wondered if he should have disclosed Mephibosheth's condition earlier. He silently reassured himself that full disclosure was necessary and right. The girl's father needed to know.

Hanon brought his hands to his face, then lifted them up across his forehead, over and down his long red hair. Taking a deep breath, he let it out with a sigh. "Do you remember what Moses said to the

Lord when the burning bush was not consumed?" Hanon's words were more of a statement than a question.

"Yes, of course."

Hanon continued, "Moses said to God, 'Pardon your servant, Lord. I have never been eloquent, neither in the past nor since you have spoken to your servant. I am slow of speech and tongue.'"[2]

Ziba smiled and nodded, "My father told me this story many times."

"I suppose that in the presence of Yahweh, we are all crippled," Hanon said. "My daughter will learn to love Prince Jonathan's son."

Ziba's face softened with relief.

Hanon was not quite finished. "They will have children who will be a blessing to their parents ... and their grandparents." Hanon's eyes twinkled. "I will speak to my daughter," Hanon added. "I know her heart. She will agree."

And so it was.

Hanon's daughter was radiant on the day of her betrothal. The rabbi waited to seal the marriage contract as Mephibosheth's friends carried the young prince forward for the ceremony.

Several months later, the couple was wed, and in the years that followed, Mephibosheth loved his wife for her kindness and resolve. She loved him for his humility and wisdom. He was often overwhelmed with gratitude for her gentle spirit and necessary compensations.

Their lives were shaped and seasoned by mutual support. And when their son, Mika, was born, Mephibosheth and his wife celebrated the tender beauty of God's kindness to them.

---

2. Exodus 4:10.

Their Life and Times

Tuesday

Betrothal and Marriage Ceremonies

Betrothal ceremonies in ancient Israel inaugurated an engagement period that could not be broken without a legal certificate of divorce. The later wedding ceremony — including the procession from the bride's house to the groom's — was a jubilant event in the towns and hamlets where they were held. Everyone celebrated ... family, friends, and neighbors.

In some instances, parents made agreements with each other at the time of their children's births, hoping that when the boy and girl grew up they would marry. Provision was made, however, for the possibility that one of them was not well suited for the other or simply did not want to marry the one chosen.

When no childhood agreement was made by parents, the prospective groom or his father — or if he was not alive, a surrogate — would initiate a betrothal and approach the prospective bride's father. A bride-price was offered for the right to marry a daughter and could be paid in money, a gift, or a service rendered.[3]

Next came the ceremony of betrothal, a formal and binding procedure in which the terms of the marriage were contracted and sealed before witnesses. A rabbinic blessing was pronounced over the couple, who were then considered legally married. Unfaithfulness by the prospective bride- or groom-to-be was regarded as adultery and could be punishable by stoning.[4]

Betrothals usually lasted for a year, though sometimes as long as two years or as short as a few months. The length of time was determined by the groom's ability to deliver the bride-price. If he had promised to work for the bride's father for a specific period of time, then that was the duration of the betrothal. In cases where money was paid, the groom would determine the time needed to accumulate the funds.

---

3. See Genesis 29:18.
4. See Deuteronomy 22:23–24; Matthew 1:19.

The culmination of the betrothal period was a festive ceremony — the wedding procession. This was often quite a spectacle and a time of great joy. Wedding ceremonies occurred at night — as late as midnight — so those who worked during the day could participate. The groom's attendants would travel to the bride's home to accompany her back to the residence her husband had prepared for them.

In the meantime, the bride and her attendants spent hours preparing for the ceremony. Her entourage assisted her while she bathed and put on her wedding attire. When the groom's men arrived, they would light torches and candles to illuminate the pathway to the groom. The veiled bride followed the lights to her husband.

As the procession passed, townspeople shouted congratulations and good wishes from their balconies and roofs at the parade below. As the men held their torches and candles high, the bride's attendants lifted their voices in a distinct wedding "cry" or song, alerting people along the route. The pageantry of removing the bride from her father's house and parading her to the groom's residence displayed to everyone that the groom was formally taking her as his own.

After arriving at the groom's house, the bride and groom greeted each other and sat down as guests of honor at the wedding supper. The feast could last as long as seven days.

There was no formal exchange of vows at the wedding celebration. That had been done during the betrothal. The actual consummation of the marriage occurred when the couple entered the "chamber" (a bedroom) in which stood the canopied bridal bed. The bride's face remained veiled until after consummation.[5]

Ancient Israel's betrothal and marriage ceremonies painted a striking picture of what marriage is intended to be — beginning a new home together and a binding promise of devotion and faithfulness. Marriage is a portrait of God's love for His people, a covenant to be honored and cherished.

---

5. This practice explains Laban's deception of Jacob with Leah in Genesis 29:22–25.

Can You Imagine?

Wednesday

Mephibosheth had not walked since he was a young boy, and his betrothed must have known that marrying him would be a special challenge. Can you imagine the resolve required for a marriage to flourish with this kind of adversity?

In 1982, a high school history teacher living in Southern California married the most amazing woman he had ever met. During their wedding ceremony, the groom's eyes filled with tears as his bride moved toward him down the aisle. Almost thirty years later, when asked about the experience of being married to this remarkable woman, the groom responded, "God gave me the privilege of having a wife like Joni."

In this case, the groom was Ken Tada, and when he married Joni Eareckson, she had already been a quadriplegic for almost fifteen years. Their marriage has provided inspiration for tens of thousands around the world. Ken has surrounded Joni with the kind of love that Mephibosheth's wife would have needed to display. Heart, soul, mind, ability ... and disability.[6]

When you married, you may have secretly and naively determined that the person you love would need "a few necessary adjustments" down the road. Your spouse may have thought the same about you.

By now, you both realize that the inadequacies are still there. As husband and wife, you are both members of the human race. You are both flawed and sinful.

But God has given you to each other to serve and encourage. To love and support each other ... regardless. Sacrificial love is fueled by an encounter with the kind of perfect love that God has demonstrated for "sinfully disabled" people like each one of us.

A thriving marriage is not something you find; it's something you work for.

---

6. Joni and Ken Tada's story is chronicled in the book *Joni & Ken: An Untold Love Story*, published by Zondervan (April 2013).

Martin Luther, regarding a husband's marriage to an invalid wife (one who suffers from disease or disability):

"Let him serve the Lord in the person of the invalid and await His good pleasure. Consider that in this invalid God has provided your household with a healing balm by which you are to gain heaven. Blessed and twice blessed are you when you recognize such a gift of grace and therefore serve your invalid wife for God's sake."[7]

From God's Word . . .

"Therefore we do not lose heart. Though outwardly we are wasting away, yet inwardly we are being renewed day by day ... So we fix our eyes not on what is seen, but on what is unseen, since what is seen is temporary, but what is unseen is eternal."

2 CORINTHIANS 4:16, 18

---

7. Martin Luther, "The Estate of Marriage (1522)," in *Martin Luther's Basic Theological Writings*, ed. Timothy F. Lull (Minneapolis: Augsburg Fortress, 2005), 157.

Their Legacy in Scripture

Thursday

1. According to the customs of the day, Mephibosheth's marriage to his wife was prearranged. The Bible talks about another prearranged relationship. "[God] chose us in him before the creation of the world to be holy and blameless in his sight. In love he predestined us for adoption to sonship through Jesus Christ, in accordance with his pleasure and will" (EPHESIANS 1:4–5).

   God knows our faults and weaknesses. But even before we were born, He understood us and knew how His love would transform us. In what ways does this kind of love impact your marriage?

2. "Brothers and sisters, think of what you were when you were called. Not many of you were wise by human standards; not many were influential; not many were of noble birth. But God chose the foolish things of the world to shame the wise; God chose the weak things of the world to shame the strong" (1 CORINTHIANS 1:26–27).

   The task of your spouse is not just to fill out or complete you. The goal of your marriage is also to make you more like Jesus. In what ways were you "disabled" when your spouse married you?

3. "Mephibosheth lived in Jerusalem, because he always ate at the king's table" (2 SAMUEL 9:13).

   It was a special distinction to be seated at the king's table. When David discovered that an heir of his friend, Jonathan, was still alive, the king welcomed this disabled man to sit at a place of highest honor.

   A husband and wife are to value each other as best friends. How can you honor your spouse with words of affirmation and admiration and with acts of kindness?

Their Legacy of Prayer

Friday

Reflect On: 2 Samuel 9; 1 Chronicles 8:34–35 (Merib-Baal was another name for Mephibosheth)

Praise God: For His handiwork and His wisdom, power, and ability to work through human affliction.

Offer Thanks: That God is refining you and your spouse through the very weaknesses that trouble you.

Confess: That you entered into marriage with selfishness and pride. That instead of looking to God, you often expect your spouse to satisfy and complete you.

Ask God: To help you struggle successfully and shape you into His likeness as you serve your spouse.

Listen: "My children, when I look at you, I see the beauty I created and long for you to display a loving sacrifice for each other. As you meditate on My life and My Word, you will learn how to be a servant. I will empower you and make you strong when you are weak so you can support and encourage your spouse."

Pray: *Father in heaven, we thank You for each other. You created us to be complete in Your love and to sacrifice for one another. Thank You for strengthening our feeble hands and steadying our weak knees and for saying to our fearful hearts, "Be strong and do not fear." Thank You for coming to save us. We want to be like You in the way we treat each other. Amen.*

Heart Trouble

Solomon and Foreign Wives

Meaning of Names: Solomon means "peace" or "peaceful." In the Bible, Solomon's wives were simply called "foreign women."

Their Character: He was given great wisdom, wealth, and power but mistrusted God and succumbed to pride, lust, disobedience, and sin. His wives were daughters of pagan kings who worshiped false gods.

Their Challenge: Solomon did not believe God was able to empower him to conquer foreign kings without the sinful alliances he made with them. The wives' idols, customs, and heathen practices blinded them from worshiping the one true God.

Their Outcome: Solomon's final years were chaotic with political uprisings and personal misery. His sinfulness led to the division of Israel into two separate nations.

Key Scripture: 1 Kings 11:1–23

Their Story

Monday

"How did I get here?" Solomon wondered aloud to no one in particular. He was not asking about his physical location. His question was far more important than that. He was lamenting the condition of his soul.

Solomon had been Israel's king for forty years. Today he felt no joy. Only regret. The kind of regret that can suffocate a man.

As someone would unroll the pages of an ancient scroll, Solomon slowly began reviewing his life, back to the early years of his reign following the death of his father, David. Israel's great king—the man after God's own heart—had taught his son to honor the Lord. Solomon loved God with all his heart. He really did. Following the example of his father, he had walked in obedience to the Lord as best he could. And the Lord had richly rewarded him.

A faint delight crossed Solomon's face as he recalled that day long ago when God came to him in a dream and said, "Ask for whatever you want Me to give you."[1] At that time, the young king's love for God was untainted, his motives pure. He could have asked for riches. Or power. Or glory. But no, these things meant little to him then. As a new monarch he carried a heavy burden. He was inexperienced —a child in his own estimation—and had an entire nation to lead. It was an overwhelming responsibility.

He knew of only one way to rule successfully. "Please give me a discerning heart to govern Your people," Solomon had prayed. "Help me to understand the difference between right and wrong so I am able to lead this nation."

The request had been humble and desperate.

And the Lord was pleased.

Solomon was granted his request—as well as other things he had not requested. He became one of the wisest, wealthiest, and most powerful rulers to ever live.

In the process of bestowing such glory on Solomon, the Lord had added, "And if you walk in obedience to me and keep my decrees and commands as David your father did, I will give you a long life."[2]

So what had gone wrong?

It all started with his desire for the daughter of Siamun, the pharaoh of Egypt. Even though he knew God had forbidden such an alliance.[3] Solomon rationalized the marriage as a way to protect the Israelite nation. His quest for power through marital alliances continued with other daughters of local chiefs and clan leaders from pagan nations—Moab, Ammon, Edom, and Sidon.

---

1. See 1 Kings 3:5.
2. 1 Kings 3:14.
3. See Deuteronomy 7:1–4.

God would have provided Solomon all the resources necessary for Israel to conquer these nations. Sadly, Solomon settled on his own strategy and molded power alliances with enemy kings, sealing treaties by marrying their daughters and bringing them to Jerusalem.

But there was a problem Solomon hadn't planned for. His foreign wives brought their carved idols with them to Jerusalem—along with amulets, charms, incense, and fetishes.

And Solomon allowed it. His fallen heart willfully embraced his wives' immoral customs. Their gods were less demanding and their worship more tantalizing than the solemn worship of Yahweh.

And so, along with his worship of Yahweh, Solomon—the king who should have known better—worshiped and built altars for Molek.

And Chemosh. And a host of foreign deities.

There was an appealing mystery and indulgence about them that tarnished the soul of David's son.

Boasting 700 wives and 300 concubines, Solomon amassed a harem that was the envy of every world monarch. He was obsessed with owning women.

And their deities.

He no longer knew the presence and closeness of the God of Israel.

Although only sixty, Solomon felt much older. As he looked at his life, he saw nothing but corruption, vanity, and shame. "Wise old Solomon," he mocked himself, the words stinging his lips. "Old fool is more like it! For with much wisdom comes much sorrow; the more knowledge, the more grief."[4]

He had trifled with Yahweh and squandered the gift of wisdom.

He had accommodated his wives and bowed to their deities.

And now his soul was bankrupt.

"Meaningless! Meaningless!" he cried out. "Everything is meaningless."[5] How far Solomon had fallen.

---

4. See Ecclesiastes 1:18.

5. See Ecclesiastes 1:2.

Their Life and Times

Tuesday

Truth and Consequences

Considering Solomon's impressive start as the king of Israel, it's tragic that he didn't finish well. Of his beginnings, we are told, "Solomon showed his love for the LORD by walking according to the instructions given him by his father David" (1 Kings 3:3).

The problem began when he signed a peace agreement with Siamun, the pharaoh of Egypt, and sealed it by marrying his daughter. It was a common practice among pagan kings to build alliances as a means of national security. The nuptials were intended to guarantee safe international relations. However, Solomon became obsessed with the power, marrying an unfathomable 700 wives and keeping 300 concubines as trophies for his harem.

This collection of women was in open defiance of God, who had gifted him, saying, "I will give you a wise and discerning heart, so that there will never have been anyone like you, nor will there ever be" (1 Kings 3:12).

In Israel's early history, God had cautioned His people regarding their future king: "He must not take many wives, or his heart will be led astray" (Deuteronomy 17:17). This truth did not apply only to kings. Forty years earlier, when Israel was wandering in the wilderness, God warned the people that when they entered the Promised Land and would "choose some of their daughters as wives for your sons and those daughters prostitute themselves to their gods, they will lead your sons to do the same" (Exodus 34:16). God fully understood the power of the marriage relationship.

This was no idle warning. Decades later, "while Israel was staying in Shittim, the men began to indulge in sexual immorality with Moabite women, who invited them to the sacrifices to their gods. The people ate the sacrificial meal and bowed down before these gods" (Numbers 25:1–2). The result of such open rebellion against God was severe and brutal. "The LORD said to Moses, 'Take all the leaders of these people, kill them and expose them in broad daylight before the LORD, so that the LORD's fierce anger may turn away from Israel'" (Numbers 25:4).

Solomon had been repeatedly reminded of God's specific instructions regarding marrying foreign women. He knew the consequences Israel faced when they disregarded Him. But history's wisest man disobeyed the Lord. "As Solomon grew old, his wives turned his heart after other gods ... He followed Ashtoreth the goddess of the Sidonians, and Molek the detestable god of the Ammonites" (1 Kings 11:4–5).

Solomon not only defied God's standards; he also tolerated and sponsored the worship of foreign gods. Molek was the god of Ammon. While in the wilderness shortly after fleeing Egyptian bondage, the Israelites received this warning from God: "Do not give any of your children to be sacrificed to Molek, for you must not profane the name of your God. I am the LORD" (Leviticus 18:21).

The image of Molek, a Canaanite fire-god, was large, well over fifteen feet, and was made of brass and was hollow within. His face was that of a calf, and his hands were outstretched. An ugly and unsettling figure.

What made the worship of Molek repulsive was child sacrifice. In order to receive "blessings" from Molek—such as healthy crops, rain, large homes—worshipers would sacrifice their firstborn children. The worship of Molek also involved perverted sexual practices, usually with a shrine prostitute. God had strongly warned His people to stay away from both child sacrifice and sexual sins.[6]

Solomon compromised the integrity of his relationship with God and strayed far from the first commandment, which he knew well. "You shall have no other gods before me" (Exodus 20:3).

Led by women who did not know or love the true God, unable to guard his own heart, Solomon's tragedy was self-inflicted. Instead of becoming an extraordinary leader of the Hebrew nation as the Lord had called him to be, Solomon became an ordinary idol worshiper.

---

6. See 1 Kings 14:23–24.

Can You Imagine?

Wednesday

In ancient Israel, when a man married a woman they entered into a legal partnership. At the close of the ceremony, a *ketubah*, or marriage contract, was sealed.

Your marriage license is like your articles of incorporation. Signed "before God and these witnesses," this agreement gives you and your spouse the authority to do whatever is necessary to protect the assets of your own corporation. This bond carries with it the duty to speak the truth in love to each other.

Can you imagine how Solomon's life—and the history of an entire nation—would have benefited if he had chosen one wife—only one—who assumed her role as his full partner?

Solomon's downfall was incremental. One foolish choice, one small indiscretion at a time. And perhaps it was because he was so powerful that no one challenged him to remain faithful to the God he had promised to serve. Driven by a thirst for power and surrounded by unthinkable excesses, Solomon had no ally to speak God's truth to his soul. It cost him his heart.

Like the guardrails on a mountain road, you and your spouse are boundary keepers. You help to shape and define each other. And the one who follows God's Word, prays, and models faithfulness can be the one who will make a difference in their spouse's life, one small, wise choice at a time.

When your spouse is dangerously close to the precipice of poor choices, ask God for the wisdom to lovingly speak the truth so your spouse—the co-owner of your partnership—can clearly see the certain peril ahead.

The spouse God blessed you with is your most important asset. His counsel can bring perspective. Her words can protect you. And together you can display the wisdom of God's plan for your marriage.

From God's Word ...

"'My command is this: Love each other as I have loved
you. Greater love has no one than this: to lay down one's
life for one's friends. You are my friends if you do what I
command.'"

JOHN 15:12–14

Their Legacy in Scripture

Thursday

1. **"King Solomon, however, loved many foreign women ... As Solomon grew old, his wives turned his heart after other gods, and his heart was not fully devoted to the LORD his God"** (1 KINGS 11:1, 4).

   Solomon sacrificed to the deities of his pagan wives, but at the same time he continued to worship in his own temple. His depravity caused him to adjust his view of God downward. God was displeased and took the kingdom away from him.

   What does it mean for your heart to be "turned"? What will your children need to deal with years from now if you choose to continue certain habits, indiscretions, or sins? How can you help your spouse stay "fully devoted" to the Lord?

2. **"You were taught, with regard to your former way of life, to put off your old self, which is being corrupted by its deceitful desires; to be made new in the attitude of your minds; and to put on the new self, created to be like God in true righteousness and holiness"** (EPHESIANS 4:22–24).

   What idols—things you cherish more than God—have snared you or continue to challenge the purity of your relationship with Him? What things have you and your spouse determined to do or to avoid in order to guard against "creeping idolatry" in your lives?

3. **"Your beauty should not come from outward adornment, such as elaborate hairstyles and the wearing of gold jewelry or fine clothes. Rather, it should be that of your inner self, the unfading beauty of a gentle and quiet spirit, which is of great worth in God's sight"** (1 PETER 3:3–4).

   This idea about the source of beauty is not something you'll find celebrated in the grocery checkout lanes, the mall, or in the media. What things define beauty to you? Why is it easy for a woman to be drawn into "outward adornment"? How can a wife nurture qualities of a godly woman? What can you do to encourage a godly heart in your spouse?

Their Legacy of Prayer

Friday

Reflect On: 1 Kings 11:1–13

Praise God: That He alone is worthy of our worship and for His mercy and power and goodness.

Offer Thanks: That God has chosen you to be His and that He has shown you what He expects of you. For giving you the power to resist immorality and sin, and for His forgiveness and restoration when sinners go to Him in repentance with contrite hearts.

Confess: That you accommodate idols, make alliances with sin, and tolerate an inaccurate or inadequate view of God's holiness.

Ask God: To give you faith and a deep love for Him. That God's Spirit will enable you to surrender your selfishness and pride so the distractions of this world fade away in light of God's wonderful deeds.

Listen: "My children, I created all things for you to enjoy, but nothing in this world is to capture your heart and turn you away from Me. I am able to satisfy your deepest desires and will fulfill you when you trust and obey My Word."

Pray: *Heavenly Father, we worship You alone. You deserve the power, the glory, and the focus of our lives. We want to be fully devoted to You in whatever we think and do. When the things of this world distract us or tempt us to make sinful alliances, please remind us of Your better purpose and power. Quiet our wandering hearts so that we may yearn to put You first in all things. Fill us with one holy passion. You are our only God. Amen.*

32

Oh, Jezebel

Ahab and Jezebel

Meaning of Names: *Ahab* means "uncle" or "father's brother." *Jezebel* means "not exalted," "impure," or "Baal exalts."

Their Character: Though a brave soldier, he was weak willed and unable to restrain his wife. He was an immoral, greedy, and selfish king. She was a ruthless pagan, treacherous toward followers of the Lord, manipulative, and unscrupulous.

Their Challenge: Ahab adopted his father's evil ways, became even more evil, and disregarded the command to marry a follower of God. Jezebel was a pagan Phoenician who promoted Baal worship and plotted the murders of many of God's people and prophets in Israel.

Their Outcome: Ahab built monuments to pagan gods and led the Hebrews into Baal worship. He had a brief time of repentance before his dishonorable death. Jezebel suffered a violent death.

Key Scripture: 1 Kings 16:29–33; 19:1–2; 21:1–28

Their Story

Monday

Ahab was dying, and he knew it. Despite his efforts to conceal himself during the battle against the Arameans, an enemy arrow had found its way between his breastplate and the scale armor that covered his abdomen, mortally piercing Israel's king. Warm blood drenched his lower body, seeping onto the floor of his chariot. Ahab ordered his driver to prop him up. He would not give the Arameans the satisfaction of watching him slump.

As the shadow of death crept over him, the carnage around him was a fitting metaphor of what his marriage to Jezebel had been. All of this was an apt postscript to Ahab's rebellion against God.

The son of Israel's wicked King Omri, Ahab had inherited a blatant disregard for the God of Abraham, Isaac, and Jacob. As a young man he bowed to his father's wishes and set in place his own perilous future. Ahab did not protest when Omri, in defiance of God's command, orchestrated a marriage for his son with a foreigner. Wanting a secure alliance with the neighboring Phoenicians, King Omri arranged a marriage between his son and the daughter of the Phoenician king, Ethbaal. Omri hoped the marriage would strengthen Israel's security, especially when Ahab succeeded him as king.

Ahab must have known of God's command, yet he agreed to marry Jezebel anyway. His "prize" was an aggressive, determined, and evil princess who dominated him. Jezebel had grown up in a pagan land where kings ruled with no regard for God, the law, or their subjects' welfare. Ahab and the entire Hebrew nation were sentenced to her ruthless influence because of this marriage.

When his father died, Ahab seized the reins and established his own regime. Taxing his people mercilessly, King Ahab constructed a dazzling ivory palace in the capital city of Samaria, and he filled other cities with his magnificent monuments.

Architecture and military might were Ahab's passions. And to keep marital peace, he acquiesced to his wife's demands. So, with the people's money, Ahab built a breathtaking and ornate temple to the male fertility god Baal, which became the playground for every sort of sexual perversion imaginable. Ahab also consented when Jezebel invited 450 priests of Baal and 400 priests of the female fertility goddess Asherah to Israel. These pagan religious leaders infested the land with the ways of their deities.

And when Jezebel determined to systematically purge Israel of all God's prophets, the king stood silent. Ahab did not restrain his wife when she also methodically threatened and murdered other faithful followers of the Lord. He didn't even try. Ahab had other priorities.

He didn't care what his wife did as long as she allowed him to build his lavish construction projects, engage in his wars, and indulge in lecherous living. In the eyes of the Lord, Ahab committed more evil than any of the kings before him.[1]

Now Ahab was mortally wounded, unable to lead his troops on the battlefield. He was as weak and powerless here as he had been in the palace with Jezebel. His mind wandered back to an incident many years before, when he had built his summer pleasure-palace in the beautiful Jezreel Valley. He loved that home—especially when Jezebel was away in Samaria entertaining her 850 priests—but there was a problem.

The king had wanted to plant a vegetable garden adjacent to the palace. But the neighbor who owned the property, a God-honoring Israelite named Naboth who had inherited the land from his ancestors, refused to sell. There was an established decree in Israel stating that all personal property "must not be sold permanently," because the land is the Lord's, and His people are but foreigners and His tenants.[2]

Unable to acquire Naboth's property, Ahab's plan for a garden was thwarted. The king went to his room angry, sulked like a little boy, and refused to eat. Annoyed by his behavior, Jezebel confronted him and asked, "Why are you so sullen? Why won't you eat?"[3]

When Ahab told her that Naboth would not sell him the land, Jezebel was disgusted, and said, "Is this how you act as king over Israel? Get up and eat! Cheer up. I'll get you the vineyard of Naboth the Jezreelite."

With the king's signet ring in hand, Jezebel forged ahead with her plan. Fabricating charges of blasphemy against Naboth, she had him tried and then stoned to death by his own people.

Ahab had his vegetable garden. But while he was on the very land he had stolen from Naboth, a messenger arrived with a word from the Lord for King Ahab. It was the "troubler of Israel"—as Ahab called him—Elijah the prophet.[4] "I am going to bring disaster on you," Elijah spoke God's verdict to the king. "I will wipe out your

---

1. See 1 Kings 16:30.
2. See Leviticus 25:23.
3. 1 Kings 21:5.
4. See 1 Kings 18:17.

descendants and cut off from Ahab every last male in Israel—slave or free."

The holy man of God had ruined Ahab's revelry.

"When Ahab heard these words, he tore his clothes, put on sack-cloth and fasted."[5] Convicted of his sin, the king humbled himself and repented. This was something he had not done since the days of his youth. Although it was too late to reverse all the evil he and Jezebel had perpetuated, the Lord noticed that Ahab had humbled himself. But his belated repentance did not cancel the consequences.

Now, alone with his chariot driver and dying on the battlefield, King Ahab remembered with regret the prophet's words: "You have sold yourself to do evil in the eyes of the Lord."[6]

Focusing his blurring eyes, the king sat dying, wondering what his life could have been.

Their Life and Times

Tuesday

Baal Worship

Ahab and Jezebel will always be synonymous with sinfulness and the idolatry they promoted. An immigrant from Phoenicia,[7] Jezebel was a high priestess for the pagan gods of her homeland, Baal and Asherah. Baal was the son of the mythical god El, the supreme deity of the Canaanite people. Asherah was the wife of El and the mother of Baal, and Ashtoreth was considered to be Baal's wife. Jezebel was a follower of these goddesses.

The word *Baal* means "lord" or "possessor," a fitting description of his stranglehold on people. In Phoenicia—modern-day Lebanon—Baal worship involved animal sacrifices, ritual meals, and ceremonial dancing where almost-naked men and women gyrated in sexual frenzy. Baal temples and shrines contained inner chambers for prostitution. Even married men and women visited these temple prostitutes.

---

5. 1 Kings 21:27.
6. See 1 Kings 21:20.
7. Phoenicia was the world capital of Baal worship and home to a violent people who instituted crucifixion as the cruelest form of capital punishment.

Known as the fertility god, Baal was believed to grant fertility to the womb and productivity to the land, sending rain during dry seasons and causing crops to flourish. Statues symbolizing his fertility and strength depicted Baal as a powerful man with a bull's head. To venerate Baal was to have food and children.

Baal worship reached its pinnacle in Israel during Ahab's marriage to Jezebel. When Jezebel brought with her to Israel the 450 priests of Baal and 400 priests of Asherah, she showered these priests with lavish gifts, building them luxurious homes and feasting with them daily at palaces in Samaria and Jezreel. All at the people's expense.

The priests of Baal took turns working around the clock, watching over the perpetual flame burning in a large, dish-shaped pan on the altar. Together, the priests and people—pagan and Israelite alike—performed sexual acts in view of this altar, hoping that the gods who controlled earth and water would grant fertility to the land, animals, and people.

If "prayers" would go unanswered because Baal was too busy to notice, the people resorted to human sacrifice, throwing their first-born children into the huge pan of fire in order to summon the help of Baal and Asherah.[8] Loud music played during these gruesome episodes in an attempt to drown out the screams of the victims ... and their parents.

After the passing of only one generation—following the deaths of Joshua and the elders who led the nation—the Hebrews succumbed to the sinful passions of their Canaanite neighbors and the worship of their gods. In spite of Yahweh's faithful mercy and protection for centuries, "the Israelites did evil in the eyes of the LORD and served the Baals ... and the Ashtoreths" (Judges 2:11, 13). In the face of this treachery among the people God loved and led, He sent messengers like the prophet Elijah and future righteous kings to end Baal worship in Israel.

---

8. See 1 Kings 18:27.

Can You Imagine?

Wednesday

"It's mine."

"No, it's mine. I want it."

If you have ever volunteered for church nursery duty, you've heard these words, sometimes at earsplitting decibels. It's understandable that little ones will selfishly battle for things that please them, but when grown-ups do it—when the spiritual survival of an entire nation is involved and the squabblers are the king and queen—that's a different story.

"I don't like your God; I want my idols and my rituals," Jezebel insisted.

"I want my monuments. I want my wars. I want my vegetable garden," responded Ahab. "I want my way, and I don't care who pays for it."

Can you imagine a more pathetic scene between a husband and wife?

At the heart of every great marriage is a spirit of giving. Of mercy. Of selflessness. Before you said "I do," you didn't need to share your things or schedule your life around someone else. Sentences never began with "Can I borrow your …?" or "Does this fit into your plans?" But now you're living in shared space. What once was "mine" is now "ours." Your rights to personal property and individual freedoms have been traded for "I won't stubbornly demand what I want. No, I want what's best for you—even if it costs me something." Or, "I choose to serve you, even though it's inconvenient."

Is this hard work? Does this require self-denial and discipline every day? Are there times when you would rather demand your own way? Yes to all of these.

But God calls us to selflessness and service. To humility and caring. To want the highest good for our spouse regardless of the sacrifice, so that we together can mirror the extravagant love of God.

From God's Word . . .

"Do nothing out of selfish ambition or vain conceit. Rather, in humility value others above yourselves, not looking to your own interests but each of you to the interests of the others."

PHILIPPIANS 2:3–4

Their Legacy in Scripture

Thursday

1. **"There was never anyone like Ahab, who sold himself to do evil in the eyes of the LORD, urged on by Jezebel his wife"** (1 KINGS 21:25).

   When we trifle with obedience to God, we are capable of foolishness and great evil. What does it mean that Ahab "sold himself" to do evil? What part did Jezebel play in the loss of his spiritual moorings? What have you and your spouse decided to embrace in order to fully obey God?

2. **"Love must be sincere. Hate what is evil; cling to what is good. Be devoted to one another in love. Honor one another above yourselves"** (ROMANS 12:9–10).

   Ahab and Jezebel selfishly pursued their own interests with no regard for pleasing God or faithfully serving the people they ruled. What truth do you need to speak in love to your spouse in order to push back evil? What do you consider "good" and how can you "cling" to it? In what ways does your spouse honor you?

3. **"Let us consider how we may spur one another on toward love and good deeds, not giving up meeting together, as some are in the habit of doing, but encouraging one another"** (HEBREWS 10:24–25).

   What spiritual strengths and loving qualities does your spouse display to you and others? In what ways can you acknowledge, admire, and encourage your spouse in these areas? What habits are important to cultivate in order to deepen the spiritual bond in your marriage?

Their Legacy of Prayer

Friday

Reflect On:	1 Kings 21
Praise God:	That He is the one true and holy God, and He cannot be controlled or defeated by any earthly evil or power.
Offer Thanks:	That God forgives you and offers salvation when you repent. For the new heart He has given you, one that delights in serving your spouse with sacrificial love.
Confess:	That without God's power you are capable of foolishness and any sin. That you selfishly make excuses and rationalize in order to avoid facing your sin.
Ask God:	To remind you of His holiness so you will not trifle with obedience to His Word. To strengthen you to resist anything that is not wholesome and good.
Listen:	"My children, seek My wisdom and humble yourselves before Me. With My Spirit, you will be able to stand against evil and lead others to find salvation and peace. I am the way and the truth. I offer eternal life to all who come to Me with contrite hearts of repentance and belief."
Pray:	*Heavenly Father, You know the deep and secret thoughts of our hearts and minds. We want You to take possession of our lives so we may please You. We need Your help to rid our lives of the idols that capture us and sometimes overwhelm us. You have made us new creations in Christ Jesus and have given us Your Spirit. You graciously give us the privilege to walk together in righteousness. Please give us the courage to be faithful to each other and to You. Amen.*

33

More Than Just a Pretty Face

Xerxes and Vashti

Meaning of Names:	*Xerxes* means "the lion king," "prince," "head," or "chief." *Vashti* means "thread" or "beautiful."
Their Character:	He was a self-absorbed, sensual monarch who flaunted his privilege and possessions and indulged his appetites. She was an exceptionally beautiful, courageous woman who, as queen, risked banishment for her virtuous ideals.
Their Challenge:	Though he used women for his own purposes, he had married a woman of self-worth who was willing to do what was right. She risked her life when she refused her drunken husband's order to display her body and beauty before the men at his party.
Their Outcome:	He repeatedly lost battles, including the war against the Greeks. Even though she was deposed as queen, she became the mother of the successor to her husband's throne.
Key Scripture:	Esther 1

Their Story

Monday

Xerxes had entered his third year as the king of Persia and was preparing for a major campaign against Greece. Anticipating a victorious conquest, he proclaimed an extravagant and lavish banquet

—six months of revelry to wine, dine, and dazzle his nobles, officials, military leaders, and princes. The party would be interrupted by strategy meetings, but Xerxes' primary intent was to impress his subjects with his majesty and splendor.

Queen Vashti, the most beautiful woman in the land and the one who would ordinarily sit on her throne next to Xerxes for such a celebration, was not invited. If a feast included lots of wine and raucous behavior, custom dictated that the queen be dismissed. But that was fine with her. Knowing that her self-indulgent husband was planning an excessive and sensuous affair, Vashti had no interest in attending. Like everything else in his life—including her—this party was all about Xerxes.

When she and Xerxes were first married, Vashti hoped she would be cherished. From among the women in the entire realm, the king had chosen her. But she soon realized that Xerxes had not wed a companion; he had selected an ornament. The king wanted her for one reason: Vashti was gorgeous.

His collection of women did not stop with Vashti. King Xerxes was famous for owning an impressive harem, acquiring beauties of every color and nationality, accessories for his own stature and pleasure.

Because she held the official title of queen, Vashti may have thought she would be regarded more highly than the rest of the women. She soon learned otherwise. Besides occasional conjugal visits, her time with the king was purely political. She accompanied him on diplomatic missions and hosted dignitaries from other parts of the realm. Visitors ogled at the queen's resplendence, something Xerxes intentionally cultivated. Vashti knew exactly why Xerxes paraded her. And it insulted her personhood. A silent chasm grew, separating their souls.

When the six months of feasting ended, Xerxes announced he would throw one more party, this one solely for those who served in the palace. It lasted seven days. Queen Vashti also gave a banquet for the women in the royal palace.[1] Despite her disenchantment with her husband, Queen Vashti enjoyed entertaining the ladies of the court. They provided the friendship and conversation she needed.

---

1. See Esther 1:9.

On the final day of both banquets, Vashti was surprised to see seven men from her husband's court walking into her party. "Queen Vashti," one of them announced, "the king commands you to put on your royal crown and come immediately to his banquet."

Vashti knew the king was drunk and wanted his intoxicated friends to feast their eyes on her. This was a gross insult, and Vashti would have none of it, saying, "I will not come to his banquet."

The seven servants gasped at the danger of saying no to the king. "But Your Highness …" They trembled.

"I am the queen of Persia," she replied. "Am I to be treated as a common harlot, humiliated at the king's hall? I refuse this indignity."

The servants said nothing. But they feared for Vashti.

As the attendants left, the queen knew retribution would follow. Of this she was certain. No one — not even the queen — could embarrass the king and escape unpunished. When Xerxes heard that Queen Vashti had refused his demand, he was furious and burned with anger.[2]

Vashti's defiance had caused an uproar in the citadel. The king consulted his wisest men. "According to law, what must be done to Queen Vashti?" he asked. "She has not obeyed the command of King Xerxes that the eunuchs have taken to her."

The council agreed on the verdict. "Queen Vashti has done wrong, not only against the king but also against all the nobles and the peoples of all the provinces of King Xerxes." And then the king's wise men suggested an appropriate sentence. "Let him issue a royal decree and let it be written in the laws of Persia and Media, which cannot be repealed, that Vashti is never again to enter the presence of King Xerxes. Also let the king give her royal position to someone else who is better than she."

Vashti was guilty. She was to be deposed.

The queen was banished, moving a short distance from the palace to another part of Susa. But she was granted the guarantee that she could still live comfortably with the king's protection because she was pregnant with Xerxes' child, who would eventually ascend to the throne of Persia.

Years later, even though she sometimes missed the privileges that

---

2. See Esther 1:12.

came with being the queen, she had no regrets. What she did on that extraordinary night four years before she would do again.

Her dismissal had not disgraced her dignity. Vashti had protected her honor.

Their Life and Times

Tuesday

The Law of the Medes and the Persians

The law of the Medes and Persians was an undisputable, established edict in the Medo-Persian Empire. When a king formally signed and instituted a decree, it was so binding that not even the king himself could change it. This was because the king was thought to be a god and could therefore speak for gods. Kings were deities who were considered infallible and therefore never needed to change their minds.[3]

Bound by this law, King Xerxes ruled over the vast Persian Empire, which stretched west to Greece, east to India, and south to Ethiopia. Vashti, the queen of Persia, was a figurehead and politically expendable. She did not hold any official power but was expected to serve as the king's companion on diplomatic trips and, when necessary, host foreign dignitaries who visited the palace.

When Xerxes gave an order, the kingdom's subjects — including his wife — defied it at the immediate cost of their lives. His word was law and not to be disobeyed.

It is possible that Vashti was courageous in standing up to her husband and willing to risk her life by defying the king's command because she was pregnant. She would have had good reason to protect herself and her baby — the successor to the throne. No wonder the king acquiesced.

Xerxes, who ruled from 486 to 465 BC, was succeeded by his son Artaxerxes, who ruled from 465 to 424 BC. Artaxerxes was born in the year 483 BC, the same year Vashti was summoned to display her

---

3. See David Guzik, "Daniel 6: In the Lions' Den," Enduring Word Media, http://goo.gl/uvW0j (accessed July 25, 2012).

beauty to Xerxes' guests. Bearing the heir to the throne carried with it some rare benefits, and apparently rebuffing the king and living to tell about it was one of them.

Regardless of her status as mother of the successor to Xerxes' throne, Vashti was nonetheless punished for her defiance. She never again was allowed the privilege of entering the presence of the king. It was the law. Xerxes was reminded of the finality of his decree by Memukan, one of the kingdom's wise men, an expert in matters of law and justice.

"Therefore, if it pleases the king," Memukan said to Xerxes, "let him issue a royal decree and let it be written in the laws of Persia and Media, which cannot be repealed, that Vashti is never again to enter the presence of King Xerxes" (Esther 1:19).

The decree—according to the law of the Medes and the Persians—had been issued. But this is not the first time the law is mentioned in the Bible. It was also cited less than fifty years before Xerxes' decree.

The king who preceded Xerxes on the Persian—modern-day Iran—throne was Darius.[4] He ruled when Daniel and his Hebrew friends were taken from their homeland and exiled to Persia.

Darius had proclaimed an unchangeable law that anyone praying to another god or person other than himself would be thrown into the lions' den.

Far from his country, Daniel had resolved to pray three times a day to the true God of Israel. When Daniel heard of the king's edict, he went home, knelt at an open window facing Jerusalem, and prayed.

Although the king admired Daniel and had great plans for his future in Persia, Darius, the most powerful man on earth, could not rescind his own law.

"The decree stands," Darius declared, "in accordance with the law of the Medes and Persians, which cannot be repealed" (Daniel 6:12).

---

4. Sometimes Darius is referred to as Cyrus. This is the same person.

Can You Imagine?

Wednesday

Her skin was smooth, her features symmetrical and flawless. Vashti was a vision. Yet her dark eyes flashed a confidence that trumped all her beauty. Vashti knew who she was, and she would not let her husband—even though he could have had her executed—disregard her dignity. She would not be his shimmering, sensuous toy. So the queen refused, embarrassing the king in front of his subjects. Can you imagine the virtue and courageous confidence required to take this kind of risk?

To Xerxes, Vashti was a decoration, not a friend or a partner he loved. He did not see her as a person, and he misjudged the resolve of her soul.

Healthy relationships are not made up of two people who are together because of what the other person does for their ego or public image. "You complete me" may be a spine-tingling thing for two infatuated lovers to say to each other, but it's no way to build a strong foundation for your marriage.

One day, Jesus summarized the importance of unselfish love in just a few words. "Love your neighbor as yourself," He said.[5]

Mutual respect is a nonnegotiable in every loving relationship. Especially marriage. Even though Vashti was beautiful and had everything her culture afforded her, she did not have what every married person wants ... a spouse who loves unselfishly.

In your marriage, you want someone who thinks about your interests and what pleases you. And your spouse needs the same. Mutual respect loves the other person in the way he or she needs to be loved. Only with God's help can we begin to set aside our wants and love the other person well.

---

5. See Matthew 19:19.

From God's Word ...

"By the grace given me I say to every one of you: Do not think of yourself more highly than you ought, but rather think of yourself with sober judgment, in accordance with the faith God has distributed to each of you."

ROMANS 12:3

Their Legacy in Scripture

Thursday

1. **"When King Xerxes was in high spirits from wine, he commanded the seven eunuchs who served him ... to bring before him Queen Vashti ... for she was lovely to look at. But ... Queen Vashti refused to come"** (ESTHER 1:10–12).

   The queen felt dishonored by her husband's request. What was the purpose for summoning Vashti and why did she refuse? When does your spouse feel disrespected by your behavior? What is your attitude when your spouse confronts you?

2. **"Let the message of Christ dwell among you richly as you teach and admonish one another with all wisdom through psalms, hymns, and songs from the Spirit, singing to God with gratitude in your hearts"** (COLOSSIANS 3:16).

   As a follower of Christ, you carry with you the dignity of someone who is loved by the Creator. Marriage partners are truth tellers and each other's teachers and coaches. What has your spouse taught you? This verse also challenges you to admonish or correct one another. When have you benefited from your spouse's warning?

3. **"Even if you should suffer for what is right, you are blessed"** (1 PETER 3:14).

   Vashti was more concerned about doing the right thing than retaining her wealth and position. It is possible that if you stand for God against evil, you may suffer loss, slander, and isolation. When have you acted properly and been unfairly tested? According to this verse, what is God's promise to you and your spouse for doing right?

Their Legacy of Prayer

Friday

Reflect On: Esther 1

Praise God: For His unlimited, all-powerful ability to take authority over every dominion, ruler, and realm.

Offer Thanks: That God has provided all the resources you need for godly living, and that He offers His presence to be with you in the midst of your weakness.

Confess: That you often fear the future and do not believe God can handle your difficulties. That your heart is more devoted to temporal things than to pleasing God.

Ask God: To give you the desire to put Him first. To inform your conscience and instruct your behavior in ways that please Him.

Listen: "My children, fill your thoughts with My Word. Whatever is good and pure and lovely will allow you to behold My beauty and character. The things of this world are passing, but I am eternal. Devote yourself to My truth, and I will give you eternal riches that will never fade."

Pray: *Father in heaven, our hearts' desire is to worship You forever. We want to love You more than anything else, but too often we devote ourselves to unimportant things. Give us strength and courage to do what is right. Nothing compares to the promise and hope we have in You. Help us to honor You in the way we treat each other. Amen.*

34

God's Timing

Xerxes and Esther

Meaning of Names:	*Xerxes* means "the lion king," "prince," "head," or "chief." *Esther* means "star."
Their Character:	He was at times naive but had a soft spot for his Hebrew bride. She was willing to risk her life for the survival of her people.
Their Challenge:	A decree was issued that would annihilate the Hebrews.
Their Outcome:	Esther's bold actions led to the deliverance of the Jews and an elevation of status for Esther's cousin Mordecai.
Key Scripture:	Esther 2–10

Their Story

Monday

Esther was filled with trepidation and resolve as she glided along the polished hallways of the palace toward the king's inner court where her husband, Xerxes, sat on his throne.

Thirty days had passed since she had worn her royal robes. Although she was the queen of Persia, she wondered if the king's displeasure was the reason she had not been summoned.

This meeting was far too important for Esther to be distracted by anything. She had spent the last three days fasting and praying about how to approach her husband, but she did not know how he would respond. Her execution was a possibility. Esther's solemn vow—"if I perish, I perish"—was irrepressible in her thoughts as she anticipated her unscheduled and uninvited audience with the king.

Only a few steps from the open door of the throne room where her husband was sitting, Queen Esther closed her eyes and took a deep breath. Her mind swept over the events that had led to this improbable moment.

Esther's parents had died years earlier, and she was raised by her older cousin, Mordecai, who had been like a loving father to her. Her welfare was his greatest concern, and he fussed over the orphan who had come under his charge.

One day, news circulated throughout the realm that King Xerxes would be holding a beauty pageant to fill the vacancy left by the deposed Queen Vashti. Hundreds of young candidates were rounded up to be taken to the citadel. Esther's elegance had not gone unnoticed, and she was among those chosen to move to the next round.

Mordecai had explained the significance of the king's plan to young Esther. He told her that she and other maidens would be taken to the king's harem to receive extensive beauty treatments. Then, by appointment, each girl would be expected to spend a night with the king, leaving his quarters the next morning. King Xerxes would select the woman who most pleased him to be his new wife and queen.

Mordecai warned Esther not to reveal her nationality or family background when she arrived at the court, because her people, the Jews, had once been despised captives in Persia.

Esther was brought to the king's palace along with many other young girls. Hegai, who was responsible for the harem, was so impressed with Esther that he favored her above the others. He ordered a special menu for her, provided her with her beauty treatments, and gave her seven female attendants from the king's palace and the most luxurious living quarters available.

When it was Esther's turn to go to the king, she dressed in regal simplicity, perfectly complementing her natural features and gentle manner.

The king was so delighted with Esther that he set a royal crown on her head and declared her queen instead of Vashti.

To celebrate the occasion, he gave a great banquet—Esther's banquet—for all his nobles and officials. Proclaiming a holiday throughout the provinces, he lowered the taxes and gave generous gifts to everyone.

Queen Esther accepted her new role with grace and dignity and gave Xerxes no reason to be displeased with her. He exulted in her simplicity of spirit and stunning good looks.

However, Xerxes' loyalty to his queen was about to be tested.

The nation's second-highest-ranking official, Haman, hated the Hebrews and had devised a scheme to have them exterminated. Not knowing that his noble queen was a Jew, Xerxes naively consented. The date for the carnage was set for eleven months from that day.

When Esther's cousin Mordecai heard the gruesome news, he tore his clothing, put on sackcloth, and sat down in the dirt to mourn. Word reached Esther that Mordecai was grieving, so she dispatched a servant to find out the reason. Mordecai sent the messenger back to Esther with a copy of the king's edict, a death sentence pronounced on every Jew in the land.

Mordecai urged Esther to seek the king's mercy. But she sent a reply to Mordecai that no one, including the queen, could approach the king without first being invited into his presence.

Mordecai was undaunted. He sent another message to Esther. "Do not think that because you are in the king's house you alone of all the Jews will escape," Mordecai said. "If you remain silent at this time, relief and deliverance for the Jews will arise from another place, but you and your father's family will perish. And who knows but that you have come to your royal position for such a time as this?"[1]

Esther's determination was ignited.

"Go, gather together all the Jews who are in Susa, and fast for me," she told the messenger. "Do not eat or drink for three days, night or day. I and my attendants will fast as you do. When this is done, I will go to the king, even though it is against the law. And if I perish, I perish."

And now Esther stood just outside the king's hall, uninvited, unwarranted, unannounced—a perilous breach of Persian law. She stepped into the doorway of the interior court where her husband could see her. A herald's voice pierced the air. The startled king looked up and gazed at her exquisite beauty and simple radiance,

---

1. Esther 4:13–14.

and he stood to receive her. He reached for his scepter and extended it to her, inviting his queen to approach.

The danger had passed. She had pleased the king.

Esther then requested the honor of her husband's presence at a special banquet she would prepare. Xerxes agreed to attend. In God's providence, Esther's plan saved the Jews.

Their Life and Times

Tuesday

Purim

The Jewish holiday that honors the triumph of Queen Esther is called Purim.[2] It marks the miraculous rescue of the Jews living in Persia during the reign of Xerxes. The road to that celebration, however, goes back hundreds of years before Esther.

It all began in Israel's infancy when the nation was under the leadership of Moses in the Sinai desert. Speaking through Moses, God warned the disobedient Hebrews, "If you will not listen to me and carry out all these commands, and if you reject my decrees and abhor my laws and fail to carry out all my commands and so violate my covenant, then I will do this to you: ... I will scatter you among the nations and will draw out my sword and pursue you. Your land will be laid waste, and your cities will lie in ruins" (Leviticus 26:14–16, 33).

God began to carry out this sentence against Israel in 722 BC when King Sargon II of Assyria conquered the ten tribes of northern Israel and exiled them to "the towns of the Medes" (2 Kings 17:6). More than a century later, the Southern Kingdom experienced God's punishment as the Babylonian emperor Nebuchadnezzar carried the people into exile in three separate deportations (597 BC, 586 BC, 581 BC).[3]

The exiled Jews remained under Babylonian control until that

---

2. The word *Purim* actually refers to casting lots, which Haman did to determine the specific day when the Jews living in Persia would be exterminated.

3. See 2 Kings 25:11; Jeremiah 52:28–30.

empire was overthrown by the Medo-Persian Empire (539 BC).[4] At that time, Cyrus, king of Persia, gave the Jews permission to return to Jerusalem, and nearly 50,000 of them returned to their homeland.[5] However, because thousands of exiled Hebrews had lived in Persia for seventy years and had become acclimated to life there, many more decided to remain in pagan territory. The Jews who stayed included Mordecai and Esther.

Xerxes unknowingly chose a Jewish maiden as his queen after Queen Vashti was deposed. But Xerxes' chief adviser, Haman, hated the Jews. Because Haman was second in command, protocol required all people to bow to him. However, Mordecai refused to acknowledge Haman as lord over his people and would not bow to him.

Mordecai's insolence so infuriated Haman that he demanded Mordecai's execution and the extermination of the entire Jewish race. King Xerxes approved, giving Haman his signet ring and the authority to carry out the treachery. In April 474 BC—the fifth year of Queen Esther's reign—Haman issued an edict stating that eleven months later, March 473 BC, all the Jews of the empire were to be destroyed.[6]

To decide on a date, Haman cast a *pur*, or lot. Lots were small stones with designs carved or painted on them that were tossed or rolled like modern dice. Once the day was determined, the law was written. Couriers riding the swiftest horses from the royal stables carried Haman's death decree throughout the 127 provinces of the empire. Within two weeks the edict reached villages fifteen hundred miles away.

Esther was shrewd by withholding her complaints or requests until after she had honored her husband with special meals. When she prepared a banquet for Haman and Xerxes, she secured the king's approval for her plan. The king gave her exactly what she requested, and a new directive was issued on June 25, 474 BC, two months and ten days after Haman's original mandate. Eight months later, March 7, 473 BC, the Jews were given "the right to assemble and protect themselves; to destroy, kill and annihilate the armed men of any

---

4. See Daniel 5:30.
5. See Ezra 1:1–4; 2:64.
6. See Esther 3:8–9.

nationality or province who might attack them and their women and children" (Esther 8:11).

The Jewish people were victorious, and Xerxes elevated Mordecai to a place of high honor. Letters were sent from the king to the Jews of the empire, declaring, "These days should be remembered and observed in every generation by every family, and in every province and in every city. And these days of Purim [plural of *pur*] should never fail to be celebrated by the Jews — nor should the memory of these days die out among their descendants" (Esther 9:28).

Purim was to be commemorated on the 14th of Adar (March) by Jews living in the villages, and on the 15th by city dwellers. The joyous observance was to be characterized by feasting and the exchanging of presents.[7]

Purim is one of two festivals not included in Mosaic law. Hanukkah, or the Festival of Lights, is the other.

Can You Imagine?

Wednesday

The story of this biblical couple is filled with graphic contrasts.
Xerxes, who makes no claim to know or believe in the God of the Hebrews, is the raucous and philandering king of a vast empire. When he meets Esther, she is a virgin.

Xerxes is surrounded by indescribable opulence and luxury. Esther is an orphan being raised by her uncle.

Xerxes is a man of indulgence, impulse, and great passion. Esther is a humble worshiper of Yahweh.

Xerxes lives in a royal bubble, protected from uninvited visitors and isolated from unplanned conversation. Esther is a woman at the mercy of her husband's station.

Even for the most prepared brides whose grooms are of like faith and character, meaningful conversation in marriage is a challenge. Can you imagine what Esther faced?

When it came time for a life-and-death discussion with her hus-

---

7. See Esther 9:19.

band, how was Esther successful in helping her husband understand? What melted these extremes and opened his heart? The Bible tells us that because she knew the critical importance of this encounter with Xerxes, Esther fasted and prayed. Before she approached her husband, she approached God.

For three days, instead of eating or drinking, she bowed before the Lord and pleaded for His mercy. And wisdom. We don't know how many of the details she may have shared with her friends, but we know that Esther also invited them to join her. She even called for a season of prayer among the entire Hebrew population living in Persia.

Then as Esther entered into the conversation with her husband, she was polite, gentle, gracious, and humble. She didn't blame; she didn't whine or complain. Because she had thought it through, she chose not to disclose her entire request but to use her opening conversation to invite her husband to talk about the details later, over dinner.

The Lord gave Queen Esther great discernment when she talked to her spouse. He can do the same for you, if you seek His guidance.

From God's Word . . .

"Love must be sincere. Hate what is evil; cling to what is good. Be devoted to one another in love. Honor one another above yourselves."

ROMANS 12:9–10

Their Legacy in Scripture

Thursday

1. "'If I perish, I perish'" (ESTHER 4:16).

Every relationship is challenged by the hard conversations. But relationships are often hurt, not by what *is* said, but by what is *not* said. Esther had to tell her husband she was a Jew. Your life may not be in danger if you dare to initiate a difficult conversation with your husband, but the strength of your relationship may depend on it. What difficult conversation topic have you been avoiding with your spouse? What do you need to reveal in order to move to a deeper level of intimacy?

2. "May these words of my mouth and this meditation of my heart be pleasing in your sight, LORD, my Rock and my Redeemer" (PSALM 19:14).

Before speaking to her husband, Esther not only took time to think about what she would say; she also carefully prepared her heart.[8] What did she do to get ready for this important conversation? What can you learn from Esther?

3. "Let us then approach God's throne of grace with confidence, so that we may receive mercy and find grace to help us in our time of need" (HEBREWS 4:16).

Esther had spent three days before the heavenly throne of God before she approached the earthly throne of King Xerxes. She relied on God's providence more than the king's power. When you and your spouse face a crisis, what is typically your first response? Do you go to the throne or the phone? What confidence do you have that Jesus is able to help you? When have you experienced God's mercy and grace, perfectly timed, when you needed resources or faced difficulties?

---

8. See Esther 4:15–16.

Their Legacy of Prayer

Friday

Reflect On: Esther 3–5

Praise God: For His perfect timing and His ability to work mightily to accomplish His will.

Offer Thanks: That God is orchestrating events and providing on your behalf when difficult situations arise, and that He has given you the gift of faith to walk forward with confidence in His mercy.

Confess: That you often do not trust God's timing, and that you tend to be consumed by a fear that drives you to turn to people or to some other power outside of His provision.

Ask God: To give you discernment, hope, and confidence in His plan and His timing. For His strength and ability to rescue you from the forces that would destroy your marriage.

Listen: "Dear children, I am a very present help in time of trouble and have made all the resources of heaven available to you. Come boldly into My presence, and I will give you grace and mercy and all you need. Do not worry about anything. Pray about everything. You are Mine, and I will never forsake you."

Pray: *Father in heaven, we are weak and often fearful, but You are strong and have settled the future. You are the Creator and Ruler of all things. We need Your help to trust Your Word and rely on Your promises. Please equip us to face every challenge in our marriage with prayer, grace, and courage as we put our hope in You. Thank You for Your amazing plan and perfect timing. Amen.*

Unsound Advice

Haman and Zeresh

Meaning of Names:	*Haman* means "magnificent" or "illustrious." *Zeresh* means "gold," "splendor," or "dispersed inheritance."
Their Character:	He was arrogant, cruel, manipulative, and full of revenge. She was cunning, conceited, wicked, and self-centered.
Their Challenge:	Haman wanted to destroy the Jewish people in Persia, but didn't realize that Persia's queen was a Jew. Zeresh gave Haman bad advice.
Their Outcome:	When Haman's wickedness was revealed to the king, he was hanged and their ten sons put to death. The Jewish people were saved.
Key Scripture:	Esther 3–9

Their Story

Monday

Haman found in Zeresh his perfect match. She was tenacious, cynical, and ruthless. Driven by bigotry and selfish ambition, they indulged the same thirst for power.

The couple boasted ten sons, a badge of honor and indisputable evidence that Baal, the god of fertility and Baga, the god of prosperity and wealth, had favored them above all others. At night Haman and Zeresh lay awake in animated conversation, reveling in fantasies of the next commendation King Xerxes would confer on Haman.

They dreamed of prestige and power in Persia. Intoxicated with the possibilities of rising in rank, they slept soundly.

Then the day came when Haman and Zeresh's dream was fulfilled. Xerxes promoted Haman to prime minister, making him the most powerful official in the empire next to the king himself. All the royal officials were commanded to bow before Haman in deep reverence when he passed by.

Wine flowed freely in their home that night as Haman and Zeresh celebrated with their sons. Haman's sons raised their goblets, toasting their father's new royalty. They were all drunk on wine and apparent success.

It was an exhilarating time for the couple postured at the heights of Persian power. Every man and woman in the realm was required to kneel in Haman's presence. Happy and in high spirits, Haman strode daily to the palace, flaunting his position and expecting humble gestures from all the commoners he passed along the way. But one stubborn holdout rankled Haman's pride. Mordecai the Jew neither feared nor knelt. Haman's lieutenants inquired, "Are you going to tolerate this Jew?"[1]

Furious and embarrassed, Haman resolved to destroy Mordecai. Driven further by his deep ethnic hatred, Haman decided to exterminate all the Hebrews. He gathered his subordinates, and they cast a lot (called the *pur*) to select a date for the holocaust.

Needing permission for the extermination, Haman went to King Xerxes and proposed, "There is a certain people dispersed among the peoples in all the provinces of your kingdom who keep themselves separate. Their customs are different from those of all other people, and they do not obey the king's laws; it is not in the king's best interest to tolerate them. If it pleases the king, let a decree be issued to destroy them."

Xerxes said, "Do with the people as you please."[2]

The lot had been cast. The date had been set. In exactly eleven months there would be no more Jews in Persia.

Couriers on horseback were dispatched throughout the land to pronounce the edict.

That night over dinner with his wife and friends, Haman bragged

---

1. See Esther 3:4.
2. Esther 3:11.

about his wealth, his many children, and promotions the king had given him. He boasted that Xerxes had elevated him above the other nobles and officials. "And that's not all," Haman added. "Queen Esther has invited only me and the king to the banquet she prepared for us. And tomorrow we are invited again."

"But yet," he added, "all this is nothing as long as I see that Jew Mordecai sitting at the king's gate, refusing to kneel before me."

Not willing to have her access to power threatened by a Jew, Zeresh spoke up. "Well," she said, "set up a seventy-five-foot-high pole, and in the morning, ask the king to have Mordecai impaled on it. When this is done, you can go to the banquet with the king and enjoy yourself."

The suggestion pleased Haman, and he ordered the pole to be set up.[3]

That very night, King Xerxes could not sleep and requested that the record book of his reign be brought to him. As he read, the king discovered that five years earlier, a man named Mordecai had exposed an assassination plot. Because of this man's courage, the conspiracy had been foiled.

Calling his attendants the next morning, the king asked, "What honor and recognition has Mordecai received for this?"

"Nothing has been done for him."

Pondering how he could reward Mordecai, Xerxes sought counsel from his senior adviser who had just arrived at the palace. The king asked Haman, "What should be done for the man the king delights to honor?"[4]

Haman thought to himself, *Who is there that the king would rather honor than me?*

Imagining that the tribute was about him, Haman suggested a parade, complete with the king's royal robes and horses and a noble prince proclaiming, "This is what is done for the man the king delights to honor!"

Pleased with Haman's counsel, the king commanded, "Go at once. Get the robe and the horse and do just as you have suggested for Mordecai the Jew." Shocked and humiliated, Haman obeyed,

---

3. See Esther 5:14.
4. Esther 6:6.

leading the royal parade and escorting Mordecai through the streets of Susa, shouting accolades for the man he detested.[5]

After the procession, Mordecai returned to his assignment at the king's gate. But Haman hurried home, utterly humiliated, and told Zeresh and all his friends everything that had happened.

Seeking sympathy, Haman discovered that Zeresh had no capacity for it. A cynic with a dead soul, Zeresh pronounced her husband's demise. "Since Mordecai, before whom your downfall has started, is of Jewish origin, you cannot stand against him—you will surely come to ruin!"[6]

Just then the king's officials came to escort Haman to Esther's second banquet. At the feast, Esther disclosed to Xerxes that someone was planning to murder her and slaughter her people. "Who is he? Where is he—the man who has dared to do such a thing?" the king shouted.[7]

Esther unmasked her adversary. Pointing to Haman, she replied, "The enemy is this vile Haman!"

Xerxes stood to his feet and ordered Haman's execution. As soon as the words left the king's mouth, his troops covered Haman's terrified face and whisked him away. Zeresh watched in horror as her husband died on the pole he had built for Mordecai.

A counteredict was then issued, and on the appointed day, the Jews were triumphant, killing their enemies, including Haman's ten sons.

There would be no legacy for Haman and Zeresh.

---

5. See Esther 6:11.
6. Esther 6:13.
7. Esther 7:5.

Their Life and Times

Tuesday

The Story behind Mordecai's Defiance and Haman's Hatred

Even for an evil man like Haman—and his wife, Zeresh—it seems extreme to destroy an entire race of people based on the absence of decorum from just one man. After all, Mordecai simply refused to kneel before Haman. Did he really consider the extermination of the Jewish people as fair retribution? Or was there more to the story?

About a thousand years before the time described in the book of Esther (483–473 BC), Israel was freed from slavery in Egypt. As the Hebrews wandered through the Sinai desert, they came to the territory occupied by the Amalekites, a people descended from Amalek, a grandson of Esau.[8]

While the Israelites were camped at Rephidim, "the Amalekites came and attacked the Israelites" (Exodus 17:8). What ensued was a daylong battle between the two nations, with Joshua leading Israel to victory. However, this one victory wasn't severe enough punishment for the Amalekites. God's justice would not overlook the unprovoked attack on His people. The Lord said to Moses, "Write this on a scroll as something to be remembered and make sure that Joshua hears it, because I will completely blot out the name of Amalek from under heaven" (Exodus 17:14).

Despite the somber vow, God did not immediately fulfill it, giving the Amalekites time to repent of their behavior. The Lord had given them more than four hundred years to change their ways and turn from their sin.

In 1030 BC, when Saul was the king of Israel, God sent him on a mission. Speaking through the prophet Samuel, God told Saul, "This is what the LORD Almighty says: 'I will punish the Amalekites for what they did to Israel when they waylaid them as they came up from Egypt. Now go, attack the Amalekites and totally destroy all that belongs to them. Do not spare them; put to death men and

---

8. See Genesis 36:12.

women, children and infants, cattle and sheep, camels and donkeys'"
(1 Samuel 15:2–3).

God's command was to eliminate the Amalekites, including Agag,
their king.

But Saul disobeyed. After leading his troops to a decisive victory,
he spared what God had told him to destroy. "[Saul] took Agag king
of the Amalekites alive ... Saul and the army spared Agag and the best
of the sheep and cattle, the fat calves and lambs ...These they were
unwilling to destroy completely" (1 Samuel 15:8–9).

This act of defiance by Saul eventually cost him the kingdom.
After admonishing the wayward monarch, Samuel took it upon himself to strike Agag down with the sword, not a typical assignment for
a prophet (1 Samuel 15:33).

This episode created a blood feud between the descendants of
Saul and those of Agag that culminated 550 years later in Persia.
Mordecai was a direct descendant of Saul, the man appointed to kill
Agag.

Haman is referred to as "the Agagite" (Esther 3:1). He and his ten
sons were among the remnant of the Amalekites.

There is no doubt that Mordecai and Haman knew each other's
pedigree. To Mordecai, Haman was the wicked offspring of a wicked
king whose people should have vanished long ago. No wonder Mordecai refused to kneel before him.

To Haman, Mordecai was the descendant of the king who exterminated most of his people. Haman had carried a lifelong hatred for
the Jews, and Mordecai's defiance further fueled his disdain. Haman's
high rank allowed him access to the king and the endorsement
needed for a decree that all Jews in Persia be killed.

Haman would finally have his revenge.

Can You Imagine?

Wednesday

"How was your day at the palace, honey?" Haman may have heard this question each time he finished his workday and arrived at home. Zeresh wanted to know what was happening with her husband's career so she could manipulate the outcome for her own benefit. She offered her unwise counsel, feeding Haman's ego and unholy passions.

Can you imagine the power of a wife's words? They can either lead a man to indulge his pride or stop him in his tracks and avert evil.

A spouse who studies God's Word will have discernment. Godly wisdom gives perspective and arrests unhealthy attitudes, such as the desire for power and prestige. Zeresh gave bad advice to her husband. You may understand the temptation.

"Yes, take that promotion. Even though it will mean extra hours, we could use a few more dollars around here."

"He said *that* to you? Who does he think he is? You should give him a piece of your mind."

As part of a covenant relationship with your spouse, you have the privilege of being a personal counselor. You can listen to his hopes and dreams. You can embrace her longings. And you can speak the truth in love.

In your marriage, unlike any other relationship, you have the freedom to be the voice of truth and a godly influence. You can understand his weaknesses and inspire righteousness. You can pray for her and encourage contentment and peace.

Haman and Zeresh did none of these things for each other. And it cost them everything.

From God's Word . . .

"My mouth will speak words of wisdom; the meditation of my heart will give you understanding."

PSALM 49:3

Their Legacy in Scripture

Thursday

1. **"Live in harmony with one another. Do not be proud, but be willing to associate with people of low position. Do not be conceited"** (ROMANS 12:16).

   Zeresh and Haman fed each other's pride and spirit of revenge, which led to their downfall. They thought they were better than other people. According to this verse, how does God want us to treat everyone, including our spouse?

2. **"'My mouth would encourage you; comfort from my lips would bring you relief'"** (JOB 16:5).

   Your words—and your facial expressions—are powerful in your marriage. Why is it sometimes difficult to speak supportive words and smile at your spouse? When you ask God to change your attitude, He gives you the desire and power to change. What attitudes do you need to cultivate in order to encourage your spouse?

3. **"Be wise in the way you act toward outsiders; make the most of every opportunity. Let your conversation be always full of grace, seasoned with salt, so that you may know how to answer everyone"** (COLOSSIANS 4:5–6).

   Your words are the greatest witness of your walk with Jesus. How do you "speak" Christ to your husband, your family, your friends, or unbelievers?

Their Legacy of Prayer

Friday

Reflect On: Esther 6–7

Praise God: For His justice and His sovereignty over all people and circumstances.

Offer Thanks: That vengeance belongs to God and that He will make all things right in His perfect time. For His Word, which instructs in wisdom and righteousness.

Confess: The dangerous pride that leads you to selfishly evaluate situations with impure motives. Any unwholesome words —words of criticism or revenge spoken in anger—that do not build up others.

Ask God: To fill your heart and will with His Spirit of love and forgiveness and show you how to use your words for good at all times, and to give you the courage to respond correctly in all circumstances, even when others do you harm.

Listen: "My children, I know everything that is unfair and unjust. I see your heart. It pleases Me when you desire to do what is right in My eyes. When people slander or hurt you, do not respond with angry and hostile words. I will strengthen you and give you discernment to speak truth and words of peace. Your reaction to injustice will show others the power of My Spirit."

Pray: *Father in heaven, within the kingdom of Your might, all is just and right. Help us trust in Your ability to overturn evil plans and bring about salvation for others. We want our motives to be pure and good. When we have been hurt, we want to respond in a way that pleases You. Teach us to speak only words that build up, encourage, and enlighten. Amen.*

Where Is God When It Hurts?

Job and Wife

Meaning of Names: Job means "persecuted," "hated," or "afflicted." The name of Job's wife is not given in the Bible.

Their Character: He was a respected leader and the most righteous man on the earth. He clung to his faith despite personal tragedy. She was the loyal wife of a godly man, and she nurtured her close-knit family. When calamity struck, she became embittered.

Their Challenge: They suffered the devastating loss of everything they had, including their ten children. Job's wife tempted him to despair and curse God.

Their Outcome: God revealed His majesty to Job and his wife and restored their fortune. God also gave them ten more children.

Key Scripture: Job 1–2, 42

Their Story

Monday

Job was sitting in his spacious home when suddenly a servant came running into the room. "Master," he sputtered, "traveling merchants invaded your land and have carried off the oxen and donkeys and killed your servants."

Job stood. His face ashen, his heart ambushed by the news.

While he was trying to picture the carnage in his mind, another messenger rushed in. "A fire from heaven has killed your sheep and servants." The words staggered Job.

"Fire?" Job drew in a breath. "From heaven?"

But no sooner had this messenger spoken when another hurried in bearing more terrible news. "Raiding parties of savage Chaldeans have stolen all three thousand of your camels and killed your servants."

Dazed by the magnitude of the catastrophe, Job slumped into a chair, blinking away tears. "Chaldeans? I don't know any Chaldeans."

Then one more traumatized messenger barged into Job's home. The servant was hysterical. "All ten of your children are dead! They perished together in the house where they were feasting. It collapsed under the force of a fierce desert wind."

With no strength left, Job leaned forward, burying his face in his hands. "My children," he cried out. "My children … gone? How can this be?"

He rose from his chair. Tearing his robes, he called for a servant to bring a razor, and then he shaved his head.

Upon hearing the noise, Job's wife entered the commotion. When she was told all that had happened, she stood speechless. As she gazed at her bald husband, her legs gave way.

Job also fell to his knees. Lifting his hands toward heaven, he trembled. "Naked I came from my mother's womb, and naked I will depart. The LORD gave and the LORD has taken away; may the name of the LORD be praised."[1]

His wife watched the good man she knew so well grieve with anguished heaves. In an act of submission to the Creator, Job lowered his face to the ground. He had no answers, but Job did not charge God with wrongdoing.

After enduring many nights of sleepless torment, he awakened one morning with his body throbbing. Burning lesions and boils covered him from the soles of his feet to the crown of his head. Job doubled up in pain. Stumbling to the ash heaps outside the city reserved for lepers, the once prominent and respected man retrieved a piece of broken pottery and began scraping himself.

Setting aside her own dignity, his wife followed her husband.

---

1. Job 1:21.

Unable to cope with her loss or suppress her anger against the injustice of the Almighty, cynicism bubbled out of her mouth. "Are you still maintaining your integrity?" she taunted. "Curse God and die!"

Woefully, Job looked up at his despondent wife. Tears welled in his eyes. The woman who had borne him ten children—the beloved wife of his youth—had turned against God. With her children gone, her faith had buckled.

From the dust heap, Job's resolve came to full stature, and he responded, "You are talking like a foolish woman. Shall we accept good from God, and not trouble?"[2]

Unable to convince Job to give in to self-pity and despair, the woman looked down at her husband and let the tears flow. They stared at each other for a few silent moments. Job's wife began to turn away, stopped, reconsidered, and turned back.

"My children are all dead."

Her words hung in the air. Leaving the man she loved sitting in the city dump, Job's wife returned to their home.

News of the calamity spread throughout the region. Not knowing what to say and paralyzed with confusion, townspeople kept their distance. But three of Job's friends came to visit.

When they saw the person who at one time had been the most admired man in their community, they broke down and wept. For seven days, these three sat quietly with their friend. No one said anything. The right words were impossible to find. Mercifully, they chose not to speak. Job was strangely heartened by their presence.

Finally, he spoke. "Why did I not perish at birth, and die as I came from the womb?"

The three men were silent no longer. Reaching for something —anything—that might explain the unexplainable tragedy that had fallen on Job, they delivered shallow counsel to their hurting friend.

"If I were you," one of them naively announced, "I would appeal to God."

The notion was insulting. All of his life Job had sought the Lord and had prayed diligently for his wife and children. And he had continued to cry out to God after receiving the news of the staggering atrocities.

---

2. Job 2:10.

Back and forth went the conversations with his friends. They pried into Job's personal life. He tried to defend himself. They accused. He pushed back. Finally Job had had enough. "You are miserable comforters, all of you!" he snapped. "Will your long-winded speeches never end?"[3]

Steeped in frustration and confusion, Job brought his case before God. Concluding his lament, Job finally resigned himself to divine providence. "God stands alone, and who can oppose him? He does whatever he pleases ... That is why I am terrified before him; when I think of all this, I fear him. The fear of the Lord—that is wisdom."[4]

Then God spoke. He hammered Job with questions. "Where were you when I laid the earth's foundation? Tell me, if you understand. Who marked off its dimensions? Surely you know! Who stretched a measuring line across it?"[5]

God's words halted Job. "I am unworthy," the depleted man said. "How can I reply to you? I put my hand over my mouth. I spoke once, but I have no answer—twice, but I will say no more ... My ears had heard of you but now my eyes have seen you."[6]

When Job and his wife finally surrendered to God's unmistakable sovereignty and greatness, their healing began. Their lives were restored. God blessed their marriage with ten more children. Their property and possessions were replenished ... twofold.

Contemplating their blessings once again after all they had been through, Job gently whispered to his wife, "May the name of the Lord be praised."

---

3. See Job 16:2–3.
4. See Job 23:13, 15.
5. Job 38:4–5.
6. See Job 40:4–5; 42:5.

Their Life and Times

Tuesday

Why Job Suffered

Although the book of Job is found in the Bible right after Esther, the events described in Job probably took place during the patriarchal period, hundreds of years earlier. Its placement connects it to the "wisdom literature," which also includes Psalms, Proverbs, Ecclesiastes, and Song of Songs.

Like other wisdom literature, the purpose of the book of Job is not primarily historical. Instead, Job unpacks the deep emotion — the despair and the ecstasy — of walking with the Sovereign God. The prominent theme in the story of Job highlights God's involvement in human suffering.

Ironically, throughout the horrific trials they endured, Job and his wife did not know that suffering was the result of a wager between God and Satan.

Having just finished a tour of the earth and its people, Satan and his angels entered the Lord's presence to report their findings. Their purpose was to identify possible righteous targets they could attack.

God said to Satan, "Have you considered my servant Job? There is no one on earth like him; he is blameless and upright, a man who fears God and shuns evil" (Job 1:8).

"Of course he's a righteous man," Satan sneered. "Look at all the things You've given him. You have put a hedge of protection around him, his household, and everything he owns. Job would be a fool to not honor You. Take his stuff away and see what he does. Stretch out Your hand and strike everything he has, and he will surely curse You to Your face."

So God gave Satan permission to persecute Job. "Very well, then," God said. "Everything he has is in your power, but on the man himself do not lay a finger" (Job 1:12).

Within a short time, four different messengers brought Job tragic news. The last one reported that all ten of his children were dead. But Job did not curse God. Satan was wrong.

Then God and Satan talk again and the adversary presses further. "You have only touched the man's possessions," Satan says. "But now stretch out your hand and strike his flesh and bones, and he will surely curse you to your face" (Job 2:5).

So God removed the hedge of protection and Satan was granted permission to afflict Job's body. Still Job remained faithful, even though his wife demanded that he profane God. "Job did not sin in what he said" (Job 2:10).

The story of Job reveals the truth that God's ways are beyond our understanding.

Where does this leave Job? The few times he is allowed to speak, he defends his righteousness and blames the Lord for his situation. "The arrows of the Almighty are in me, my spirit drinks in their poison," Job wails. "God's terrors are marshaled against me" (Job 6:4).

After a long silence, God finally speaks. "Then the LORD spoke to Job out of the storm ... Who is this that obscures my plans with words without knowledge? Brace yourself like a man; I will question you, and you shall answer me" (Job 38:1–3). Job trembles at the awesomeness of God and is humbled.

Job and his wife learn that no one is exempt from suffering—but no matter how great the trial, the presence of the peace of God is greater still. God never explained to Job why he had suffered. Job's friends presumed it was for punishment. Job thought God wanted to destroy him. Instead, Job suffered in order to reveal the very nature of the Creator—His majesty, glory, and sovereignty—and to shape Job's capacity to trust Him more fully.

Can You Imagine?

Wednesday

In a matter of a few moments, Job's servants, livestock, and children are gone—destroyed, stolen, or killed. We read how Job dealt with this horrific tragedy. But we hear nothing from his wife. Then Job's body is assaulted. Lesions cover him from the top of his shaved head to the soles of his feet. At this point, Job's wife enters the story. She has seen enough.

Can you imagine how she must have felt as she endured all these catastrophes? It wasn't only her husband who had suffered loss. She, too, shared in the tragedy. "Are you still maintaining your integrity, Job?" she fumes. "Curse God and die!"

Job's wife's outburst is severe ... and understandable. But her words are misguided. At the very moment when Job's wife has an opportunity to support and encourage her husband, she mocks him and blasphemes God's name.

God's grand design is not always clear to us. Whatever God's providence may bring to you and your spouse, you can encourage each other by accepting the circumstances and acknowledging that God is in control. By directing your minds to trust God's mercy and goodness, you can glorify Him in times of suffering.

From God's Word ...

From the depths of despair and fear, David wrote these words:

"[God] has not despised or scorned the suffering of the afflicted one; he has not hidden his face from him but has listened to his cry for help."

PSALM 22:24

Their Legacy in Scripture
Thursday

1. **"Are you still maintaining your integrity? Curse God and die!"** (JOB 2:9).

   Over the centuries, Job's wife has been criticized for speaking these words to her suffering husband. But many of us can empathize with her situation and the way she expressed herself. What do you think she should have said? When have you offered words to your spouse that were misguided or not helpful? What could you have said instead?

2. **"Since we have been justified through faith, we have peace with God through our Lord Jesus Christ, through whom we have gained access by faith into this grace in which we now stand. And we boast in the hope of the glory of God. Not only so, but we also glory in our sufferings, because we know that suffering produces perseverance; perseverance, character; and character, hope"** (ROMANS 5:1–4).

   Although it seems strange to talk about the glory of suffering, these verses describe the benefits of trials. What are they? What perspective can you offer when your spouse is in pain? How can you say these things in a way that is truly helpful and not glib or trite sounding?

3. **"But [the Lord] said to me, 'My grace is sufficient for you, for my power is made perfect in weakness.' Therefore I will boast all the more gladly about my weaknesses, so that Christ's power may rest on me. That is why, for Christ's sake, I delight in weaknesses, in insults, in hardships, in persecutions, in difficulties. For when I am weak, then I am strong"** (2 CORINTHIANS 12:9–10).

   These words from the apostle Paul reveal that he is suffering from "a thorn in the flesh" and a lifetime of pain. What weakness has God used in your life to make you strong? How can you help your spouse face suffering? What habits and attitudes can you cultivate now to prepare you for unknown trials you will face as a couple?

Their Legacy of Prayer

Friday

Reflect On: Job 2

Praise God: For His majesty, mercy, and sovereignty, and for His vast wisdom and His many good gifts.

Offer Thanks: That God speaks to you through His Word and reveals Himself through creation, and that He takes everything that happens to you—both the good and the bad—and uses it to mold you into the image of Christ.

Confess: That you often forget to thank God for all His benefits, but when things go wrong, you question His ways and complain.

Ask God: To help you focus on His greatness rather than on your distress, and to teach you how to endure with patience the path He has chosen for you, and to give you faith to believe that He will work out all things in conformity with the higher purpose of His will.

Listen: "My children, I know the plans I have for you, and they are for your good. Trust Me moment by moment, and I will sustain you with My peace. I am your compassionate God; I will care for you. Call to Me, and I will bring healing to your soul."

Pray: *Father in heaven, You are the Potter; we are the clay. You have all knowledge, and we are often confused by our circumstances. We need Your divine wisdom to walk into the unknown future. Help us to consider who You are without doubting Your ability to give us what You know is best. We are Your children. You have given Yourself, and we are grateful. Thank You for the gift of salvation. Our future is in Your hands. Amen.*

Here Comes the Bride

Beloved and the Shulammite

Meaning of Names: *Beloved*, believed to refer to King Solomon, means "peace" or "peaceful." *Shulammite* is the feminine form of Solomon, meaning "Solomon's girl."

Their Character: He was a man of noble birth who was romantic and delighted with the woman he loved. She was a working woman who longed to be with her beloved and was devoted to him.

Their Challenge: At first, they had to wait to consummate their marriage. Later, they faced responsibilities that challenged their closeness.

Their Outcome: Their affirmation and admiration of each other were openly expressed, and they enjoyed a deep and mature love.

Key Scripture: Song of Songs 6

Their Story

Monday

She had waited for this day since she was a little girl. She and her young friends would take turns pretending they were the bride. When the festive sounds of wedding processions were heard on the streets in her town, she imagined the day when all eyes would be on her because she was the bride. As a youngster, the girl was filled with unanswerable questions. She often wondered, *Who will my husband be? What will he look like? Where will we live? How many children will we have?*

Then one day when she was grown, a notable and respected man came to the vineyard where she worked. She knew of his reputation as a fair man, a man of character. She and her friends had heard other girls speak of his charm. She doubted he would pay any attention to a humble Shulammite woman.

But he did. Her skin was dark from years of toil under the sun, yet there was a gentle deep beauty radiating from her that he found captivating. He pursued her, and they fell in love.

To her delight, this man would become her husband. She had hardly dared to think of him loving her, but in her most untamed dreams she had bravely entertained the thought.

Her groom-to-be was just as delighted in her. From the moment he had been introduced to the Shulammite, he extolled her elegance. "Your cheeks are beautiful with earrings, your neck with strings of jewels," he praised. "We will make you earrings of gold, studded with silver ... How beautiful you are, my darling! Oh, how beautiful!"[1] His words quickened her heart. When she was alone, she marveled over them one at a time, and they had the same delicious effect as when he first spoke them.

Eagerly, she answered with her own words of devotion. "How handsome you are, my beloved! Oh, how charming!" the Shulammite's words flowed like poetry. She felt completely free. Her adoration was audible. And she shared her admiration for her betrothed with anyone who listened.

Their engagement was a joyous occasion of exchanging promises that sealed her to him. Following the celebration, she returned to her father's home. Consummation would have to wait until after the marriage ceremony.

In the months between their betrothal and their marriage, she expressed her longing for her beloved with many beautiful words. "Your love is more delightful than wine ... your name is like perfume poured out. No wonder the young women love you!"[2]

The bride and the groom-to-be used their words to introduce their hearts to each other. His touch — even his scent — fueled her

1. Song of Songs 1:10-11, 15.
2. Song of Songs 1:2-3.

eagerness for their wedding night. Their chastity and patience would be richly rewarded as the Shulammite and her beloved anticipated the wonder of one another.

Their wedding day was all they had hoped for. Consummation was the ecstatic reward for their patience. Intimacy and lovely words now entwined their hearts and bodies.

"How delightful is your love, my sister, my bride! How much more pleasing is your love than wine, and the fragrance of your perfume more than any spice! ...Your plants are an orchard of pomegranates with choice fruits, with henna and nard ...You are a garden fountain, a well of flowing water streaming down from Lebanon."[3]

In the years that followed the wedding, they experienced inevitable threats to their friendship and intimacy. At times the Shulammite longed for her husband; however, he was not there—work and other responsibilities had taken him away.

"I slept but my heart was awake," she said.[4]

One time her husband unexpectedly returned home during the dark, early hours of the morning. Because she was tired and nestled in bed, the Shulammite considered his return an intrusion. To remedy the breach, the Shulammite and her husband determined to remember the commitment they had made to be on the alert for anything that could ruin their marriage.

With resolve, the couple renewed their love. He told her, "You are beautiful, my darling. Turn your eyes from me; they overwhelm me. Your temples are like the halves of a pomegranate. Your lips drop sweetness as the honeycomb; milk and honey are under your tongue."

As the early years of their marriage passed, the Shulammite continued to esteem her husband and delight in his presence. He was considerate and kind.

Weaving their lives together, the couple grew in stability and security. Body, soul, and spirit—they were God's good gifts to each other.

Because her heart was devoted to him and his desire was for her, expressions of intimacy were full and free. The union of their bodies celebrated their love.

---

3. Song of Songs 4:10, 13, 15.
4. See Song of Songs 5:2.

Their Life and Times

Tuesday

The Betrothal Contract

Although Jewish betrothals and weddings in the ancient world were characterized by days of joyful celebration, the initial transaction itself was a serious matter. It was a legal covenant, binding and permanent.

Contracts are familiar documents in the modern world. For example, when a couple decides to buy a house, they search for the right neighborhood and home, and they negotiate a fair price. Then they sit down with the seller and realtor and sign legal documents securing the transaction. During this procedure there is no music or reading from ancient poetry. The couple and all those around the conference table are dressed in business attire. No fancy — expensive — dress for her; no tuxedo for him. And no overdressed children dropping flowers petals.

A house closing is a solemn event with life-altering implications. Sobriety hangs in the air like a thick mist.

So it was for the events surrounding the marriage of a couple in ancient Israel. A Hebrew man and woman were entering a pact that was to last a lifetime, and they signed a written betrothal contract. This was serious business.

This document promised that the groom would provide and care for his bride in every way. Once the papers were signed, a couple could wait up to a full year before they were officially married.

Following the waiting time, a date was set for the couple to be joined in marriage. Because they had exchanged vows at the betrothal and signed an agreement, no vows were exchanged at the wedding. However, during the ceremony, the rabbi performed a ritual baptism of the bride, which symbolized her turning away from old ways and former relationships. She was starting a new life with her beloved.

After the baptism, the marriage was official. The couple was declared husband and wife.

While the wedding guests waited, the couple left to consummate their marriage. When they returned to their guests, the festivities began. It was no ordinary wedding reception. This party lasted for a whole week.

On each of the seven days of celebration, the rabbi prayed a different blessing over the couple. These blessings underscored the solemnity and holiness of the wedding and the responsibility of the newlyweds to frequently renew their love for God as well as their vows and passion for each other.

1. You are blessed, Lord our God, the sovereign of the world, who created everything for his glory.

2. You are blessed, Lord our God, the sovereign of the world, the creator of man.

3. You are blessed, Lord our God, the sovereign of the world, who created man in His image, in the pattern of His own likeness, and provided for the perpetuation of his kind. You are blessed, Lord, the creator of man.

4. Let the barren city be jubilantly happy and joyful at her joyous reunion with her children. You are blessed, Lord, who makes Zion rejoice with her children.

5. Let the loving couple be very happy, just as You made Your creation happy in the garden of Eden so long ago. You are blessed, Lord, who makes the bridegroom and the bride happy.

6. You are blessed, Lord our God, the sovereign of the world, who created joy and celebration, bridegroom and bride, rejoicing, jubilation, pleasure and delight, love and brotherhood, peace and friendship ...You are blessed, Lord, who makes the bridegroom and the bride rejoice together.

7. You are blessed, Lord our God, the sovereign of the world, creator of the fruit of the vine.

In ancient Israel, betrothals and marriage were treated with somber respect. The celebration that followed a wedding was spirited; but the beauty of the wedding was the worship.

Can You Imagine?

Wednesday

Although the story of the Shulammite woman and her husband is enough to steam the windows, the result of all this intimate love talk is quite simple. And not surprisingly, it's the bride who best summarizes the goal of the marriage: "This is my beloved, this is my friend" (Song of Songs 5:16).

Can you imagine, after all the passion and sexual imagery of Song of Songs, that the safe harbor of this fantastic voyage is ... friendship? Once the candles have been extinguished, the oils and lotions have been washed off, and the passion for lovemaking has subsided, what remains is devoted friendship. Closeness. The deep desire for intimacy and companionship.

We can learn a lot from this bride and groom about the language of friendship. They spoke words of praise, admiration, and affirmation.

"How great is your name!" she says.

"You are the most beautiful woman in all the world," he replies. "You have ravished my heart, my lovely one. You have captivated my heart with one glance of your eyes."

And right in the middle of more than one of his eloquent soliloquies to her delicious charms, the groom uses an enduring term for friendship and calls her his "sister" (Song of Songs 4:9–10).

In addition to the joy you bring to each other physically, your marriage needs to be strengthened by the things that make for lasting friendship: spontaneous presents, thoughtful words and conversation, pleasant facial expressions, and selfless serving of one another.

Study your spouse. Become an expert on the person you married. Lavish your best friend with gifts of kindness. Abandon criticism. Experience the euphoria of remarkable closeness. Then, celebrate your friendship on the playground of sexual intimacy.

Choose to be each other's closest friend.

From God's Word . . .

"Drive out the mocker, and out goes strife; quarrels and insults are ended. One who loves a pure heart and who speaks with grace will have the king for a friend."

PROVERBS 22:10–11

Their Legacy in Scripture

Thursday

1. "A friend loves at all times, and a brother is born for a time of adversity" (PROVERBS 17:17). "One who has unreliable friends soon comes to ruin, but there is a friend who sticks closer than a brother" (PROVERBS 18:24).

   Sometimes a married couple forgets what first drew them together. Because of obligations and mundane tasks, friendship is neglected and even sex can become routine. Why is it important to treat your lover as your best friend? What is likely to happen to your sexual intimacy when you do?

2. "May your fountain be blessed, and may you rejoice in the wife of your youth" (PROVERBS 5:18).

   Why does the writer refer to the past ("the wife of your youth") in the above verse? What did you enthusiastically celebrate about your spouse when you first fell in love? How can remembering the enthusiasm you felt in the early days of your courtship rekindle the joy in your marriage now?

3. "Love is patient, love is kind. It does not envy, it does not boast, it is not proud. It does not dishonor others, it is not self-seeking, it is not easily angered, it keeps no record of wrongs" (1 CORINTHIANS 13:4–5).

   A great marriage, like a great friendship, is hard work. In your marriage, which of the things listed in these verses above require your focused attention?

Their Legacy of Prayer

Friday

Reflect On: Song of Songs

Praise God: For His gracious character and His good gift of marriage and intimacy, and for pursuing you, loving you, and sacrificing for you.

Offer Thanks: For your spouse and for the protection, pleasure, and partnership God designed for your marriage.

Confess: That you are often self-focused and do not value your spouse or cultivate the friendship you once shared.

Ask God: To fill you with His love and creativity so that you willingly offer affirmation, admiration, and affection to your spouse. To rekindle your joy and the desire to build a deep friendship and a marriage that will go the distance.

Listen: "My children, I designed your marriage to teach you how to grow in passionate love that honors Me. When I brought you and your spouse together, it was for life. I watch over you with delight and will quiet you with My love. My strength and wisdom will guide and guard you always."

Pray: *Father in heaven, You have demonstrated to us the kind of love that sacrifices and overwhelms with grace. We are humbled and grateful for the provision You have made for our love to grow fuller and richer as we rely on You. We want to stay committed to You and need Your help to honor our vows to live as You intended. Thank You for the rest, joy, and friendship You designed for our marriage. Help us to grow more in love with each other and with You. Amen.*

38

Till Death Do Us Part

Ezekiel and Wife

Meaning of Names: Ezekiel means "the strength of God" or "may God toughen." The name of Ezekiel's wife is not given in the Bible.

Their Character: He was a righteous priest and loyal prophet who obeyed God and remained faithful in tragedy. She was a delightful, gentle, and loving companion to her husband.

Their Challenge: They lived among rebellious people. God called them to display sin's consequences and to preach repentance.

Their Outcome: God used Ezekiel's wife as an object lesson, and Jerusalem was destroyed shortly after she died.

Key Scripture: Ezekiel 24:15–27

Their Story

Monday

In the early days of Ezekiel's ministry as a priest and prophet, he and his wife shared the call of God to serve His exiled people living far from their homeland.

As a priest and member of the tribe of Levi, Ezekiel went regularly to the temple, faced the altar with his back to the congregation, and pleaded for God's mercy for his sin and the sin of the Hebrews, crying out, "Have mercy on me, O God, according to your unfailing love; according to your great compassion blot out my transgressions."[1]

As a prophet, Ezekiel spoke for God. After pleading for God's mercy as the priest, he would turn and face the people, proclaiming, "Thus says the LORD." God had commissioned Ezekiel to speak like a compassionate and stern father calling His children to repentance.

"I am sending you to My rebellious people," God commanded Ezekiel. "They have turned away from following Me and have become obstinate and morally depraved. They and their fathers have kept on sinning against Me to this very hour. This is what the Sovereign Lord says."

God continued. "I will put My message in your mouth. And whether or not they listen to you, they will at least know that a prophet has been among them."

Roundly mocked by his own people, Ezekiel was only able to fulfill the task God had given him because he was committed to the job and empowered by the God who had commissioned him when he was thirty years old. And the prophet was blessed to have a companion by his side — the wife he adored and cherished. They were two righteous souls living among a shamelessly sinful people destined for doom. They had walked as one as thousands of Israel's citizens were deported to Babylon. When the Babylonians came to tear the Hebrews from their homes, Ezekiel and his wife went willingly.

In Babylon, they quickly settled in, but being away from Jerusalem and their homeland was a trial. At least they had each other. On earth, this would be enough.

And then came the most crushing blow in Ezekiel's life. Though Ezekiel was still a young man, God gave him a shocking assignment. Early one morning when he was in bed, the prophet heard the voice of God. "Ezekiel, I am going to take away your precious wife. She will die suddenly, but you must show no sorrow. You may quietly sigh, but do not weep. Let there be no tears or wailing at her grave. Keep your turban fastened and do not unsandal your feet or accept the food brought to you by mourners."[2]

---

1. Psalm 51:1.
2. See Ezekiel 24:16–17.

Ezekiel rose with a terrifying start. His wife stirred in their bed at his unexpected jolt, but did not awaken. His eyes scanned her soft and familiar face. If she had awakened, her countenance would have smiled a blessing on his day. Ezekiel left her sleeping.

Barely able to breathe, the prophet dressed and walked into the chilled silence outside. He dreaded the day ahead, but somehow the Lord strengthened him for the unbearable mission of showing the people what they were to face because of their sin. God was going to take away their beautiful temple and their protection. Their relationship with Him would be ended.

Throughout the long day, Ezekiel warned the Hebrews that their treasured temple was destined to be destroyed unless they repented. Their houses and every important building in Jerusalem would be burned down.

As Ezekiel walked throughout the city preaching repentance, God's earlier words concerning his wife's death haunted him. His precious wife was about to be taken from him. Her soon-coming death symbolized the devastation the people were going to experience. Shortly after she died, the temple, the place of the Hebrews' intimate worship with the Lord God, would be turned to rubble.

Later that day, Ezekiel returned home to his wife. She greeted him with an embrace. They kissed.

"You left so early today," she smiled, "I didn't have a chance to say good-bye."

Heartbroken, Ezekiel could not speak. He gently wrapped his arms around his beloved.

Sensing that her husband was very upset, she whispered, "May God's will be done. He will give you the strength to obey whatever has been ordained."

No more words were spoken. Ezekiel held his wife and prayed for her death to happen quickly and painlessly.

He listened to her breathe. He heard the mild staccato as she exhaled a final, short sigh. Her warm body grew limp. His wife was now with God.

Ezekiel was alone.

Their Life and Times

Tuesday

Mourning in Bible Times

Biblical mourning involved a wide range of customs. Ordinarily, mourning was marked by a very public display, as well as by various prescribed ceremonies. Here are some of those practices:

- *Tearing clothes.* Jacob tore his clothing when he believed his son Joseph has been killed by a wild animal (see Genesis 37:34).

- *Wearing sackcloth.* This was a garment made of coarse, black goat's hair. David ordered the people of Judah to wear sackcloth to commemorate the death of Israel's great general, Abner (see 2 Samuel 3:31).

- *Sprinkling dust or dirt on the head.* Job's friends expressed their mourning for Job in this way (see Job 2:12).

- *Looking disheveled and ripping your clothes.* The high priest Aaron and his two surviving sons were commanded to avoid this accepted practice following the death of their brothers, Nadab and Abihu. Moses told them, "Do not let your hair become unkempt and do not tear your clothes" (Leviticus 10:6; see Matthew 6:16–18).

- *Fasting.* Sometimes mourners abstained from food and drink after the death of someone close to them. David fasted when he received news of the deaths of King Saul and his son Jonathan (see 2 Samuel 1:12).

- *Covering not only the lower face but also the entire head.* David and his supporters did this when fleeing the wrath of his son Absalom: "His head was covered and he was barefoot. All the people with him covered their heads too and were weeping as they went up" (see 2 Samuel 15:30).

- *Pounding the chest.* Ezekiel displayed his grief in this way as well: "Cry out and wail, son of man, for it is against my people; it is against all the princes of Israel. They are thrown to the sword along with my people. Therefore beat your breast" (see Ezekiel 21:12).

- *Hiring professional wailers.* As Jeremiah prophesies divine judgment, he records the Lord's words: "Consider now! Call for the wailing women to come; send for the most skillful of them" (Jeremiah 9:17). The synagogue leader Jairus hired mourners to lament the death of his daughter (see Matthew 9:23). This was one of the more dramatic forms of mourning.
- *Sitting or lying on the ground while weeping.* Abraham did this after the death of his wife, Sarah (see Genesis 23:2–3).

The Lord was compassionate and made provision for His people to mourn. Knowing the anguish of broken hearts, He was sympathetic and gracious, allowing people to express their deep pain in ways that would bring comfort.

Yet, in one command, God prohibited Ezekiel from participating in six of these practices when his beloved wife died. God instructed, "Do not lament or weep or shed any tears. Groan quietly; do not mourn for the dead. Keep your turban fastened and your sandals on your feet; do not cover your mustache and beard or eat the customary food of mourners" (Ezekiel 24:16–17).

Because Jerusalem's fall had been foretold by the prophets, and the people were to lose their beloved sanctuary as judgment on them, Ezekiel became an example of how the regular rituals of mourning would be insufficient to express the remorse that God's people would soon feel for their loss.

Can You Imagine?

Wednesday

Early one morning, the Lord spoke to Ezekiel. The message could not have been more terrifying. "Son of man, with one blow I am about to take away from you the delight of your eyes" (Ezekiel 24:16).

Can you imagine being told you only had one more day with your spouse?

What would you do on the last day with the one you love? How would you treat your spouse? Would you make certain there were no unsettled issues? What tender words would you use to express your love? Would you be kinder and more thankful than usual? Would you look for ways to serve more eagerly? And how do you think your spouse would respond to all this special treatment?

About 350 years before Ezekiel received this stunning message from God, King Solomon put life and death in perspective: "It is better to go to a house of mourning than to go to a house of feasting, for death is the destiny of everyone; the living should take this to heart" (Ecclesiastes 7:2). It is wise to live with the end of your life in mind and treasure each other while you can.

"But my spouse and I are young and healthy," you might be tempted to say. "We have many good years ahead."

Six hundred years after Ezekiel, James wrote, "Now listen, you who say, 'Today or tomorrow we will go to this or that city, spend a year there, carry on business and make money.' Why, you do not even know what will happen tomorrow. What is your life? You are a mist that appears for a little while and then vanishes" (James 4:13–14).

Your spouse is a treasure to be cherished. Treat every day with each other as if it were your last.

From God's Word . . .

> "Teach us to number our days, that we may gain a heart of wisdom."
>
> PSALM 90:12

Their Legacy in Scripture

Thursday

1. **"'Son of man, with one blow I am about to take away from you the delight of your eyes. Yet do not lament or weep or shed any tears'"** (EZEKIEL 24:16).

It is difficult to imagine how Ezekiel must have felt when God told him his wife was going to die. How do you imagine Ezekiel handled this shocking news? How would this have tested Ezekiel's walk with God? How do you think you would respond if you suddenly lost your spouse? How would it test your relationship with God?

2. **"'[God] will wipe every tear from their eyes. There will be no more death or mourning or crying or pain, for the old order of things has passed away'"** (REVELATION 21:4).

We live in the land of the dying. Heaven is the land of the living, and your true home. What difference does it make for you and your spouse to know this truth?

3. **"'As long as it is day, we must do the works of him who sent me. Night is coming, when no one can work'"** (JOHN 9:4).

You may have experienced the tragedy of loss. Someone you loved is gone. But you are alive. You have today. What does this verse challenge you to do? How can you and your spouse serve in God's kingdom together?

Their Legacy of Prayer

Friday

Reflect On: Ezekiel 41:15–27

Praise God: For the strength He gives you to endure the most devastating times of life.

Offer Thanks: That though you have suffered or are suffering, God is always with you in the midst of your pain and sadness. For all the people who have blessed you, even if some of them are no longer with you.

Confess: That instead of being grateful for those who were in your life, you sometimes feel angry with God for taking them away.

Ask God: To allow you to view loss through different eyes—to give you comfort.

Listen: "My children, I understand how difficult it is to lose someone you love. I watched My only Son die. I am acquainted with your grief. I am here to wrap my arms around you and carry you through the sorrow of your loss. With each passing day, I will continue to strengthen you and bring you into a greater understanding of who I am and of how much I love you."

Pray: *Dear Lord, You are the One who heals our emotional wounds. You know the anguish of our souls and how much we hurt. We are so grateful we can express to You how we feel. You hear and care. Lord, in our grief, help us to display your goodness. As You bring healing to our souls, help us to bring glory to Your Name. Amen.*

Come Back Home

Hosea and Gomer

Meaning of Names:	*Hosea* means "salvation." *Gomer* means "perfect," "complete," or "to finish."
Their Character:	He was an obedient prophet who displayed God's merciful heart, endured grief, and chose to forgive. She was a discontented and unfaithful wife and mother who chose to pursue self-indulgence and sin instead of loving her family.
Their Challenge:	Hosea preached, and no one listened. God told him to take an adulterous wife. Gomer's lovers used her, and she ended up forsaken and for sale in the slave market.
Their Outcome:	Their marriage was restored and became an illustration of God's love for Israel.
Key Scripture:	Hosea 1–3

Their Story

Monday

Hosea had never been a buyer at the slave market until today, but now he had no choice. God had instructed him to purchase his wife, Gomer. To buy her back.

The slave auction in Samaria was a beehive. One by one, slaves were paraded in front of the people as the auctioneer shouted out the victim's marketable qualities and potential owners called out a price. The needs of the buyers determined the kind of slaves they would purchase. Strong-backed men went to farmers. Able-bodied women went to families with an abundance of children to care for and feed. Sometimes a woman who was beautiful, like Gomer, was purchased in order to satisfy the sexual desires of the buyer.

Years before, while walking the hills near his home, God spoke to Hosea, telling him it was time to turn the page on his single life. God wanted Hosea to marry. Good news.

But then God told him he was not to marry someone of his own choosing. God instructed him to marry a woman who would eventually break Hosea's heart. God warned him that his wife would quickly become bored with married life and abandon Hosea and their children, trading the privilege of marriage for serial infidelity.

"But why?" Hosea pushed back.

"Because there is no faithfulness, no love, no acknowledgment of God in the land," God answered.

Hosea was shocked. God wanted more than the prophet's words; He wanted Hosea to live — to embody — the message.

It took a few days to grasp it all, and no matter how much Hosea prayed, the Lord did not relent. God told Hosea to marry Gomer, a woman who would cheat on him, so that He could use the couple as an object lesson for the Hebrews. The disastrous marriage Hosea soon entered mirrored Israel's unfaithful relationship with God.

Dread filled Hosea as he walked the road to the home of Gomer's father, Diblaim. Diblaim summoned his daughter. Hosea's heart pounded as the blushing teenage girl slowly bowed before him. Hosea helped her to her feet and gently kissed her hand. He had never seen such beauty and promise.

He paid the bride-price Diblaim required, and wedding arrangements were soon made. On the day of their celebration, Hosea's eyes drank in the sight of his bright and lively bride. In spite of what he knew about the heartache that awaited him — how she would betray him — Hosea fell in love with Gomer.

The first year of their marriage, Gomer seemed to love Hosea. He protected and provided for her, lavishing her with kindness and affection. But something unsettled Gomer. She did not understand why her husband was constantly preaching and announcing things in public that made the people angry. She also didn't like hearing the whispers in the marketplace—"That's Hosea's wife. Poor girl. She's married to a religious fanatic."

That year ended with the birth of a son. Gomer wanted to name him after someone in Hosea's family. God, however, had instructed Hosea to name the child Jezreel.

"But that makes no sense," Gomer objected. "Jezreel is the name of a city. And it will remind people of disaster."[1]

Hosea told her the name meant "God will scatter."

"The people will understand," he told his wife. But Gomer didn't like it, and she grew more and more distant. She began spending time away from home; sometimes she was gone all night. When she told Hosea she was pregnant again, he suspected he was not the father.

This time the baby was a daughter. God said, "Name her Lo-Ruhamah," which means "not loved."

"But why such a dreadful name, Hosea?" Gomer argued. "That will make our neighbors scorn us. Of course she is loved."

Hosea explained what the name meant. Gomer wasn't convinced.

A third pregnancy. A son. Lo-Ammi, which means "not my people."

This time, Gomer didn't argue with Hosea about the name. A month after giving birth, she was gone, leaving the children in the care of their father.

Hosea searched for his wife, asking everyone if they had seen her. She had been spotted with a man. Then another. And another. A year passed. Then another. Hosea never saw Gomer but occasionally heard reports. To support herself, Gomer lived as a mistress to men who would house her. When they were through with her, they discarded her like rubbish. She would then seek another man, who soon would do the same.

Hosea agonized over his wife's infidelity and abandonment. He felt desperate and alone. Then one day as he stumbled through the hills, God spoke to him again. "Hosea, go show your love to your wife again, though she is loved by another man and is an adulteress."[2] It had been three years since Hosea had last seen Gomer. Three years of loneliness. And heartbreak.

---

1. See 2 Kings 9–10. Ahab and Jezebel died and their seventy sons were killed in Jezreel.
2. Hosea 3:1.

Then Hosea was told that the queue of men had ended. Unable to find a man willing to take her in for sexual favors, Gomer was to be auctioned as a slave. She was no longer desirable.

Hosea approached the slave market as the bidding began. Scanning the row of prospects, he recognized Gomer immediately. What he saw broke his heart. Oh, how she had aged. She looked tired, hardened. Her innocence had been destroyed, her beauty gone hollow.

Gomer stepped up to the block, and the auctioneer began the bidding. No one made an offer.

Hosea strengthened his resolve and spoke. "I will give fifteen shekels of silver and fifteen shekels worth of barley for this woman."[3]

Gomer stared at her husband in disbelief. She looked away. He saw despair and fear.

His offer went unchallenged, and the transaction was soon complete. "Unchain her," Hosea demanded.

Gomer stood with her head down, barely clothed, shivering in the cold.

Filled with compassion, Hosea approached his wife. Even though she had been unfaithful to him, he still loved her. He slipped off his cloak and wrapped it around her naked shoulders.

Gently raising her chin, Hosea bent down and kissed her cheek. "I have missed you," he whispered.

Cradling Gomer with his arm so she would not fall, Hosea led his wife back to their home and children. One day he would explain to her the meaning behind all that had happened, but now was not the time.

He would love her as he always had.

---

3. See Hosea 3:2.

Their Life and Times

Tuesday

God's Reason for the Tragedy of Hosea

God treasured the Hebrews and loved them. They were His very own. His bride. He had rescued them from slavery in Egypt and sustained them in the wilderness. He had provided everything they needed. He had empowered them to conquer the ruthless inhabitants of the Promised Land. And because of His favor they had prospered.

But the Hebrews took God's faithfulness for granted and became unfaithful to Him. Instead of loving their Provider, they dallied among idols, sacrificing to images of wood and stone and committing spiritual adultery.

In biblical times adultery—unfaithfulness within a marriage—was a capital offense:

> If a man commits adultery with another man's wife—with the wife of his neighbor—both the adulterer and the adulteress are to be put to death."
>
> LEVITICUS 20:10

> If a man is found sleeping with another man's wife, both the man who slept with her and the woman must die. You must purge the evil from Israel.
>
> DEUTERONOMY 22:22

According to the law, Gomer should have been put to death for her adultery. Her death sentence should have been irrevocable. But God's mercy overruled. He told Hosea to reclaim her instead of ordering her execution. God told the prophet to buy his wife back at the slave auction. To redeem her. Hosea brought Gomer home.

Hosea was an eighth-century BC prophet who was called to preach repentance to Israel. God's chosen people had abandoned Him and had willfully absorbed their sinful surroundings.

And so Hosea preached, desperately trying to persuade the rebels to return to the One who loved them. The prophet reminded the people that, in spite of their waywardness, they had a merciful Savior who is "the LORD, the compassionate and gracious God, slow to anger, abounding in love and faithfulness, maintaining love to thousands, and forgiving wickedness, rebellion and sin" (Exodus 34:6–7). But Hosea's words evoked no contrition. No confession. No repentance.

So God instructed Hosea to do something dramatic. Something that would demonstrate forgiveness and sacrificial love. Something that would show the world God's unmerited mercy.

So Hosea obeyed and married Gomer, the one who would have multiple adulterous affairs.

This couple's story, their relationship, is a metaphor — a picture — of God's relationship with His chosen people, the Israelites. In the Old Testament, God regarded Himself as betrothed to Israel. He was her spiritual husband and she was His wife. Just as Gomer was unfaithful, so Israel was unfaithful to God. Whenever the Israelites worshiped pagan deities, the Lord equated this to adultery: "'But like a woman unfaithful to her husband, so you, Israel, have been unfaithful to me,' declares the LORD" (Jeremiah 3:20).

The story of Hosea and Gomer is a story of God's love and forgiveness, even in the face of our unfaithfulness.

Can You Imagine?

Wednesday

At your wedding ceremony, your minister asked you and your spouse a series of questions. "Will you have this man?"

"I will," you said.

"Do you promise to love, honor, and cherish?"

"I do."

As important as these words were, they were only that. Words. But now that you have been married for a while, you've faced the challenge of turning what you promised to do into actions and heart-driven attitudes. Can you imagine how hollow marriage vows would be without the resolve to keep them?

With God's help you are able to be a faithful spouse. He will enable you to become the person—the forgiving lover—God created you to be in your home.

Throughout history, when God wanted to teach His people an important lesson, He often sent a person ... not only as a teacher and helper, but as an example. A living metaphor.

God handed Hosea an assignment that transcended talking and tasks. God asked him to live out grace. To embody forgiveness. To demonstrate unbiased love.

God has called us to "be kind and compassionate to one another, forgiving each other, just as in Christ God forgave you" (Ephesians 4:32). This is an impossible assignment in our own strength. But God understands the challenge, and so He sent Jesus. By the power of His Spirit, we are enabled to be God's person in our marriage, reflecting His forgiving love.

To save Gomer from ruin, God sent Hosea on a mission to bring her home. To redeem you and me, God sent His only Son. To empower us to go the distance in our marriages, God sends His Holy Spirit.

From God's Word ...

> "God demonstrates his own love for us in this: While we were still sinners, Christ died for us."
>
> ROMANS 5:8

Their Legacy in Scripture

Thursday

1. "As high as the heavens are above the earth, so great is
his love for those who fear him; as far as the east is from
the west, so far has he removed our transgressions from us"
(PSALM 103:11–12).

   Describe ways God has demonstrated His love for you and your
   spouse before you were married and since. What are some ways your
   spouse has shown you love and forgiveness? How can Hosea's story
   help you to show Christlike compassion?

2. "You see, at just the right time, when we were still powerless,
Christ died for the ungodly ... God demonstrates his own
love for us in this: While we were still sinners, Christ died
for us" (ROMANS 5:6, 8).

   The Bible makes it clear that we are all sinful and in need of a
   Savior. Every married couple is made up of two sinners in need of
   grace. When has your spouse demonstrated sacrificial love for you?
   How did you respond? What are some ways you can be a picture of
   unconditional love to your spouse?

3. "'You are the light of the world. A town built on a hill cannot be hidden. Neither do people light a lamp and put it
under a bowl. Instead they put it on its stand, and it gives
light to everyone in the house. In the same way, let your light
shine before others, that they may see your good deeds and
glorify your Father in heaven'" (MATTHEW 5:14–16).

   Your marriage is on display to show others how the love and
   forgiveness of Jesus are lived out. You don't have to be perfect people,
   but you can reflect the transforming light of Christ. How would your
   neighbors describe your marriage? What one thing could you work
   on to brighten your witness?

Their Legacy of Prayer

Friday

Reflect On: Hosea 1, 3

Praise God: For His compassion and forgiveness and for His pursuit of sinners with mercy and grace.

Offer Thanks: That He gives you the ability to do the seemingly impossible — to forgive when you have been hurt. For giving you a tender, forgiving heart toward your spouse.

Confess: That you would much rather cling to your anger and bitterness than relinquish it to God and allow Him to display His kindness through you.

Ask God: To make you a new creation with a heart like His, and to remove your resentment and bitterness and replace it with His tenderness and forgiveness.

Listen: "My children, I love every unlovable sinner and desire to show mercy and grace to the vilest offender. You are My hands and feet to display kindness to your spouse. I am calling you to forgive freely, just as I forgive you because of My Son's sacrifice. Resolve to love and forgive — I will give you the strength to carry it through."

Pray: *Father in heaven, thank You for loving us so deeply. You sent Jesus to rescue us while we were still offending You with our sin. Help us to forgive each other as You have forgiven us. We can't do it on our own. We need Your Spirit to enable us to exhibit grace and mercy. Without You, we would act selfishly and nurture our resentment. But with Your help, we are empowered to carry the gospel of Jesus Christ to the people who need it most. We want to live to please You in our home and in our world. Thank You for Your astounding compassion. Amen.*

40

God Surprises

Zechariah and Elizabeth

Meaning of Names: *Zechariah* means "pure" or "Yahweh remembers."
Elizabeth means "oath of God."

Their Character: He was a priest, an upright and righteous man. She was a dignified woman who quietly bore the heartbreak of barrenness.

Their Challenge: Zechariah displayed a lack of faith. Elizabeth's inability to have children led to feelings of shame.

Their Outcome: The Lord rewarded the godly couple with a child who would grow up to be the forerunner of the Messiah.

Key Scripture: Luke 1

Their Story

Monday

Zechariah was in a hurry. Despite his advanced years, he deftly navigated the rock-strewn hill country of Judea. The wind blew a shock of white hair across his wrinkled face.

Not since the days of his youth had he conquered these rugged hills with such ease. Zechariah had an urgent message for his wife, Elizabeth, and he was determined to reach her as quickly as he could. This was an unforgettable day, and his spirit soared with anticipation when he imagined his wife's response to the news he had received that morning.

He had gone to the temple in Jerusalem as usual. Lots had been cast, and Zechariah was the priest chosen to enter the Holy Place and burn sweet-smelling incense just in front of the Holy of Holies. The aroma of prayers rose to God. The other priests and the Hebrew people remained outside, worshiping as their advocate humbly bowed and prayed inside.

Having long awaited his turn to be the priest on duty to offer prayers and sacrifices, Zechariah was completely awed to be in the presence of God. "O Lord, our God," Zechariah whispered, "You alone are worthy. We worship You."

Suddenly the Holy Place shimmered. An incandescent angel of God stood before the altar. Zechariah winced in terror and covered his face, but his fear evaporated when the angel spoke.

"Do not be afraid, Zechariah," the angel said. "Your prayer has been heard."

Which prayer? the old man wondered. *The one I was just praying for the people and the nation?*

The angel continued, "Your wife Elizabeth will bear you a son, and you are to call him John … And he will go on before the Lord, in the spirit and power of Elijah, to turn the hearts of the parents to their children and the disobedient to the wisdom of the righteous — to make ready a people prepared for the Lord."[1]

"My wife?" The angelic message astonished Zechariah. It was both wonderful and impossible to believe. Zechariah and Elizabeth had prayed for decades for a child … a son who could carry on his father's priestly lineage. Now they were old, and still no child.

He pictured Elizabeth's gentle face, laced with soft wrinkles and the tears she had shed. She had abandoned dreams of motherhood long ago.

"How can I be sure of this?" Zechariah asked, wanting a sign. "I am an old man and my wife is well along in years."

The heavenly messenger spoke a stern rebuke. "I am Gabriel. And I stand in the presence of God, and I have been sent to speak to you and to tell you this good news. And now you will be silent and not able to speak until the day this happens, because you did not believe my words, which will come true at their appointed time."

---

1. Luke 1:13, 17.

As quickly as he had appeared, the angel was gone. But something had happened to Zechariah. He tried speaking. No sound came from his mouth. *Where's my voice?* he thought, with an overpowering feeling of fear.

The priest struggled to his feet and walked outside to the courtyard where the worshipers awaited his spoken blessing. All eyes were on him. The people were full of questions because the old priest had lingered in the Holy Place longer than usual. In vain, Zechariah tried again to speak. He nodded and signaled with his hands, but no one could understand what he was trying to say.

Excusing himself with a bow, Zechariah wove his way through the crowd and busy Jerusalem streets, past the city gate. Eager to reach Elizabeth, he hastened into the hill country toward his home.

Elizabeth was startled to see her husband so soon. His lips were moving as if he were speaking to her, but she heard nothing. There was no sound. Zechariah gazed into her face, his wide eyes brimming with confusion and frustration.

"What happened to your voice?" Elizabeth asked. "What are you trying to tell me?"

Zechariah gestured, forming a cradle with his trembling hands.

She understood and exclaimed, "We are going to have a son?" Blinking away tears, she repeated the words again. Taking her face in his hands, Zechariah began nodding. He believed everything the angel had promised was true.

Elizabeth wanted details, but her husband could not tell her more. At least not now. The old man and woman fell together, their eyes shining.

There would be plenty of time later for Zechariah to tell Elizabeth about his heavenly visitor. He resolved to confess his earlier unbelief to his wife and explain the news that their son would bring joy to many people and someday announce the coming of Israel's Messiah.

But for now, the couple, sheltered in each other's embrace, simply pondered the sacred message.

Their Life and Times

Tuesday

The Role of a Priest

Zechariah was one of eighteen thousand priests who served God by offering sacrifices and prayers on behalf of the people. As a priest, he was expected to live a holy and righteous life.

He was also required to marry an honorable woman because the character of a priest's wife could adversely reflect on her husband's reputation and fitness to minister the holy things of God.[2] In Elizabeth, Zechariah fulfilled this part of the priest's duties very well. "Righteous in the sight of God" (Luke 1:6)—she was a suitable partner for Zechariah in his sacred work.

Priests were responsible to watch over the fire for burnt offering and keep it ablaze day and night by adding wood. Through the sacrificing of animals without any blemish, priests secured a temporary atonement for Israel's transgressions. "In fact, the law requires that nearly everything be cleansed with blood, and without the shedding of blood there is no forgiveness" (Hebrews 9:22).

At the top of the priestly hierarchy was the high priest. Although all Levitical priests offered sacrifices daily, once a year a special day was set aside—the Day of Atonement (also known as Yom Kippur). On that day, only the high priest could enter the Most Holy Place in the temple. Inside the small, sacred room, he sprinkled the blood of the sin offering on the top of the ark of the covenant.

However, the sacrificial system could not permanently cleanse and redeem the people. The old covenant system of sacrifices revealed to the people that their sins were a serious offense to God's holiness and required a covering. Because their sins were perpetual, the sacrificial system had to be perpetual. Although the animal sacrifices could not remove sin and guilt once and for all, they pointed to the future time when the perfect "Lamb of God," the Messiah, would give His life one time for all sins for all time: So when "the set time had fully come, God sent his Son, born of a woman, born under the law, to redeem those under the law" (Galatians 4:4–5).

---

2. See Leviticus 21:7.

Jesus became Israel's new High Priest. He "offered up prayers and petitions with fervent cries and tears to the one who could save him from death" (Hebrews 5:7). Just as the high priest made requests to God, interceding to spare the lives of the Israelites, Jesus, the High Priest, intercedes on our behalf: "He is able to save completely those who come to God through him, because he always lives to intercede for them" (Hebrews 7:25).

Jesus Christ invites all believers to come into His holy presence: "We do not have a high priest who is unable to empathize with our weaknesses, but we have one who has been tempted in every way, just as we are—yet he did not sin. Let us then approach God's throne of grace with confidence, so that we may receive mercy and find grace to help us in our time of need" (Hebrews 4:15–16).

Jesus, the final High Priest, lived a sinless life. He was qualified to become the complete and perfect sacrifice, satisfying God's wrath toward mankind's sin.

Can You Imagine?

Wednesday

In ancient times, children were considered to be a clear and visible sign of God's blessing on a marriage. But Zechariah and Elizabeth could not conceive. Month after month, year after year, they prayed. Still there was only barrenness.

Can you imagine Zechariah's and Elizabeth's amazement and gratitude when God finally answered their prayers for a child? The message was impossible from their human point of view, and the timing was not close to anything they expected. Despite her advanced age, Elizabeth was going to have a son, who they were to name John. From God's vantage point, the day of John's birth was perfect. He would be born just before the birth of Jesus, making it possible for John to prepare the way for the Messiah.

Like Zechariah and Elizabeth, you may have to wait for God to answer some of your prayers. What are you and your spouse doing to prepare for times of disappointment, grief, embarrassment, and weakness? The regular habit of worshiping God together allows you to focus on His transcendent character rather than on your unanswered prayers. He will strengthen you and your spouse as you affirm God's truth together. "We wait in hope for the LORD; he is our help and our shield. In him our hearts rejoice, for we trust in his holy name" (Psalm 33:20–21).

Sometimes God answers prayer with a swift reply; sometimes He doesn't. But you can be absolutely certain that He is always listening. And His timing is perfect.

From God's Word . . .

> "Wait for the LORD; be strong and take heart
> and wait for the LORD."
>
> PSALM 27:14

Their Legacy in Scripture

Thursday

1. **"Without faith it is impossible to please God, because anyone who comes to him must believe that he exists and that he rewards those who earnestly seek him"** (HEBREWS 11:6).

   Elizabeth and Zechariah hoped and prayed for a son who could carry on his father's priestly legacy. What is something that you or your spouse long for? According to this verse, what pleases God? In what ways has God already rewarded you? How can you encourage your spouse to wait for answers?

2. **"'The Lord has done this for me,' she said. 'In these days he has shown his favor and taken away my disgrace among the people'"** (LUKE 1:25).

   The Bible describes Zechariah and Elizabeth as "righteous in the sight of God, observing all the Lord's commands and decrees blamelessly" (Luke 1:6). What do you learn from Elizabeth's words in the above verse? When have you personally experienced the Lord's unexpected favor? What can you do to regularly offer moments of grace to your spouse?

3. **"'Ask and it will be given to you; seek and you will find; knock and the door will be opened to you. For everyone who asks receives; the one who seeks finds; and to the one who knocks, the door will be opened'"** (MATTHEW 7:7–8).

   Prayer ushers you and your spouse into God's presence. You are closer to Him and to each other every time you call on the Lord. Why is this true? Prayer at mealtimes, as you're saying good-bye each morning, before you go to sleep at night, sitting next to one another in church ... these are sacred moments when you as a couple are in God's presence. When do you pray together? How can you begin to experience the closeness of God more often with your spouse?

Their Legacy of Prayer

Friday

Reflect On: Luke 1:1–25, 57–80

Praise God: For His redemptive plan and faithfulness to accomplish His purpose.

Offer Thanks: That God has His hand on you and your spouse, and that He is sustaining you in times of disappointment and giving you a heart to worship Him.

Confess: That you too often focus on what you don't have rather than on God's ability to accomplish His will in His time. That you often fall into doubt and unbelief, and that you tend to complain instead of thanking God for the blessings you have.

Ask God: To help you view your circumstances through His eyes, and to strengthen you to accept His will and be satisfied with the life He has called you to — not the one you wish you had. To teach you what He wants you to learn in this season of your marriage.

Listen: "My children, I have given you everything you need for godly living. Trust me to fulfill My plan for you at the right time. You are earthbound pilgrims whom I love. My perspective is eternal. I am your good Shepherd and will care for you. I know you and will lead you. Come to Me with a heart of worship, and I will fill you with My peace that surpasses all understanding."

Pray: *Dear Father in heaven, You have already given us so much, and we worship You today for Your wisdom, mercy, and generosity. Forgive us for discontented and ungrateful thoughts. Give us a vision of how You want to use our marriage to magnify You and to bless others. Help us to cherish each other and to embrace what You have called us to be — a picture of faith, hope, and love. Help us to honor You by becoming people who say, "Not my will, but Yours be done." Amen.*

It's a Savior

Joseph and Mary

Meaning of Names: *Joseph* means "may God add" or "increase." *Mary* means "a tear," "sea of bitterness," or "star of the sea."

Their Character: He was kindhearted and upright, a diligent student of the law who lived by faith. She was a simple peasant girl, devoted to worshiping God and willing to be His humble servant.

Their Challenge: While they were betrothed, she became pregnant, facing scorn and the possibility of being stoned to death. He thought she had been unfaithful and sought to divorce her quietly.

Their Outcome: She became the mother of Jesus Christ. Together, Mary and Joseph raised the Savior of the world.

Key Scripture: Matthew 1:18–25; Luke 1:26–38

Their Story

Monday

Joseph gently guided his mule along the rocky path that twisted through the Judean hills between Nazareth and Bethlehem. A thin moon and some timid stars peeking into the low haze provided just enough light for the travelers. Joesph was attentive to his pregnant wife, who was riding sidesaddle.

Less than a year before this journey, Joseph and Mary's lives had been simple and unheralded. Now they were awash with the

astonishing events that had led them on this trek to David's city.
Up until nine months ago, Mary was an ordinary Hebrew teenager,
betrothed to a suitable and good man named Joseph. He was a carpenter, the son of Jacob of Nazareth, and a descendant of King David.
Mary was living at her parents' home, preparing for her wedding day.

And then something happened.

A brilliant light filled Mary's small room, and in its midst floated
an angel. Astonished, Mary stood mute, eyes squinting at the bright-
ness, body trembling. When the angel spoke, his words both calmed
and mystified her. He identified himself as Gabriel and said, "Do not
be afraid, Mary; you have found favor with God. You will conceive
and give birth to a son, and you are to call him Jesus. He will be
great and will be called the Son of the Most High ... his kingdom
will never end."[1]

"But how can I have a baby?" Mary asked the angel. "I am a
virgin."

Mary was confused. She had not slept with Joseph and was saving
her purity until after their wedding.

The angel answered, "The Holy Spirit will hover over you, and
the power of the Most High will overshadow you. So your baby will
be holy, the Son of God."

Gabriel continued with news about Mary's older relative who
had faithfully endured years of scorn. "Six months ago, Elizabeth
— the woman they called barren — became pregnant in her old age.
For every promise from God will surely come true."

Mary was stunned and humbled. "I am the Lord's servant," she
said. "And I am willing to do whatever He wants."

Then the angel disappeared.

After the angel was gone, Mary wanted to talk to someone and
pondered how to tell Joseph all that had happened. Knowing that
Elizabeth would understand and validate her vision and predicament,
Mary gathered a few belongings and hurried to her relative's home
in the Judean hill country.

When Joseph heard that his fiancée was pregnant, he was hurt and
bewildered. He wondered how his pure and upright betrothed could
have fallen into such sin. Being a devout follower of the Mosaic law,

---

1. Luke 1:30–33.

Joseph decided to divorce Mary privately rather than demanding the death penalty, which was his legal right. Mary's conception was not by him, and they both knew it. But his love for her would never permit such severe punishment. So he resolved to protect her virtue and send her far away from the wagging tongues in Nazareth so she could have her child in secret.

Exhausted one night after wrestling with the anguish of Mary's mysterious betrayal and deceit, Joseph fell into a deep sleep. An angel appeared to him in a dream and said, "Joseph son of David, do not be afraid to take Mary home as your wife, because what is conceived in her is from the Holy Spirit. She will give birth to a son, and you are to give him the name Jesus, because he will save his people from their sins."[2]

Fully convinced of Mary's purity, Joseph obeyed the angel's command. Rather than waiting for the one-year betrothal time to pass, he brought Mary into his house as his wife. But he had no union with her until after she gave birth.

During the months that followed, Mary and Joseph spent hours in lively conversation, talking about the angel visits. They recalled the words of Isaiah the prophet. "Therefore the Lord himself will give you a sign: The virgin will conceive and give birth to a son, and will call him Immanuel."[3]

"That was written seven hundred years ago!" Mary marveled.

Joseph nodded. "The Lord is fulfilling what He planned long ago."

There was so much to discover. As Joseph scoured through the scrolls at Nazareth's synagogue, he read a prophecy regarding the Messiah. "But you, Bethlehem Ephrathah, though you are small among the clans of Judah, out of you will come for me one who will be ruler over Israel, whose origins are from of old, from ancient times."[4]

When Joseph told Mary what he had found, her voice echoed with uncertainty. "We live in Nazareth. Bethlehem is far away."

Joseph was silent. He had no answer.

---

2. Matthew 1:20–21.
3. Isaiah 7:14.
4. Micah 5:2.

Then one day he brought timely news to his wife. He told her about a census the Roman Emperor Caesar Augustus had just issued. Mary did not understand her husband's enthusiasm.

"Don't you see?" Joseph reported. "I must return to my ancestral home, the city of David."

Smiling, Joseph gave Mary a moment to contemplate his words. Her eyes widened. "Bethlehem ... the prophecy ... yes, we must go to Bethlehem, just as God has ordained!"

And now, as Joseph and Mary navigated the rugged hill country of Judea on their way to Bethlehem, they contemplated God's intricate plan. He had prepared them, led them, and sovereignly cared for them. In a few days, Israel's long-awaited Messiah would be born ... of a virgin.

In Bethlehem. Jesus. Immanuel.

And He provided salvation for His people.

God had planned this long ago.

Their Life and Times

Tuesday

Daily Life in Nazareth

When thinking of Nazareth—the hometown of Joseph, Mary, and Jesus—think small. Very small. In fact, with a population of less than two hundred citizens, think "hamlet." This is all Nazareth was.

It is no wonder that when Philip told his friend Nathanael that he had "found the one Moses wrote about in the Law, and about whom the prophets also wrote—Jesus of Nazareth, the son of Joseph," Nathanael replied, "Nazareth! Can anything good come from there?" (John 1:45–46).

Like any other town in Galilee, Nazareth had a synagogue and marketplace, both of which served as the main gathering spots. In addition to being the place of worship, the synagogue was where men met to discuss theological matters. The marketplace served as a venue for commerce, and it gave women a respite from their cease-less chores at home and the rare opportunity to socialize with one another.

Nazareth was nestled in beautiful surroundings at the northern edge of the Plain of Esdraelon, one of the most visually stunning locations in all of Israel. Its breathtaking vistas included rolling, green hills from which on clear days townsfolk could survey for miles vast tracts of lush land to the west and south.

Israelites from Jerusalem, and even those from the larger areas in Galilee such as Capernaum, unfairly regarded Nazareth as a rural backwater town populated with bumpkins and peasants. In their opinion, Nazareth produced little, if any, men of higher rabbinic education. Also, the dialect of that region was coarse compared to the more refined-sounding Aramaic spoken in the southern cities.

Even in a town as small as Nazareth, Joseph's work as a carpenter would have been regarded as lowly. Trades such as silversmith, pot-ter, engraver, and stonecutter were considered more respectable than that of humble carpenter, perhaps because carpenters earned smaller wages than that of other skilled craftspeople. Since most trades were handed down from generation to generation, it is likely that Joseph's father, grandfather, and great-grandfather were also carpenters.

Joseph probably spent his days making chairs, benches, tables, cattle yoke, plows, and window frames. The constant sawing, hammering, smoothing, and crafting would have toughened and gnarled his hands. Like other carpenters of his day, Joseph may have had a chip of wood dangling from one of his ears as a way of drawing business and informing potential customers of his profession.

While Joseph was laboring in his workshop—probably located right next to the house—Mary would have been equally hard at work at home, spinning yarn for clothing, bedsheets, and cloths; weaving baskets; washing clothes on a large scouring stone; and culling curds from goat's milk. And, of course, cooking.

Joseph and Mary's morning fare would have been simple, consisting of curds and bread, either left over from the night before or freshly baked if Mary rose particularly early. Other than fruits, vegetables, and bread, lunches were relatively light. Dinner, their most substantial meal of the day, probably included the always-present bread, wine, salted fish or boiled chicken, beans, lentils, cucumbers, leeks, and onions. This evening meal may also have featured nuts, melons, figs, and grapes.

Most Galilean homes were umbrellaed by thatched or mud roofs. Leaks during heavy rainstorms were a constant problem, and someone had to repair the breaches through which the water dripped. That someone was often the woman of the house, so this would have been something Mary had to do as well.

Can You Imagine?

Wednesday

When we read the familiar story of Mary and Joseph and the babe lying in a manger, it's hard not to default to a charming Christmas card scene. But the real story of the first Christmas is an account of danger, treachery, survival ... and faith.

The unanticipated adjustments you faced when you were first married were challenging. But can you imagine the puzzling events Joseph and Mary had to navigate? Even though supernatural messengers had visited and instructed both of them individually, they lived in a real world of doubt and uncertainty. Surely Joseph and Mary must have wondered, *Is this really where we're supposed to be going? Is this really what God wants us to do?*

You and your spouse cannot see the future. But your obedience can be informed by God's faithfulness in the past and your confidence in His perfect character. Trusting Him for tomorrow requires faith ... dependence on God's goodness.

So when the two of you are confused, what does God really promise? How do you know when you're following His lead, when you're living within the walls of His will?

Mary and Joseph would have been familiar with the stories of men and women of faith. Noah and his wife, Abraham and Sarah, Boaz and Ruth — couples who prayed and acknowledged God, trusting Him to lead them despite their doubts. Mary and Joseph also benefited from mentors — Zechariah and Elizabeth — who understood their struggles and validated their mission. These mentors would have given them encouragement and hope. "His mercy extends to those who fear him, from generation to generation. He has performed mighty deeds" (Luke 1:50–51).

Whatever you're facing as a couple, God is faithful. Depend on Him to lead you. He intends for your marriage to bless others.

From God's Word ...

"Without faith it is impossible to please God, because anyone who comes to him must believe that he exists and
that he rewards those who earnestly seek him."

HEBREWS 11:6

Their Legacy in Scripture

Thursday

1. **"Praise be to the LORD God, the God of Israel, who alone
does marvelous deeds"** (PSALM 72:18).

   When we think of the "marvelous" works of God, our minds
lean toward His vast creation, His great plan of salvation, His future
kingdom. But what about the amazing creation of ... your marriage? What marvelous deeds has God worked on behalf of you and
your spouse? In what ways do you see God at work now in your
relationship?

2. **"'See, I am doing a new thing! Now it springs up; do you not
perceive it? I am making a way in the wilderness and streams
in the wasteland'"** (ISAIAH 43:19).

   God visited Mary and Joseph separately in completely unexpected ways, confirming God's words to both of them. They each
had to quickly process an angel's message, accept the call of God on
their lives, and then learn to walk together by faith. When have you
and your spouse experienced something new and unexpected in
your marriage, and how did you respond? How do you validate or
confirm each other's hopes and ideas?

3. **"Now to him who is able to do immeasurably more than all
we ask or imagine, according to his power that is at work
within us, to him be glory"** (EPHESIANS 3:20–21).

   God is able to make your marriage "immeasurably" better than
it is now. What has He already done in and through you and your
spouse that you could not have accomplished without Him? Where
do you need God's power now to have a better marriage?

Their Legacy of Prayer

Friday

Reflect On: Matthew 1:18–24; Luke 1:26–38; 2:1–21

Praise God: For sending Jesus, His gift too wonderful for words.

Offer Thanks: That God fulfills His plan in history and also gives you new and exciting opportunities to serve Him.

Confess: That often you question God's call and doubt His ability to guide you in puzzling times. That you worry instead of worshiping Him.

Ask God: To give you confidence in His character and a greater vision of His purpose in your lives.

Listen: "Dear children, I have designed your marriage to display My limitless power. I will confirm to both of you what you need to know. I have gone ahead of you and have prepared the way. My kingdom has no limits, and you have an important part in it. Whatever seems impossible to you is possible with Me. I will do great things for you as you trust and obey."

Pray: *Dear Father in heaven, when we are confused by the circumstances in our lives, we are tempted to panic and overlook the magnitude of Your wisdom. Help us to be open to Your special call on our lives and trust Your faithfulness. We are available to serve You in any way that pleases You so that Your will may be done on earth through us as You have planned it in heaven. We are Your servants. Thank You for leading us with tender mercy. Amen.*

God Knows

Joseph and Mary

Meaning of Names:	*Joseph* means "may God add" or "increase." *Mary* means "a tear," "sea of bitterness," or "star of the sea."
Their Character:	He was a patient and trustworthy man, resting in the providence of God. She worshiped while waiting on God and willingly followed her husband's prayerful lead.
Their Challenge:	They were misunderstood, faced danger, and received information they did not fully understand while raising Israel's Messiah.
Their Outcome:	They faithfully trusted God and received timely affirmation, instruction, and protection for their family. Jesus grew up to fulfill God's plan for redemption.
Key Scripture:	Matthew 1:18–25; Luke 1:26–38

Their Story

Monday

Two and a half years had passed since Mary and Joseph had traveled to Bethlehem. Now they were back in Nazareth. It was good to be home and settled. It had been a busy day chasing their toddler. Their young son, Jesus, was asleep in His father's arms.

The couple relaxed on the ground outside their small home. The brilliant stars reminded them of the night when their son was born.

Crickets chirped as the young parents enjoyed quiet conversation. They reminisced with words of wonder. God had included them in His eternal plan. How they marveled at His kind providence!

Mary remembered again the angel Gabriel's surprise visit when he had told her she was going to have a baby. Then there was the sixty-five-mile journey to Judea to see her aged cousin Elizabeth, who was also pregnant. The thrill of their greeting lingered. Mary could still picture her relative resting her hands on her stomach and exclaiming, "Oh, Mary, you are favored by God above all other women, and your child is destined for God's mightiest work. What an honor this is — to have the mother of my Lord visit me."

Elizabeth cried with excitement. "When you greeted me, the instant I heard your voice, my baby kicked and moved in me for joy. You believed that God would do what He said. He has given you this wonderful blessing."

How amazing that she knows! Mary had thought. *God is so kind to encourage me with her words.*

The Holy Spirit had revealed to Elizabeth that Mary was carrying the Lord, Israel's Messiah. For Mary, this had been the first clear confirmation of God's purposes for her and her baby.

And there were more astounding affirmations to recall.

Like the night Jesus was born. Joseph had just finished swaddling the baby, settling Him in an animal feeding trough, when he had heard voices outside. Joseph went to investigate and found a cluster of foul-smelling shepherds standing there.

"What do you want?" Joseph asked.

One of the shepherds spoke. "Sir, no more than an hour ago, a host of heavenly angels appeared to us. One of them said, 'Today in the town of David, a Savior has been born to you; He is the Messiah, the Lord. This will be a sign to you: You will find a baby wrapped in cloths and lying in a manger.' We have come here to see Him."[1]

How amazing that they know about His birth! Joseph had thought. *God has told the shepherds.*

After Joseph escorted the shepherds to the trough, they acknowledged Mary with a bow of their heads and then turned toward the

---

1. Luke 2:10–12.

child. In unison, they knelt in worship. One by one the shepherds backed out of the stable. Mary gazed at the baby in awe.

Another confirmation came a little more than six weeks after Jesus' birth, when the couple had traveled to Jerusalem to dedicate the child. As they entered the temple courts, an elderly gentleman approached them.

"I am Simeon," the man said, his eyes brightening at the sight of the child. "Praise the Lord, for He told me I would see the Messiah before I die. And now the promise is fulfilled."[2]

Simeon reached for the baby. Mary hesitated and looked to Joseph for guidance. Her husband nodded. Mary gently handed the child to Simeon. The old man's eyes glistened. Then he lifted his face toward heaven and spoke. "Sovereign Lord, as You have promised, You may now dismiss Your servant in peace. For my eyes have seen Your salvation, which You have prepared in the sight of all nations: a light of revelation to the Gentiles, and the glory of Your people Israel."

How does he know this about our baby? the couple had wondered.

But Simeon was not finished. Looking directly at Mary as he lowered the infant into her arms, he said, "This child is destined to cause the falling and rising of many in Israel, and to be a sign that will be spoken against, so that the thoughts of many hearts will be revealed. And a sword will pierce your own soul too."

Deeply troubled by Simeon's words, Mary had wondered, *What does this mean?*

Just then, a very old woman stepped toward the young family. Her name was Anna, and she lived in the outer court of the temple. Because she remained there day and night, fasting and praying, the Jewish officials had given her a place to stay. Anna did not ask to hold the child. She adoringly laid her hand on His tiny form, closed her eyes, and thanked God for at last providing "the redemption of Jerusalem."[3] When she finished, Anna smiled at the couple and walked away rejoicing.

How does she know? the couple had wondered.

Two years later, while still living in Bethlehem, there was another encounter, this one with strange visitors from the east. Unlike the

2. See Luke 2:25–26.
3. Luke 2:36–38.

others, these men were not Hebrews, yet they declared the child as "king of the Jews" and bowed down to worship Him.[4]

How do they know? Joseph and Mary had again wondered.

And now, as Mary and Joseph nestled together on this cool Nazareth evening, they were still amazed and filled with awe. They knew they could never fully comprehend all that the Lord had done or why He had chosen them.

God knew. That was enough.

Their Life and Times

Tuesday

The Magi

When Joseph and Mary were visited by a contingent of travelers —Magi—from the east, they were surprised. They did not expect such unusual-looking guests. They were even more shocked when the distinguished men got on their knees and paid homage to the child Jesus.

Who were these men?

The Magi were members of a priestly caste in ancient Persia who studied the stars to determine future events. Kings employed them to gain advantage over their enemies. The Magi were part of King Nebuchadnezzar's inner circle of advisers. While in Babylon, the Magi were influenced by a God-fearing Hebrew exile named Daniel, who had been promoted to "chief of the magicians, enchanters, astrologers and diviners" (Daniel 5:11).

When the Jews were exiled to Babylon—and later migrated farther east to Persia—they took with them their holy writings and scrolls, including the Old Testament law, wisdom books, and prophetic works. Though God was punishing the Israelites for their disobedience and idolatry, some of them had learned their lesson while in exile. Those with contrite hearts of repentance turned back to the one, true God. They revered the Scriptures—especially Isaiah—that promised the coming Messiah.

One of the exiles, Daniel, who oversaw the Magi in Babylon,

---

4. See Matthew 2:1–2, 11.

must have taught them about the precise time when this Messiah would arrive.[5] Over the course of the next five hundred years, these prophecies were handed down among the generations of Magi. By the time Jesus was born, rumors circulated within the civilized world that a powerful Hebrew child would be born and grow up to usher in a "golden age" on the earth.

In describing this ruler, Isaiah had written, "He will not judge by what he sees with his eyes, or decide by what he hears with his ears; but with righteousness he will judge the needy, with justice he will give decisions for the poor of the earth" (Isaiah 11:3–4). The kingdom of this promised leader would also be characterized by peace. "The wolf will live with the lamb, the leopard will lie down with the goat, the calf and the lion and the yearling together; and a little child will lead them" (Isaiah 11:6).

When Jesus Christ was born, the Magi were looking for signs of this King. When an unusually brilliant "star" appeared in the sky one night, the Magi recognized its glory and immediately set out to find the "one who has been born king of the Jews" (Matthew 2:2).[6] The "Shekinah" of God guided them.

The contingent of Magi who left Persia for Israel is significant. The myth that there were only three kings was based on the three gifts they later gave to Jesus, but the traveling party of Magi was probably dozens of men. Travel in those days — especially for an extended number of months — was dangerous. A virtual army was required to safely navigate the journey.

By the time the Magi arrived in Bethlehem, Jesus would have been a toddler, nearly two years old. King Herod questioned the Magi about when they had first seen the "star." Based on their reply, Herod issued his decree to kill all boys in Bethlehem two years old and younger.

When the Magi found Jesus, they worshiped and honored Him with gold, frankincense, and myrrh — expensive gifts fit for a king.

---

5. See Daniel 9: 20–27.

6. Many scholars believe this was the Shekinah glory of God that first appeared to the Israelites during their wilderness wanderings when the Lord led the nation in a pillar of cloud by day and a pillar of fire at night (see Exodus 13:21).

Can You Imagine?

Wednesday

Simeon and Anna were much older than Joseph and Mary—perhaps old enough to be their grandparents. The young couple confirmed God's direction through the words of these godly, elderly people at the temple.

Mary also enjoyed a sweet friendship with her elderly cousin, Elizabeth. After Mary was visited by the angel, she hurried to the older woman and spent three months with Elizabeth and Zechariah. This was the kind of multigenerational relationship that Titus had in mind when he wrote, "[The older women] can urge the younger women to love their husbands and children, to be self-controlled and pure, to be busy at home, to be kind, and to be subject to their husbands, so that no one will malign the word of God" (Titus 2:4–5).

Can you imagine the affirmation and benefit you and your spouse can experience when you encounter the wisdom of people who have been transformed by God and have listened to His voice for many years?

It's easy to choose only friends with whom you identify, couples who are about your age. And why not? Your children are on the same soccer team, you're in the same book club, and they speak your language. But have you considered the wise perspectives you might be missing?

Joseph and Mary were inspired by saints whose advanced age offered them the kind of wisdom that only real-time years could provide.

As a couple, you will be enriched when you seek out older people who love Jesus. Ask them the lessons they've learned. Find out the secrets of walking with God and finishing well. These friends will be a treasured gift to your marriage.

From God's Word . . .

"You are God my Savior, and my hope is in you all day long. Remember, LORD, your great mercy and love, for they are from of old."

PSALM 25:5–6

Their Legacy in Scripture

Thursday

1. **"We are God's handiwork, created in Christ Jesus to do good works, which God prepared in advance for us to do"** (EPHESIANS 2:10).

   What does this verse tell you about God's purpose in your life? In what ways have you and your spouse been designed by God to complement each other? How has God prepared both you to do His good works? What have you learned that has equipped you?

2. **"In their hearts humans plan their course, but the LORD establishes their steps"** (PROVERBS 16:9).

   Mary and Joseph had their own plans interrupted. But God confirmed and validated His leading as they trusted Him. When have your plans been interrupted and what did you learn? What or who has God used to encourage you and your spouse and to establish your steps as you seek His direction?

3. **"Oh, magnify the LORD with me, and let us exalt his name together!"** (PSALM 34:3 ESV).

   Joseph and Mary shared a deep partnership of worship and humble obedience. They chose to enlarge their view of God and focus on His work on their behalf. In what situations do you need to focus on the goodness of God rather than on your own problems? How can you as a couple display faith and hope when trouble comes?

Their Legacy of Prayer

Friday

Reflect On: Matthew 1:9–12; Luke 2:1–40

Praise God: That He is Ruler over all times, places, and people, and that He has given us the gift of salvation through Jesus Christ.

Offer Thanks: That God chose you from before time began to be His, and that He has prepared you as a couple to be His chosen vessels for the advancement of His kingdom.

Confess: Any affections and sins that blur your vision of the role God has for both of you in His kingdom.

Ask God: To empower you with His Spirit to do His work here on earth, and to show you specifically which good works He has called you to do.

Listen: "Dear children, I called you long before you were born. I designed you and will enable you to carry out My plans. Seek My kingdom first, and I will provide everything you need to do My work. My Spirit and My Word are adequate to prepare you for the mission I have chosen for you. Trust Me, and I will show you great and awesome things."

Pray: *Father in heaven, You are worthy to direct all our plans and dreams. Your ways are beyond our understanding, but we trust in Your majesty and mercy. We want to let go of everything that isn't important so we can follow You completely. Help us to pursue Your kingdom with passion and urgency. Amen.*

43

The Last Dance

Herod and Herodias

Meaning of Names:	*Herod* means "song of the hero." *Herodias* means "to monitor" or "to watch over."
Their Character:	He was prideful and narcissistic and indulged in sensual pleasures. She was manipulative and evil and used her daughter Salome for wicked schemes.
Their Challenge:	John the Baptist was confronting their sin and they wanted to silence him. Herod did not want to lose face in front of his guests.
Their Outcome:	Herodias and Salome schemed to have John the Baptist killed. John's death resulted in inner turmoil and guilt for Herod.
Key Scripture:	Matthew 14:1–12; Mark 6:14–26

Their Story

Monday

Even though John the Baptist was dead, his voice still resounded in the thick silence of the night. Herod Antipas could not escape it. He had learned long ago that covering his head with pillows was no match for noises that made their home in his mind, and right now, that's where John the Baptist's voice lived, rent free.

But the voice wasn't the only thing that stalked Herod; there was also his ruthless wife, Herodias.

And his seductive stepdaughter, Salome.

And the platter.

The one that carried the head of John from daughter to mother.

And, of course, there was his own blundering tongue. The one that spoke those lamentable words, "Whatever you ask I will give you, up to half my kingdom."[1]

That's what Herod had promised to Salome.

And it cost John his head.

And Herod his sanity.

As the ruler of Galilee and Perea, Herod Antipas was a man of many appetites. Like his father, Herod the Great, Antipas had a hunger for building projects. He also had a passion for fame. And riches. And power.

And women.

One in particular.

A woman he should not have taken — Herodias, the wife of his half brother Herod Philip I.

But Herod wanted her, and he resolved to have her.

One night, while a guest in Philip's home, Herod arranged time alone with Herodias. Just a brief encounter and a little talk with her would be enough. Whatever he propositioned worked — Herodias agreed to leave Philip and marry Herod. And in the deal, Herod would also acquire Herodias's teenage daughter, Salome.

The fact that Herod was already married was a mere technicality. He made quick work of his own divorce and quickly married Herodias.

But one problem loomed large: A religious zealot a few miles away was preaching repentance in preparation for the coming of Israel's Messiah. John the Baptist was calling people to righteous living and obedience to God's laws. Sadly for Herod, those cumbersome rules included, "Do not have sexual relations with your brother's wife; that would dishonor your brother."[2]

The marriage of Herod and Herodias was a clear breach of this command. The Baptist would not let it pass. Incensed, Herodias demanded that her husband kill the Baptizer and be done with him. Herod, too, wanted John dead, but he knew this would be bad

---

1. Mark 6:23.
2. Leviticus 18:16.

politics. The Israelites regarded John the Baptist as a prophet and might revolt if Herod killed him.

So the king did what he could—he threw John into prison. But even though he was out of circulation, John was not silent. From his cell the Baptist continued to preach condemnation. Herodias was furious and became consumed with killing John.

During the two years of John's imprisonment, however, Herod grew curious at—perhaps convicted by—John's words. Herodias would not—could not—let it go, and Herod knew it. He protected John from her schemes.

Until the night of Herod's birthday.

Wanting to honor himself—a favorite pastime—Herod threw a raucous party. He was intoxicated within the first hour and pontificating his greatness the next hour. By the third hour, he was slurring his words. And by the fourth hour, he was ready to be had.

Feeling frisky, he asked young Salome to dance for him. Her lewd and provocative gyrations sent Herod into a frenzy. When at last Salome had finished, Herod was a soft target for catastrophe. "What is it you want, Salome?" the aroused Herod asked loudly enough for all his high-ranking officials to hear. "Just ask it of me and it is yours—up to half my kingdom."

He watched as she strutted over to confer with her mother.

Herod's heart sank. He was trapped. This would not be good.

Salome walked up to her stepfather with a smug smile on her face. "My lord," she said, her dark eyes chilling Herod's soul, "I want you to give me the head of John the Baptist on a platter. Right now."

A hushed silence blanketed the palace.

"No, Salome, no."

"You promised ..."

"But Salome ..."

"In front of all your guests!"

Herod looked around the room. Men and women—his subjects—were all watching him now. Like spears, every eye pierced him.

Herod's heart pounded with panic. No, not the Baptist. He's a righteous man. He doesn't deserve to die.

"You promised, Herod; you promised."

"No, Salome ..."

"I danced for you!"

Herod dropped his eyes in surrender. Salome and her devious mother had won, and it was clear to everyone. Defeated, he obediently gave the order to the captain of his guard. "Bring the head of the Baptist."

Save for scattered murmurings, a dreadful silence seized the banquet hall.

Soon the soldier returned with a platter. On it was the severed head of the Baptist.

Herod watched in horror as the platter was handed to the girl. Then she delivered the grand prize to her mother.

Herod had been manipulated by his wife's cunning, and for this he despised her.

And now, distant months later, in the silence of the night, he was wide-awake. The quiet of his palace mocked the screams of his soul. Pounding in his head were the thunderous words of the Baptist. The voice that had once mesmerized Herod was louder than ever. Guilt terrorized his soul.

He turned to look at his wife in the darkness.

She was sound asleep.

Their Life and Times

Tuesday

The Herodic Dynasty

Herod Antipas, the ruler responsible for the execution of John the Baptist, was the son of Herod the Great. This loathsome ruler had cast a huge shadow across the land of Israel by the time John the Baptist and Jesus were born. Herod the Great was the one who was threatened by the Magi's prophecy about the Christ child. He ordered the murder of all Jewish baby boys under the age of two. So Joseph and Mary fled with their toddler, Jesus, from Judah to Egypt in order to escape Herod's edict.

A few years later, after Herod the Great was dead, Joseph and Mary left Egypt, believing it was safe to return to their home in Nazareth.

Because Herod the Great had died with no succession plan in

place, his kingdom was divided into four regions, each headed by a "tetrarch" or "ruler of a fourth." These four rulers included three of Herod's sons. One was Herod Antipas, who reigned over Galilee and Perea on the eastern side of the Jordan River valley. The second son was Philip II, who controlled Iturea and Traconitis (north of Galilee). The third son was Archelaus, who ruled Judea, Idumea (Edom), and Samaria. The fourth region went to Lysanias, who presided over Abilene (located on the western slopes of Mount Hermon). Herod's son Philip I did not rule.

The Herod who killed John the Baptist, Herod Antipas, was first married to the daughter of Aretas IV of Arabia. But Herod fell in love with another woman, Herodias, the wife of Philip I, his half brother. Because she was his sister-in-law, marriage to her would have been unlawful. But Herod Antipas lived by his own rules. No doubt his wealth, power, and charm—which far exceeded Philip's—helped Herodias to see her suitor's point of view.

When Herod divorced his first wife and married Herodias, John the Baptist refused to sit quietly. He was not going to look the other way as these people thumbed their noses at God's law. Denouncing their marriage publicly, John predictably drew their wrath. He was imprisoned for two years until the day when Herod made a glib promise to do whatever his salacious, dancing stepdaughter wanted.[3] She demanded that her stepfather have John beheaded. So he did.

Herod's problems did not end with John the Baptist's death. They intensified. The news of Jesus, another prophet, began to spread across the region. Confused and paranoid, Herod exclaimed. "John, whom I beheaded, has been raised from the dead!" (Mark 6:16).

Several years later, Herod cross-examined Jesus before he was put on trial for claiming to be the Messiah. But Jesus was silent. In frustration, Herod returned Jesus to Pilate, who would preside over the crucifixion.

A few years after his encounter with Jesus, Herod Antipas fell from power, due in large part to an aggressive and defiant young man named Agrippa, his nephew, the brother of Herodias. Herod Antipas had tried to placate his scheming wife, but her own brother toppled him from the throne.

---

3. See Luke 3:19–20.

Can You Imagine?

Wednesday

When Herod met Herodias, the fact that they both were married did not deter them. His desire for her and his ability to get what he wanted trumped any moral imperative. Herod's unbridled lust over his stepdaughter's dancing led to the murder of John the Baptist. Sexual temptation is powerful. And it can be lethal.

Can you imagine why, in God's perfect wisdom, He set boundaries for human sexuality? Intimacy is one of God's good gifts to married couples. As the expression of our love for our spouse, sex is intended to be the blending of shameless vulnerability and selfless celebration. Fidelity—one man and one woman for life—protects us, body, soul, and spirit.

One of the most stunning and poetic directives about fidelity in marriage is found in the book of Proverbs: "Drink water from your own cistern, running water from your own well ... Let them be yours alone, never to be shared with strangers. May your fountain be blessed, and may you rejoice in the wife of your youth" (Proverbs 5:15, 17–18). Herod and Herodias probably had access to these words written centuries earlier, but if so they disregarded them.

Sex is meant to be celebrated by two people who love deeply and exclusively. Lust and impurity cannot satisfy the longing for intimacy and security. God gave us marriage to fulfill those longings. The promise of sexual satisfaction outside of God's boundaries is a lie. Do all you can to protect the purity of your exclusive sexual relationship with your spouse.

From God's Word ...

"Enjoy life with your wife, whom you love."

ECCLESIASTES 9:9

Their Legacy in Scripture

Thursday

1. **"Above all else, guard your heart, for everything you do flows from it"** (PROVERBS 4:23).

   Herodias was angry with John the Baptist because he pointed out her sin. Her contempt led her to manipulate her husband. We believers have the Holy Spirit to point out our sin. How can you keep your heart tender toward the conviction of God and guard against sexual temptation?

2. **"Now that you know God—or rather are known by God—how is it that you are turning back to those weak and miserable forces? Do you wish to be enslaved by them all over again?"** (GALATIANS 4:9).

   Herod was driven by his unlawful and unbridled lust. Why do you think he was drawn to John's preaching? How do you think his wife would have reacted if he had embraced John's message and repented? What temptations pose a threat to the sexual intimacy of your marriage? What would your spouse say has the potential to enslave you?

3. **"The wisdom that comes from heaven is first of all pure; then peace-loving, considerate, submissive, full of mercy and good fruit, impartial and sincere"** (JAMES 3:17).

   From this list, what do you need to cultivate to demonstrate heavenly wisdom toward your spouse? What can you plan in word or action (send a loving text message, hold hands in church, write a love note, prepare a special meal) that will positively affect your physical, emotional, or spiritual intimacy with your spouse?

Their Legacy of Prayer

Friday

Reflect On: Ecclesiastes 9:9

Praise God: For His holiness and purity, and for His gift to you—
His Holy Spirit.

Offer Thanks: For the gift of a spouse with whom you can share
physical love as God intended, and for covering your
marriage with truth and sincerity.

Confess: That you are often motivated by selfishness and
sometimes crave unholy things. Repent for holding
on to bitterness and neglecting to enjoy your spouse.

Ask God: To point out any attitude that could weaken your
marriage, to replace contempt with consideration,
and to give you the tenderness you felt for your spouse
when you first married.

Listen: "Dear children, I created your union to display My
goodness. Your marriage is designed to bring happiness
to your hearts and to draw you closer to Me. Put aside
harmful attitudes and rejoice in each other today."

Pray: *Holy Spirit, we need You to preach to our hearts so we may
become the people You created us to be. We repent of our
waywardness. Many things pull us away from You, but we want
to trust You and cling to Your Word. Grant us the capacity to
delight in each other. Help us to rekindle the hope and wonder
of our marriage. We want to love each other the way You love us.
Amen.*

44

We Bow Down

Jairus and Wife

Meaning of Names: *Jairus* means "whom God enlightens" or "he shines." The name of Jairus's wife is not given in the Bible.

Their Character: He was a respected and upright man who was not afraid to humble himself. She was a grieving mother who was given the gift of faith.

Their Challenge: They had a twelve-year-old daughter who was terminally ill and died. He was a synagogue leader who, at first, feared scorn for believing in Jesus.

Their Outcome: Jesus miraculously restored their daughter to life, and they believed in Him.

Key Scripture: Mark 5:21–43

Their Story

Monday

It had been a week since the young girl had told her parents she was sick. Over the past few days, she had grown worse. Her fever was so severe that it threatened to end her life.

The village doctor had been summoned, but his treatment had proven ineffective. The girl was going in and out of consciousness.

Her father, Jairus, wasn't sleeping. Her mother was numb with uncertainty. Day and night, the anxious parents kept vigil. At times they wondered if their daughter was alive, carefully watching to see if her chest raised and lowered with her breathing. It did. Barely.

Jairus and his wife could do nothing but wait.

On the seventh day, Jairus's wife lifted her head and turned to her husband. "I think it's time."

Jairus swallowed hard. "You mean the Rabbi from Nazareth?"

His wife nodded and turned her face back toward their sleeping daughter.

But what will my friends at the synagogue say? Jairus wondered, immediately regretting the shallowness of his thought.

His wife pleaded. "Our daughter is dying, Jairus."

Her words contradicted his pride and were enough to persuade him. Without speaking to the people gathered outside his home, Jairus hurried on his way. His face was etched with focus and determination as he anxiously moved through the narrow, busy streets of Capernaum down to the shoreline of the Sea of Galilee. He knew the Rabbi was likely to be there.

Jairus's heart pounded. He had heard much about the Rabbi from Nazareth, especially His miracles. Jairus was intrigued and wanted to believe the stories. But one question haunted him: What was the source of Jesus' healing powers? He claimed He was sent from God. The Jewish leaders mocked Jesus and said His strength came from Satan.

Jairus was undecided. As a synagogue ruler, he was often asked about the Rabbi. He diplomatically avoided expressing an opinion.

But now his daughter was near death. And his wife was about to collapse from exhaustion. Jairus was afraid of losing them both. His skeptical mind was undone. The Jewish leaders could not help him. The physicians could do nothing to save his little girl.

The Rabbi was his only hope.

The desperate father reached the shoreline just as the Rabbi and His disciples were stepping away from their boats. Jairus's heart soared when he caught a glimpse of Jesus. But a huge crowd was in the way, making it nearly impossible to get close to Him.

Pushing forward, Jairus told several men standing near that his daughter was dying and he must reach the Rabbi. A few people recognized Jairus as the synagogue leader and helped to clear a path.

Finally standing directly in front of the Rabbi, Jairus collapsed at Jesus' feet. He had never bowed before a man. "My little daughter is dying," he wept. "Please come and put Your hands on her so she will be healed and live."

The Rabbi's eyes were fixed on Jairus. He nodded, agreeing to go. They were on their way.

And then ...

The Rabbi stopped.

"Who touched Me?" He asked. "I felt power go out from Me."

What is this interruption? Jairus silently agonized. *We have no time for this delay.*

Hoping to be healed from twelve years of hemorrhaging, a woman had touched the edge of Jesus' robe. When Jesus turned and saw her, she fell down in worship. "Daughter, your faith has healed you," the Rabbi told her. "Go in peace and be freed from your suffering."[1]

Just then, some frantic men pushed through the crowd toward him. They had come from Jairus's home. "Your daughter is dead, Jairus," they said. "Why bother the teacher anymore?"

Jairus stood motionless, trying to breathe. The Rabbi paid no attention to the news. "Don't be afraid, Jairus, just believe." Jairus wasn't sure what to do.

Jairus and Jesus continued to walk.

When they arrived at his home, Jairus was stunned by what he saw. Paid professional mourners were already wailing. His daughter was dead. His faith was shaken.

But the Rabbi was unfazed.

Stepping through the chaos, Jesus and Jairus slipped into the house. "Why all this commotion and wailing?" Jesus asked. "The child is not dead but asleep." Some of the people standing nearby laughed derisively.

Jairus's wife reached for her husband and dropped into his arms. "The Rabbi is here," Jairus whispered.

Jesus gathered the couple, and together they entered the dead girl's room. She appeared lifeless, but was as beautiful as an angel. Jairus tried to keep his composure, holding his trembling wife as Jesus approached the bed.

Leaning down, He took her cold hand. "Little girl," He said. "I say to you, get up!"

The girl blinked. Opening her eyes wide, she looked around and

---

1. Mark 5:34.

immediately stood up, rushing to her mother and father's arms. The three held each other and did not let go. Their faces were wet with tears.

Jairus and his wife stared gratefully at the Rabbi but were unable to speak.

What could they say?

Their Life and Times

Tuesday

The Position of Prayer

After Jairus and his wife had exhausted all other options to save their twelve-year-old daughter's life, Jairus set out to find the Healer. For a respected Jewish leader to bow before Jesus and solicit His help would have been an admission that the Rabbi was a superior. It could also have been an indication that Jairus considered Jesus to be the Messiah.

Jairus went further than just bowing when he caught up with the Rabbi. The sick girl's father fell down at Jesus' feet.[2] For his colleagues at the Capernaum temple, this would have been seen as blasphemy. To them, Jesus was at best an imposter, at worst a demon.

So was Jairus's visible homage to the Rabbi significant? Yes, extremely significant.

A learned man, Jairus would have known the meaning of the Hebrew verb *ḥāwāh*. It meant to "bow down." Jairus knew the history of *ḥāwāh*.

When Abraham was hoping to bury Sarah in Hittite land, he bowed down before the people as he made his request.[3] Bowing meant respect.

When the conniving Jacob met up with his brother Esau many years after having stolen their father's birthright, he bowed down.[4] Doing this demonstrated repentance and contrition.

Moses had left Zipporah, his wife, and their two sons under the

---

2. See Mark 5:22.
3. See Genesis 23:7.
4. See Genesis 33:3.

care of her father, Jethro, in Midian to travel back to Egypt. His assignment was to free the Hebrews from Egyptian captivity. Then his family and father-in-law rejoined Moses in the wilderness. As an act of deep gratitude for his help, Moses bowed down to Jethro.[5]

When Boaz displayed surprising kindness to Ruth, a foreigner with no standing in his country, she bowed down in his presence.[6] Why Boaz had been so kind to her, she could not understand. Bowing down was a sign of humility and wonder.

David's life was being threatened by King Saul. When Jonathan, Saul's son and David's closest ally, warned David that his father had plans to kill him, David bowed down to his friend.[7] This gesture represented a pledge of loyalty.

Abigail had hurried to meet King David. Her husband, Nabal, had done a foolish thing and David's plan was to get even with the scoundrel. When Abigail met David, she bowed down before him.[8] Bowing was an act of mediation and intercession. She was not bowing for herself; she was asking for a special kind of mercy for someone else.

But when Jairus found himself in the presence of Jesus, he did not simply bow down; he fell down. The Hebrew word indicating this intense form of bowing down is *artzah* ("to the ground").[9] A person could "bow" and remain standing.[10] But falling down to the ground meant the highest measure of respect, repentance, gratitude, humility, loyalty, and intercession.

Setting aside all pretense and pride, Jairus went to the Rabbi as his final hope for his daughter's life. He was out of options. There was nothing Jairus could do on his own, and he knew it.

Jairus was in the presence of Jesus. *Yeshua.* The Christ. The Savior. The Anointed One. The Healer. And regardless of any temporal rank or status, in that moment, Jairus was just a desperate husband and father.

Simply bowing down would not do. So Jairus fell down.

---

5. See Exodus 18:7.
6. See Ruth 2:10.
7. See 1 Samuel 20:41.
8. See 1 Samuel 25:23.
9. See Ruth 2:10.
10. See Hebrews 11:21.

Can You Imagine?

Wednesday

You or someone you know has suffered indescribable loss or is now in the middle of a debilitating trial or illness. When a couple arrives at the point of no return with all their options exhausted, sometimes all they can do is cling to each other ... and worship. As their daughter lay motionless at the threshold of death, Jairus and his wife huddled together. Can you imagine you and your spouse holding on to each other in sheer desperation? Maybe you have.

Little by little, we prepare our spiritual muscles for these times. The habits that you and your spouse have established—praying and worshiping together, mutual encouragement and confession—build your spiritual strength so you can endure tough times with God's grace. And then, when your faith is tested with a crisis—and it will be—you can keep your eyes on Jesus and run with perseverance the race that has been set before you.[11]

Jesus was never anxious or disturbed by circumstances. Even death was not an obstacle beyond His power. Jairus and his wife looked to Him, and Jesus told them not to be afraid. Though the couple struggled with believing, Jesus both initiated and matured their faith.

When you and your spouse bow in humility before the Lord, He welcomes you and increases your faith. His comfort becomes real.

From God's Word ...

"Therefore we do not lose heart. Though outwardly we are wasting away, yet inwardly we are being renewed day by day. For our light and momentary troubles are achieving for us an eternal glory that far outweighs them all. So we fix our eyes not on what is seen, but on what is unseen, since what is seen is temporary, but what is unseen is eternal."

2 CORINTHIANS 4:16–18

---

11. See Hebrews 12:1–2.

Their Legacy in Scripture

Thursday

1. "In my distress I called to the LORD; I cried to my God for help. From his temple he heard my voice; my cry came before him, into his ears" (PSALM 18:6).

   Jairus went to Jesus to ask Him to heal his daughter. Do you think this was the couple's first response when their little girl's condition grew more serious? Prayer ushers us into God's presence in good times and in times of crisis. When have you and your spouse cried out to the Lord for help? What can you do each day to become spiritually strong?

2. "In your righteousness, rescue me and deliver me; turn your ear to me and save me" (PSALM 71:2).

   These could have been the words Jairus and his wife prayed. At times of severe crisis, words like *rescue*, *deliver*, and *save* make perfect sense. But the kind hand of God's providence rescues, delivers, and saves you every day in ways you do not know. What praise can you offer God for the blessings in your life right now? How can words of gratefulness change your attitude and strengthen your marriage?

3. "'Take my yoke upon you and learn from me, for I am gentle and humble in heart, and you will find rest for your souls'" (MATTHEW 11:29).

   What does it mean to have a restless soul? What was the condition of Jairus's heart before his encounter with Jesus? Following Jairus's example, what are the steps for healing an anxious soul? What can you do to experience the peace Jesus offers?

Their Legacy of Prayer

Friday

Reflect On: Mark 5:21–43

Praise God: That He is the all-present God who has the power to redeem, rescue, and deliver His children, and that He is the God of all comfort who sends His peace that passes human understanding.

Offer Thanks: That God has given you the gift of faith to believe He is at work on your behalf and will strengthen your heart. For hearing your prayers when you pour out your deepest fears, hurts, and anguish.

Confess: That in your most desperate times you often rely on your own power rather than on His, and that in your unbelief, you sometimes seek God as a last resort rather than your first thought.

Ask God: To help you understand that He is the supreme rescuer and sustainer of not only your soul but of your physical life as well. For faith to believe that everything is in God's control and perfectly timed, and for His peace in your heart.

Listen: "My children, I will never leave you or forsake you. My presence will sustain you when you are confused and hurting. Do not be afraid. I am the resurrection and the life. I am the light that will drive out the darkness. Give Me all of your fears. Be still, and I will lift you into My presence."

Pray: *Heavenly Father, You are the light of the world. You are eternal life. We fall at Your feet and rely on Your mercy. Rescue us from fear and give us faith to trust You. Thank You for sustaining us and giving us Your Holy Spirit to encourage our desperate hearts. You are the only One who can save us. We have hope because of You. Amen.*

45

Satisfied

Samaritan Woman and Lover

Meaning of Names: Neither the name of the Samaritan woman nor the name of her lover is given in the Bible.

Her Character: She was a sinful woman from a despised region who was receptive to hearing the truth of God.

Her Challenge: After having been married five times, she was living with a man who was not her husband.

Her Outcome: She met Jesus and believed He was the Messiah. Because of her witness, many Samaritans were converted.

Key Scripture: John 4:1–42

Their Story

Monday

The sun lifted high over the countryside, sending down its harshest rays. A short distance outside the city limits was a well belonging to the town of Sychar. Because of the extreme heat, only a few of the townspeople ventured out during the scorching hours of midday ... unless the goal was to avoid seeing others. Or to avoid being seen, which was the case of the woman making her way to draw water that afternoon.

As she approached the well, she saw a man sitting on the stone edge. The woman hesitated. Her mind raced ahead of her feet. *Do not speak with this stranger. Draw the water you need and be gone.*

The closer she came to the well, the greater her apprehension. If the water source hadn't been such a distance from town and the jug so heavy, she would have turned around. But she had traveled far, and she was thirsty, so the woman continued. Relieved because men did not speak with unknown women in public, she determined to fill her water pot and be on her way without conversation or incident.

She was wrong on both counts.

She was drawing water when the sound of His voice startled her. "Will you give me a drink?" the man asked.[1]

While she was trying to figure out whether or not this was a trick of some kind and if she should even answer Him, she studied His face. He looked like a Hebrew. If this were true, she was even more astonished. Hebrews—men or women—did not speak to lowly Samaritans. But His countenance calmed her. His eyes were gentle, His voice welcoming.

Because He had spoken first, the law allowed her to reply or even to ask a question. So she did. "You are a Jew and I am a Samaritan woman. How can you ask me for a drink?"[2]

This inquiry began an intriguing conversation, a dialogue that loosened the woman's knotted soul.

The man looked up at the woman. "If you knew the gift of God and who it is that asks you for a drink, you would have asked him and he would have given you living water."[3]

Confused because the traveler had no goatskin bucket in His hand, the woman said, "Sir, You have nothing to draw with and the well is deep. Where can You get this living water?"

His reply puzzled her. "Everyone who drinks this water will be thirsty again, but whoever drinks the water I give them will never thirst. Indeed, the water I give them will become in them a spring of water welling up to eternal life."

Desperately seeking what the man offered, she said to Him, "Sir, give me this water so that I won't get thirsty and have to keep coming here to draw water."

"Go, call your husband and come back."

Attempting to appear righteous, the woman replied, "I have no husband."

---

1. John 4:7.
2. John 4:9.
3. John 4:10.

"You are right when you say you have no husband," the man replied. "The fact is, you have had five husbands, and the man you now have is not your husband. What you have just said is quite true."

How does He know who I am and what I have done? She had never seen this man before. His words confounded her.

"Sir," the woman said, "I can see that You are a prophet ... I know that Messiah is coming. When He comes, He will explain everything to us."

Then Jesus declared, "I, the one speaking to you—I am he."[4]

Chills shot through the woman's body. *Could this man be the Messiah?* she wondered.

The Samaritan woman looked at Jesus. Something new and beautiful was welling up inside her. Something fresh and powerful. *Could this be the living water He was talking about?*

Alive with excitement, the woman left her water pot and hurried back to Sychar. Running through the streets like a herald, she announced to anyone who would listen, "Come, see a man who told me everything I ever did. Could this be the Messiah?"

She, an outcast, had met Jesus and been redeemed by the encounter. Everyone needed to know. Quite taken by her witness and the possibility that the man at the well was really the Messiah, the people came out of the town and made their way toward Jesus.

The woman did not follow them. A wave of urgency stopped her. Her thoughts went to the house where her lover was waiting. She must tell him all that had happened. But would he understand about the living water?

As the people of Sychar streamed past the woman and out of town toward the well, she knew what she must do.

Turning toward her street, the woman bravely walked home.

---

4. John 4:26.

Their Life and Times

Tuesday

Water Wells

Jesus met the Samaritan woman at a well. Wells were a common meeting place because they were the daily source of water, essential for life. Wells also represented God's goodness and were symbols of His blessings on a village.

Wells were especially important in Canaan, where rainwater was quickly absorbed by the sandy landscape. Though it is believed that "Jacob's well" (mentioned only in this Bible story) was located outside the town of Sychar, most wells were situated in the centers of communities—near homes, synagogues, and the marketplace.

Community wells were beehives of conversation. Women gathered there six mornings a week to draw what they needed for the day. They filled their vessels and caught up on the latest news. Once their water pots were filled, they would balance them on their heads and walk home.

Wells were valuable assets that required constant maintenance. To keep debris from falling in and spoiling the water, well openings were often protected by heavy stone lids that could only be removed by three or four strong men. This is the kind of stone covering that the love-struck Jacob single-handedly removed for Rachel.[5]

Besides supplying water for domestic needs, wells were often necessary for nourishing thirsty flocks of sheep and goats when there were no available streams. These wells were usually located far outside of town in pasturelands. This was the way the young shepherd David —long before he became king of Israel—watered his flocks in the surrounding hill country of Bethlehem. Large drinking troughs were often built alongside these wells. Shepherds would lower their vessels into the well, fill them, pull them out, and pour the water into the trough. When the trough was full, their flocks could drink.

There were two primary types of wells. The first was dug by hand. With backbreaking labor, the digging continued until water was discovered. So valuable were these wells in the water-starved

---

5. See Genesis 29:10.

Near East that wars were often fought over them. Following Abraham's death, the Philistines stopped up his wells as a way to drive his descendants away from what they regarded as their land. Years later, Abraham's son Isaac reopened the wells.[6]

The second kind of well was the treasured—and much rarer—spring-fed well, which rarely ran dry. Constantly replenished by underground reservoirs, these highly prized wells provided communities with a steady water supply.

Jacob's well, where Jesus met with the Samaritan woman, was unusual. The initial word used to describe this well is *pēgē*, meaning "spring" or "fountain."[7] Later the word *phrear* is used, meaning "cistern" or "pit."[8] This well was first dug out by hand and then fed by an underground spring.

Jesus was using the uniqueness of this two-thousand-year-old well to provide a gospel metaphor. When He spoke of the living water as "springing up," He used a word that actually meant "leaping up" as from a spring-fed source. He painted a picture of water eternally bubbling up, so alive and powerful that it would satisfy the woman's thirst and never run dry.

Though "Jacob's well" is no longer in existence, the spring that fed it is still active.

6. See Genesis 26:18.
7. See John 4:6.
8. See John 4:11–12.

Can You Imagine?

Wednesday

For the woman from Sychar, the midday walk to the well was probably routine. But the ordinary complexion of this day was about to blush full crimson. As she approached from a distance, she saw someone sitting on the stone edge. It was a man. *What is He doing there? And who is He?*

Seeing her approach, the man spoke. And in a few minutes the anxiety of who this might be was replaced with an overwhelming sense of wonder. Even though this woman's life had been a mess, Jesus did not treat her like damaged goods. His countenance and His words spoke of love. Once she knew who He was, it is reasonable to assume she was convicted about her lifestyle and resolved to make some changes.

Once she met Jesus, she saw herself in a new light.

Can you imagine what it would be like to actually meet Jesus face-to-face? What do you think He would point out in your life that needs to be changed? How would you tell your spouse about the encounter? How should you respond when your spouse becomes convicted about something he or she is doing?

We live in a culture that shrugs off the gravity of sin. And too often we are tempted to compromise what we know to be right and true. For the woman, meeting Jesus turned out to be both good news and bad news. The good news was that she had met the Savior who could release her from her sin. The sobering news was that she would need to go home and live differently.

With all that you have done, Jesus sits on the edge of the stone well and gently says, "Come. Be new."

From God's Word ...

"Jesus said, 'Come to me, all you who are weary and burdened, and I will give you rest ... for I am gentle and humble in heart, and you will find rest for your souls.'"

MATTHEW 11:28–29

Their Legacy in Scripture

Thursday

1. **"'I am he'"** (JOHN 4:26).

    When she approached the stranger, the Samaritan woman had no idea He was Jesus. What do you think were the qualities of God's Son that drew her to open up to Him? What draws you to Jesus now? What do you think He would point out that displeases Him?

2. **"'The LORD will guide you always; he will satisfy your needs in a sun-scorched land and will strengthen your frame. You will be like a well-watered garden, like a spring whose waters never fail'"** (ISAIAH 58:11).

    People today are bombarded by empty promises. If you buy this or wear that or eat this or do that—or if you marry him—you'll be satisfied. These can be alluring guarantees. The woman at the well had tried to find happiness by marrying five different men and living with another, but she was still thirsty for fulfillment. Jesus offered her something eternal. What did He mean by "living water"? What does the satisfaction that Jesus promises look like to you?

3. **"As high as the heavens are above the earth, so great is his love for those who fear him; as far as the east is from the west, so far has he removed our transgressions from us"** (PSALM 103:11–12).

    The Samaritan woman came to the well as an outcast with plenty of issues. Describe the transformation she experienced when she met Jesus. Why is it sometimes hard to believe that God has truly forgiven all of your sins? How far is the east from the west? Why is it sometimes difficult to forgive your spouse? What would this kind of complete forgiveness mean in your marriage?

Their Legacy of Prayer

Friday

Reflect On: John 4:1–42

Praise God: For pursuing you and offering forgiveness, hope, and new life in Christ.

Offer Thanks: That God has removed all of your sins as far as the east is from the west and remembers them no more, and that He is providing deep springs of contentment for your marriage that will never run dry.

Confess: That you often are enticed by worldly desires and seek satisfaction outside of what is pleasing to Christ, and that you tend to rationalize your sin and refuse to repent.

Ask God: To give you the faith to believe that He alone can satisfy the longings of your heart. To help you be a winsome witness of His grace in your life, and to give you courage to break away from all known sin and do what is right in His sight.

Listen: "My children, I have known all about you from before you were born. I know how to satisfy the deepest longings of your soul. I will provide springs of living water for your marriage. I am a forgiver of sin—past, present, and future—and you have been completely forgiven. I have made you a new creation. Live in the joy of your redeemed life with Me."

Pray: *Heavenly Father, thank You for removing our transgressions and giving us eternal life. Your promises are sure and Your love is powerful. We want to run to tell everyone about Your amazing mercy and salvation. With Your Spirit living inside us, our marriage is renewed each day. You are the God who redeems. We are thirsty for the love You offer. We want to be a couple that honors You. Amen.*

46

Thunder and Lightning

Zebedee and Salome

Meaning of Names:	*Zebedee* means "the gift of God." *Salome* means "peaceful."
Their Character:	He was a passionate businessman whose faith allowed his sons and his wife to follow and serve Jesus. She was an assertive woman who actively sought the best for her sons and was transformed by Jesus.
Their Challenge:	Their two sons left the successful family business in order to follow Jesus, leaving them shorthanded.
Their Outcome:	Their sons, James and John, became disciples and were two of the three closest associates of Jesus. John wrote a gospel, three epistles, and the book of Revelation. Salome witnessed the crucifixion and was one of the first to see the empty tomb.
Key Scripture:	Matthew 20:20–28; Mark 15:40; 16:1

Their Story

Monday

Salome was usually content with her independence, but she never needed Zebedee more than she needed him right now.

Though she took comfort in the companionship of the other women gathered with her, she missed her husband's broad shoulders. Although at times her dominant will had clashed with his consuming passion for expanding his business, Salome longed to breathe in the familiar smell of fish and salt water and nestle again in Zebedee's strong arms.

But Salome's husband was ninety miles away in Capernaum, plying his trade on the Sea of Galilee. During the day's early hours, she wondered if he had secured a good catch of fish, and as the day approached noon, she suspected he was mending his nets.

Zebedee's wife was in Jerusalem. The city felt dark and hopeless.

Salome's mind was a flurried mix of confusion and sorrow. The wailing of the other mourners surrounded her. She never thought she would witness the execution of her Savior.

As much as she could, Salome had spent the past three years following Jesus, and this is where her journey had led her.

Now she stood near the crest of the rounded hill. Although it was not chilly, her small frame shivered. She drew her cloak in, wrapping it as tightly as possible. Not far ahead, close to the spot where Jesus' cross met the earth, she could see her son, John. The responsibility had been given him to care for Mary of Nazareth, the mother of Jesus. Salome was thankful for John and was pleased to loan him to her friend Mary.

Salome scanned the crowd. She could not see her other son, James, or any of the other disciples. She guessed they were hiding somewhere, afraid of being arrested by the Jewish leaders who had apprehended Jesus the previous night.

After a hasty trial earlier that day, a brutal scourging, and a torturous march through the streets of Jerusalem to a place outside of the city gates, Jesus had been nailed to a cross.

It had been four hours since the nails had been driven into Jesus' hands and feet and His cross dropped with a thump into a deep hole. Standing there, Salome had watched in horror, unable to take it in. Her mind floated back over the years to when this all began.

She remembered the day Zebedee strode home with a bemused look on his angular face. Salome inquired. Zebedee paused. He was not one to wait before speaking, but this time he weighed his words. "Our sons are up to something," he said. "James and John left the boat to follow a stranger. A rabbi."

"What do you mean 'follow'?"

"Well, the Rabbi called to our sons and said, 'Follow me.' We were sitting on the shore mending our fishing nets after a big catch. James and John were immediately captivated. They stood, dropped the nets, and followed Him."

That was not enough information for Salome. She grilled her husband. He expected her questions. After all, they were a fierce couple filled with Jewish zeal for the God of Israel. And they had raised their two sons with the same passion. James and John were thunderous, enthusiastic young men with a sincere yearning for truth. They were not given to shirking responsibility or impulsively pledging their allegiance to just anyone.

But in that moment when the Rabbi called them by name, James and John left their father standing knee-deep in the snarled nets, wondering what would become of the family business.

The next morning, after a fitful night, Salome headed out to get some answers. "I'll be back," she said to Zebedee. "I must find our sons ... and see this for myself."

When she reached the fishing district of Capernaum, a throng of people hovered near a lone man who was sitting in a boat close to shore. The Teacher's voice rang through the captivated multitude as He spoke. The Galileans listened intently.

Drawing closer, Salome soon became one of the crowd following Jesus. Like the others, she wondered, *Could this be the Messiah?* This was the question that had the people talking and taking sides. Swathes of dissension swept the region.

After finding her sons and discussing the words of the Teacher, it became clear to Salome why James and John had left everything to become His disciples. He was the One.

As often as she could in the months that followed, Salome joined a contingent of women who served the needs of Jesus the Teacher and His followers.

One day she heard Jesus say to His disciples, "Truly I tell you, at the renewal of all things, when the Son of Man sits on his glorious throne, you who have followed me will also sit on twelve thrones, judging the twelve tribes of Israel."[1]

The words of Jesus ignited Salome's imagination. In a valiant

---

1. Matthew 19:28.

attempt to secure highest honors for her sons, she went to the Teacher and said, "Grant that one of these two sons of mine may sit at your right and the other at your left in your kingdom."[2]

"You don't know what you're asking," Jesus told her.

And now, as the early afternoon sky darkened, Salome was beginning to realize what Jesus meant. His love had taken hold of her, and she was strengthened with bold faith.

Salome's thoughts turned back toward her home and her husband in Capernaum. She was eager to tell Zebedee everything she had seen.

Their Life and Times

Tuesday

Going Fishing

Much of Jesus' earthly ministry took place on or near water, especially the Sea of Galilee — a body of fresh water measuring nearly sixty-four square miles.[3] Jesus traveled along its coast to towns with names like Capernaum and Bethsaida. He visited other villages like Nazareth, Cana, and Nain within a few miles of the sea. It was along the shoreline of the Sea of Galilee where Jesus met and invited the sons of Zebedee to follow Him. They were career fishermen.

Because of the abundance of underwater vegetation and plankton, the Sea of Galilee was a good place for business. It was a reservoir for several varieties of plentiful fish. These included sardines, as well as carp-like fish called barbels with visible spines near their mouths. The sea was also home to a fish we now call "St. Peter's Fish," which sported a long dorsal fin resembling a comb. This fish could weigh more than three pounds and be up to eighteen inches long.[4]

Zebedee was a commercial fisherman whose livelihood depended on the abundant resources in the Sea of Galilee. His business was robust enough to employ men other than his sons, so Zebedee was

---

2. Matthew 20:21.

3. In the Bible, the Sea of Galilee is identified with several names, including the Sea of Kinnereth (see Numbers 34:11), Lake of Gennesaret (see Luke 5:1), and Sea of Tiberias (see John 6:1; 21:1).

4. See "Sea of Galilee," BiblePlaces.com, http://goo.gl/ItRx0 (accessed September 13, 2012).

likely a man of means. When Jesus called James and John to become His disciples, they left behind Zebedee and his hired men.[5]

To collect the daily catch, Zebedee and his crew used weighted dragnets pulled behind their boats. Sometimes lighter nets were thrown across the surface of the water and then gathered back.[6]

Fishermen were usually sinewy and strong because of the manual labor required to lift heavy nets filled with fish. Toughened and leathery from their daily exposure to the elements, they were a community of robust and persevering men.

Because of the relatively high cost of meat, fish provided nutrition at an affordable cost. Zebedee's business flourished because he was able to catch enough fish to market to people in two towns.

The Bible references fish and fishing to help people understand spiritual truth. Old Testament writers compared human helplessness to fish trapped in a net.[7] Jesus explained to His disciples that they would fish for people when He called them to go out and gather souls for the kingdom of God.[8]

In early Christian churches, the Greek word for fish (*ichthys*) took on a special meaning for believers. The word *ichthys* is an acronym formed from the first letters of the Greek words meaning "Jesus Christ, God's Son, Savior." The fish symbol was used by early Christians to associate themselves with others who were followers of Jesus Christ and is still used today.

5. See Mark 1:20.
6. See Matthew 4:18; John 21:8.
7. See Ecclesiastes 9:12; Habakkuk 1:14.
8. See Matthew 4:19.

Can You Imagine?

Wednesday

On the day when Zebedee and Salome were married, the priest could have said, "Salome, will you take Zebedee to be your husband? I now pronounce you Mr. and Mrs. Thunderbolt." Can you imagine the possibilities for excitement and trouble in the marriage of Miss Assertive and Mr. Thunder?

You and your spouse may not have nicknames like these, but your personalities will eventually clash. Your strong differences were the very things that drew you to each other. In the early days, you probably found them to be the source of admiration and amusement. But after a while, these assets may have become liabilities. He loved your creativity, but now he thinks you're too disorganized. You loved his determination, but now you think he's bullheaded.

It is tempting in an argument to rationalize, "That's just the way I am." But in a Christ-centered marriage, we are called to be like Jesus. Your walk with God gives you the chance to be new. To be changed by His power. "So we have stopped evaluating others from a human point of view ... This means that anyone who belongs to Christ has become a new person. The old life is gone; a new life has begun!" (2 Corinthians 5:16–17 NLT).

As disciples of Jesus, we spend time with Him and study His character. Then with His Spirit inside us, we can abandon our need to be right and celebrate again how God designed our spouse. When we willingly honor each other, our marriages can display the glory of Christ.

From God's Word ...

> "Just as each of us has one body with many members, and these members do not all have the same function, so in Christ we, though many, form one body, and each member belongs to all the others. We have different gifts, according to the grace given to each of us."

ROMANS 12:4–6

Their Legacy in Scripture

Thursday

1. **"Get rid of all bitterness, rage and anger, brawling and slander, along with every form of malice. Be kind and compassionate to one another, forgiving each other, just as in Christ God forgave you"** (EPHESIANS 4:31–32).

   In light of Zebedee's nickname, it's possible there were occasional fireworks or there was at least conflict in their home. Look at the first list above. Which of these troubling issues would you like to eliminate in your relationship? What are some specific ways you can begin to focus on the wise counsel offered in the second list?

2. **"'I hold this against you: You have forsaken the love you had at first. Consider how far you have fallen! Repent and do the things you did at first'"** (REVELATION 2:4–5).

   Although these verses addressed the people's relationship to God, they can also apply to your marriage. What qualities and strengths first attracted you to your spouse? How did you celebrate those things? What can you do now to renew that "first love"?

3. **"Do not conform to the pattern of this world, but be transformed by the renewing of your mind. Then you will be able to test and approve what God's will is—his good, pleasing and perfect will"** (ROMANS 12:2).

   What negative or "worldly" attitudes about marriage are portrayed in broadcast media and in books and magazines today? What issues in your marriage need to be conformed to God's "good, pleasing and perfect will?"

Their Legacy of Prayer

Friday

Reflect On: Matthew 20:20–22; 27:55–56; Mark 16:1

Praise God: For His great wisdom and creativity in the way He designed you and your spouse. For Jesus, who is the pioneer and perfecter of faith.

Offer Thanks: That God provides spiritual strength for every sacrifice you make when you seek first His kingdom, and that He gives you the opportunity to follow Him by loving and serving your spouse.

Confess: That you often want to control every situation instead of surrendering to God's way of humble service, and that you often seek the gifts but not the Giver and want what Jesus offers instead of His presence.

Ask God: To give you a submissive heart that exalts God above all else and is willing to glorify and follow Jesus without receiving any power, position, or recognition.

Listen: "My children, My ways are not your ways, and My thoughts are not your thoughts. The way of My kingdom is the way of love, surrender, and sacrifice. I will fill you with joy and strength when you follow Me. When you are filled with My Spirit, your marriage will demonstrate gracious service. Great things will be accomplished when you serve each other in love."

Pray: *Father in heaven, You alone are worthy of highest honor. Forgive us for selfishly trying to use You to get what we want. When we are tempted to place our own interests above Yours, remind us of the sacrifice of the cross and of Your great love. Strengthen us to serve You and each other with humility, and give us Your joy as we focus on pleasing You. Amen.*

47

Passing Notes

Pilate and Claudia

Meaning of Names:	*Pilate* means "armed with a spear" or "skilled with a javelin." *Claudia* means "lame" or "crippled."
Their Character:	A Roman governor blinded by his power, he sinned against his conscience and was unwilling to follow his wife's advice. She was a bold, intuitive woman who recognized Jesus' innocence.
Their Challenge:	He was a politician who gave the people what they wanted instead of what was right. She had a dream but was unable to convince her husband of the truth about Jesus.
Their Outcome:	Pilate ordered Jesus to be crucified.
Key Scripture:	Matthew 27:19

Their Story

Monday

It had been the longest day of Claudia Procula's life, and yet she couldn't understand why.

The governor's wife had a dream that disturbed her, but who was she to be imagining the guilt or innocence of a Jewish rabbi? As the wife of Pontius Pilate, she rarely was involved with his politics. But sometimes he invited her counsel.

During his four years of governing Israel, Pilate had come to trust his wife. She was wise, and he valued her opinion. "Would you have done the same thing, Claudia?" he often asked. Her discernment made him feel safe, one of the reasons he sometimes took her with him when he traveled.

Today, however, Claudia wished she were back at their other home in Caesarea, on the Mediterranean coast. She loved being there. When time allowed, she would escape and stroll along the shore, her bare feet soaking in the cool of the foamy tide.

But right now she was at the palace in Judea. And this day had been the most troublesome since her husband had been in office. Pilate had been summoned exceptionally early that morning, just after daybreak. More than twelve hours later, he still was not back.

How she wanted to speak with him.

The day wore on. Claudia paced, anxiously waiting for her husband. Deep in thought, she paid little attention to the beauty of the paintings, intricate tapestries, or elaborate furniture that surrounded her. Finally, as the sun was setting, Pilate arrived home and entered their living quarters. Immediately sensing that his spirit was churning, Claudia moved to greet him.

Pilate stopped, his unfocused eyes staring past his wife. She sensed he had much to say but was still trying to make sense of it himself. Wanting to break the silence, she asked, "Shall I have the servants prepare you something for dinner?"

"No," Pilate sighed. "I don't want to eat right now."

She held her breath and readied herself for what he would do next. Going to his private chambers would mean he wanted to be alone and would not be seeing her for the rest of the evening. Staying in the room and sitting comfortably, however, would be her invitation to join him.

Pilate slumped into his favorite chair. She gathered at his feet.

"Claudia," he began, "I received your message today. Tell me more about this dream of yours."

Only the night before, Claudia had experienced the disturbing dream. It so haunted her that when she awoke that morning and realized Pilate had already left for the trial of a Jewish holy man, she panicked. So she had sent him an urgent message: "Don't have anything to do with that innocent man, for I have suffered a great deal today in a dream because of Him."[1]

---

1. See Matthew 27:19.

Pilate had been stung by the message when he had received it, and now he looked at his wife for an explanation. "You can imagine my surprise," he said to Claudia. "What made you think the rabbi Jesus was innocent before I even had an opportunity to question Him?"

"I can't explain it. But it was more than a dream."

"What do you mean?"

"I don't know. It was an ominous message that circled my mind and wouldn't release me. That is all I can say."

Pilate was seized with conviction. Having interrogated Jesus and sensing something supernatural that day, Pilate was undone. Claudia's warning rang with truth. The weary governor looked down, considered his words, then met his wife's eyes. "Are you certain He is innocent?"

She nodded and swallowed hard, waiting to hear what had happened at the trial.

"I sentenced Jesus to death," Pilate confessed. "He was crucified this afternoon, and His body was buried in a tomb provided by one of His countrymen."

Claudia's eyes filled with dismay. *Did my husband drink the fatal poison of irresponsible power?*

"What do you think of me, Claudia?" Pilate asked.

She folded her arms across her chest and shook her head.

"There would have been a riot," he rationalized. "The mob was getting out of control."

She studied his ashen face as he continued. "This is why we came to Jerusalem for the Passover, Claudia — to keep the peace."

Claudia summoned enough breath to speak. "Some people called Him the Son of God."

"I don't know what that means."

"Neither do I, Pilate, but ..."

"But you believe it."

"I don't know."

"But you do believe I killed an innocent man."

For a moment she was motionless, then slowly nodded.

"I did everything I could to free the rabbi."

She said nothing.

"I had no choice. I was forced into it. I did what I had to do."

She said nothing.

"I tried to release Him."

She looked down at the floor.

He took her hand.

"You know I value your opinion, Claudia."

She nodded.

"This won't be easy to live with," Pilate conceded.

The governor and his wife sat silently in the darkened room.

Their Life and Times

Tuesday

Claudia Procula

It was AD 30, and Claudia was married to the sixth governor of Judea. She was with Pilate in Jerusalem during this very important time. Their primary residence was in Caesarea Maritima, about seventy-five miles north of Jerusalem on the Mediterranean coast. Pilate had come down to Jerusalem for Passover to keep the peace between the Jews and the Romans. It would have been an easy matter to leave Claudia in Caesarea, especially for the few days he would be away. The fact that Pilate brought her with him suggests a closeness between them.

Although there is no absolute certainty about Pilate and Claudia's relationship, it is clear that Claudia has become a figure of great respect.

In his *Homilies on Matthew*, the second-century Christian scholar and theologian Origen suggested that God sent her the dream so she may come to know Christ. Other theologians have supported this view that her vision was given for her personal salvation.

On the other hand, it has also been suggested that Satan gave her the dream to persuade Pilate to commute the death sentence and prevent Jesus from going to the cross, which was His earthly mission all along.

Two Christian churches—the Eastern Orthodox and the Ethiopian Orthodox—have bestowed sainthood on Claudia, and each celebrates a special day in her honor. In the Eastern Orthodox

Church, she is celebrated on October 27; the Ethiopian Orthodox Church celebrates Pilate and Procula together on June 25.

During the twentieth and twenty-first centuries, books of historical fiction have been written about Claudia, and she has been a frequent character in movies and stage plays.[2]

Despite the lack of certainty regarding Pilate's wife, one thing is known: at a time when so many people were turning against Jesus, Claudia boldly defended Him.

This has given her a place of distinction in the hearts of believers.

---

2. See "Pontius Pilate's Wife," Wikipedia.org, http://goo.gl/i4m2Y (accessed September 13, 2012).

Can You Imagine?

Wednesday

The story of Pilate and Claudia provides a fascinating and intimate portrait of how spouses provide discernment for each other. He was an extremely powerful man. She was the first lady of the territory. As the governor of Judea, Pilate had the authority to act as a judge, sentencing Jesus to death or granting Him a pardon.

A dream informed Claudia about Jesus' innocence. She was certain of it. And so she penned a message and commissioned a servant to deliver it to her husband. There was no doubt in her mind, and she was determined to warn Pilate, even if it interfered with a capital trial. Can you imagine the urgency she must have felt?

Claudia pushed past any protocol anxiety and sent her note to Pilate because she was convinced that Jesus was innocent. But Pilate, who was responsible for a peaceful Judea, was caught between his wife's wisdom and the hostile mob. He chose to ignore her warning and to follow the opinion of the crowd. Ceremoniously washing his hands, he declared, "I am innocent of this man's blood" (Matthew 27:24).

In marriage, your spouse can be an invaluable resource. Invite your spouse to pray about the decisions you are facing. You may say, "I trust your wisdom. What do you see that I don't see." Then listen carefully to each other's concerns and learn from your spouse's perspective.

God is using your spouse to shape you, and He is using you to shape your spouse. Seek God's truth and ask for discernment.

From God's Word . . .

"If we walk in the light, as he is in the light, we have fellowship with one another, and the blood of Jesus, his Son, purifies us from all sin."

1 JOHN 1:7

Their Legacy in Scripture

Thursday

1. **"Where there is strife, there is pride, but wisdom is found in those who take advice"** (PROVERBS 13:10).

    Taking good counsel is wise. This is especially true when the advice comes from someone who knows you, loves you, and wants the best for you. But often we judge our spouses and do not listen to them. What strength does your spouse have that you lack? Why do you sometimes resist his or her advice?

2. **"'Which of them has stood in the council of the LORD to see or to hear his word? Who has listened and heard his word?'"** (JEREMIAH 23:18).

    Two important words in the above verse are *hear* and *listened*. These are the keys to wisdom. What voices vie for your attention? How has your spouse influenced your decisions in the past? In what ways can you and your spouse hear and listen to God's voice?

3. **"My dear brothers and sisters, take note of this: Everyone should be quick to listen, slow to speak and slow to become angry"** (JAMES 1:19).

    According to this verse, what are the secrets to effective communication? Which of these habits is the greatest challenge in your marriage? Why is your spouse one of your most important resources?

Their Legacy of Prayer

Friday

Reflect on: Matthew 27:18–20

Praise God: For His eternal wisdom and that His counsel is always perfect.

Offer Thanks: That God has given you a spouse who knows you and can be a valuable resource in shaping who you are and what you do.

Confess: Your pride and rebellion when you disregard God's Word, neglect to pray about decisions, or ignore the gift of your spouse's godly warnings.

Ask God: To give you and your spouse insight, discernment, and humility as you seek Him for direction and wisdom.

Listen: "My children, I possess all the depth and riches of wisdom and knowledge. I have given you a spouse to be your resource. I designed and gifted your spouse with strengths and sensitivities. I want you to seek Me in all things. When you search for Me, My wisdom will be poured into your marriage."

Pray: *Dear Father in heaven, You alone have all the resources of wisdom and truth and goodness. When we do not know which way to turn, our eyes are on You. Thank You for this marriage partnership You have given us. Teach us to lean on You for every provision and each decision. We cannot see the future, but You can. Hear us in mercy, and show us Your favor. Amen.*

48

Liar, Liar

Ananias and Sapphira

Meaning of Names: *Ananias* means "God is gracious." *Sapphira* means "sapphire."

Their Character: He was an ambitious deceiver who sought the praise of people. She was driven by greed and pretense and joined her husband in his hypocrisy.

Their Challenge: They wanted the acclaim of other people and lied to the Holy Spirit.

Their Outcome: God pronounced a death sentence on both of them for their deceitfulness.

Key Scripture: Acts 5:1–11

Their Story

Monday

Sapphira liked her husband's idea.

In fact, it thrilled her.

"Just imagine, Ananias," Sapphira prattled, "being so highly regarded. Everyone will be impressed. You heard the good things being said about Barnabas — how wonderful he is. And he is, of course."

Ananias smiled broadly and sat down, taking Sapphira's hand. The thought of such admiration thrilled them as they talked in their modest home, looking at the large pile of coins on a nearby table. The money made them happy. It gave them confidence and pride.

As a young husband and wife, Ananias and Sapphira were members of a new, flourishing church in Jerusalem. Over the past few months, they had paid close attention to the commotion about the Rabbi of Nazareth, including His crucifixion and reported resurrection. They were sympathetic toward Jesus' claim to be the Messiah. The young seekers were intrigued with the way He had shaken up the Jewish establishment, and they were fascinated by His teachings, boldness, and compassion.

Ananias and Sapphira were also impressed by the charisma of Jesus' disciples, especially Peter and John. These uneducated men spoke with power and even performed miracles.

So Ananias and Sapphira started attending the meetings in homes across the city where the followers of Jesus gathered. Caught up in the fresh wave of spiritual energy, the couple was amazed at the movement's mounting popularity.

They watched as the men and women of this new faith began voluntarily selling their houses and property, generously depositing the proceeds at the feet of the apostles ... some rather impressive sums of money.

One day, a follower of Jesus named Barnabas delivered a particularly large gift to the apostles. Ananias and Sapphira watched as everyone celebrated his good-heartedness.

Until this time, no one had paid much attention to the obscure newcomers. And as praise was heaped on Barnabas, a plan was born. The desire for acclaim overtook them.

Now, one week later, Ananias and Sapphira sat gazing at their stack of coins like doting parents.

"At last," Ananias said to his wife. "You will be a woman of honor."

"And you will be a man of respect," she replied.

Ananias suddenly stopped gawking at their coins and stared into the distance. His wife noticed.

"Is something wrong?"

"You know, Sapphira," he said haltingly, "this is a rather large sum of money."

She nodded. "I was thinking the same thing. This piece of property has been in your family for years."

Ananias's face brightened. "You're right. There's no reason we shouldn't keep some of the proceeds for ourselves."

"But ..."

"What Sapphira? But what?"

"Well," she said, "Barnabas told us he was giving the entire amount from the sale of his field. Can we really do any less and still expect the same praise?"

The two sat in silence, mulling over the dilemma.

"I know what we will do," Ananias announced. "If we give what Barnabas gave—perhaps a shekel more—that will be good enough. Then we can keep some for ourselves. No one has to know. Many people will still benefit from our generosity."

"And they will honor us because of it," Sapphira said with a smile.

Ananias began scraping most of the coins into a leather pouch. The remaining pieces glistened on the table.

"Shall we go together and deliver this, Sapphira?"

"No, you go ahead, Ananias. I have some work to do. I'll join you soon."

Ananias picked up the money pouch. "By the time you join me," he said confidently, "we will be a couple worthy of honor and praise."

She smiled as she watched her husband head for the door, unable to imagine what awaited both of them before long.

Their Life and Times

Tuesday

God Is Holy, Yet Merciful

Ananias's and Sapphira's sin was not in keeping the money for themselves. That would have been their right.[1] Their treachery was in saying that what they were laying at the apostles' feet was the full amount. This lie incurred God's wrath and brought almost instant death—first to Ananias and then a few hours later to his wife, Sapphira, when she corroborated her husband's lie.

God is gracious and patient with His people, not wanting any to perish because of their sin.[2] However, He demanded obedience, and His punishment was strong when His people did not confess and turn from their open rebellion against Him.

A number of stories in the Bible reveal God's displeasure against unrepentant sin.

- God expected holiness from the two sons of Aaron the priest. When they defiantly performed an unauthorized sacrifice before the Lord, Nadab and Abihu were consumed by fire (see Leviticus 10:1–2).

- When the Israelites defeated Jericho, the rules were clear: do not take any spoils. But Achan took a few forbidden items, and God commanded Joshua to stone Achan and his entire family (see Joshua 7:24–25).

- Uzzah kept the ark of God from falling into the mud by reaching out his hand and taking hold of it as it was being transported on a cart. He knew that touching the ark was against God's law. Uzzah was immediately struck dead (see 2 Samuel 6:6–7).

The Bible is clear about the eternal consequences of unrepentant sin. "The wages of sin is death" (Romans 6:23). Even so, there are biblical accounts that display God's great mercy. Cain killed Abel —and lived. Joseph's brothers sold him into slavery and lied to their

---

1. See Acts 5:4.
2. See 2 Peter 3:9.

father about it—and lived. David committed adultery and plotted Uriah's death—and lived.

So what can be made of the disparity?

The Lord answered this question when He told Moses, "I will have mercy on whom I will have mercy, and I will have compassion on whom I will have compassion" (Exodus 33:19).

Asking why God dealt so harshly with sin is the wrong question. Because God is holy and His laws are sure, the correct question is, *Why does He show mercy at all? Ever?* He is not obligated to do anything other than give sinners what they deserve. But He graciously offers blessings to those who cry out to Him for mercy.

We see a vivid picture of the holiness of God when the prophet Isaiah entered the temple one morning. Even though he was familiar with the temple, on this day Isaiah was suddenly aware of the awesome presence of a righteous God who was not to be trifled with. Isaiah's immediate response was an admission of his own sinfulness: "'Woe to me!... I am ruined! For I am a man of unclean lips, and I live among a people of unclean lips, and my eyes have seen the King, the LORD Almighty'" (Isaiah 6:5).

What a difference it would have made if Ananias and Sapphira had understood who it was they were defying. Even so, they were given time to repent and receive God's mercy. Ananias could have changed his mind on his way to the church gathering. Sapphira had three hours to think it over, and Peter's final question gave her another chance to repent: "Tell me, is this the price you and Ananias got for the land?"

"Yes, that is the price" (Acts 5:8).

Ananias and Sapphira lived without regard for the sacredness of God. This was a tragic miscalculation.

Can You Imagine?

Wednesday

The sin of Ananias and Sapphira stemmed from their desire to win praise. Can you imagine how different this story would have been if they had been truthful about their actions? What if they had realized that everything belongs to God? What if they had been able to think of their possessions as tools for helping others? If they had followed the first nudging of the Holy Spirit to be generous and truthful, God would have been pleased and others would have been blessed.

You and your spouse have the privilege of listening to divine promptings and furthering God's work. When you prayerfully and truthfully evaluate what God wants you to do and give, when you obey the first urgings of God's Spirit, then you can trust God for amazing results.

A wise couple carefully appraises their prosperity, pride, jealousy, feelings of inferiority, and other human tendencies that would mar the beauty of God's intended plan for His people.

Listen to God's voice in response to these questions: "Are our lives too submerged in stuff and position and power? How much is enough? Are we really following Jesus?" When we believe God is worthy of all our plans and dreams, we will feel the urgency to use every resource of person and purse to further His kingdom.

Don't ignore creeping deception. Ask the Holy Spirit to stop you when you start making excuses. Pay close attention to the pleasures and pursuits that drive you to disobedience. Your lives were created to make God's glory known.

From God's Word . . .

"Let us hold unswervingly to the hope we profess, for he who promised is faithful. And let us consider how we may spur one another on toward love and good deeds, not giving up meeting together, as some are in the habit of doing, but encouraging one another."

HEBREWS 10:23–25

Their Legacy in Scripture

Thursday

1. "Do not be deceived: God cannot be mocked. A man reaps what he sows. Whoever sows to please their flesh, from the flesh will reap destruction; whoever sows to please the Spirit, from the Spirit will reap eternal life" (GALATIANS 6:7–8).

   Making excuses for sin of any kind harms our relationship with God and each other. Every spending decision is a spiritual decision. In what ways are your resources impacting someone else's life for the future? What hoarding, overspending habit, or unholy pretense has God's Spirit highlighted in your life that needs to be rooted out?

2. "Love the LORD your God with all your heart and with all your soul and with all your strength" (DEUTERONOMY 6:5).

   Ananias and Sapphira may have been willing to say they loved God. But they loved other things even more. What were they? Sin is sin, regardless of how many virtuous motives surround it. What entices you or your spouse to compromise or make excuses?

3. "What we have received is not the spirit of the world, but the Spirit who is from God, so that we may understand what God has freely given us" (1 CORINTHIANS 2:12).

   As God's child, what spiritual blessings have you received? As a couple, what temporal blessings and resources have you received? What do you think God is saying to you about your attitude regarding these things? How can you and your spouse please God with what He has generously given you?

Their Legacy of Prayer

Friday

Reflect On: Acts 5:1–11

Praise God: That He is a God of eternal truth whose holy nature
cannot be trifled with.

Offer Thanks: For God's Holy Spirit who convicts, guides, and corrects
you and your spouse, and for the church, which He
established to further His kingdom and to provide
instruction and correction for believers.

Confess: The contempt you display when you disregard God's
holiness and when you rationalize your sin and
marginalize the truth in order to benefit yourselves.

Ask God: To let you see your sin as He sees it and to give you His
saving mercy and grace in temptation's hour. For a clean
heart and generous hands.

Listen: "My children, I require righteousness and purity at
all times. I see your motives and am pleased with pure
hearts and honest lips. Truthfulness will guard your lives
and your marriage. I shower blessings on My children
who give generously to others in order to glorify Me,
not themselves. The church is My body and your family.
Share what I have given you with those in need. I love
cheerful givers."

Pray: *Father in heaven, Your holiness demands our utmost respect
and honor. We admit we have tried to surround our sin with
enough virtue to appear noble, but we cannot fool You or clear
away our guilt. We confess our greed and our desire for human
praise. We plead for Your mercy. Thank You for the blood of Jesus
that cleanses us from every sin and makes us new. You have
created us in Your image and have called us to truthfulness and
generosity. We need pure hearts and a strong desire to do what
pleases You. With Your help, all things are possible. Amen.*

49

Singular Faith

Unbelieving Husband and Eunice

Meaning of Names: The name of Eunice's husband is not given
in the Bible. *Eunice* means "good victory" or
"victorious."

Their Character: He was a Greek unbeliever, but he allowed
his son to be raised as a Jew. She was a Jewish
believer who made sure her son knew God
and His Word.

Their Challenge: They came from different cultures and were
spiritually unequally yoked.

Their Outcome: Their son Timothy became a strong believer
in Jesus and a missionary traveling companion
of the apostle Paul.

Key Scripture: Acts 16:1–4; 2 Timothy 1:1–5

Their Story

Monday

Eunice was privileged to be mentored by her godly mother, Lois.
Their Jewish home and community were tucked inside the
pagan culture of the city of Lystra. As a young woman surrounded
by a concourse of Roman culture, Eunice observed those who did
not worship in the synagogue or esteem the laws of her mother's
Jewish Scriptures.

When Eunice reached her mid-teenage years, she married a
Greek who did not hold to strict marriage customs. He was tall and

handsome and was attracted to this young Jewish girl who also did not highly regard strict tradition.

A year later, the couple had a baby and named him Timothy. As Eunice held their infant son, her heart began to yearn for God's presence and protection. She wanted to cover her baby with the same godly love and wisdom that she had experienced as a youngster.

Eunice regretted that she had ignored her mother's pleas to embrace their ancestors' faith. Even though she was married to an unbeliever, Eunice determined to follow God. She discussed with her husband her desire to raise their son as a Jew. He had only one objection. "That's fine — as long as you don't get him circumcised," he demanded. "You know what I think about that barbaric ritual."

Eunice enlisted her mother's help in teaching her son the sacred writings. From his earliest infancy, Scripture, prayers, and songs were poured over Timothy. His mother taught him about Abraham and Isaac and Jacob. About Joseph and his brothers and the time of slavery in Egypt. About Moses and Joshua and the judges. She told him the stories of Kings Saul, David, and Solomon and all of Israel's other kings, even the very wicked kings like Ahab and Manasseh. She taught him about the great prophets like Elijah, Elisha, Isaiah, and Jeremiah. Even as a young boy, Timothy displayed a hearty appetite for God's Word.

As her son grew, Eunice cried to the Lord to help her raise a boy who would love God with all his heart, soul, strength, and mind. Her highest priority was to prepare him to be a man of God.

When Timothy was fourteen years old, a respected missionary named Paul came to Lystra to preach in the synagogue. Eunice was overjoyed that her son had an opportunity to meet the apostle. Timothy went to the synagogue to hear him speak and was stirred by Paul's powerful message and his ability to explain the Scriptures and their fulfillment in Jesus Christ — the Jewish Messiah.

For years, Eunice had been diligently praying for her son and equipping him for God's service. When the believers from Lystra who knew Timothy saw him speaking to Paul, they recognized the important role the young man could someday play as the apostle's traveling companion. With his strong faith and background, Timothy would be able to influence people in both Jewish and Greek cultures.

Six years later, when Paul visited Lystra a second time, Timothy was ready to join him.

And Eunice was grateful. Although a mother's heart always longs to be with her child, she was delighted by Timothy's assignment. Now a man of twenty, her boy accepted an invitation from the great apostle Paul to accompany him throughout the Roman world, preaching the saving grace of Jesus Christ.

Eunice knew that her son was where God wanted him to be. She had raised Timothy for this purpose.

Their Life and Times

Tuesday

Growing Up Jewish

Eunice and Lois were not Timothy's only teachers. Much of his learning would have also been conducted outside their home. Growing up Jewish, Timothy's formal education began at age six.

Throughout the Jewish communities of the Roman world, boys ages six to sixteen (unless required to work in the fields for financial reasons) walked to the synagogue school following breakfast each day. Hebrew school was for boys only. Girls learned at home, if their mothers chose to give them an education.

Once at school, the boys were greeted by their teacher, who was usually the rabbi. If the rabbi didn't have the time — or the propensity — to teach youngsters, a learned elderly gentleman would sometimes assume the duties. To the younger boys, the instructor was a rather intimidating figure dressed in a long, white tunic with a tasseled prayer shawl draped over his head. This fabric shadowed his bearded face, making him seem almost ominous. Once the teacher was seated, the boys, from youngest to oldest, sat around him in a semicircle on the floor.

Lessons always included reading and speaking ancient Hebrew. In Israel, Hebrew was not the language of common street conversations, so Jewish parents were keen that their sons learn their ancestors' tongue. The Scriptures were only written in Hebrew, so all Jewish boys received a thorough Hebrew-language education.

The classroom featured a small, curtained chest housing the sacred scrolls of the Hebrew Scriptures (the Old Testament). In front of the chest—also called the ark—were lamps that continually burned. After an opening prayer, the rabbi slowly walked to the ark and ceremoniously removed one of the scrolls. As Timothy and the other boys watched, the teacher carefully removed the scroll's linen shroud and leather case and returned to his seat.

The rabbi would then recite selected passages from the scroll, perhaps those he considered to be most important for the boys' training. Spoken slowly and clearly, every word was a gem worth treasuring. The boys were deeply respectful of the rabbi and were rarely restless. This was serious business, and they knew it. The rabbi often recited the text in a distinct rhythmic pattern, a method of teaching that made memorizing Scripture songlike and easier. Many of the older boys learned lengthy passages by heart and were able to recite them without forgetting a single word. Eventually, the younger boys would learn to do the same.

Following the reading, the rabbi returned the scroll to the ark, taking the same care in putting it away as he had in removing it. The boys then practiced writing Hebrew by copying the twenty-two letters that comprised the alphabet.

Each student wrote on a wooden tablet covered by wax, using a pointed stylus of bone, bronze, or wood as a writing utensil. Once the younger students proved proficient in writing letters and short passages, they moved on to copying longer lessons on sheets of parchment using reed pens dipped in black ink.

If parents were particularly diligent, further instruction was provided in the home, often at dinnertime, where the daughters could also participate. Fathers would generally teach about the laws and history of Israel.

Can You Imagine?

Wednesday

Being married to someone who does not share your faith can be a huge challenge. Can you imagine the challenges Eunice faced with a spouse who was indifferent—perhaps hostile—to her faith?

The apostle Paul wrote about being unequally yoked. "If a woman has a husband who is not a believer and he is willing to live with her, she must not divorce him. For the unbelieving husband has been sanctified through his wife, and the unbelieving wife has been sanctified through her believing husband" (1 Corinthians 7:13–14).

Having a spouse who is a nonbeliever does not give you a reason to leave the marriage. You are called to love your mate and live in such a way that your love and behavior draw your spouse to Christ. In fact, God's blessing on you will spill over onto your spouse. Because you are a recipient of God's grace, the benefits accrue to your spouse as well. When your spouse is talking with friends about you, he or she should rave about the way you honor and serve him. Your love and respect will be more effective in winning your spouse to Christ than taping Bible verses to his shaving mirror or secretly loading a preacher's message onto her iPhone.

If you have an unbelieving spouse, you cannot afford to display a judgmental or self-righteous attitude. Ask yourself, *Does my spouse see Jesus in the way I love and esteem them?* And continually pray that the Holy Spirit will give your spouse the gift of faith—the same gift that drew you to the Savior.

Winning a lost spouse calls for you to be Jesus in your home.

From God's Word . . .

> "In your relationships with one another, have the same mindset as Christ Jesus: Who, being in very nature God, did not consider equality with God something to be used to his own advantage; rather, he made himself nothing by taking the very nature of a servant."
>
> PHILIPPIANS 2:5–7

Their Legacy in Scripture

Thursday

1. **"You will keep in perfect peace those whose minds are steadfast, because they trust in you. Trust in the LORD forever, for the LORD, the LORD himself, is the Rock eternal"** (ISAIAH 26:3–4).

   Without a spouse who shares your love for God, the struggle for peace can be relentless, especially peace that would be described as "perfect." The word *steadfast* means "to lean on" or "to take hold of." What a strong picture of how the Lord wants your mind and heart to depend on Him, even when you feel spiritually alone in your marriage. What habits can you develop in your own walk with Jesus that will help you at home?

2. **"I am reminded of your sincere faith, which first lived in your grandmother Lois and in your mother Eunice and, I am persuaded, now lives in you also"** (2 TIMOTHY 1:5).

   Wouldn't it be wonderful if someday a pastor would say of your child, "I am reminded of your sincere faith, which first lived in your mother and father"? This would be the supreme compliment for a Christian parent. What specific steps can you and your spouse take to help secure this kind of future for your children?

3. **"May the Lord direct your hearts into God's love and Christ's perseverance"** (2 THESSALONIANS 3:5).

   This verse expresses the Bible's instructions for a successful life and marriage. It takes spiritual discipline to offer gentleness and mercy instead of obsessing over your spouse's shortcomings. Think of husbands and wives you know who model this kind of love and perseverance with each other. What are the qualities of their relationship that you admire?

Their Legacy of Prayer

Friday

Reflect On: 2 Timothy 1:3–5

Praise God: For being a compassionate and holy God who redeems and walks with His children throughout life on earth and who has planned a perfect eternal home for them in heaven.

Offer Thanks: That He strengthens you in your marriage to be lovable and loving and to display Christlike attitudes to your spouse.

Confess: That you often complain about your spouse rather than looking at every difficulty as an opportunity for spiritual growth — in your spouse and in you — and that you often focus on your spouse's faults rather than asking God to point out your own shortcomings.

Ask God: To give you a persevering desire to see your spouse become the person God intended him or her to be. For His power to become a winsome witness in your home and for God's Word to dwell in you richly.

Listen: "My children, I am your source of joy, satisfaction, and spiritual fulfillment. I know the desires of your heart and have planned what is good for your future. Be steadfast in faith and fervent in hope. Rely on My Spirit to help you live together in harmony. Love, worship, and obey Me. When you open your Bible, I speak to you. I am with you always, to the very end of the world."

Pray: *Father in heaven, You are a merciful God who redeems. Thank You for choosing us and preparing us from childhood to follow You. We want our lives to honor You by the way we honor each other. Give us grace to be the people You want us to be and to view our marriage as a blessed privilege to increase our dependence on You. Every good gift is from Your hand. We are grateful for Your Word and for every blessing on our marriage. Amen.*

50

Mr. and Mrs. Missionary

Aquila and Priscilla

Meaning of Names: *Aquila* means "eagle." *Priscilla* means "old-fashioned simplicity."

Their Character: He was a Jewish believer and tentmaker who was willing to use his resources to spread the gospel. She was a prominent Roman believer who partnered with her husband in business and ministry.

Their Challenge: They were exiled from Italy to Corinth and faced persecution because of their faith in Jesus and their hospitality toward Paul.

Their Outcome: God blessed them with a rich ministry in the growing early church.

Key Scripture: Acts 18

Their Story

Monday

Aquila and Priscilla had been living in Corinth for less than a year, exiles from their beloved Italy. They had been part of the exciting and burgeoning church in Rome where many Jews gathered who believed in Jesus as their Messiah. The Roman officials had seen the new sect as a threat to its government and had ousted them.

Additional opposition had come from Jewish zealots who considered any Christ followers as heretics. Openly harassing the converts, they disrupted meetings and engaged in noisy protests aimed at the church. When the upheaval had become unbearable, Emperor Claudius issued an edict in AD 49 ejecting all Jews — those for and against Christ — from Italy.

Because he was Jewish, Aquila was among the exiled. His Gentile wife, Priscilla, a mature believer who was ready for whatever lay ahead, stayed by her husband's side as they ventured to a new life in the city of Corinth. Although the journey across the Adriatic Sea had been harrowing, they were now thanking God for this extraordinary opportunity for ministry. Corinth was also a good place to establish their joint tentmaking trade. Business was robust, and Aquila and Priscilla enthusiastically used their success as a chance to tell people about Jesus.

One day a bold and friendly Jewish man named Paul visited their booth in the marketplace. A vibrant Christ follower, Paul told the couple he had just arrived in Corinth. He too was a tentmaker and wondered if they could use another hand. Paul also asked for a place to live. He would help Aquila and Priscilla in their business during the day and preach whenever he was able.

Paul was not unknown to Aquila and Priscilla. They had heard about his persuasive preaching and the opposition he had endured while establishing churches throughout the region. The couple told him they appreciated his willingness to work and that they would discuss his request to stay with them.

That night, Aquila and Priscilla lay in bed discussing Paul's appeal for lodging. Priscilla took Aquila's arm, wrapped it under her head, and snuggled close to him. "There is tremendous risk," she admitted. "But this could be what God has been preparing us for ... the most rewarding adventure we've ever taken."

The two lay silently for a few moments, thinking through their options and discussing whether they should partner with Paul.

"What do we know about Paul?" Aquila said. "He is a fearless witness for Christ, but he has a tendency to instigate riots wherever he goes. And often those who are with him are punished severely, beaten, and stoned."

"I know all this," Priscilla said. "But isn't this the cost for spreading the gospel of Christ?"

"You're right, Priscilla. It is."

"Shouldn't this be the call of all followers of the Way?"[1]

"To be stoned? Or killed?"

"It is if the Lord so wills it. God will take care of His servants."

Even though he had been married to Priscilla for many years, Aquila was always amazed at her perspective. And courage. Aquila could tell his wife was growing more excited by the challenge.

"Paul said several times that he is willing to die for Christ," Priscilla said.

"I'm aware of this."

"Shouldn't we be willing to die for our Savior too?"

Aquila sighed. "Yes, we should be."

"And just think what we can do to help Paul spread the gospel." Even though it was dark, Aquila could tell his wife was smiling. "He is obviously anointed and has heavenly visions," Priscilla continued. "The Holy Spirit instructs him. I think he was sent to us for a reason."

"True, Priscilla. What else?"

"He boldly preaches in synagogues every Saturday. He has a way of explaining Jesus as the Messiah so clearly." Priscilla's voice was lifted far louder than necessary. Aquila was familiar with this ... and loved his wife's intensity. Usually.

"Imagine how much we could learn from Paul, Aquila."

Catching a vision for their own ministry and growing more enthusiastic, Aquila agreed.

Priscilla looked at her husband. "I think we have our answer. Let's invite Paul to live in our home. We will be his partners in ministry."

"I'm all in," he said.

"First thing in the morning," Priscilla said, "we'll prepare the guest room for Paul. I think he'll enjoy living here."

---

1. Early Christians were often called "followers of the Way." This description of Christians, derived from Jesus' description of Himself, appears several times in Acts. This is an appropriate title because Christianity is the way of God, the way into the Holy Place, and the way of truth.

Their Life and Times

Tuesday

Partners in Ministry

In biblical times, it was unusual for a husband and wife to work together in business or ministry. Roles were separate and well-defined. Husbands worked outside the home or in a trade and supported the family. Wives stayed close to home and took care of the domestic needs of their families.

Aquila and Priscilla's marriage represented a startling contrast to ordinary marriages of the day. As a couple working together in their tentmaking vocation, they used their resources to spread the gospel throughout Asia Minor.

Aquila and Priscilla were not the Bible's only couple to join forces for the sake of God's kingdom.

Though little is said about Noah's wife, it's clear she partnered with her husband in obedience to the Lord's assignment. She was one of eight people the Lord spared when He destroyed the inhabitants of the earth in the flood.[2] Providing comfort and encouragement to Noah as he worked for years building the ark, she endured public ridicule aimed at their family.

Moses and Zipporah were also teammates in marriage, participating together in God's call. After they had been married for forty years, they were sent by the Lord to Egypt where Moses would lead the enslaved Israelites out of bondage. Somewhere along the 350-mile journey, an event occurred that threatened Moses' life. Because he had failed to circumcise his firstborn son—an egregious violation of God's covenant with the Hebrews—the Lord was about to kill Moses.[3] Zipporah interceded and did for her son what Moses should have done long before. Though unhappy about having to circumcise the boy herself, Zipporah's fear of the Lord and her instinctive actions preserved her husband's life. Her willingness to obey God kept her husband alive to play a key role in God's plan to release the Israelites from bondage.

---

2. See Genesis 7:13.
3. See Exodus 4:24.

Zechariah and Elizabeth were used together to prepare the way for the Messiah. He was a priest, and she was a priest's daughter who would have been expected to raise a large family. But they were childless. Then the Lord rewarded this godly couple's years of long service and faith by granting them a child. The one who would be born to them—John the Baptist—would become the forerunner to Israel's Messiah.[4] His parents worked together to raise John according to the Lord's specific—and restrictive—requirements.[5]

The most significant ministry couple in the Bible was Joseph and Mary. The angel Gabriel announced to Mary that she would conceive and give birth to a son to be named Jesus. Gabriel also visited Joseph, confirming the miracle inside Mary's womb. Together they protected Mary's honor and God's secret. With constant instruction from the Holy Spirit, they followed every detail of His plan.

Joseph and Mary traveled together to Joseph's ancestral home of Bethlehem according to the dictates of a Roman census. Together they shared the birth of the Savior in a stable. Together they fled to Egypt to protect baby Jesus from the murderous Herod. Together Joseph and Mary returned to Nazareth after Herod's death and raised the Christ child.[6]

Following in the great train of godly couples who faithfully toiled together, Aquila and Priscilla were equipped for ministry by their upbringing, their business, and their mutual passion for Christ.

Aquila and Priscilla were partners in tentmaking, in hospitality, in teaching, and in faithful service to the church.

---

4. See Luke 1:76.
5. See Luke 1:15.
6. See Luke 2:1–4, 6–7; Matthew 2:13–15.

Can You Imagine?

Wednesday

G od is worthy of your plans and dreams. He has a mission especially designed for you as a couple. Together.

Aquila and Priscilla are never mentioned separately in the Bible. They were teammates. They did everything together. They worked in their tentmaking business, were evicted from their house, relocated from Rome to Corinth after taking a treacherous boat trip, joined a new fellowship of believers, volunteered to host Paul in their home, and then joined him in ministry for sixteen years.

Have you and your spouse ever talked about why you married each other? Sometimes in retrospect those reasons make you smile. His athletic ability. Her beautiful hair. But have you thought about what God had in mind when He chose you for each other? Aquila and Priscilla are a picture of teamwork in marriage.

God's plan for you as a couple is to glorify Him. Can you imagine that He drew you and your spouse together to serve Him ... together?

When you volunteer to do something beyond yourselves, the results are more significant than just feeding homeless people, encouraging shut-ins, tutoring inner-city kids, or building a school somewhere in the developing world. As husband and wife, doing ministry in Jesus' name binds you together in sacred ways that cannot be measured.

Like Aquila and Priscilla, when you serve others in God's name, empowered by the Holy Spirit, you will experience His miraculous presence. A self-focused marriage is a hollow marriage. But fulfillment comes when a couple joyfully serves God.

From God's Word ...

> "In him you too are being built together to become
> a dwelling in which God lives by his Spirit."
>
> EPHESIANS 2:22

Their Legacy in Scripture

Thursday

1. **"Calling the Twelve to him, he began to send them out two by two and gave them authority over impure spirits"** (MARK 6:7).

   This verse, while not specifically about spouses, gives an account of Jesus' sending His disciples in pairs. It's the power of two. Jesus understood this when He sent out missionaries. Where do you and your spouse already participate in ministry as a team—in your work, your neighborhood, and your church?

2. **"'The harvest is plentiful, but the workers are few. Ask the Lord of the harvest, therefore, to send out workers into his harvest field. Go! I am sending you out like lambs among wolves'"** (LUKE 10:2–3).

   Aquila and Priscilla saw their tentmaking business as an opportunity to spread the gospel. They were diligent workers who reaped a great harvest. Where do you go every day that is a mission field? Where can you and your spouse find daily opportunities to turn ordinary activities into ministry? What challenges and blessings can you expect?

3. **"I have fought the good fight, I have finished the race, I have kept the faith. Now there is in store for me the crown of righteousness, which the Lord, the righteous Judge, will award to me on that day—and not only to me, but also to all who have longed for his appearing"** (2 TIMOTHY 4:7–8).

   Read these verses again, but this time substitute "we" for "I" and "us" for "me." In what ways do your love for God and a common vision for mission bind you and your spouse closer together?

Their Legacy of Prayer

Friday

Reflect On: Acts 18

Praise God: For His omniscience—knowing the entire story of every life from beginning to end—and for His faithfulness to bring people together for His kingdom work.

Offer Thanks: That God has chosen you and your spouse to be His and has given you a mission in the world, and that He has equipped you and granted you the privilege of serving Him.

Confess: Your tendency to doubt that God is able to bring every resource and the right people into your lives at the right moment, and that you too often ignore a holy nudge to invite someone into your home.

Ask God: To give you enthusiasm and courage to speak about Jesus and do the work He calls you to do, and to give you discernment to know when to say yes and when to say no to mission opportunities.

Listen: "My children, kingdom work will be accomplished with My resources and the people I choose. I am sending you out as a couple and have prepared and equipped you to serve with vision and passion. Speak up when I lead you to tell others about Me. After you pray and study My Word and listen to Me, watch for well-timed opportunities and the people I will send into your lives."

Pray: *Father in heaven, You are an awesome God. Thank You for orchestrating thousands of things to further Your kingdom on earth that we are unaware of now. We offer our lives, our business, and our home for Your service. Bring to our minds those You want us to encourage this week. We are Your grateful servants. Thank You for the privilege of sharing the gospel. Help us to stand firm in Your strength, knowing that our labor with You is not in vain. Amen.*

51

Lost Leader

Felix and Drusilla

Meaning of Names:	*Felix* means "happy" or "prosperous." *Drusilla* means "watered by the dew."
Their Character:	A former slave who became a ruthless governor, he overrode his conscience and rejected the truth about Jesus. She was a Jewish woman of royalty who left her husband to marry Felix and ignored the claims of Christ.
Their Challenge:	They both had been unfaithful in past marriages and did not want to hear Paul's preaching about self-control and God's judgment.
Their Outcome:	Because of Felix's brutality, they were forced to leave Judea and move to Rome. From what Scripture reveals, they died without acknowledging Christ as Savior.
Key Scripture:	Acts 23–24

Their Story

Monday

The governor and his young wife loved their royal home —Herod's Palace— in Caesarea. At the palace, built on the western shores of the Mediterranean Sea, Felix and Drusilla were surrounded by plenty of luxury and an abundance of servants. Lavish tapestries hung from the ceiling, and beautiful paintings and sculptures were scattered throughout the compound. Felix and Drusilla preferred this place over their city-bound and more spartan residence in Judea. It provided them with plenty of distance from the commoners they ruled ... and despised.

When a skirmish broke out among the Jewish leaders in Jerusalem, it was brought to the governor's attention. His primary mandate from Rome was to keep the peace in Judea. Felix's life soon became snarled by a conundrum—a preacher named Paul.

From what he could discern from the reports, Felix concluded that Paul was the cause of the trouble. Although Felix considered the details of Hebrew law a complete waste of his time, he knew how zealous the Jewish leaders were about the purity of their sacred writings and lineage. Apparently this rabble-rouser was creating so much unrest that the Sanhedrin—the collection of Hebrew holy men—was ready to kill him. The governor was forced to intervene.

In order to avoid civil unrest, a Roman commander issued a hasty decree: "Get ready a detachment of two hundred soldiers, seventy horsemen and two hundred spearmen to go to Caesarea at nine tonight. Provide horses for Paul so that he may be taken safely to Governor Felix."[1]

Bringing an official letter with him, the commander was about to drop Paul into Felix's lap. The document was hand-delivered to Governor Felix. It read:

> This man was seized by the Jews and they were about to kill him, but I came with my troops and rescued him, for I had learned that he is a Roman citizen. I wanted to know why they were accusing him, so I brought him to their Sanhedrin. I found that the accusation had to do with questions about their law, but there was no charge against him that deserved death or imprisonment. When I was informed of a plot to be carried out against the man, I sent him to you at once. I also ordered his accusers to present to you their case against him.
>
> ACTS 23:27–30

Pending further examination, Paul was arrested and held under palace guard. Five days later, the high priest, Ananias, arrived in Caesarea with some of the Jewish elders and their attorney. Their

---

1. Acts 23:23–24.

mission was an audience with the governor to present their case against the preacher. Once the Jewish leaders were in Felix's presence, Paul was brought in.

The high priest's attorney was the first to speak to Felix, his monologue filled with flattery toward the governor. "We have enjoyed a long period of peace under you, and your foresight has brought about reforms in this nation. Everywhere and in every way, most excellent Felix, we acknowledge this with profound gratitude."

The governor's ego swelled.

Turning his attention to the prisoner, the lawyer continued. "We have found this man to be a troublemaker, stirring up riots among the Jews all over the world—a violation of Roman law. He is a ringleader of the Nazarene sect—a violation of Jewish law—and even tried to desecrate the temple—a violation of God's law; so we seized him. By examining him yourself you will be able to learn the truth about all these charges we are bringing against him."[2]

Then Paul spoke. His rebuttal was straightforward and respectful toward Felix. "I know that for a number of years you have been a judge over this nation; so I gladly make my defense."

In the time that followed, the apostle summarized his life and ministry. He denied creating a disturbance in Jerusalem and carefully articulated his humble allegiance to God and his loyalty to the growing fellowship of Christian believers.

Unable to make a decision regarding the prisoner's fate until the commander Lysias could come, Felix imprisoned Paul in the palace. Thoroughly fascinated with the preacher, Felix often summoned him to the royal quarters. One day, when Paul arrived to speak to Felix, Drusilla was also there. Feigning political interest in the apostle's message, Felix queried Paul about the meaning of "faith in Christ Jesus."

As Paul reasoned with them concerning "righteousness, self-control and the judgment to come," Felix was alarmed. "Go away. That's enough for now. When I have a more convenient time, I will send for you."

Felix had lured Drusilla away from her former husband, so Paul's

---

2. Acts 24:5–8.

words about self-control and judgment terrified him. Felix quickly removed Paul from his presence.

Paul had been confined to the palace prison for two years when Rome sent word that Felix was being dismissed as the governor of the region.

"I suppose I'll miss this place," Felix said aloud to his wife, gazing out the window westward over the Mediterranean Sea. The setting sun touched the horizon and brilliantly colored every cloud. Felix paid no attention to the beauty.

"What about Paul? Will you miss him?" Drusilla probed.

"This job was bearable until two years ago," Felix responded. "My job would have been much easier if not for Paul," Felix dropped his voice and turned back to the window. "The man is a plague."

Felix hesitated. "Wouldn't you agree that at least some of what he said was quite convincing?"

"Do you mean to tell me, Governor Felix," she said, "that this Jew, or Christian or whatever he is, actually made sense to you?"

"Well, it isn't as if he is some uneducated fanatic," Felix countered. "He used to be a Pharisee."

"What does that mean?"

"He knows the Jewish law back to front," Felix replied. "But the Jews hate him because he preaches that the only way to God is through the crucified rabbi, Jesus—whom Paul claims is no longer dead."

"And you believe that?"

"I don't know what I believe," Felix said, brushing back his graying hair with his hand. "He's very persuasive!"

"Am I on the verge of becoming the wife of a Christian?"

"You're Jewish, Drusilla. Why does it strike you as so strange?"

"You know I consider myself Roman. Emperor Nero would not be pleased with any embracing of Christianity," she warned.

"Then don't tell him!"

Felix paced a few steps, rubbed his hair again, and sat down.

By this time tomorrow, the governor and his wife would be on their way back to Rome, far away from the preaching of Paul.

Their Life and Times

Tuesday

Why Wait?

Felix, the governor of Judea, and his Jewish wife, Drusilla, had the opportunity to sit under the teaching of the great apostle Paul for two years. Neither of them were believers in Christ when they were introduced to Paul and his teachings on redemption, faith, self-control, and eternity. Felix and Drusilla rejected Paul's clear message of salvation.

Felix and his brother Pallas were born in Rome as slaves. They were able to attain their freedom and began climbing toward political power. Pallas was so successful that he became a Roman official and was well esteemed by Emperor Claudius. Pallas's influence helped Felix gain the position of governor of Judea from AD 52 to 58. One of Felix's predecessors was Pontius Pilate, who served in the same post from AD 26 to 36.

One of the primary responsibilities of Roman governors was to keep peace in the provinces over which they were assigned. Felix was successful, but he was a brutal, violent man who performed his duties with fury. The Roman historian Tacitus wrote that Felix, "thought he could commit every sort of iniquity and escape the consequences." Tacitus also referred to Felix as "a master of cruelty and lust who exercised the powers of a king in the spirit of a slave."[3]

Drusilla was Felix's third wife. Very little is known about his first two marriages, but information about his marriage to Drusilla is plentiful. At the time he met Drusilla, Felix was in his second marriage. He wanted the sixteen-year-old Jewess for himself, but Drusilla was also married. Taking advantage of his political position and favor with Emperor Claudius, Felix made quick work of securing Drusilla for himself, ending both of their marriages and beginning a new one with her.

In marrying Drusilla (her formal name was Drusa), Felix aligned himself with royalty—the notorious Herod family. Drusilla was the daughter of Herod Agrippa I, who was the first to martyr one of

---

3. Tacitus, *Historiae* 5.9.

the apostles: "[Agrippa] had James, the brother of John, put to death with the sword. When he saw that this met with approval among the Jews, he proceeded to seize Peter also" (Acts 12:2–3). So not only was Agrippa an enemy of Christianity; he was also one of its earliest persecutors.

Wishing to make stronger political ties in the north, Agrippa I arranged for his daughter Drusilla to marry King Azizus of Emesa (western Syria) when she was just fifteen years old. A year later, Drusilla was seduced by Felix.

When Paul was brought before Governor Felix and Drusilla as a prisoner—on false charges of inciting a disturbance—Drusilla was only nineteen years old.

As governor, Felix feared for the peace of his province. If he had allowed Paul to go free and return to Jerusalem, those who hated the preacher would have incited a massive riot. To avoid an outbreak, Felix placated the Jewish leaders by keeping Paul locked up in the palace at Caesarea.

Scripture reveals that Felix was hoping Paul would try to bribe him in exchange for freedom, so Felix sent for Paul frequently while the captive was imprisoned.[4] The substance of their conversations is not recorded, but given Paul's zeal for the gospel, Felix must have heard much of the teaching found in Paul's New Testament letters. Though possibly convicted about his violence and immorality, Felix was also intrigued enough with the preacher to summon him for many visits. But the prideful Felix never repented or changed his mind about his need for a Savior.

For Felix and Drusilla, their "day of salvation" came near, but sadly they let it pass.[5]

---

4. See Acts 24:26.
5. See 2 Corinthians 6:2.

Can You Imagine?

Wednesday

I n marriage, many decisions we make are fairly inconsequential—"Who is going to pick up the kids from gymnastics?" or "Should we do Mexican or Chinese on Friday night?" But sometimes, a significant decision presents itself to you and your spouse—"Should we take the new job and move to Cleveland?" or "Should we adopt a baby?"

For Felix and Drusilla, the greatest decision they faced was ... *What should we do with Jesus?* They were terrified because of their guilt when they heard Paul talk about righteousness, self-control, and their ultimate destiny. Can you imagine the conversations between them? Conversations that had eternal implications. *Do you think Paul is telling the truth?* Felix and Drusilla must have wondered.

Quenching the Holy Spirit's conviction, Felix and Drusilla chose to dismiss the message. Denying their sin, Felix sent Paul away.

What we know of Felix is that there was no thread of faith in his fabric. But as a Jewess, Drusilla would likely have been exposed to lessons concerning the one true God. It's possible that the rejection of her ancestral religion turned her into a cynic. Sadly, neither of them had any interest in pursuing the claims of Jesus Christ.

Your marriage is designed to grow and flourish when it is built on the foundation of God's truth. It's a prudent man who embraces the claims of Christ. It's a sensible woman who studies God's Word and clings to His design for her marriage. And it's a grounded couple who pray and seek God's will together.

"I'm not sure what we should do here," you may say to your spouse when faced with a dilemma. "Let's pray about this and ask for God's leading."

If Felix and Drusilla had listened to the truth and sought the Lord, their checkered pasts and their marriage could have been redeemed.

From God's Word ...

"By the grace given me I say to every one of you: Do not think of yourself more highly than you ought, but rather think of yourself with sober judgment, in accordance with the faith God has distributed to each of you."

ROMANS 12:3

Their Legacy in Scripture

Thursday

1. **"'That's enough for now! You may leave. When I find it convenient, I will send for you'"** (ACTS 24:25).

   Neither Felix nor his wife, Drusilla, wanted to hear about their sin or face the truth. So they shut their ears and allowed more calluses to grow on their consciences. When our marriages expose our flaws — our pettiness, selfishness, pride, or even cruelty — we may want to run from our spouse, deny reality, and delay confession. God designed marriage to force us to face ourselves and to mature spiritually. When your spouse points out something deceptive, sinful, or unacceptable in your behavior, how do you respond? What attitude, habit, or disposition do you need to address and change so your marriage can grow in love?

2. **"Do not be wise in your own eyes; fear the LORD and shun evil. This will bring health to your body and nourishment to your bones"** (PROVERBS 3:7–8).

   Sometimes arguments start because one of you is certain you're absolutely right and your spouse isn't. You may deceive yourselves into thinking your spouse always brings out the worst in you and fantasize that someone else would be easier to live with. In his wisdom, Solomon offers a sober warning. His prescription, which also applies to a healthy marriage, is to "fear the LORD." In the heat of a disagreement with your spouse, what attitude could you display that would nourish your relationship?

3. **"Come, let us bow down in worship, let us kneel before the LORD our Maker; for he is our God and we are the people of his pasture, the flock under his care. Today, if only you would hear his voice, 'Do not harden your hearts ...'"** (PSALM 95:6–8).

   God's Word is His voice to you and your spouse. His Holy Spirit convicts, instructs, and comforts you. How can you and your spouse keep your hearts from becoming hardened to the things of God? Compared to last year, how have you and your spouse grown spiritually?

Their Legacy of Prayer

Friday

Reflect On: Acts 24

Praise God: That He is the God of all truth and that He sent His Son, Jesus, to redeem lost and guilty people.

Offer Thanks: That God has preserved His Word and has called people in every generation to proclaim the truth of Jesus Christ, and that He has sent the gospel message to you and your spouse and has given you the Holy Spirit, who confirms that the gospel is true.

Confess: That you often hesitate to speak the truth about your love for Jesus to unbelievers who are in positions of power or seem disinterested in things of faith. That you procrastinate and put off God's prompting to be a faithful witness in your neighborhood and workplace.

Ask God: To give you the gift of faith and His Spirit to make you a bold follower of Christ, and to help you and your spouse to study, set aside time to pray, and deal with the issues in your marriage that hinder you from displaying His forgiveness, love, and transformation.

Listen: "Dear children, I chose you and you are Mine. I have forgiven and redeemed you by the blood of My Son and have called you to good works in Him. When doubts arise, seek Me, and I will reveal Myself to you. My Word is truth. My Spirit will lead you through your wrestling to firm belief in My character and provision for your salvation. I am waiting to enter your hearts with My presence and peace."

Pray: *Father in heaven, You are a gracious and loving God who welcomes the doubting heart. Thank You for patiently waiting for us to deal with the sin in our lives and to turn to You for hope and healing. We want to honor You by the way we love each other, deal with our problems, and trust You for our future. You are the Creator and Sustainer of heaven and earth, and You are able to reconcile our hearts to each other and increase our faith. You are able to do more than we can ask or imagine. Amen.*

Here Comes the Church

Christ and His Bride

Meaning of Names: *Christ* means "the Anointed One." *Church* means "called-out assembly."

Their Character: He is the King of kings and Lord of lords, the mighty and holy One. She is the chosen bride awaiting the marriage to her Husband.

Their Challenge: The bride longs to live in peace with her Husband but faces great challenges in this present wicked world.

Their Outcome: Perfection for the church and eternal bliss with the Bridegroom Christ when He returns to take her to be with Him.

Key Scripture: Revelation 19:6–9

Their Story

Monday

The music swelled. It was the most glorious sound history had ever heard. The Groom was stationed at attention, His eyes fixed on the center aisle where His bride was ready to begin her long procession. The celebratory walk that led her to Him.

The congregation stood to its feet, some watching the veiled bride, others looking into the face of the Groom. His eyes did not wander from her. His countenance radiated anticipation and wonder. And perfect love.

Instead of silently nodding as the bride glided past, the congregation — actually a multitude of wedding guests — loudly proclaimed their approval. The cacophony of sounds from the gathered host blended into the finest choral singing ever performed. This was a grand harmonic symphony, each voice taking its part perfectly.

"Hallelujah! Salvation and glory and power belong to our God ..."[1]

Those outside the sanctuary who heard the sound stood on tiptoe, wondering, *Who is this bride? And why is the Groom so enthralled with her?* Although they had received an invitation to the wedding, these outsiders had neglected to respond. The description of the Groom, the glorious bride, and the ceremony had been printed for all to read:

> You are a chosen people, a royal priesthood, a holy nation, God's special possession, that you may declare the praises of him who called you out of darkness into his wonderful light. Once you were not a people, but now you are the people of God; once you had not received mercy, but now you have received mercy.
>
> 1 PETER 2:9–10

Was the bride born this beautiful? Had her clothing ever shimmered like this ... had her gown always been this dazzling? Did she grow up in the kind of privilege that would have provided these things for her?

No. This now-radiant bride was once a waif. She was without resources, no standing, no wealth ... no worth. A most miserable creature, she had been utterly hopeless.

Then the Groom saw her. Though she was clothed in rags and lived in squalor, He loved her. The Groom decided she was to become His royal bride.

Mocking voices throughout the universe questioned His choice. "Why would You stoop to marry someone so unworthy of You? A King with such pedigree — and perfection — can do much better than this."

---

1. Revelation 19:1.

The skeptics were right, of course. But the Groom was undistracted. This would be an arranged marriage by a Father handselecting His Son's bride. A story of a Groom reaching down. An act of mercy. Of forgiveness. Of transformation.

The Groom had pursued the girl, provided the resources of His kingdom, and readied His bride for this day. He had strengthened her and empowered her. For millennia she had been His helper, His voice in the land of scoffers. He had watched over her and protected her and told her about His kingdom,

Saints in the congregation stared in wide-eyed amazement. Gratitude and deep emotion filled even the most stoic of guests. The bride's elegance was indescribable.

They knew what she had endured. They knew that, from the beginning of time, there had been a Rival who loathed the Groom and detested the thought of this wedding day.

The Rival had raised up adversaries to persecute the betrothed and had tried to defeat her. At times she wondered if she would survive the relentless war waged against her. But her Groom had protected her. He had prevailed. On this day, she walked toward her Beloved with poise and purity.

As His bride drew nearer to Him, the Groom smiled, delighting in her beauty. He took a deep breath. She was His treasure and would reign with Him forever.

Their Life and Times

Tuesday

The Perfect Groom

Throughout the Bible, God uses the imagery of a husband and wife to illustrate His relationship to His people. To Israel, God said, "'Your Maker is your husband—the LORD Almighty is his name—the Holy One of Israel is your Redeemer; he is called the God of all the earth'" (Isaiah 54:5). God is the loving Husband; His people are His beloved bride.

The prophet Hosea echoes God's tender love for His people: "'I will betroth you to me forever; I will betroth you in righteousness and justice, in love and compassion'" (Hosea 2:19).

Again presenting earthly marriage as a picture of a heavenly reality, the apostle Paul wrote these words:

> Husbands, love your wives, just as Christ loved the church and gave himself up for her to make her holy, cleansing her by the washing with water through the word, and to present her to himself as a radiant church, without stain or wrinkle or any other blemish, but holy and blameless.
>
> EPHESIANS 5:25–27

In the last chapters of the Bible, the imagery of a bride and groom crescendos in a glorious picture of Christ and the church. "Let us rejoice and be glad and give him glory! For the wedding of the Lamb has come, and his bride has made herself ready. Fine linen, bright and clean, was given her to wear" (Revelation 19:7–8).

In Bible times, there were three distinct events involved in the joining of a man and a woman in marriage.

First, there was the betrothal, the legal transaction when a couple became engaged. The groom's father had sought out the bride's parents, making clear he had selected their daughter to be his son's bride.

The betrothal of believers is highlighted in the New Testament. "I promised you to one husband, to Christ, so that I might present you as a pure virgin to him" (2 Corinthians 11:2). Here the church is being admonished to remain pure for the Groom until He comes for her. This is where the church is today—between the choosing and the wedding.

Second, the groom "fetches" his bride. This fetching represents the return of Christ and the rapture of the church when Jesus will return to earth and claim His people.

> The Lord himself will come down from heaven, with a loud command, with the voice of the archangel and with the trumpet call of God, and the dead in Christ will rise first. After that, we who are still alive and are left will be caught up together with them in the clouds to meet the Lord in the air. And so we will be with the Lord forever. Therefore encourage one another with these words.
>
> 1 THESSALONIANS 4:16–18

Finally, there is the wedding feast. After the exchanging of the vows and the betrothal were made complete, this marriage supper usually lasted several days. The feast was a celebration marking the unbreakable covenant. "What God has joined together, let no one separate" (Matthew 19:6).

The book of Revelation describes this extravagant event—when Jesus comes for His bride and takes her to His heavenly home: "I saw the Holy City, the new Jerusalem, coming down out of heaven from God, prepared as a bride beautifully dressed for her husband" (Revelation 21:2).

This home—heaven—will be glorious.

The royal Groom and His cherished bride together. Forever.

Can You Imagine?

Wednesday

Thousands of years ago, before creation, God was acquainted with you. Long before there was anything at all, He knew your name. And like a father in ancient Israel pursuing a bride for his son and willingly paying a dowry for her hand, it was God's great desire that you would belong to Jesus.

In his letter to the church in Corinth, Paul reminds you and me of the dowry the Father paid to claim us for His Son: "You are not your own; you were bought at a price" (1 Corinthians 6:19–20).

Like a father knocking on the door of his son's bride-to-be, God took the initiative. None of us could have imagined being worthy enough to belong to Him, so He stepped toward us. He embraced us as we were and gave us the capacity—the faith—to accept His offer. "We love because he first loved us" (1 John 4:19).

> *The church's one foundation is Jesus Christ her Lord,*
> *She is His new creation by water and the word;*
> *From heaven He came and sought her to be His holy bride;*
> *With His own blood He bought her, and for her life He died.*[2]

God paid the bride-price for you with the blood of His own Son. He loves you and has claimed you for His very own. You are God's betrothed. You are His.

When you and your spouse go for a walk in your neighborhood, people see you and think, *She's his wife. He's her husband.* Can you imagine that your kindness and the way you treat each other display that you belong to Jesus"?

You are His bride.

---

2. "The Church's One Foundation," lyrics by Samuel J. Stone, 1866.

From God's Word . . .

"Praise be to the God and Father of our Lord Jesus Christ, who has blessed us in the heavenly realms with every spiritual blessing in Christ. For he chose us in him before the creation of the world to be holy and blameless in his sight."

EPHESIANS 1:3–4

Their Legacy in Scripture

Thursday

1. "All glorious is the princess within her chamber; her gown is interwoven with gold. In embroidered garments she is led to the king; her virgin companions follow her—those brought to be with her. Led in with joy and gladness, they enter the palace of the king" (PSALM 45:13–15).

   What do you remember about the anticipation and excitement of your wedding day? How can you rekindle loving thoughts toward your spouse that will restore the joy and gladness of that day?

2. "I delight greatly in the LORD; my soul rejoices in my God. For he has clothed me with garments of salvation and arrayed me in a robe of his righteousness, as a bridegroom adorns his head like a priest, and as a bride adorns herself with her jewels" (ISAIAH 61:10).

   God loves His bride—the church—and provides everything for her well-being. He is constantly thinking about everything you need for godly living. What does your spouse need most from you? What kindness can you provide that would demonstrate compassion, tenderness, and love?

3. "'Your Maker is your husband—the LORD Almighty is his name—the Holy One of Israel is your Redeemer; he is called the God of all the earth'" (ISAIAH 54:5).

   God is your perfect Provider and Companion. When you love Him with all your heart, soul, mind, and strength, He enables you to love your spouse well. How should knowing the spiritual significance of your marriage inspire you to treat your spouse with more honor, respect, and love?

Their Legacy of Prayer

Friday

Reflect On: Revelation 19:6–9

Praise God: That He is the King of Glory who seeks and prepares
His bride for a glorious future, and that His covenant
love cannot be broken.

Offer Thanks: That God sought you when you were unfit to be His,
and loved you into loveliness, and that He has given you
His robe of righteousness and His garment of salvation.
Thank Him for His sustaining provisions and care
for you.

Confess: That you often take your heavenly Groom for granted
and forget the price He paid to be in relationship with
you, and that you sometimes accept His gifts but neglect
to spend time cultivating the intimacy He desires.

Ask God: To rekindle the love you first experienced when you
became the bride of Christ, and to give you a glimpse
again of the deep love He has for you. To increase your
desire to spend time with your heavenly Groom, and to
reveal how you can best love and serve your spouse.

Listen: "My bride, I love you with an everlasting love. I came to
earth, sought you, and gave My life in order to make you
My beloved forever. You will spend eternity with Me.
I think about you every moment of the day and night.
Your welfare is My concern. Nothing will ever separate
you from Me. I have provided everything you need for
life here on earth so your joy may be full, and someday
I will bring you into My glorious home in heaven."

Pray: *Our King of Glory, You have bestowed on us the honor of being Your beloved. You ride forth victoriously on behalf of truth, humility, and righteousness. We are filled with gratitude because You have chosen to love us through all eternity. We want to honor Your great Name by the way we love and serve each other. Thank You for providing everything we need for our marriage to display Your grace. And someday in heaven we will rejoice in the splendor of the grand eternal home You have prepared for us. To be with You forever will be more glorious than we can imagine. Thank You for loving us with such incredible love. We are Yours. Amen.*

Acknowledgments

In some ways, writing a book is like marching off to war. There are long days in the trenches, dark mornings and lonely weekends of isolation, and the ever-present danger of being frozen up with fear or overwhelmed with doubt. In the two years of working on this book, while we were holed up and surrounded by pages of manuscript, ever pounding away on our computers like Schroeder at his piano, an army of support troops has kept us well supplied and covered with encouragement.

Friends, colleagues, family members, and literary experts have come alongside at just the right time and offered invaluable help. For these who joined us in the bunkers, we are grateful.

Our married children, Jon and Missy Schrader and Christopher and Julie Tassy, have provided a solid base of accountability and support. They cheered for us, generously shared their ideas with us, and faithfully prayed for us throughout this entire project. We are blessed parents.

The "Amazing Women" in Bobbie's church Bible study circle have been a rich resource of wisdom, encouragement, and feedback for what it takes to build a marriage relationship that goes the distance. Their fresh and honest assessment of what Christian couples need has been a laboratory for ideas and a reservoir of love. For these young mothers and the husbands they adore, we give thanks.

Because this book covers centuries of ancient Jewish history and Old Testament stories steeped in Hebrew richness, a depth of knowledge way beyond our ability to uncover was required. It has been our privilege to have a Jewish believer alongside to provide essential Hebrew insights. David Ettinger is a rare and trustworthy historian and writer who knows the Old Testament intimately and embraces the New Testament fully as a believer in Yeshua (Hebrew for Jesus). His expertise in Jewish law, customs, and history is woven into nearly every page of this book. As our comrade in arms, David's commitment to join us in the

446

writing and his tireless dedication to familiarize us with Jewish culture are deeply appreciated.

For our friends at Zondervan who encouraged us to tackle this daunting project and trusted us with this treasured task, we are humbled. Sandy VanderZicht first approached us with the idea of enlisting for this mission and then provided a full war chest of ideas. With skill and grace, Sandy strategized and lovingly coached us along the way. Then she handed us off to Dirk Buursma to do the fine-tuning. Thanks to Dirk for his excellent work and notes of encouragement in the margins of the manuscript. We are also thankful for Don Gates, Tom Dean, Madeleine Hart, and the entire marketing and design team at Zondervan.

We are deeply grateful for our colleagues at Wolgemuth & Associates, Inc. Erik Wolgemuth, Andrew Wolgemuth, Austin Wilson, and Susan Kreider covered our backs many days and allowed us freedom to maneuver with the manuscript without distractions. They are faithful comrades.

And to our friends who have spent years fighting the good fight for strong homes and godly marriages, we thank Dennis and Barbara Rainey for graciously writing the foreword and thereby adding their good names to this project. We are also humbled by others who kindly offered their endorsements of the book. We are also humbled by other friends who kindly offered their endorsements of the book: Philip Yancey, Joni Eareckson Tada, Darryl and Ann Voskamp, Michael and Gail Hyatt, Jerry B. Jenkins, Ann Spangler, Larry and Autumn Ross, Ron and Judy Blue, Alistair Begg, Ryan and Laura Dobson, and Jerry and Cristie Jo Johnston. Thank you to Robert's aunt, Ruth Dourte, and Joy Jacobs for inspiration from their book, *One I Love: A Devotional for Couples*.

As with any endeavor that is bigger than we can handle on our own, are thankful to God for hovering over us as we wrote and edited, rewrote and reedited. Our prayer throughout the process was that these stories would challenge and inspire and inform godly relationships. While we were writing, we asked that we might experience a glimpse of God at work in our hearts and in our own marriage so we could become the people He created us to be. And for all who will read these pages, may our good and gracious Redeemer surround you with His presence.

For His faithfulness and provision, count us grateful.

Alphabetical Index
of Couples

Index of Names

Index of Themes:
Issues Married Couples Face

Index of Scripture

Men of the Bible

A One-Year Devotional Study
of Men in Scripture

Ann Spangler and Robert Wolgemuth

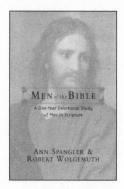

Men of the Bible offers both men and women a fresh way to read and understand the Bible — through the eyes and hearts of the men whose stories unfold in its pages. This unique book takes a close-up look at fifty-two men in Scripture — complex flesh-and-blood characters whose strengths and weaknesses will seem strangely similar to your own. Heroes and villains, sinners and prophets, commoners and kings ... their dramatic life stories provide a fresh perspective on the unfolding story of redemption.

Designed for personal prayer and study or for use in small groups, *Men of the Bible* will help you make Bible reading a daily habit and will help you grow in character, wisdom, and obedience as a person after God's own heart.

Women of the Bible

A One-Year Devotional Study
of Women in Scripture

Ann Spangler and Jean E. Syswerda

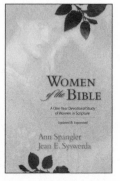

Women of the Bible, by Ann Spangler and Jean E. Syswerda, focuses on fifty-two remarkable women in Scripture — women whose struggles to live with faith and courage are not unlike your own. The women in this book encourage you through their failures as well as their successes. You'll see how God acted in surprising and wonderful ways to draw them — and you — to himself.

This yearlong devotional will help you slow down and savor the story of God's unrelenting love for his people, offering a fresh perspective that will nourish and strengthen your personal communion with him.